SLAVES OF ONE MASTER

SLAVES OF ONE MASTER

Globalization and Slavery in Arabia in the Age of Empire

Matthew S. Hopper

Yale UNIVERSITY PRESS
New Haven & London

Copyright © 2015 by Yale University.

All rights reserved.

This book may not be reproduced, in whole or in part, including illustrations, in any form (beyond that copying permitted by Sections 107 and 108 of the U.S. Copyright Law and except by reviewers for the public press), without written permission from the publishers.

Yale University Press books may be purchased in quantity for educational, business, or promotional use. For information, please e-mail sales.press@yale.edu (U.S. office) or sales@yaleup.co.uk (U.K. office).

Set in Galliard type by IDS Infotech Ltd., Chandigarh, India.
Printed in the United States of America.

Library of Congress Control Number: 2015931443
ISBN: 978-0-300-19201-8 (cloth: alk. paper)

A catalogue record for this book is available from the British Library.

CONTENTS

Preface vii

Introduction 1

1 The East African Slave Trade and the Making of the African Diaspora in Arabia 18

2 Slavery, Dates, and Globalization 51

3 Pearls, Slaves, and Fashion 80

4 Slavery and African Life in Arabia 105

5 Antislavery and Empire: Paradoxes of Liberation in the Western Indian Ocean 142

6 Globalization and the End of the East African Slave Trade 181

Conclusion: Silencing and Forgetting 212

Notes 223
Bibliography 261
Index 293

PREFACE

Salama was nineteen years old when war came to her town in Ngindo-speaking southeastern Tanzania in 1869. Her father was killed, and her home was destroyed. She and her sister were sold to slave traders who forced the women to walk a month's distance to the coastal city of Kilwa. From there, Salama and her sister were sent by boat to Zanzibar, where they were separated and sold to different slave traders. Off the coast of Oman, the ship that carried Salama was stopped by a British naval patrol, which suspected the ship of transporting slaves to the Arabian (Persian) Gulf ("the Gulf") in violation of a treaty with the sultan of Muscat. British officers boarded the ship, seized the Africans aboard, and recorded some of their testimonies. Salama's story is preserved in the records of that seizure, but there is no account of what happened to her sister. If she survived the journey, Salama's sister likely became one of the hundreds of thousands of Africans taken from East Africa to the Arabian Gulf in the nineteenth century.[1]

Salama and her sister highlight the central problem of this book. Historians know much about the Africans who were captured by British antislavery patrols in the Indian Ocean and something about those who were enslaved on the coast of East Africa. But we know remarkably little about the African captives who were transported to many destinations around the Indian Ocean. A growing scholarly literature has begun to explore the history of this branch of the African diaspora, but Arabia—which received a considerable number of captives from East Africa—has remained largely unexplored by historians. The aim of this book is to fill this gap in the literature by recounting the story of the Africans who were enslaved in the Gulf in the late nineteenth and early twentieth centuries.

I first read Salama's story as a doctoral student, and it profoundly moved me. Inspired in part by stories like hers and in part by my exposure to Pan-Africanism as a student at Temple University and my readings in diaspora studies with Edward Alpers at UCLA, I drafted research proposals, received financial support, and departed in the summer of 2001 to begin work on this project in Yemen and Oman. With a theoretical and methodological background and years of training in both Swahili and Arabic, I anticipated uncovering the kinds of documentary sources that would allow me to fill a significant gap in the historical literature and bring stories like Salama's into clearer view. I hoped that Arabic manuscripts would reveal the inner workings of the slave trade and allow me to draw the kinds of concrete conclusions made by historians of the transatlantic slave trade and provide a non-Eurocentric framework for understanding this rich history. I imagined that hitherto elusive documents would provide me a portal into the lives of slaves themselves and that interviews with the descendants of enslaved Africans in Arabia would provide additional depth of understanding of African cultural retentions, survivals, coping mechanisms, and diasporic consciousness.

No research project turns out exactly as planned, and I was unprepared for the shifts that would be required in both my framing and conducting of this research. My first adjustment was geographic. Four months into my stay in Yemen, the September 11 attacks and their aftermath presented challenges for my research agenda in that country. Moving eastward to the Gulf was expedient in the short term but also proved logical in the long term, as the origins of African communities on the Gulf side of Arabia differ from those of the Red Sea side (chapter 1). With some adjustments to my research plans, including a temporary shift in location to Zanzibar, I was ultimately able to spend more than a year, cumulatively, in Oman, the United Arab Emirates (UAE), Bahrain, and Qatar, where I attempted to visit every town and village in those countries that was accessible by paved road at the time. The "Arabia" of this book's title is thus limited to eastern Arabia and the Gulf.

That experience led me to a further revelation and another adjustment. I found that those whose ancestors had been forcibly taken to eastern Arabia as slaves did not by and large identify themselves as African, speak African languages, talk openly to strangers about their ancestry, or celebrate aspects of their African heritage. Moreover, the sensitivity of the topic of slavery discouraged my inclusion of interviews in subsequent applications for research clearance in those countries. The sensitivity of the subject also contributed to the limited accessibility of documentary sources. The Arabic sources related to the slave trade that I cite in this book come primarily from archives in Zanzibar and London. And unlike documentary sources from the transatlantic slave trade, where banking, insurance, and governmental demands created inducements for both the specificity and preservation of records, Arabic documents related to the slave trade in the Indian Ocean proved more uneven. Some of the most promising Arabic documents, those captured aboard slaving vessels in the Indian Ocean in the nineteenth century, yielded little useful information about slaves themselves other than gender and price, and provided only limited insights into the workings of the slave trade.[2]

Specialists in this field may be disappointed by the preponderance of European (mainly British) sources in this book, particularly as the voices of the Africans whose lives this book seeks to uncover will necessarily be contained behind several mediating layers. This limitation demands explanation. The question of whether the enslaved or subaltern may actually speak for themselves was raised provocatively by Gayatri Spivak and has been revisited variously since. Spivak's interrogation of the representation (and "re-presentation") of the subaltern subject in theoretical and historical texts has presented a challenge to cultural historians of imperialism and slavery that endures today. Her determination that the "subaltern as female cannot be heard or read" is exemplified poignantly by descriptions of colonial and post-colonial forces claiming to represent the silent dead. Whether it is Victorian imperialists justifying a civilizing mission in India through the mistranscribed names of widows of *sati*, male independence movement leaders interpreting a female activist's suicide, or the contemporary historian/critic attempting to represent the motives/actions of masses/workers/subalterns, she concludes that "one cannot put together a 'voice.'"[3]

Eve Troutt Powell has recently reiterated Spivak's challenge for scholars attempting to find a voice of enslaved Africans in the historiography of the Middle East.[4] In an important essay, Troutt Powell expands on Spivak's criticism to show how historians in the twentieth century have been complicit in the muting of slave voices by reinforcing artificial geographic divisions, accepting monolithic and universal constructions of race and religion, and placing a blind faith in the word of nineteenth-century British "men on the spot." Perhaps most important, Troutt Powell challenges us to consider the influence of Atlantic slave narratives on nineteenth-century European conceptions of Middle Eastern slavery and their lingering influence on twentieth-century historiography. Echoing scholars of African American studies, she acknowledges the limits of freed slaves' authorial autonomy and reminds us that Atlantic slave narratives often reflected the editorial supervision of white American abolitionists to the extent that the experience of slavery itself becomes the subject of these stories, while the former slave remains the object. Thus, in the absence of the voices of the slaves themselves, historians have tended to "speak for" them, allowing nineteenth-century perspectives to shape the grounding assumptions of twentieth-century historiography.

More recently, Ehud Toledano, in examining the history of enslaved populations in the Ottoman Empire, has concluded that in the absence of a significant number of slave narratives—"which increased the difficulty in reconstructing the voices of the enslaved"—the research requires that one "adopt a more flexible approach to the interpretation of the available sources." Toledano suggests using techniques of "voice recovery" or "experience reconstruction," processes that expand the definition of "voice" from speech alone to action—as both commission and omission—relying on careful examination of silences and the use of at least some measure of imagination, which he employs to read complex documentary material.[5] The pioneering work of Troutt Powell and Toledano inspires much of my use of sources in this book.

Despite the obvious limitations of European sources, there are numerous examples of enslaved Africans "speaking"—or at least attempting to convey first-person narratives—to a variety of European officials in various capacities around the Indian Ocean. These narratives indeed suffer from many of the same "layers of mediation" identified by Kathryn Joy

McKnight and reiterated by Toledano.⁶ These accounts are complicated by problems of transcription, translation, and representation but are nevertheless of immense value. In this book I draw particularly on manumission testimonies recorded at British consular and agency offices in the Gulf; these present unique possibilities and problems. While the manumission testimonies can be a valuable source for historians interested in the lives of the enslaved in the Gulf, they must also be treated with a degree of caution. It would be an error to regard these testimonies as representative of the entire enslaved population of the Gulf because numerous factors have limited the number of testimonies that were recorded. For a variety of reasons, enslaved Africans who sought manumission certificates were overwhelmingly male. Additionally, many of the recorded testimonies came from the British residency agent at Sharjah (UAE). The agent, a man of Persian ancestry, appears to have tended to treat enslaved Baluchis (from Baluchistan or Persian Mekran) graciously but was known to have returned a great many of the enslaved Africans who appealed to him back to their masters in exchange for bribes or to bolster his tenuous position as British agent on the coast. As a result, most manumission testimonies from Africans enslaved on the Trucial Coast (today's UAE) come from those who were able to escape and walk to Muscat or sail to Bahrain to appeal for manumission. The format of manumission testimonies also varied over time. British agents did not always ask those who appealed to them for manumission for details about their arrival in Arabia, and that information has not always been recorded. In some cases, testimonies of Africans who were kidnapped are missing too much information to be useful in calculating back the dates of their capture. Furthermore, not all manumission testimonies have been preserved. Despite these limitations, the manumission testimonies provide significant details that help us better understand the nature and extent of slavery in this part of the Indian Ocean. When evaluated carefully and critically, as I hope to have done here, they can be invaluable resources for understanding African life in Arabia. My hope is that my limited contribution using these selective sources will inspire and provide a contextual framework for future work by historians and anthropologists who will make use of Islamic jurisprudence *(fiqh)*, oral tradition, and other sources that proved beyond my own capacity in this project.

Transliterations from Arabic sources in this book follow the guidelines of the *International Journal of Middle East Studies* system except in quotations and for names and words with commonly accepted anglicizations. Portions of chapter 2 have previously appeared in "The Globalization of Dried Fruit: Transformations in the Eastern Arabian Economy, 1860s–1920s," in *Global Muslims in the Age of Steam and Print*, ed. James L. Gelvin and Nile Green (Berkeley: University of California Press, 2014), 158–182.

The research behind this book would not have been possible without the help of many kind and generous people. First and foremost, I am grateful to my mentor, Edward A. Alpers, who supported and encouraged me through the process of training for this research and writing this book. His inexhaustible energy and knowledge have been an inspiration to me. James Gelvin's insights through both his instruction and conversation have influenced much of this project. Christopher Ehret's help on various stages of this research was invaluable. Thomas Hinnebusch, whose Swahili instruction initially brought me to UCLA, supported me throughout this project. Richard von Glahn's instruction in world history inspired the global focus of this project from the outset and inspired me to broaden my theoretical horizons. I am also grateful to my professors at UCLA whose instruction directly influenced my approach to this topic in various ways, especially Perry Anderson, Robert Brenner, Sondra Hale, Robert Hill, Lynn Hunt, Michael Lofchie, Ghislaine Lydon, Aamir Mufti, Gabriel Piterberg, Daniel Posner, and William Worger.

William Gervase Clarence-Smith and Nelida Fuccaro in London, Abdul Sheriff in Zanzibar, and Anne Bang and Reda Bhacker in Muscat provided me with vital advice during the early stages of my research. Stimulating dialogues with Jeremy Prestholdt challenged my perspectives, broadened my horizons, and strengthened my arguments throughout this project. Thomas McDow's insight and connections made much of my research in East Africa and Oman possible. Pier Larson graciously provided critique, encouragement, and inspiration throughout this project. Gwyn Campbell provided essential feedback at conferences and in conversations over the past several years. Special thanks are also due to my colleagues at various universities, with whom I discussed elements of this project at various stages at home and in the field. Thanks especially to James Brennan, Thomas Burgess, Jacob Dorman, Steve Fabian, Pedro Machado, Lahra Smith, Laith Ulaiby, and Steve Urgola. Over the past several years, I have presented portions of this project to workshops, conferences, and classes. I am grateful for the feedback I have received from scholars at each of these and am particularly indebted to those who offered thoughtful criticisms that have strengthened this project: Felicitas Becker, Fahad Bishara, Sugata Bose, Joel Cabrita, Robert Carter, Kevin Dawson, Dale Eickelman, Jonathon Glassman, Nile Green, Robert Harms, Victoria Hightower, Ahmed Kanna, Martin Klein, Michael Laffan, Paul Lovejoy, Joseph Miller, Jonathan Miran, Farah Al-Nakib, James Onley, Michaela Pelican, John Peterson, Lawrence Potter, Scott Reese, Michael Salman, Maho Sebiane, Ahmed Alawad Sikainga, Christina Snyder, Elke Stockreiter, Hideaki Suzuki, Eric Tagliacozzo, James Warren, and Molly Warsh, among others. My students and colleagues in my department at Cal Poly, and George Cotkin and Andrew Morris in particular, have been a source of strength and encouragement. Dr. Linda Halisky, former Dean of the College of Liberal Arts (CLA) at Cal Poly, facilitated my research trip to the University of Wyoming to work with the Paul Popenoe papers, and more recently CLA Dean Douglas L. Epperson helped make possible my research trip to work with the David Fairchild papers at Fairchild Tropical Botanic Gardens in Florida.

Research abroad for this project was funded by the Social Science Research Council's International Pre-Dissertation Fellowship Program with funds from the Ford Foundation, the Fulbright-Hays Doctoral Dissertation Research Abroad Program with funding from the U.S. Department of Education, and the Social Science Research Council's International Dissertation Research Fellowship Program with funds from the Andrew W. Mellon Foundation in partnership with the American Council of Learned Societies. I am particularly grateful for the support of the Social Science Research Council's Book Fellowship and especially to the editorial insights of Mara Naselli on the organization and structure of this project. This research would not have been possible without language training in Swahili and Arabic, portions of which were supported by U.S.

Department of Education Foreign Language Area Studies (FLAS) fellowships for study at UCLA, Yale University, and the College of William and Mary. Foreign language study abroad in Morogoro and Sana'a was made possible by grants from the Fulbright-Hays Group Projects Abroad Program and the American Institute for Yemeni Studies. Thanks to my colleagues on these projects for their support. I am especially grateful to my language instructors: Jamal Ali, Muhammad Al-Anasi, Najat Al-Kalbani, Michael Cooperson, John Eisele, Michael Fishbein, Thomas Hinnebusch, Masangu Matondo, John Mugane, and Yumi Odom. The staff and fellows at the Gilder Lehrman Center for the Study of Slavery, Resistance, and Abolition at Yale University provided wonderful support and encouragement during a fellowship there in fall 2009. Special thanks to Dana Schaffer, Melissa McGrath, Thomas Thurston, and David W. Blight. I am also grateful for the hard work of the editorial staff at Yale University Press, especially Christopher Rogers, Christina Tucker, and Erica Hanson; my copy editor, Bojana Ristich; and two anonymous reviewers. The maps in this book were completed with the assistance of Trevor M. Hooper at Cal Poly.

The librarians, archivists, and administrators at the various research centers I used in the course of this research deserve special thanks, especially the following: Hedley Sutton at the British Library India Office Reading Room, Philippa Bassett at the University of Birmingham, 'Abdullah El-Reyes at the Centre for Documentation and Research in Abu Dhabi, Sarah White at the Beit Al-Zubair Museum in Muscat, Ibrahim Soghayroun at Sultan Qaboos University, Christopher Edens at the American Institute for Yemeni Studies, Ali Abdulrahman Abahussain at the Historical Documents Center in Bahrain, Nancy Korber at the Fairchild Tropical Botanic Gardens, Russell Gassero at the Reformed Church in America Archives, and Abdul Sheriff and the staff at the Zanzibar National Archive. I am also very grateful for the assistance of David Hirsch and Ruby Bell-Gam in the Charles E. Young Research Library at UCLA.

I am especially thankful for the support of my family throughout this process and particularly during my travels abroad to research this project. My parents, my sisters, my in-laws, and my grandparents were all incredibly supportive through the research and writing of this book, and I am truly thankful for all of their love and encouragement. My son, Silas, has given me inspiration, hope, and courage. Most of all, I am grateful to my wife, Sada, who made travel and research fun, helped me write, and went surfing when I needed to work alone. Thank you for making my life brighter and encouraging me when I needed it most.

INTRODUCTION

As the sun rose over the Gulf of Oman on the morning of May 21, 1896, the silhouette of a ship became visible as it passed through the rocky inlet of Bander Khairan, fifteen miles south of Muscat. The *baghla* (or dhow) hugged the coast and passed between the inlet's steep cliffs and islands in order to keep out of sight as it sailed north from its home port of Sur toward Muscat. Despite its attempt to avoid detection, the morning light exposed its presence to the awaiting cutter (rowboat) of the HMS *Lapwing*. The Royal Navy cruiser was on antislave-trade duties, and its cutter had spent a warm night beneath a quarter moon keeping lookout over the channel. Philip Francklin, the twenty-two-year-old lieutenant commanding the detachment, spotted the dhow around 5:30 a.m. and immediately grew suspicious when it quickly reversed course upon seeing the British patrol. The dhow ran south and disappeared around a point. Francklin and the cutter made chase, the crew rowing hard to catch up. The cutter fired two blanks and a live shot across the dhow's bow to no effect. The dhow raced ahead. It made for a sandy beach about a mile away, where it ran ashore, dropped its sail, and quickly dislodged its cargo—sixteen African children, who were shooed up the rocky outcrops by their captors.[1]

Five minutes later, Francklin and his crew hit the beach and charged after them with rifles in hand. Francklin scrambled up the rocks in one direction with his translator. He caught up with one child after a quarter of a mile and one of the slave traders after another mile and escorted both back to the beach. Four of Francklin's men meanwhile caught up with

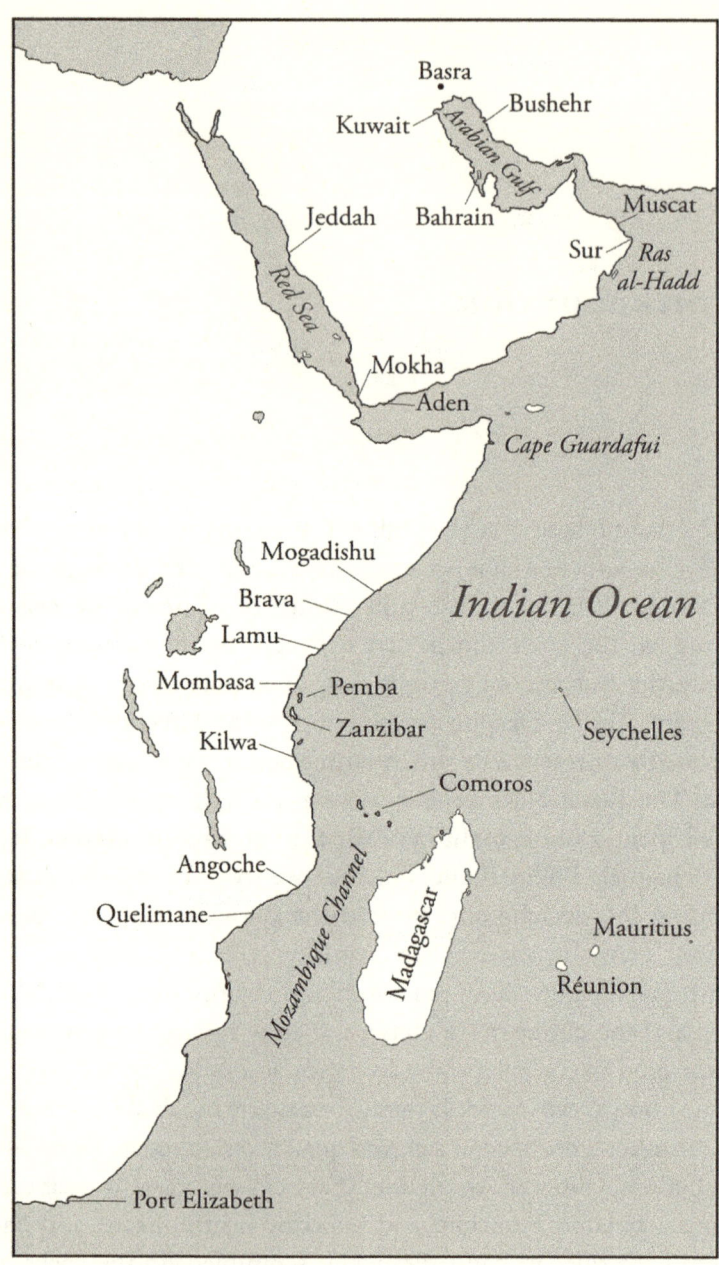

Western Indian Ocean

another slave trader and thirteen of the captives. Questioning revealed that two additional slave traders had escaped, along with two more captives, who were nowhere to be found. In all, fourteen African children were seized. Francklin ordered three of his crew to ready the dhow and place the rescued captives aboard to be brought back to Muscat for presentation to the British consul. A mile into the voyage, the dhow's rudder became detached—a casualty of its run on shore—and the boat capsized, plunging the children and crew into rough seas. In the desperate minutes that followed, all of the children were rescued and pulled into the cutter, but one British sailor drowned. The exhausted crew of the overloaded cutter rowed the children through high surf for several more hours before eventually reuniting with the HMS *Lapwing* and returning to Muscat.[2]

At Muscat, the fourteen rescued captives were handed over to the British consul, F. G. Beville, who just days earlier had personally seized a dhow in Muscat harbor containing 27 African captives, also mostly children. These were not just isolated incidents—a few months later, another British ship, the HMS *Sphinx*, captured two more dhows north of Muscat containing 198 and 35 slaves each.[3] For a few busy days after the arrival of the *Lapwing*, the British consulate was crowded with rescued African youngsters. Following protocol, Beville sent the African girls onward by steamer to Bombay to be consigned to a Catholic mission. But Beville elected to break with tradition and hand 16 of the rescued boys over to a new American missionary in Muscat instead of sending them to India. As a result of Beville's decision, the stories of some of these youngsters have been uniquely preserved in the record of the mission. The Reformed Church in America (RCA; better known as the Dutch Reformed denomination) began a mission to Arabia in 1891 under the leadership of Samuel Zwemer and James Cantine, two New Brunswick (New Jersey) seminarians who were inspired by the zeal of their Old Testament professor, John Lansing, for spreading the gospel in the land of his birth (his parents had been Presbyterian missionaries in Damascus).[4] The RCA mission stations that Lansing inspired—virtually the only Christian missionary efforts in all of eastern Arabia—would eventually develop into medical clinics, schools, and hospitals at Basra, Muscat, Bahrain, and Kuwait. But their first educational effort was the Industrial School for Freed Slaves (or Freed Slave School), founded at Muscat in 1896.

The RCA missionary at Muscat was Peter Zwemer, the younger brother of founder Samuel Zwemer. He had previously expressed interest in opening a "school for liberated slave boys" when he heard about a group of manumitted boys at Bushehr in Persia. When Peter learned of the capture of the two dhows in May 1896, he "at once went to the Political Agent and requested that the boy slaves be given to me for training and support." On May 27, Beville consigned sixteen boys over to Zwemer, who personally pledged to feed and clothe them until they were eighteen years old. Peter Zwemer was convinced that the boys could grow up to be "vigorous spiritual helpers to us in all of our stations some day."[5] He intended to model the school on Lovedale, the Glasgow Missionary Society's station in Cape Colony. A register listing the original boys of the Freed Slave School, signed by Zwemer, contains the following information:

No.	Name	Tribe	Age	English Name
1	Feeekrin	Matumbi	15	John
2	Suleiman	Mrima	14	Solomon
3	Nulleidee	Matumbi	13	Phillip
4	Baroot	Matumbi	13	Thomas
5	Muftah	Managuru	12	Stephen
6	Ferooz	Manyema	12	David
7	Saadulla	Matumbi	12	George
8	Farhan	Ndegereko	12	Isaac
9	Mabrook	Zaramo	11	Joseph
10	Mabrook	Matumbi	11	Peter
11	Mabrook	Yao	11	Andrew
12	Nasani	Matumbi	11	Mark
13	Fatak	Nyassa	11	Nathan
14	Nulleidee	Nyassa	11	Alfred
15	Hajiboo	Yao	10	Henry
16	Boyi	Yao	10	Edwin[6]

The names, ages, and ethnicities of the boys are consistent with enslaved populations in coastal East Africa and the islands of Zanzibar and Pemba at the time. Their ethnic origins are from southern Tanzania, northern Mozambique, Malawi, and eastern Congo. Given the timing of the boys' capture, however, it is likely they had recently arrived at the Omani port town of Sur after having embarked from Pemba or from the coast of northern Mozambique, where an extensive slave trade continued through at least 1902. The boys all spoke Swahili, and several already possessed Muslim names or ones common among enslaved males (three were named Mabrūk [literally "congratulations"], a common slave name, and one was named Boyi [derived from the English "boy," familiar in Zanzibar]), indicating that some may have been born into slavery on the East African coast. An active, covert slave trade involving traders from Sur and Batinah in Oman operated through Pemba in the 1880s and 1890s, so it is likely many of the boys had come from there. Two other boys, Samuel and James, were added to the group later.

Zwemer recalled that when he received the boys, half of them were emaciated with starvation, but within four months they were all restored to "robust health."[7] A year later, a mission publication could boast that the boys had proved "docile and tractable" and were making "good progress in the training, educational, religious, and industrial, provided for them."[8] Zwemer noted that he preferred instruction in English instead of Arabic "in order to keep them separate from Muscat and Moslem influence."[9] By all accounts, the boys of the Freed Slave School admired Zwemer and took kindly to his instruction until his untimely death two years later. The school persevered in Zwemer's absence, and the boys continued to learn English. Many of them eventually found employment aboard British naval ships, in consulates, or with missionaries. Some kept in correspondence with RCA missionaries into adulthood. One of the boys, Suleiman, served aboard the HMS *Fox* during World War I and ultimately found his way to New York City, where he settled in the heart of Harlem a few blocks from Marcus Garvey and changed his name to William H. King Solomon (chapter 4).

The boys of the Industrial School for Freed Slaves were extraordinary. Most enslaved Africans imported to the Arabian Gulf from the nineteenth to the early twentieth centuries were not caught at sea by British cruisers or sent to mission schools. They lived out their lives in eastern Arabia under rather different conditions. Although historians have produced volumes on the African diaspora in the Atlantic world, scholarship on dispersed Africans in the Indian Ocean world has emerged much more recently and remains more limited in scope.[10] Re-creating the history of the African diaspora in eastern Arabia requires some breaks with convention. The standard histories of the Indian Ocean tell us that the slave trade from East Africa to Arabia was eliminated by the diligent work of the British Royal Navy in the second half of the nineteenth century and should have been, at the very least, cut to only "a trickle" by the last decades of the century. But the captures of 1896 attest to a thriving slave trade to Arabia through the turn of the twentieth century.[11] With a few notable exceptions, much of the conventional literature on Middle Eastern slavery (sometimes mislabeled "Islamic" or "Arab" slavery) tends to emphasize nonproductive labor outside of the economic sector, strengthening the stereotype that most slaves in the region were elite slaves or domestic slaves; yet in the Gulf a great number were part of a labor force geared toward export production.[12] Economic historians tell us that the Gulf should have been too poor to account for significant demand for slaves following the region's loss of trade after the Napoleonic Wars, the rise of competition from steamships, and the opening of the Suez Canal in 1869.[13] Likewise, historiography produced within the Gulf has tended to further reinforce a "rags-to-riches" image of a region long impoverished before the development of oil under the benevolent tutelage of the region's sheikhs and sultans.[14] But evidence suggests that the late nineteenth century was a period in which the Gulf economy was expanding dramatically. Between the 1860s and the 1920s, two industries in particular—dates and pearls—underwent rapid expansion and created new demands for labor. In many ways the existing historiography is insufficient to contextualize stories like the dhow captures in Oman in 1896 that led to the creation of the Freed Slave School. Conventional interpretations of slavery and the economy in the Gulf and Western Indian Ocean are strained to explain the growth of enslaved populations in this late period. This book argues that the growth of African communities in the Gulf should not be seen as part of an isolated "Islamic" slave trade but part of an economy that—like its predecessor in the Atlantic—was influenced by global forces.

Demand for slave labor in the Indian Ocean grew for a host of reasons, most notably the expansion of commodity production for global consumption in the nineteenth century. On the East African coast, growth in demand accompanied the development of a massive plantation complex that produced cloves, coconuts, grain, copra, oil, and sugar for both domestic and global consumption.[15] Likewise, in Arabia and the Gulf, the rise in demand for slave labor accompanied the expansion of production of commodities such as dates and pearls for global markets. But these commodities have received considerably less attention, perhaps because trends in the existing historiography have tended to obfuscate the connections between slavery and global commodity chains in the Middle East. Imperial Britain, which nominally controlled much of eastern Arabia and made abolition of the Indian Ocean slave trade a centerpiece of its nineteenth-century imperial policy, tended to see slavery as a permanent fixture of Arab society and therefore largely missed the connection between the growth of the slave trade and growing global demands for Gulf products. As Abdul Sheriff has poignantly argued, British imperial agents and their early historians regarded Arabia as "a convenient bottomless pit that allegedly consumed any number of slaves that their lively imagination cared to conjure up."[16] Arabs were assumed to demand slaves simply because they were averse to hard work and partisans of a religion or culture that "condoned" slavery rather than for any economic reason. Until very recently, scholars of "Islamic slavery" could argue that slavery in the Middle East differed fundamentally from Atlantic slavery in three timeless ways: an overwhelming preference for women over men, a preponderance of "elite" slavery (soldiers, eunuchs, women in harems, and retainers) over manual labor, and labor limited to the nonproductive sector.[17] Thus, while the Atlantic historiography could debate the extent to which slavery in the Western Hemisphere was the by-product of European economic expansion or may have contributed to it,[18] slavery in the Middle East was frequently regarded as a permanent and fundamental element of Islamic civilization or Arab character. In *Orientalism*, Edward Said noted, "Whereas it is no longer possible to write learned (or even popular) disquisitions on either 'the Negro mind' or 'the Jewish personality,' it is perfectly possible to engage in such research as 'the Islamic mind,' or 'the Arab character.'"[19] Said's criticism might be applied to studies of "Arab" or "Islamic" slavery; historians tend not to label slavery in the Atlantic world as inherently "Christian" or "European."[20] Without question, Islam regulated who could be enslaved and how slaves were treated, just as it encouraged the manumission of slaves for religious purposes,[21] but the demand for slave labor in nineteenth-century eastern Arabia was driven by economics rather than religion. To be sure, old patterns of slave ownership for conspicuous consumption endured and employment of slaves as elites and domestic servants persisted, but a fundamental shift in the use and acquisition of slaves accompanied the spread of global capitalism in the Indian Ocean and Middle East in the nineteenth century.

Not long ago, the historiography on slavery in the Middle East was so limited that older stereotypes about Middle Eastern slavery could be accepted uncritically. More recently, however, historians of the Middle East, led foremost by scholars of the Ottoman Empire, have presented far more sophisticated and nuanced histories of slavery in the region.[22] Methods of enslavement, sources of slaves, and use of slave labor differed widely throughout Ottoman history and within the empire's vast territory. Elite slavery and domestic slavery typified the slave experience in some but not all of the empire's history. At various times, slave labor was employed in agriculture and industry.[23] Taken in conjunction with new research by historians of Indian Ocean slavery, it is now clear that for much of the region's history slave populations were drawn largely from Eurasian populations, were predominantly female, and were probably engaged primarily in domestic labor or were acquired as "symbols of conspicuous consumption, to reflect the power and wealth of slave owners."[24] But dramatic quantitative and qualitative shifts in slavery occurred in the nineteenth century as a result of a confluence of economic forces. By the late nineteenth century, slavery in the Gulf was typified by African males laboring in pearling or date farming. Older modes of slavery persisted, but they were augmented or overwhelmed by new ones. As the Middle East, including the Arabian (Persian) Gulf, was drawn into the expanding global economy in the nineteenth century, dependence on global markets subjected the Gulf economy to the whims of international consumer tastes and supply and demand.[25] In the nineteenth century, the Gulf experienced a boom in date exports, fueled in part by new markets in North America and Europe. The lucrative American date market grew as Salem and New York merchants expanded American trade in the Indian Ocean with places like Muscat, Zanzibar, and Aden.[26] Likewise, the pearling industry expanded dramatically as pearl fashion experienced a revival in Europe and created new markets in North America. Pearl exports skyrocketed in the first decades of the twentieth century as the desire for pearls spread beyond royal and aristocratic classes. As early as 1863, Sheikh Muhammad bin

Thānī of Doha, Qatar, could remark to William Palgrave, "We are all from the highest to the lowest slaves of one master, [the] Pearl," lamenting the growing dependence of the region on the caprice of global markets.[27] Ironically, some of the same countries that pushed for the abolition of slavery were also the largest consumers of the commodities produced by slave labor.

Growing demand for labor in the date-farming and pearl-diving sectors of the Gulf economy created increased incentives for importing slave labor. In the nineteenth century, the primary (although not exclusive) source of this labor became East Africa. Arabia's long-standing trade connections with coastal East Africa facilitated early Arab participation in indigenous slave trading networks in the Mozambique Channel, Madagascar, and Indian Ocean islands. Mariners from the Gulf helped supply African captives to French planters on the Mascarene Islands in the eighteenth century and witnessed rising demand for East African laborers from Atlantic powers like Portugal, Brazil, and the United States in the early nineteenth century. The collapse of extensive European demand following British abolition, the Napoleonic Wars, and Atlantic antislave-trade measures drove prices down and encouraged Arab traders to begin employing large numbers of enslaved Africans on plantations of their own on the coast of East Africa and its nearby islands, as well as to transport them to Arabia.[28] By the 1820s, European visitors described sizable populations of enslaved Africans in Gulf port cities.[29] By the turn of the twentieth century, the demographics of the African diaspora in the Gulf were clearly visible. In 1905, Africans reportedly accounted for 11 percent of Kuwait's population, 22 percent of Qatar's population, 11 percent of Bahrain's population, 28 percent of the Trucial Coast's population, and 25 percent of Muscat and neighboring Mutrah's population. J. G. Lorimer estimated that Africans made up roughly 17 percent of the total population of coastal eastern Arabia between Oman and Kuwait.[30]

Telling the story of the African diaspora in the Gulf also requires departure from some traditional understandings of globalization and the history of capitalism. Popular understanding of neoliberal economics holds that globalization promotes free markets and free labor and should therefore tend to eliminate slavery and coerced labor. Received wisdom is that globalization and slavery should not coexist since the former tends to eliminate the latter. In this cheery narrative, greater connectivity precipitates greater freedom, modernity replaces tradition, tyrants yield to democracies, and slavery gives way to abolition and free labor. The reality is of course far more complicated. Similar to the case of cotton production in the Mississippi Valley and the American South, as Walter Johnson has shown,[31] in nineteenth-century Arabia (and much of the rest of the world), increased global connectivity promoted slavery and the slave trade just as it spread free markets. In the Gulf, expanding global markets for Arabian products like dates and pearls fueled demand for slave labor. Growing markets, made possible by means of faster communication and transportation, combined with new opportunities for expansion in Africa and partnerships with European imperial powers to create an expansion rather than a decline in slave trading in Africa. For the Africans caught up in the vicious Indian Ocean slave trade, the expansion of global markets meant enslavement rather than liberation.

By the late nineteenth century, Arabia and the Gulf had become economically dependent on the export of dates and pearls, commodities that relied on slave labor. The expansion of capitalism and new, faster means of transportation and communication (for example, steamships, the telegraph, the Suez Canal) transformed the Gulf's economy by creating new markets and new demands for labor. But the same forces that led to the rise of the Gulf's global date and pearl markets also helped to bring about their collapse and consequently upended Arabia's slave economy. Horticulturalists from the United States would use global shipping, communication, and consular networks to bring Gulf date palms to California. At the same time, Japanese entrepreneurs would apply industrial techniques and global marketing to mass-produce and distribute cultured pearls. California dates and Japanese cultured pearls soon undercut the Gulf's main export industries and presaged an economic collapse that in turn eliminated demand for slave labor and thrust enslaved Africans into new uncertainties. Many were cast out to fend for themselves or forced into dependent relationships with their former masters. Globalization was a two-edged sword with the power to both generate and extinguish wealth and demand for labor.

Telling the story of the African diaspora in the Gulf also requires challenging some conventions about British imperialism. Received wisdom attributes the decline of the slave trade in East Africa and the Indian Ocean to the dutiful work of the antislavery squadron of the British Royal Navy. Because the historiography of the East African slave trade was so deeply influenced by the rhetoric of abolitionism, Britain is popularly understood to have introduced manumission into societies that had promoted slavery for centuries and imposed abolition through force and diplomacy.[32] I argue instead that the British government struggled to formulate a coherent policy toward slavery in the Indian Ocean because the aims of liberal politics clashed with the aims of liberal economics. An aggressive antislavery movement pressured the British government to combat (or at least appear to combat) the slave trade in the Indian Ocean, but Gulf territories nominally under British hegemony demanded slave labor. The British administration in the Gulf therefore turned a blind eye to slavery until pressured by the League of Nations in the 1920s. Although it is true that the antislavery squadron captured many slave ships, the British antislavery campaign in the Indian Ocean was also fraught with fraud, graft, and callousness and ultimately failed to check a trade that continued well into the twentieth century. Slave traders adopted techniques to evade patrols that were sparse and underequipped. Most "freed slaves" captured early on by the Royal Navy in the Indian Ocean were sent to far-off ports, where at least a third died shortly after being disembarked. Those who survived were contracted out to local elites to work as domestics or in cash-crop production or were put to work in the ports. When deposited at mission stations in Kenya, Mauritius, Zanzibar, and the Seychelles, "freed slaves" were renamed; introduced to new clothing, religion, and language; paired off and married in group ceremonies; and required to perform labor similar to slaves in Arabia. Many free African sailors were captured and "freed" during the campaign as well. Even some wealthy Zanzibari merchants were captured by the navy and sent as "prize negroes" to South Africa, where they were contracted to perform menial agricultural labor after being "rescued" by the Royal Navy. For most of its history, the Gulf was not a British lake. It was a contested imperial space in which Britain struggled to balance controlling a territory reliant on slave labor while fulfilling its commitment to ending the slave trade in its empire. British imperialists recognized the dependence of Arabia on global markets and slave labor and bent imperial structures into contortions to preserve slavery in order to attain bigger imperial goals in the Indian Ocean.

Approaching the history of dispersed Africans in the Gulf also requires a reconsideration of the primacy of the Atlantic in diaspora studies. The editors of a recent compilation of essays on the history of race and slavery in the Middle East stated succinctly that slavery in the Middle East was characterized by "the absence of anything resembling the traumatic American experience of slavery." Among the key differences, the authors identified the absence of racial oppression, the absence of a legacy of "racial" issues in politics, no political division or civil war over slavery, and the comparatively small population in the Middle East descended from slaves.[33] To be sure, the experiences of enslaved Africans throughout the Indian Ocean world seem like conspicuous aberrations from the normative experience of the broader African diaspora. As a corollary, in the Indian Ocean, many of the key elements usually associated with the concept of "diaspora" are also absent. Many of the essential characteristics that typify the diasporic experience according to Robin Cohen's seminal treatise on global diasporas are largely missing in the Gulf, including "a collective memory and myth about the homeland," "an idealization of the supposed ancestral home," and "the presence of a return movement or intermittent visits to home." In fact, beyond the first characteristic, "dispersal," the African diaspora in the Indian Ocean seems a poor fit for Cohen's ideal type of diaspora.[34] In Arabia today the descendants of enslaved Africans do not usually identify themselves as Africans but as Arabs. Arabia has not produced a popular pan-African movement or a group of intellectuals who call for reparations for slavery. A leading scholar of the African diaspora in the Indian Ocean has noted that unlike the Atlantic world, the Indian Ocean world has not had a Western-educated class of African individuals and has therefore not produced an Equiano, a Césaire, a Garvey, or a DuBois. "In sharp contrast to the situation in the Atlantic world," Edward Alpers notes, "there is no literary tradition struggling either to recall African origins or to understand the retention and transformation of African ways in the new world in which Africans found themselves as a consequence of the slave trade." Furthermore, "not a single spokesperson has yet emerged from within the region to articulate the history or contemporary situation of any of these communities." In much of the Indian Ocean world, he concludes, "Africans have been made 'invisible' to all but the most interested outsiders."[35]

Pier Larson reminds us that "the Indian Ocean is not the Atlantic."[36] Although the Atlantic world dominates scholarship on the African diaspora, the American creole experience is but one of many contexts for the dispersion of Africans around the world. In spite of the enormity of the transatlantic slave trade—which coercively removed between 11 and 12 million Africans by the best estimates—Africans who were enslaved in the Americas were actually outnumbered by those who were internally displaced within the African continent and dispersed through the Trans-Saharan and Indian Ocean slave trades between the seventh and eighteenth centuries. Although the African diaspora in the Americas dominates scholarship on the diaspora, its experiences of slavery are not normative.[37] Internal displacement within Africa accounted for a much larger and more important part of the African diaspora. Martin Klein has estimated that even at its peak, the Atlantic slave trade produced more enslaved Africans who were relocated and kept within Africa than were sent abroad. Abdul Sheriff and Ralph Austen have drawn similar conclusions about the Indian Ocean and Trans-Saharan slave trades. If there is a normative experience of slavery in the global African diaspora, it may be the intracontinental experience.[38] Seen within the broader context of the African diaspora both within and outside of the African continent, the Atlantic experience may prove to be exceptional rather than normative. In this book, I seek to follow Larson's call for "recentering the global African diaspora onto the African continent and creating theories of diaspora that are Africa-centric and based on captives' subjective experiences." With the growth of our knowledge of the African diaspora in other parts of the world "it is no longer possible to think of the African dispersions of the western Atlantic as constituting either the demographic center of the African diaspora or as providing its core models of cultural adaptation, self-consciousness, and community formation."[39]

To decenter the Atlantic paradigm in the study of the African diaspora, we would be wise to take a page from Dipesh Chakrabarty's efforts to "provincialize" a Europe that is "deeply embedded in *clichéd and shorthand forms* in some everyday habits of thought." Chakrabarty's project developed out of the realization that political modernity was impossible to think of anywhere in the world "without invoking certain categories and concepts, the genealogies of which go deep into the intellectual and even theological traditions of Europe." The critique of colonialism itself, Chakrabarty notes, owes an intellectual debt to European enlightenment. An analogous situation faces historians of the African diaspora who venture beyond the familiar world of the Atlantic. It is challenging to explore the experiences of Africans anywhere in the world without invoking the terminology and theoretical frameworks of the Atlantic paradigm.[40] Larson urges us to "recenter," not reject, the concept of African diaspora. Our use of the term "diaspora" must be "expanded, geographically recentered, and reworked to reflect the experiences of all Africans in dispersion from their homes." Although commemorating enslavement and identifying connections with Africa may be characteristic of the Atlantic branch of the diaspora, we must be careful not to expect to find these characteristics universally throughout the global African diaspora.[41]

The Indian Ocean is indeed not the Atlantic, and we should not expect to find parallels of every aspect of the Atlantic creole experience in the Indian Ocean. Qualitative differences in slavery in both oceans abound. Aside from the geographical and temporal differences (the slave trade endured longer and later in the Indian Ocean world and peaked nearly a century later), Gwyn Campbell notes that slaves in the Indian Ocean world also "enjoyed an array of traditional and prescribed rights unknown on the American plantations." Slaves generally possessed a legal status and were immune from state corvees, and their marriages were generally respected. In the Indian Ocean world, there is no single meaning for "slavery," but a variety of terms stemming from a variety of roots signify different levels of servility. The meanings of these terms could overlap, slaves could move up and down in the hierarchy of statuses, and some slaves could also own other slaves. The enslaved populations also differed. In contrast to the Atlantic world, Africans did not constitute the majority of enslaved peoples in the Indian Ocean world even at the slave trade's peak. Campbell thus argues that "the application of the simplistic, literally black-and-white dichotomies of the Atlantic model in Indian Ocean slavery studies becomes nonsensical." The conventional dichotomy between "slave" and "free" that is central to the Atlantic model is rendered "irrelevant" in application to the Indian Ocean world, where slaves constituted one of a number of servile groups within a hierarchy of dependency and reciprocal obligations.[42] Joseph Miller adds that there were also fundamental political differences between slaving environments in the Indian

Ocean and Atlantic worlds stemming from the fact that in contrast to the Indian Ocean, European slavers in the Atlantic operated in "a political *tabula rasa*" far from their homelands.[43]

There are nevertheless important similarities between the two regions that deserve to be highlighted. The benefit of comparing experiences of enslaved Africans in the Atlantic and Indian Ocean worlds was first demonstrated by Fredrick Cooper.[44] To begin with, in parallel with the Atlantic world, as Campbell and Alpers note, the expansion of the use of slave labor in the Indian Ocean world grew with the expansion of capitalism and the growth of global markets for tropical products.[45] The economic forces that created the demand for slave labor in both environments have distinct parallels that deserve to be placed in dialogue. It is my hope that this book will help foster broader discussion between scholars of both regions and, by challenging some conventions of each, deepen that conversation.

In the following chapters, I draw on elements and methodologies from global history, diaspora studies, and microhistory. The demand for labor that formed the backbone of the slave trade to the Gulf, I argue, can be understood only in the context of the commodities that slaves were forced to produce—namely dates and pearls. To develop this point, I draw on elements of commodity histories pioneered by Sidney Mintz and others. I see the framework for this story as largely economic and global and so draw on the work of scholars of world history. I seek to make modest interventions in diaspora studies and so draw on that work as well. In addition, I also hope to draw out global themes from the particular stories of individuals and thereby seek to respond in a small way to the recent call by Francesca Trivellato and Tonio Andrade for a "global microhistory."[46]

This book is arranged into six chapters, which each explain an aspect of the story of diasporic Africans in eastern Arabia. Chapter 1 places the history of the East African slave trade and the growth of the African diaspora in eastern Arabia in global context. By following the lives of enslaved Africans from the moment of their capture in East Africa through their passage across the Indian Ocean to destinations in Arabia, the chapter challenges some myths about the East African slave trade preserved in colonial literature. Chapter 2 addresses the development of two forms of dependence in nineteenth-century Arabia: dependence on global markets and dependence on slave labor. It tells the story of how dates, a sticky, sweet fruit, became a delicacy in the United States and how the United States became the Gulf's biggest foreign customer. Producers in the Gulf expanded their date output to meet growing American demand, which further drove a demand for slave labor, much of which came from East Africa. Slaves performed much of the backbreaking work of watering, tending, harvesting, and packing the dates that fed global markets in the late nineteenth and early twentieth centuries. The chapter explores the lives of enslaved Africans who labored in agriculture in the Gulf and places them in the context of global cash-crop production in the nineteenth century.

Chapter 3 demonstrates how Africans were essential to the massive Gulf pearling industry, which by 1900 produced more wealth from pearls than all other regions of the world combined. Pearls had long been a staple of the Gulf economy, feeding regional markets centered on India and the Middle East, but in the late nineteenth century, Gulf pearls found new markets in Europe and North America. Increased demand for divers led to a rise in the slave trade from East Africa. Enslaved Africans, who accounted for as much as half of the Gulf's diving population, performed labor essential to the Gulf economy. Chapter 4 addresses aspects of everyday life, particularly family life and labor, among enslaved Africans in the Gulf. It examines how enslaved Africans negotiated the bonds of slavery and interdependence and found ways of resistance. Space for controlling aspects of their own lives was limited, but during the boom in the date and pearl industries around the turn of the century and particularly once the British began to grant manumission certificates, the possibility of flight brought greater leverage to slaves to negotiate their terms of service. This chapter further examines family life among enslaved Africans, particularly how bonds of enslavement affected marriage, concubinage, and childbirth. Chapter 5 examines British antislavery policy in the Indian Ocean, focusing particularly on the lives of enslaved Africans who were "freed" by the Royal Navy, and it illustrates how their lives were remarkably like those of slaves in the Gulf. I highlight contradictions in the British antislavery campaign in the Indian Ocean and argue that the British government struggled to formulate a coherent policy toward slavery in the Indian Ocean because the region's economy was dependent on slave labor.

Chapter 6 explains how global economic forces drove the catastrophic collapse of the Gulf's two leading industries in the 1920s and 1930s and how this collapse affected the lives of enslaved Africans in the Gulf. The more developed economies of Japan and the United States replaced the Gulf's exotic exports with products of their own, and in only a few years the Gulf's date and pearl industries declined sharply and, with the help of the Great Depression, ultimately collapsed. With the Gulf economy in tatters, African labor declined in importance, and many slaves were cast out of their masters' homes to fend for themselves, while the bonds between former masters and former slaves often remained strong. In the conclusion, I locate the African diaspora in Arabia in the context of the wider African diaspora today and address the process of "forgetting" the African contribution to the economy and culture of the Gulf region.

1

THE EAST AFRICAN SLAVE TRADE AND THE MAKING OF THE AFRICAN DIASPORA IN ARABIA

The British paddle-wheel steamer HMS *Sphinx* was anchored off the Batinah coast of Oman near Al-Musna'ah on the night of October 10, 1907, when it received some unexpected visitors. Just before 11:00 p.m. three young African men paddled a canoe from shore and begged to be taken aboard. All three professed to be slaves from the nearby village of Bu 'Abali. The commander, F. Shirley Litchfield, recorded their ages as seventeen, twenty, and twenty-two. Two of them explained that they had run away because of ill treatment, and the third said he had escaped because he was threatened with being sold. At noon two days later, while the ship was anchored about twenty miles farther north, near the town of Khaḍra', two more African men paddled out in a canoe, followed by another at dawn the following morning. One of the young men had an iron manacle fastened around his ankle that he said his master had made him wear for the past three years. Commander Litchfield ordered the iron ring sawed off the man's ankle and had the scene photographed on the deck of the *Sphinx* to submit with his report. He also had the six fugitives photographed twice, once standing side by side on the deck of the ship wearing the clothes in which they had escaped—simple waistcloths—and then a second time in a caricature, dressed up by the crew in an odd assortment of clothing and posed around an issue of the English bourgeois magazine *The Bystander*, which they pretended to read. The photographs were sent off to the magazine and subsequently published. They appeared in the November 27, 1907, issue under the headline "Where Slaves Are Slaves!"

The first photo was captioned "A British Ship for Safety," and the second photo of the men reading the magazine was captioned (intended ironically) "A Little Much-Needed Improvement."[1]

The six African fugitives were unexpected arrivals aboard the HMS *Sphinx*, but they were not altogether unusual. The *Sphinx* had a decade-long tradition of accepting fugitive slaves off the coast of Oman and may have had something of a reputation for refuge among enslaved Africans in Batinah. As the center of Oman's date production, Batinah was widely known as the home of the largest concentration of Africans in the Gulf. The commander of the *Sphinx* began granting freedom papers to runaway slaves in 1897, citing the authority of the General Act of the Brussels Conference, although some officials had reservations about his policy. Fugitive slaves also had a habit of escaping to the British consulate in Muscat, which received more than one thousand runaways between 1884 and 1905. The presence of a large enslaved African population on the

Six slaves aboard HMS *Sphinx*, 1907. Used by permission. National Museum of the Royal Navy, Portsmouth, UK.

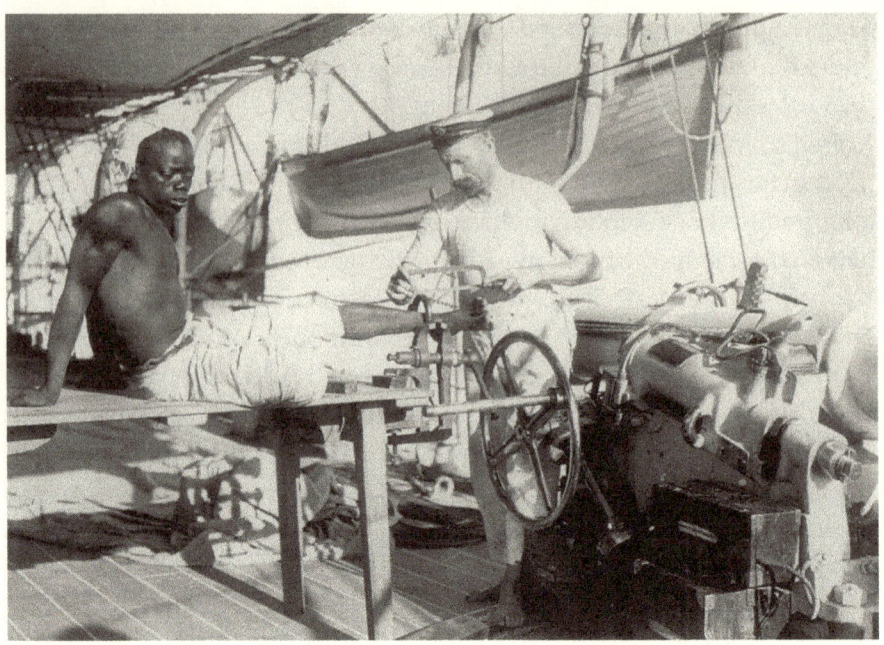

Carpenter on HMS *Sphinx* sawing off the shackles of a slave, 1907. Used by permission. National Museum of the Royal Navy, Portsmouth, UK.

Batinah coast of Oman in the early twentieth century demands some explanation. British treaties with the sultans of Muscat and Zanzibar made the importation of slaves to Oman illegal back in 1845, and the British Royal Navy's celebrated antislave-trade campaign in the western Indian Ocean had supposedly reduced the slave trade to "a trickle" in the decades that followed. Yet on the centennial of the Act for the Abolition of the Slave Trade, slavery was unquestionably alive and well in the shadow of the British Empire.[2]

This chapter provides an outline of the history of the slave trade from East Africa to eastern Arabia—a subject worthy of a book of its own and that this chapter can at best only summarize. In the following pages, I seek to provide context for the chapters that follow. In subsequent chapters I will argue that slavery and the slave trade to the Gulf were intimately connected to the economics of the region. As global markets for dates and pearls expanded, so too did demand for slave labor, and much of this labor was drawn from East Africa. In this chapter, I argue that the slave trade was neither timeless nor static. It rose and fell through various periods on account of supply and demand, with the most dramatic rise accompanying the recent spread of global capitalism into the region in the nineteenth century.[3] As mentioned in the introduction, scholars not long ago assumed that the slave trade from Africa to the Middle East emanated from the religion of Islam itself and that it was a permanent and essential feature of Muslim societies.[4] The records of the Zanj Revolt of ninth-century Basra and an ambiguous reference in the great Muslim explorer Ibn Battuta's *Rihla* were once seen as clear evidence of a millennium of extensive slave trading from East Africa to Arabia. British colonial policy in both East Africa and the Gulf was likewise informed by the popular conception that slavery was an essential element of Arab and Islamic culture.[5] As Abdul Sheriff has shown, much of British historiography on East Africa was shaped by abolitionism and colonialism.[6] The eminent imperial historian Sir Reginald Coupland wrote that the slave trade ran "like a scarlet thread" through centuries of East African history.[7] Murray Gordon theorized that slavery in Arab countries was linked to a natural Arab disinclination for work that had resulted from the early Islamic conquests of the seventh and eighth centuries. "Household slavery," he wrote, "was an indispensable form of labor in Arab society, where the people were ill-disposed to doing menial work."[8] More recently, the notion that slavery was a perpetual feature of Islam found supporters among American conservatives between September 11, 2001, and the invasion of Iraq in 2003. A critic in the *National Review* in May 2002 argued that slavery in the Islamic world was in fact both longer-lived and greater in extent than slavery in the West.[9] The reality, of course, is far more complex. Although slavery existed in the Middle East (and almost everywhere) in antiquity (earliest references to the sale of slaves in Mesopotamia date to the third millennium BCE), the sources of slaves, their treatment and rights, and the work they did varied greatly over time and location. Islam did not invent slavery, and like other monotheistic traditions, it did not entirely condemn it. Islam undoubtedly improved the lives of enslaved populations in regions it entered by giving slaves legal status and protection under the law. More than half of the nineteen references to slavery in the Quran deal with manumission and freedom.[10] The late nineteenth century and early twentieth century were a unique period in the history of slavery in the Gulf, and slavery in this

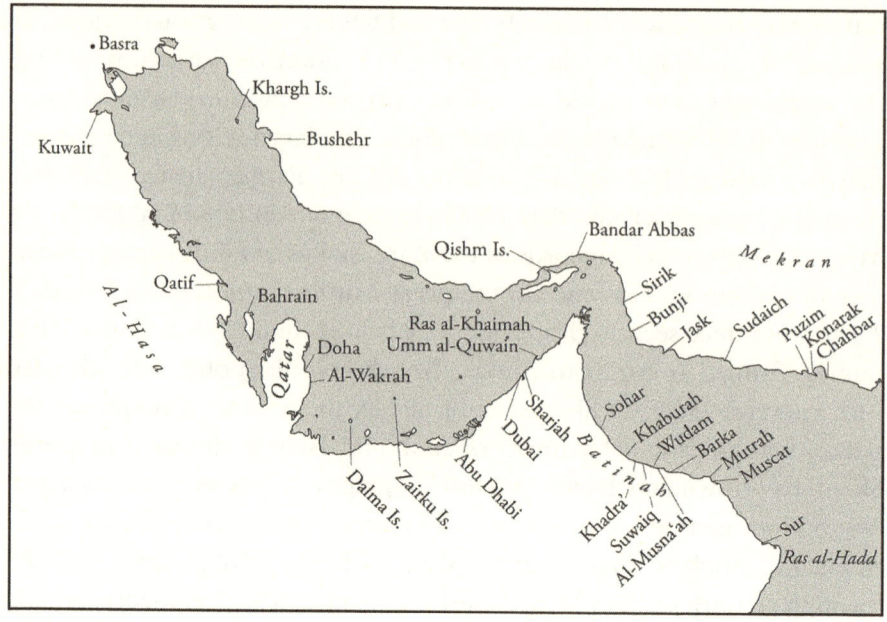

Arabian (Persian) Gulf

period must be seen as a product of a confluence of global factors, not as a timeless feature of Arab or Muslim society.

The Arabian Gulf Setting

In the second half of the nineteenth century and the first quarter of the twentieth century, the Gulf enjoyed an economic boom spurred by exports in dates and pearls, both of which were dependent on slave labor. Growing demand for labor in the date-farming and pearl-diving sectors of the Gulf economy kept the trade in enslaved men and women profitable into the twentieth century and drove many traders to participate in the slave trade from parts of East Africa and elsewhere. As a result, the African diaspora in the Gulf grew dramatically during this period, accounting for nearly a fifth of eastern Arabia's population by the turn of the twentieth century. Although Africans did not constitute the Gulf's entire slave population—men and women from Baluchistan and Persian Mekran, particularly after World War I, accounted for a significant portion of the region's enslaved community—the substantial African population stood out to numerous observers by the nineteenth century. If we could transport ourselves back in time to the Gulf that the HMS *Sphinx* patrolled over a century ago, we would find a substantial African presence just as visitors can find today.[11]

At the turn of the twentieth century, the Gulf that Africans inhabited bustled with activity. The sandy Arabian coastline that stretches along the western shore of the Arabian (Persian) Gulf between Muscat and Kuwait—a region that this book refers to as "the Gulf"—was punctuated with lively fishing villages and busy port towns. The Gulf possessed half of the world's date palms, and visitors marveled at the seemingly endless green of date plantations that stretched for miles into the interior along the coast to the north of Muscat. During the annual date harvest, the port towns teemed with stevedores—many of them African—loading ships and date packers—mostly women—working in godowns to box and bag dates for export as camel caravans delivered tons of fresh dates from the interior daily.[12] On the shore, fishermen hauled in catches of kingfish, yellow-fin tuna, skipjack, and barracuda from hand-woven gillnets and pulled up heaps of sardines and anchovies with cast nets. More than 30,000 men on 3,500 fishing boats plied the waters of Oman, and Africans were frequently among their crews. The smell of the daily catch surrounded fish markets, while on beaches, anchovies dried and fish smoked beside fishermen repairing their nets. In the pearling months, April to September, tens of thousands of men packed into boats, chanting, singing, and drumming as they rowed out into the Gulf, where they would stay for months at a time. The start and finish of the season was greeted with a frenzy of activity as pearl merchants and their intermediaries, the *tawāwīsh* (sing., *tawwāsh*), haggled with pearling captains for the best of the annual pearl catch. More than 64,000 men on some 3,400 boats worked in the pearling industry at its height in 1915.[13] Perhaps one-quarter to one-half of these diving crews were of African ancestry. The port towns teemed with Indian merchants and financiers; Arab, European, African, and Indian sailors; local residents; foreign visitors; slaves; and former slaves. Stevedores loaded ships bound for India with dates, dried limes, and ghee and unloaded bags of rice. Ships from Zanzibar brought timber, coconut fiber, tropical fruits, and spices. Slave oarsmen rowed merchandise out to waiting ships in the harbor and escorted ships' crews to shore and between Muscat and Mutrah. American ships took dates and hides and brought in exchange cash and their main import (ironically), oil in the form of kerosene. Enslaved Africans lived and worked in each of the major cities of the Gulf and made up a substantial portion of rural populations.[14]

The twelve-hundred-mile stretch of coast between Muscat and Kuwait was a diverse environment. Visitors to the Gulf who arrived by way of the Arabian Sea would pass the easternmost point of the Arabian Peninsula, called Ras al-Hadd, and would see the port town of Sur, Oman's major shipbuilding and slave-importing center, with a large lagoon full of long-distance ships awaiting the annual monsoon, before approaching the steep, dark mountain crags that surrounded the region's major mercantile hub: the twin harbors of Muscat and Mutrah. European steamers, French and British men-of-war, and hundreds of local craft crammed Muscat harbor, a large bay surrounded by rocky outcrops guarded by two large forts, numerous watchtowers, and the walled city of Muscat. Nearby Mutrah, accessible to Muscat only by sea, was the larger of the two cities and the terminus of the trade routes to the interior of Oman. Mutrah was the financial center of the whole coast, home to a large settler Indian Khoja community that had for generations been the financiers of Omani seaborne trade. Muscat was the political center of the Omani coast; permanent residence of the sultan of Muscat and his retinue; and home to foreign agents and ambassadors, the American mission hospital, and its school. The two cities boasted a combined population of some 24,000 in the early twentieth century, making them the largest metropolitan area in the southern Gulf, rivaled in size only by Bahrain's capital, Manama, and the populous cities of Kuwait and Dubai in all of eastern Arabia. Muscat's population was a cosmopolitan mixture of some 10,000 residents, with Arabs vastly outnumbered by Africans and Baluchis. Mutrah's population was around 14,000, more than half of the residents Baluchis and a substantial number of Indians.[15]

North of Muscat lies Oman's Batinah coast, the densest agricultural area south of Iraq and one of the most populous parts of the Gulf. To observers in the late nineteenth century, Batinah looked like one solid 150-mile stretch of date plantations that extended for seven miles into the interior. Set behind the sandy coastline were vast tracts of date gardens dotted with fortified towns. Between the palms grew fruits, vegetables, and lucerne, which fed goats and cattle. The camel, which was the main mode of inland transportation, fed on dates. More than 50,000 people lived along Batinah's coast, with another 60,000 living in the mountains and oasis towns surrounding the distant Jabal Akhdar range. Of the numerous coastal towns—Seeb, Barka, Al-Musna'ah, Suwaiq, Khaḍra', Khaburah, Saham, Sohar, Liwa, Shinas, and Kalba—the most important was the fortified town of Sohar, residence of the leading *wali* (governor) of the coast, loyal to the sultan at Muscat. Batinah was the largest date-producing region in the Gulf and, not coincidentally, also home to the region's largest African population. Many of Oman's enslaved Africans worked to irrigate and maintain the region's date palms. Oman was the most densely populated part of eastern Arabia, probably accounting for half a million people, more than all other regions of eastern Arabia combined. The region generally enjoyed widespread religious tolerance. Most Omanis were Ibadhi Muslims, with significant numbers of Sunnis and small minority populations of Jews, foreign Christians, Khojas, and Hindus.[16]

The Batinah Coast ends at the Musendam Peninsula, a rocky outcrop that juts out into the sea and comes within thirty miles of Iran at the Strait of Hormuz. Beyond Musendam's rocky fjords and around the sharp corner to the west lay the Trucial Coast, so called for its early-nineteenth-century anti-piracy treaties with Great Britain and home today to the United Arab Emirates. This stretch of the Gulf was surrounded by desert and had only limited agriculture; it subsisted largely from the sea—fishing, trading, and pearling. This sandy coast was only sparsely populated except at the urban centers of Ras al-Khaimah, Umm al-Quwain, Sharjah, Dubai, and Abu Dhabi. Its biggest city was Dubai, whose population may have seasonally approached 20,000, followed by Sharjah with a population of 15,000. Abu Dhabi, Umm al-Quwain, and Ras al-Khaimah each had populations of around 5,000 or 6,000, and other settlements were much smaller. Most of that stretch of coast was only settled around 1800. Each coastal town had its own ruling sheikh, drawn from its leading families. The cities of Ras al-Khaimah and Sharjah were ruled by members of the Qāsimī family, who followed Wahabism, while much of the rest of the coast was made up of branches of the Beni Yas, who were Sunni Muslims. Taken together, the population of this coast approached 80,000. These people imported most of their provisions and subsisted largely on their revenues from pearling. Around the turn of the twentieth century more than a quarter of the population of this coast was African. To the west of Abu Dhabi, the Trucial Coast turns gradually north, although it is almost entirely uninhabited until it turns into the Qatar peninsula.[17]

Most of Qatar is desert, so the peninsula was sparsely populated except on its eastern coast, where the cities of Al-Bidda (Doha) and Al-Wakrah had a combined population of some 20,000 residents. Nearly all of the men in these cities were engaged in one way or another in pearl diving. In the early twentieth century, at least 3,000 of Al-Wakrah's population of 8,000 were African, and two-thirds of these were slaves. Another 3,500 Africans lived in Al-Bidda, where the population was around 12,000. Most of Qatar's population of 26,000 was Sunni Muslim. On the west side of the Qatar peninsula lay the island chain of Bahrain with its majority Shi'i Muslim population, a substantial population of Sunnis (including the island's ruling sheikh), and a large presence of foreigners. Bahrain's main island was home to Manama, the political and economic center of the northern Gulf, home to the British agent (and later the British resident, the highest-ranking officer in the region), and seat of the king of Bahrain. Manama had a population of 25,000, of whom about 20 percent were estimated to be African. The island's capital was also its economic center and home to the Gulf's major pearl merchants, intimately tied to Bombay. Across a small channel from Manama was the small island of Muharraq, home to some 20,000 people, most of whom were engaged in pearling and 2,500 of whom were Africans. Bahrain's other main towns included Budeyya' and Hadd, each with 8,000 residents. Much of the rest of the island was engaged in agriculture and pearling.[18]

The stretch of the coast between Bahrain and Kuwait was Ottoman territory that later came under the control of the Kingdom of Nejd and its king, Ibn Sa'ud. Known as the Ottoman province of Al-Hasa, the region was home to an estimated 100,000 people scattered between the coast and inland oases. The largest coastal town was Qatīf, the main Ottoman outpost on the Arabian Peninsula, home to perhaps 5,000 people. Inland, the Turkish provincial capital, Al-Hofūf, and its surrounding towns contained perhaps 25,000 residents. Most of the population of this region was Shi'a, and many were involved in pearling. To the north, Kuwait was home to some 50,000 people, of whom some 37,000 lived in Kuwait City and at least 4,000 (11 percent) were African. Kuwait was the shipbuilding center of the northern Gulf and one of the largest suppliers of boats and men for the annual pearl dive. Kuwait possessed a fleet of more than four hundred boats, and more than nine thousand pearl divers. Beyond Kuwait lay the inland Ottoman provinces of Basra and Baghdad.

The African Presence in the Arabian Gulf

Scholars once assumed that the extensive slave trade from East Africa to Arabia in the nineteenth century could be traced back to ancient history, but more recent scholarship has made that perspective untenable. In fact, evidence for a large-scale ancient slave trade to Arabia is scant. In the absence of formal assessments before the modern period, it is difficult to estimate the size of African populations in the Gulf's distant past. Before the late nineteenth century, the limited sources for such estimates include descriptions by European visitors and representatives of the British East India Company; such descriptions are inherently subjective, anecdotal, and impressionistic, as European travelers seldom saw beyond the major port cities of the region and usually stayed briefly. If there was a substantial African presence in the Gulf before the late eighteenth century, it appears to have been largely invisible to outside observers, as their accounts make scarce mention of it. By contrast, European travelers from the early nineteenth century onward attest to a significant African population in the Gulf and a thriving slave trade. Such limited evidence suggests either that European visitors became more aware of Africans or that the numbers of Africans increased significantly. When considered in conjunction with the history of developments in East Africa, the latter is most likely.

Africans were undoubtedly present in the Gulf prior to the late eighteenth century, despite their limited visibility to outsiders. In the late seventeenth century John Ovington described the inhabitants of Muscat without mentioning Africans and referenced slavery only in the context of the mercy that was shown to enslaved captives taken when Muscat soldiers evicted the Portuguese from the Gulf. He does, however, relay a secondhand story in which thirty "Black Sailors" jump overboard from a ship bound from Muscat to Surat in order to evade capture by pirates.[19] The Scottish sailor

Alexander Hamilton, who visited Muscat around 1700, observed that slaves roasted fish on hot rocks in Muscat's intense heat and that the king of Muscat was attended by an army of one hundred slaves armed with matchlocks and swords at his forts in Nizwa and Rustaq.[20] Hamilton's account of date production at Basra, however, makes no mention of Africans. He describes the workers who harvested and packaged the dates (ten thousand tons annually) simply as the "poor."[21] Likewise, when Abraham Parsons visited Basra, Bahrain, and Muscat aboard the HMS *Seahorse* in 1775, he witnessed pearling, fishing, and agriculture in a variety of forms, but if he saw Africans or slaves, he did not think to mention them.[22] Likewise, Lt. John Porter (1787) described the inhabitants of Muscat as Arabs, Indians, Persians, and Baluchis and did not reference Africans.[23] The Salem sailor Daniel Saunders, who was shipwrecked off the coast of Oman in 1792, discussed Muscat in his account of his misadventures but did not allude to any Africans other than the African American members of his own crew.[24] Carsten Niebuhr did not include Africans or slaves in his description of his visit to Muscat in 1765 except to say that a previous imam of Muscat, Saif bin Sultan II (r. 1719–1743) of the Ya'rubi dynasty, had an army of "Caffer slaves."[25]

Africans were nevertheless present. The great Arabic chronicle of Omani history attests to the presence of Africans in the military and on date plantations. According to Salil ibn Razik's *History of the Imams and Seyyids of Oman*, Imam Saif bin Sultan (r. 1692–1711) of the Ya'rubi dynasty owned 1,700 slaves and a third of the date palms in Oman.[26] The same chronicle records that Imam Ahmed bin Sa'id (r. 1744–1783) obtained 1,000 East African slaves through a single purchase in the 1740s and had a standing army made up of 1,100 slaves and 1,000 free men.[27] Enslaved Africans were undoubtedly present in the Gulf before the nineteenth century, although their numbers appear to have been small enough to evade the notice of most foreign visitors.

Beginning in the early nineteenth century, however, visitors began to write unambiguously about a large African population and a robust slave trade in the Gulf, especially in Muscat. John Malcolm, a Scottish diplomatist who served as British emissary to the court of Persia from 1799 to 1801, identified Muscat as "the great mart" for slaves. He portrays the beaches of Muscat as crowded with slaves and recounts a slave seller in the market.

Malcolm describes a diverse population of enslaved peoples: Georgians, Nubians, Abyssinians, and "the Seedee, or Caffree, as the woolly-headed Africans are called," who he argued were far better treated than the slaves of the plantations of the Atlantic world. He observed that most were married and became "in a manner, part of their master's family" and "not unfrequently (with the exception of the woolly-headed Caffree) lose . . . all trace of their origin."[28] He noted, "When we take a comparative view of the fate of the victims of this commerce, from the stain of which our own country is hardly yet purified, and which is still carried on, openly or clandestinely, by almost every power of civilised Europe, we shall be compelled to acknowledge the superior humanity of Asiatic nations."[29]

When John Johnson visited Muscat in 1817, he witnessed a slave auction being held openly in the bazaar.[30] James Silk Buckingham, who visited Ras al-Khaimah in 1816, estimated the population of the town to be at least ten thousand "of whom probably three thousand are males capable of bearing arms, and certainly more than half of these are negroes, of African birth."[31] Around the same time, William Heude (1817) visited Muscat and found the heat so oppressive in the summer that "the only race of people who seem to bear living on this unwholesome spot, are the blacks of the Abyssinian coast, to the southward of the Red Sea, with curled or woolly hair." He explained that "Most of the persons, particularly the females, who are seen in the streets here either belong to this race, or may be traced as descendants from them, by their complexion and features: they are probably the offspring of Arab fathers, and of Abyssinian (slave-women) mothers." Heude also observed an open slave market, which he described in detail:

> On my return in the evening, I passed through the slave bazaar where three times a week slaves are exposed for sale, and disposed of by auction, or private contract. The sale had just commenced, as I stopped to view a scene that had at least the interest of novelty. Twenty or thirty young Africans, brought across the desert and chiefly from the coast of Zanguebar, were arranged in rows on either side of the bazaar, and according to their sex. They were in general handsomely trimmed (dressed is an improper term) for the occasion; and appeared in truth perfectly resigned; being certainly in

as clean and sleek a condition, (with a cloth girdle round their middle, for their only covering) as their owners or purchasers could have wished. The latter, indeed, in walking between the ranks, seemed extremely particular in handling and feeling the bodies and skins of their intended purchases; extending their inspections to such minute particulars as quite astonished me.[32]

Robert Mignan in 1820 found that although the sultan of Muscat had done "all in his power to suppress slavery, a great traffic is still carried on between the eastern coast of Africa and Oman, and every family retains two or more slaves of both sexes."[33] George Keppel (1824) observed that the women of Muscat were "generally speaking, the offspring of Arab men and Abyssinian negresses."[34] Keppel also witnessed a slave auction being held openly in the market. He also noted that "the suburbs of Muscat appear more populous than the town. The inhabitants are principally Abyssinian slaves."[35] By 1831, the British Resident reported an annual importation of 1,400–1,700 African slaves into Muscat, with three-fourths of these coming from East Africa and the remainder from Ethiopia. The same source references an additional 210 slaves delivered annually to Ras al-Khaimah and Sharjah, 300 to Bahrain, and 245 to Bushehr in Persia.[36] Within a decade, records showed more than 1,200 African slaves being re-exported to the far northern Gulf by way of remote Kharg Island.[37] A source from 1841 estimated an intake of 3,488 slaves arriving in the Gulf annually.[38] By the 1870s, Africans accounted for at least a quarter of Muscat and Mutrah's population.[39]

The Growth and Size of the East African Slave Trade

The increased trade in enslaved Africans to the Gulf in the nineteenth century stemmed from the brutal vagaries of economics—supply and demand. On the supply side, the development of a systematic process of slave trading in East Africa explains part of the story, and it should be noted that this global development was intimately connected to European slave trading to both the Americas and European colonies in the Indian Ocean. On the demand side, centuries-old patterns of slave ownership for domestic and reproductive purposes and for enhancement of social standing—that is, conspicuous consumption—were supplemented by requirements for labor in expanding economic activities at various times in the Gulf's history. But in no previous period was demand as great as in the nineteenth century. It is true that Arabs from eastern Arabia, who had settled in East Africa as early as the eleventh century, brought small numbers of captives to Arabia over the course of centuries of commerce.[40] But as a large-scale endeavor, the slave trade developed only much later in response to European demand for slave labor in the Indian Ocean, a demand that itself built upon indigenous slaving networks centered on the Mozambique Channel.

An early slave trade from East Africa to the Gulf certainly existed, although scholars debate its extent. Abdul Sheriff cites Abbasid scholar al-Jahiz (ca. 767–868) to make a strong case for a significant presence of East Africans from both Zanzibar and Pemba in ninth-century Basra who were presumably a large part of the Zanj Revolt (ca. 869–883), a civil war in which thousands of slaves and their allies rebelled against the Abbasid caliphate. Sheriff also cites numerous Arabic accounts of kidnappings in East Africa (often by enticing children with dates) to establish that slave trading was indeed substantial in East Africa in late antiquity.[41] By contrast, Ghada Talhami has argued that the inference that the "Zanj" of the ninth-century Basra revolt refers to the same "Zanj" of East Africa is problematic, as the term was used by some Arab geographers to refer to the Sudan, and most of the participants in the revolt had origins in the Nile and Red Sea zones rather than coastal East Africa. Likewise, Ibn Battuta makes only passing reference to slavery in his account of the major East African port city of Kilwa and provides no clear evidence that Arabs were transporting enslaved Africans to Arabia in the fourteenth century. At any rate, the political and economic devastation of the Zanj Revolt and the subsequent disruption by the Qarmatians in the Gulf seems to have discouraged any further large-scale use of imported African labor in the region for several centuries.[42] There is no evidence to suggest a large African presence in the region again for at least another six hundred years.

Thomas Vernet has argued that the East African slave trade in fact remained modest until the second half of the sixteenth century. Swahili and Comorian communities used slaves as concubines, domestic servants, bodyguards, sailors, and agricultural laborers, but their clientele relationships with mainland communities provided abundant labor, so slaves were not in great demand and, when acquired, were more valuable for prestige than productivity. In the sixteenth century, diverse factors—including the arrival of the Portuguese, who gradually encroached on the gold and ivory trades and established permanent settlements in Asia and Africa that led to new labor demands; the disruption of Red Sea slave trading networks resulting from the Oromo military expansions in Ethiopia; and the growing prosperity of Swahili city states—appear to have encouraged some Swahili merchants to turn to the slave trade. The arrival of Yemeni, Hadhrami, and Omani settlers in the sixteenth century may have facilitated the transmission of some East African slaves to Arabia, but in the sixteenth century the trade was still comparatively small. Paul Lovejoy suggests that 1,000 slaves departed the East African coast each year for the Indian Ocean, to which Pier Larson projects an additional 300 per year from Madagascar. By these rough estimates one could conclude that the slave trade total for East Africa in the whole of the sixteenth century may have amounted to 130,000.[43]

In the seventeenth century, as Vernet argues, Swahili traders were involved in the trade in enslaved Africans, mostly Malagasy, from Madagascar to the coast of East Africa, amounting to between 3,000 and 6,000 captives each year. He concludes, however, that slaving in the interior of East Africa by the coastal polities appears to have been rare before the end of the eighteenth century, except at Kilwa.[44] Vernet therefore favors a lower estimate of around 3,000 captives, with peak year exports around 4,000 for the seventeenth century. He notes that the Omani removal of the Portuguese from Muscat in 1650 was followed by significant expansion in the Omani economy and that chronicles attest that the Omani ruler, Imam Saif bin Sultan I, ordered the planting of thirty thousand date palms and a renovation of Oman's irrigation system. Imam Saif was reputed to have personally possessed one-third of Oman's date palms and to have owned between 700 and 1,700 slaves. His reign is also associated with Omani expansion in East Africa, sovereignty over the island of Pate (near Lamu), and the expulsion of the Portuguese from Mombasa. With an increased Omani presence and demand, Vernet argues that Arabia and the Gulf "absorbed the majority of the captives" in the seventeenth century, a number that may have amounted to 3,000–4,000 annually. Lovejoy estimates seventeenth-century East African exports at 1,000 per year, to which Larson proposes an additional 1,100 from Madagascar, and Jane Hooper and David Eltis document another 417 per year (between 1624 and 1700) going from East Africa to the Americas. By these estimates the East African slave trade may have ranged between 240,000 and 400,000 captives for the whole of the seventeenth century.[45]

Edward Alpers, Richard Allen, Abdul Sheriff, and others have shown that European demand was a significant factor in the growth of the East African slave trade in the eighteenth century. Portuguese demand for slave labor in Brazil and French demand for labor on sugar plantations on the newly acquired Mascarene Islands in the central Indian Ocean were important factors in the transformation of the slave trade in that period. At the same time, Omani settlers on Zanzibar had come to dominate regional trade by the mid-eighteenth century. Omani merchants participated and profited from a vibrant trade in enslaved Africans as French entrepreneurs transformed the previously uninhabited islands of Mauritius (formerly Île de France) and Réunion (formerly Île Bourbon) into sugar-producing islands modeled on the slave islands of the Caribbean. French planters sought slave labor from Africa, particularly Mozambique and Madagascar. Arab mariners, especially from Hadhramaut and Oman, actively engaged in this trade, although French producers were also able to bypass Arab intermediaries by negotiating sales directly with Portuguese Mozambique and indigenous rulers. In the best-known example, one French slave trader, Maurice, negotiated an arrangement with the sultan of Kilwa to provide him a thousand slaves annually, an arrangement that inspired the Omani re-subjugation of Kilwa in 1784.[46] French, Spanish, British, American, and Portuguese slave traders also looked to East Africa for supplies of captives for Atlantic markets, just as Omani planters sought slave labor for their expanding date plantations in Oman. Hooper and Eltis document 70,930 enslaved Africans taken from East Africa and Madagascar to the Americas in the eighteenth century (approximately 61,000 from East Africa and 10,000 from Madagascar). They argue that this increase was linked initially to the British acquisition of the Spanish Asiento in 1713 and later to the growth of French plantations on the Mascarenes.[47] The slave trade to the Mascarenes certainly grew dramatically between the 1720s and the 1770s and became most extensive between the 1770s and 1780s, when the intense competition for slaves drove the average per capita price up from MT$22 (Maria Theresa dollars) in 1770 to a peak of MT$40 in 1784. Richard Allen has concluded that 160,500–186,800 slaves may have been exported to the Mascarenes between 1770 and 1810, and he has documented 641 slaving voyages to the Mascarenes between 1768 and 1809 (229 from Madagascar, 196 from Mozambique, and 84 from the Swahili Coast). Lovejoy estimates 400,000 captives sent into the Indian Ocean in the eighteenth century from East Africa, to which Larson suggests an additional 152,000 from Madagascar (a figure that may be low, as Vernet estimates an average of 2,000–3,000 Malagasy slaves passing through Pate island alone in the second half of the eighteenth century), and Hooper and Eltis add about 71,000 going to the Americas. By these estimations the East African totals for the whole eighteenth century may have been upward of 623,000.[48]

Only after an extensive slave-trading network had developed in East Africa, at least partly created by European demand, did the slave trade have a profound demographic impact on Arabia. After Omanis took control of the key port city of Kilwa in the late eighteenth century, a significant portion of the slave trade was directed to the island of Zanzibar, where Omanis had ruled since 1698 and where Omani entrepreneurs were developing plantations of their own. Part of this transformation is attributable to the collapse of slave prices during the Napoleonic Wars, as Britain seized the Mascarenes from the French and the Atlantic market for slaves collapsed, which led to the halving of prices of slaves in East Africa. Prices dropped from an average of $40 (MT) to around $20 (MT) between 1784 and 1822.[49] Abdul Sheriff has shown that the drop in prices and the elimination of markets in Mauritius and the Americas inspired the development of a large-scale plantation complex in East Africa. As Sheriff has argued, "It was members of the Omani merchant class who were in a position to initiate the transformation of the slave sector of the economy of Zanzibar. From their acquaintance with the Mascarenes they realized that if slaves could not be exported, the product of their labor could." Omani planters in Zanzibar and on the east coast of Africa thus took advantage of the slave trading systems that had developed in response to European demand and employed slave labor on plantations of their own to produce commodities for global markets.[50] By contrast, Vernet argues that Omanis already had large estates with numerous slaves, who were mainly accumulated for prestige rather than production, as early as the 1770s on Zanzibar and from the 1790s on Pemba, where grain was produced for export. When cloves were introduced on Zanzibar in the early nineteenth century, there were already some fifteen thousand slaves on Zanzibar.[51] In any event, the available supply of African captives appears to have found a ready demand in the Gulf around this same time.

An enormous jump in demand for slave labor across the Indian Ocean accompanied the spread of global capitalism into the region and the expansion of new global markets for tropical products. On the East African coast, growth in demand accompanied the development of a plantation complex that produced cloves, coconuts, grain, copra, oil, and sugar for both domestic and global consumption.[52] Likewise, in Arabia and the Gulf, the rise in demand for slaves accompanied the expansion of production of commodities like dates and pearls for global markets. In the Americas, the massive expansion of the coffee and sugar plantation economy in Brazil, accompanied by British Atlantic antislave-trade efforts north of the equator between 1807 and 1835, created new demand for East African slaves south of the equator, mostly taken from Quelimane and Mozambique.[53] This global confluence of factors caused the nineteenth-century slave trade to dwarf any regional precedent. As Janet Ewald poignantly observed, "In no other part of Africa, and at no other time, did slavery and the slave trade expand as rapidly as in nineteenth-century East Africa."[54] In the nineteenth century, a single port in a single year could export more slaves than the entire western Indian Ocean had exported over the course of two decades during the eighteenth century. Edward Alpers considers it a reasonable estimate that 15,000 slaves were exported each year from Mozambique Island alone during the 1820s and 1830s.[55] Indeed, Mozambique Island was known to export 17,000 slaves annually by 1837, and Kilwa exported 22,000 slaves annually by 1865.[56] Hooper and Eltis document 440,023 slaves departed aboard European (mostly Portuguese/Brazilian) vessels for the Americas between 1800 and 1860.[57]

Estimates for the dimensions of the slave trade in the western Indian Ocean in the nineteenth century range widely.[58] Lovejoy estimates 1,487,000, while Larson estimates 1,312,000 (including northeast Africa), and Gwyn Campbell's figures total 3,084,000.[59] Thus, the range for the nineteenth century is between roughly 1.3 and 3 million—at least double the previous century and without question greater than the sum of the three prior centuries combined. The estimates for the size of the slave trade in the western Indian Ocean can therefore give us the following broad ranges of slaves traded for the period between 1500 and 1900:

Years	Estimate
1500–1600	> 130,000
1601–1700	240,000–400,000
1701–1800	> 623,000
1801–1900	1,312,000–3,084,000

The focus of this book is thus concentrated on the nineteenth century.

The Size of the Slave Trade to the Gulf

How many of the captives caught up in this massive trade in the nineteenth century were actually sent to the Gulf? In the absence of the kinds of documentation that exist for the Atlantic slave trade (formal insurance and banking registers, ships' manifests, etc.), historians have largely had to rely on less precise methodologies like "carrying capacity estimates" or guestimates derived from qualitative observations. Unfortunately, as Abdul Sheriff put it, "The famished qualitative data cannot be milked beyond their capacity to yield."[60] Early speculations from qualitative data were spectacularly high. R. P. Baur estimated that eighty thousand slaves were exported from East Africa per year in the 1880s. Similarly, R. W. Beachey estimated that 5 million slaves were exported from East Africa in the nineteenth century; Richard Reusch stated that "many millions" were exported from East Africa; Reginald Coupland argued that the slave trade from East Africa was "prodigious"; and C. S. Nicholls placed the annual average exports to Arabia at between fifteen and twenty thousand.[61]

Contemporary observers in the Royal Navy who were close to the slave trade provided accounts estimating the proportion of slave shipments they captured in a given year. One method of deducing how many slaves were actually sent to Arabia involved taking these accounts at their word and then applying the percentages mentioned to the numbers actually captured and recorded in the Royal Navy's meticulous records. For example, in filing his annual report for 1868, Admiral Leopold G. Heath, the commander-in-chief of the East Indies Station, wrote the following:

> I observe that it is not unusual to close these reports with an expression of the hope that the heavy blows which have been dealt at the trade during the past year will go far to check it for the future. I can express no such hope. The trade is far too profitable and will not be affected by a risk so small as that incurred by the proceedings of Her Majesty's Ships. . . . To put down this trade requires far more effort and far more energy than England has yet shown in the matter. Twenty five years have elapsed since the first treaty with Muscat and all that time we have been contented with the capture of a very small percentage of the total exports. . . . We must do far more than this to ensure success. We must double or treble our squadron.[62]

Heath estimated that British ships seized "less than 5 percent of the slaves exported" from East Africa in 1868.[63] Admiral Heath's words were echoed by nearly every naval commander, admiral, and consul involved in Indian Ocean antislavery efforts between 1858 and 1873. The records of slave captures are preserved in the Admiralty records, and when statistics are adjusted (to remove the possible cases of mistaken identity—that is, vessels captured without any enslaved Africans aboard or fewer than ten Africans aboard, who may well have been passengers or crew [more on this in chapter 5]), the numbers of captures can be easily tabulated and compared to arrive at cumulative totals.[64] In 1866, 721 (67 percent) of the total number of enslaved Africans captured by the Royal Navy (1,075) were captured at or beyond Cape Guardafui, leaving little doubt that they were bound for the Arabian Peninsula. These 721 captives were found aboard only seven vessels. Applying the number of captives in 1866 (721) to Heath's stated 1868 estimate that only 5 percent of the slaves bound for Arabia were captured would lead to a total of 14,420, a figure that may be close to what Heath assumed from his vantage point. This kind of methodology is likely what led Nicholls and others to arrive at figures of around 15,000 slaves imported per year. The frustration of British officers on the ground who may have felt the need to exaggerate to get additional support from the Treasury could have influenced these claims. In 1860, Christopher

P. Rigby, British consul at Zanzibar, estimated that 3,000–5,000 slaves were taken north from Zanzibar each year.[65] Later the same year Rigby estimated that "at least four thousand slaves are still taken north every year," about half of which he estimated were taken from Zanzibar.[66] In 1861 he estimated that at least 40–50 dhows belonging to Qāsimīs and Suris would run cargoes of slaves northward that spring alone.[67] He estimated that 2,000 had been taken from Zanzibar harbor in the spring of 1861.[68] Following that spring, he adjusted his estimates upward, concluding that 10,000 slaves were run north from East Africa annually in 150 dhows. Rigby reported that the HMS *Lyra* and *Sidon* captured 25 dhows that season, and he urged the return of two British steamers each March and April and again each September and October to put an end to the slave trade. He later estimated that "not even one per cent of the slaves taken north every year is captured by British cruisers."[69]

"Boarding a Slave Dhow" (Arab sailing vessel), ca. 1885. Used by permission. © National Maritime Museum, Greenwich, UK. Reference #F5766.

Since the 1970s, historians applying these kinds of estimates by "men on the spot" to various periods of time have produced a range of estimates. Esmond Martin and C. I. Ryan have estimated that 314,200 slaves were brought to Arabia in the nineteenth century.[70] Lovejoy makes only minor adjustments to their figures, bringing the exports from East Africa to Arabia, Persia, and India in the nineteenth century to 347,000.[71] Sheriff estimates 2,000 per year for the first half of the nineteenth century and a declining curve thereafter, from which we might extrapolate that he estimates 150,000–200,000.[72] Ralph Austen estimated 313,000 for the Gulf and 492,000 for the Red Sea for a total of 805,000 for Arabia.[73] So the expansive range of nineteenth-century estimates of imports to Arabia is between approximately 150,000 and 805,000 (anywhere between 5 and 61 percent of the total). Such diverse estimates and scant data make it impossible to gauge with any precision the proportion of slaves transported from East Africa to Arabia. However, if estimates by Martin and Ryan for Arabia are compared with those of Larson for East Africa, we might conclude that 23.9 percent of the East African trade was destined for Arabia, a ratio that is very similar to that which can be derived from Lovejoy's estimates for Arabia, Persia, and India when compared against his East African estimates: 23.3 percent. When minimum and maximum extremes of the rough estimates are avoided, it may be possible to imagine a ratio of perhaps one-quarter of the East African slave trade destined for Arabia, although historians simply do not know with any certainty. Historians of East Africa, however, generally agree that the slave trade peaked around mid-century and was centered on coastal East Africa rather than Arabia. Most Africans enslaved in East Africa remained there. Each of the existing estimates, however, presumes a sharp drop-off after formal abolition of the sea-borne slave trade in 1873.[74] This book does not introduce any new quantitative data, but it does provide a basis for questioning the presumed drop-off after 1873. In fact, the assumption of a sharp post-1873 decline has probably kept estimates artificially low, and the larger estimates may be more accurate than the lower estimates. Arabia may well have absorbed one-quarter to one-half million African captives in the nineteenth century, and higher estimates are possible.

The Experience of the Slave Trade: Routes to Slavery

Numbers tell only part of the story and are incapable of expressing the experience of the slave trade by the enslaved themselves. The passage from Africa to the Gulf was perilous, and only a handful of survivors managed to have their experiences recorded. We are nevertheless provided with a glimpse of the experience of this passage in the limited sources that have survived. These sources paint a picture of captive passages that often involved violence and alienation and frequently involved complicated and lengthy passages from original homelands to ultimate destinations.

Edward Alpers reminds us that the middle passage in the East African slave trade did not begin at Zanzibar or the coast. For the enslaved, the voyage began at the point of displacement or capture and included a march of weeks or months to coastal export centers such as Kilwa. From there, months could pass before the enslaved commenced another march to destinations further north, followed in turn by a passage to Zanzibar or Pemba. Yet more months still might pass before the slaves were sold to a buyer with intent to transport slaves away from the island.[75] Captives were often sold to professional slave dealers. In southeastern Africa, where most of these captives originated, selling often took place as part of large-scale transactions between the heads of larger commercial centers and major slave dealers. War captives were considered legitimate items of trade and sold alongside criminals, debtors, and otherwise kinless people. Cloth, brass, and gunpowder, the usual items of exchange for slaves, functioned as both currencies and commodities. Once sold, slaves were sent in caravans to the coast alongside porters who carried other items of trade like ivory and tobacco. Porters, the vast majority of whom worked voluntarily, were distinguishable from slaves by their dress and mobility. While porters marched along freely, slaves were either chained together or fastened into "slave sticks"—long, heavy forked branches fastened around the neck, referred to in some European accounts as *gorees*.[76]

In East Africa an individual could become a slave in several ways.[77] One could be born into slavery if one's parents were enslaved. One could become enslaved as a result of debt, pawnage, or subterfuge. It was also possible to be kidnapped or captured in battle and sold into slavery to a slave dealer or a passing caravan.[78] Very rarely, but during times of extreme

"Slavers Revenging Their Losses." From David Livingstone, *The Last Journals of David Livingstone, in Central Africa from 1865 to His Death* (London: J. Murray, 1880), 1:56. Courtesy Sterling Memorial Library, Yale University.

drought and famine, families might sell their own dependents into slavery in hopes that they might have a better chance of survival in servitude. However, in interviews freed slaves most frequently attested to being captured in raids or being kidnapped. In the middle third of the nineteenth century, wars and reprisals created many thousands of captives and fugitives. Attacks by groups of neighboring peoples could create large bodies of captives that in ordinary times might have been ransomed back or incorporated into the conquering society. As demand grew for slave labor on the coast, many of these captives were instead sold to slave dealers. Such attacks could demand reprisals, which would produce more raids and more captives. The cycle of violence in the late nineteenth century disrupted life for many thousands of people who were displaced in eastern and southeastern Africa.[79] European colonialists, explorers, and missionaries also often contributed inadvertently to the disruption that fed the slave trade through their expedient alliances, interference in local conflicts, and mismanagement of natural resources.[80]

The recorded testimonies of enslaved Africans reveal that raiding and war were among the most common methods of enslavement. These testimonies frequently name the attackers as "Maviti," an unfortunately imprecise term widely used in the late nineteenth century to describe any brigand rather than a specific ethnic group. Petro Kilekwa, who would later become an Anglican priest, was captured by "Maviti" in what is now northwest Zambia at the age of about ten in the 1870s. Kilekwa's mother tried to ransom him back after he was captured, but she was unable to meet the "Maviti" demands for eight yards of calico cloth.[81] A case from the Vice Admiralty court at Zanzibar in January 1872 reveals that the three slaves captured aboard a dhow bound for Zanzibar by the HMS *Wolverine* were all Kikutu-speakers (probably from around Morogoro, Tanzania) and had been captured through war.[82]

David Livingstone described in simplistic terms the way in which slave raiding took place in southeastern Africa. During his trip up the Ruvuma River in 1866, he recorded the following observation:

> The caravan leaders from Kilwa arrive at a Waiyau village, show the goods they have brought, are treated liberally by the elders, and told to wait and enjoy themselves; slaves enough to purchase all will be procured: then a foray is made against the Manganja, who have few or no guns. The Waiyau who come against them are abundantly supplied with both by their coast guests. Several of the low-coast Arabs, who differ in nothing from the Waiyau, usually accompany the foray, and do business on their own account. This is the usual way in which a safari is furnished with slaves.[83]

In the middle third of the nineteenth century, the slave trade centered on Lake Nyasa, today's Lake Malawi. Livingstone provided the famous descriptions of the slave caravans of the region that attracted the attention of antislavery activists, politicians, and missionaries in Great Britain. On his voyage up the Ruvuma River to Lake Nyasa in 1865–1866, Livingstone recorded his experiences in letters and journals that were published and widely read. In one classic account, which was accompanied by horrifying illustrations of the abuse of slaves in his published *Last Journals* in an immensely popular version published in 1875, Livingstone recalled the following: "June 27th.—To-day we came upon a man dead from starvation, as he was very thin. One of our men wandered and found a number of slaves with slave-sticks on, abandoned by their master from want of food; they were too weak to be able to speak or say where they had come from; some were quite young."[84]

The main region of slave raiding in the nineteenth century was southeastern Africa, the region bounded today by Mozambique, Malawi, and southern Tanzania. Although some limited slaving took place in what is today Kenya and Uganda, that traffic was considerably smaller by comparison. Slaving continued for a time in northern and eastern Tanzania and the eastern Congo, but this trade too was limited.[85] Ethnographic evidence compiled by British consul Edwin Seward in Zanzibar indicates that the vast majority of slaves manumitted by his office were from ethnic groups that correspond to today's Malawi, Mozambique, Zambia, and southern Tanzania.[86]

One testimony Seward recorded in 1866 described a caravan of over three hundred slaves who had been purchased for units of cotton cloth—adults for two yards and children for one yard. The party of slaves was accompanied by other caravans of traders, porters, and slaves, estimated at nine hundred all together. They began their march each morning at daybreak and continued for nine hours before camping. Slaves were fed only boiled sorghum and water once a day. They were forced to walk in a line, with men tied together with forked sticks and women and children with their hands bound. At night the men were arranged in groups of up to ten so that their sticks could be bound together at the center. They were forced to spend the night in that position and to urinate and defecate where they lay. On the way they passed at least a hundred corpses, and they described the road as reeking with the smell of corpses. They witnessed several murders along the way: children by blows in the face with a club; an infant thrown into the brush; and men clubbed, stabbed with a dagger, or strangled by being forced to sit against a tree and then having a leather strap wrapped around the tree and tightened around their necks. The caravan leader, Suleiman, did not perform the killings himself, but his orders were carried out by his servants.[87]

James Augustus Grant encountered a slave caravan in August 1890 on its way north to Kotakota on the western shore of Lake Nyasa. He relayed that the people of the Ruo River region just south of Lake Nyasa were "living in a state of terror" because their homeland had been claimed as the territory of a nearby Ngoni ruler. Grant noted that in the caravan that he witnessed the men were kept in slave sticks while the women and children were allowed to walk alongside without fetters.

> Shortly after encamping here, a caravan came in from the opposite direction. This caravan belonged to Jubi and consisted of 80 or 90 slaves. Purchased most likely from Mpiseni and on their way to Kotakota. The man slaves in most cases wore the slave stick but women and children were allowed to go free. In a very short span of time they had built a boma and good huts inside. The slaves especially the women looked well and were well dressed forming a marked contrast to the wretched natives of M'kasa's village. The Arabs in charge came over to us and begged for some necessaries but chiefly for soap, in order to look well on their arrival at Kotakota.[88]

Routes to the coast had many perils. Slave caravans themselves were not immune from capture. Caravans were sometimes ambushed and entire groups of captives stolen. One slave trader lamented to Livingstone in 1866 that all of his slaves had been taken by "Mazitu" raiders.[89] The inland route could also involve a voyage by boat across one of the lakes of the interior. Several European accounts confirm a brisk slave trade by boat across Lake Nyasa. By 1876, E. D. Young, a British naval officer, had observed five slave dhows operating on Lake Nyasa and estimated the ships carried some twenty thousand slaves across the lake each year.[90]

The Experience of the Slave Trade: From Coast to Coast

Once at the coast, captives were frequently held in barracoons, temporary shelters where they awaited sale or shipment. Many captives would remain on the coast while others would be sent to the islands of Zanzibar or Pemba, where they might remain or be sold or kidnapped and taken elsewhere. Edward Alpers has shown that it was not uncommon for slaves on the coast to change hands multiple times before arrival at Zanzibar.[91] The passage from the coast to Zanzibar could be particularly trying. Swema, a girl of perhaps ten years of age when she was swept into slavery from northwestern Mozambique in 1865, described the seaborne passage to Zanzibar as follows:

We were so closely packed that not only could I not turn, but not even breathe. The heat and thirst became insufferable, and a great sickness made my suffering even worse. At night a strong cold wind chilled us and covered us at every moment with sea foam that was raised up by the violence of the wind. The next day each one of us received a little drinking water and a piece of dry manioc root. Thus it was that we passed six long days and still more painful long days and nights. Hunger, thirst, seasickness, the sudden transition from great heat to insupportable cold, the impossibility of laying down one's head for a moment because of lack of space, finally all these sufferings combined to make me regret for the first time our painful voyage across the desert.[92]

When Swema landed in Zanzibar, her purchaser inspected her and decided she was too weak to be useful, so she was discarded and buried in a shallow grave in the sand outside of town. She survived only because she was rescued and brought to the Catholic mission in Zanzibar, which revived her and facilitated the publication of her story. In fact, the burial of slaves in shallow graves in Zanzibar was a fairly recent improvement on conditions from two decades earlier. Atkins Hamerton, agent of the British East India Company at Muscat, followed the sultan of Muscat, Seyyid Sa'id, when he moved to Zanzibar in 1840. Hamerton noted in 1842, "I beg to mention that, when I first arrived it was not the [custom] to inter the slaves. They were always thrown out on the beach when they died and devoured by the dogs of the town, but my continually talking to the Imam on the shameful practice—contrary to the law of God and men, as I used to tell him—, he has caused all dead bodies to be buried. I have seen fifty dead African men and women laying on the beach and the dogs tearing them to pieces as one sees the carrion eaten by the dogs in India."[93]

From Zanzibar captives could be transported to the island of Pemba (fifty miles north) or to the coast of today's Tanzania, Kenya, or Somalia to work on grain (or other) plantations, or they could be sold to markets in Arabia or the Gulf. Lovejoy estimates that most of the slaves brought to the coast from the interior stayed in East Africa while others were sent to places like the Gulf. Sheriff estimates that of the nearly twenty thousand slaves imported annually to Zanzibar in the 1860s, about 60 percent were retained on

Zanzibar, while the remaining 40 percent were re-exported, with 75 percent of the re-exports going to Lamu, 30 percent to Pemba, and 15 percent to Mombasa. From any of these locations they could also be sent to Arabia.[94] On Zanzibar in the 1860s, as Hideaki Suzuki demonstrates, numerous East African ethnic groups were represented in the slave population. The largest groups included the Yao (23.4 percent), Nyasa (11.5 percent), Sagara (8.6 percent), and Ngindo (8.4 percent). More than half of the slave population based on the sample provided by Rigby's manumission list of 1860–1861 came from the region between Kilwa and Angoche on the coast and its hinterland around Lake Nyasa.[95] At Zanzibar, David Livingstone visited the slave market in February 1866 and described it as follows:

> The slave owners go about in the slave market here with a woman or a child held by the hand calling out "seven dollars" "seven dollars." The highest was 20 dollars. They sit in rows looking dejected and ashamed. An Arab or a Persian comes forward and raises up a girl. Opens her mouth and examines her teeth, then her limbs and enquires how any scar was got. A wound from the lash decreases the value because it shows that she has been obstinate or disobedient. He usually ends by throwing his stick 20 yards or so and makes her walk for it to see as a horse dealer would say "her paces."[96]

Slaves were decorated, oiled, and clothed for display in the slave market. They were inspected and haggled over. Slaves could change hands many times on Zanzibar and were engaged in a variety of different forms of labor, including work on clove plantations.[97] As noted, slaves were used as a form of conspicuous consumption and incorporated as members into the lowest levels of their masters' houses. Jeremy Prestholdt has shown how "slaves were screens onto which concepts of civilization were projected." Slaves were renamed, given new clothes, and decorated as props in their masters' houses, often in ostentatious ways.[98] Child slaves in Zanzibar were also exposed to abuse and violence. Court records preserve the tragic story of a young slave girl named Kehonja, about ten or twelve years of age, who testified before Edwin Seward about how she was raped by an Indian shopkeeper after he forced her into his store as she passed on her bread delivery route.[99]

"Refractory Slave," Lamu, ca. 1860s. Used by permission. Robert Lambert Playfair Papers (msdep14/26/1). Courtesy of University of St. Andrews Library, St. Andrews, Scotland.

Children around the island were also vulnerable to being kidnapped and exported.[100] Arab traders from Trucial Oman would arrive annually, procure houses in Zanzibar, and purchase or kidnap slaves to bring back to the Gulf. In 1839 the Omani sultan, Sa'id bin Sultan, complained to the British Resident that vessels "belonging to the Arabian Ports in the Persian Gulf lying between Resel Khyma and Aboothabee" had carried off "by force or fraud three or four slaves for every one purchased" from his dominions in East Africa.[101] A report from the British native agent at Sharjah confirmed that men of that district went to Zanzibar "solely for the purpose of stealing slaves." The agent outlined some of the tactics these men used: "One plan, I am informed, is as follows: on their arrival . . . they draw up their vessels on shore and hire houses in the island . . . accompanied by many slaves formerly belonging to that part of the world. . . . These spread themselves through the place and, forming acquaintance among the slaves of the

"Slavery in Zanzibar," ca. 1890. Used by permission. © National Maritime Museum, Greenwich, UK. Reference #E9093.

Island, persuade them to come to their own houses where they entertain them with dates, sweetmeats etc. . . . This of course establishes an intimacy, and the intercourse continues until, a favorable opportunity offering, they are seized and detained in the house." Other tactics he recorded included the kidnapping of slaves who had been hired to carry goods purchased in the market, and the mixing of kidnapped slaves with slaves purchased in the slave market and embarking them to ships at night in small boats owned by merchants from Sur.[102] By the 1860s there were even reports of Suri slave traders "carrying kidnapped children through the public street in large baskets during the day, their mouths being gagged to prevent them from crying out."[103]

By 1860, Christopher Rigby explained that between December and March each year, when ships from the Gulf were in the harbor, "Zanzibar resembles a city with a hostile army encamped in its neighbourhood; every person who is able to do so sends his children and young slaves into the interior of the island for security; people are afraid to stir out of their houses, and reports are daily made of children and slaves kidnapped in the outskirts of the town; they even enter the houses and take children by force."[104] Rigby was appalled by the openness with which the slave trade was carried out by so-called "Northern Arabs," a term he applied to Arabs from "Trucial Oman" and Oman north of Ras al-Hadd. "The export of slaves was carried on by these piratical Arabs with impunity," Rigby complained in 1861. "One dhow embarked 150 slaves, and another 126 slaves within a few yards of the British Consulate. At this season of the year, the daily slave market is held outside the town as His Highness informed me, on purpose to prevent the Northern Arabs from purchasing slaves; nevertheless the market was daily crowded, morning and evening by Joasmees and Soorees openly purchasing slaves and leading them away."[105] British consuls at Zanzibar consistently noted that residents of Sur, Batinah, and the Trucial Coast were the biggest participants in the slave trade.

Arabic correspondence seized aboard dhows and preserved in Admiralty records from the second half of the nineteenth century also reveals that few traders who transported slaves to destinations in eastern Arabia owned their own dhows but instead paid captains of dhows to ship their cargos. Few dhow captains dealt in slaves in a major way, although many surely invested in some with each voyage. Owners and captains of dhows were paid transport fees for each slave safely landed in the destination port, ranging from MT$1/4 per slave for a short trip from Mbweni (near Dar es Salaam) to Zanzibar in 1872,[106] to MT$4 per slave for a trip from Zanzibar to Oman in 1865.[107] Unlike the ships in the transatlantic trade, dhows rarely carried exclusively slaves but carried mixed cargoes of trade goods, passengers, and slaves. A typical "slave dhow" would consist, in addition to captain and crew, of not one slave trader but many, each with the responsibility for feeding and paying transport for his own portion of the slaves aboard. In most antislavery captures at sea, these slave traders were assumed to be part of the crew or passengers, and the only name recorded was usually that of the captain, who was mistakenly assumed to be responsible for the entire cargo. One dhow captured in 1872 off of Ras al-Hadd carried 169 slaves (although it had departed with 200) belonging to fifteen dealers.[108] Although men dominated the business of transporting slaves from East Africa to the Gulf, correspondence seized aboard captured slaving dhows reveals that women were sometimes the principal buyers and even sent requests for specific types of slaves to be procured in Zanzibar.[109]

The East African slave trade was not a timeless feature of East Africa's history. Neither was it static. It fluctuated with time and grew exponentially in the nineteenth century in part because of European demand for slave labor. Captives could become enslaved in a variety of ways, and their long routes to their ultimate destinations could be arduous and convoluted. Their experiences varied and often involved their changing hands multiple times and traveling by both land and sea. At the same time, Arabian demand for African labor was not timeless or permanent. It expanded in the nineteenth century as a result of an expanding demand for labor created by growing global demand for Arabian products. Globalization helped fuel demand for dates and pearls and thereby expanded demand for African labor. The next two chapters address the date and pearl industries and the role of African labor in them.

2

SLAVERY, DATES, AND GLOBALIZATION

The *Glide*, an American bark, sailed into Muscat harbor on September 15, 1862, to obtain a precious payload. The ship had left Salem, Massachusetts, six months earlier and stopped first at Zanzibar and Aden to load coffee, ivory, hides, gum copal, beeswax, and chili peppers. But its most valuable cargo would be loaded at Muscat. The *Glide* was the property of John Bertram, Salem's most successful merchant. It had been built the previous year specifically for the Indian Ocean trade and was already on its second voyage to Muscat. Charles Benson, the ship's steward and the only African American member of the crew, carefully observed as the ship was loaded over four weeks in Muscat, and he recorded his impressions in his diary. For twenty days, Benson noted, workers loaded hundreds of bags of dates—2,060 in all—in intense heat. Temperatures ranged from 92 to 100 degrees Fahrenheit in the shade, and "very thick" swarms of hornets harassed the workers (they "sting severe," Benson remarked, wounding ten or twenty men a day). All of this was endured for the profits the dates would bring on arrival in the United States. In the final days before departure, the Muscat merchants who had facilitated the sale threw a party aboard the *Glide* for the crew. They covered the decks with Persian rugs; festooned the ship with lanterns, colorful flags, and an American ensign; and brought aboard a troupe of African dancers and drummers who entertained the sailors until four in the morning. After a month's stay in the harbor, the *Glide* sailed for Salem with more than two hundred tons of dates.[1]

Charles Benson and the crew of the *Glide* were agents in a vibrant trade between the United States and eastern Arabia that lasted for more than a century. The eastern Arabian date industry, which had fed local and regional diets for centuries, grew to global proportions in the late nineteenth century, serving faraway ports in Southeast Asia, Europe, and North America. The American market in particular became increasingly important in the nineteenth century. The United States eventually became the region's biggest foreign customer, importing nearly 80 million pounds of dates a year by 1925. Arabian date exports helped fuel an economic boom in the Gulf, creating new opportunities for consumption along the coast of eastern Arabia between Muscat and Basra. But dates also expanded the demand for slave labor in Arabia. Much of the labor force for the date industry came from the East African coast centered on Zanzibar.

This chapter explores the interconnections between global markets and slave labor in nineteenth-century Arabia. As eastern Arabian date exports expanded in the nineteenth century, the Gulf joined much of the rest of the Middle East (and a large portion of the world) in moving toward reliance on the production of cash crops for global consumption. As elsewhere, this trend in Arabia created both new possibilities and new complications. Foreign currency flowed into eastern Arabia as never before and created new wealth for the region's merchants, middlemen, and financiers. The growing export trade also provided new opportunities for women, who could earn cash in the date-packing industry and gain a source of independence in places like Muscat and Basra. But the expanding global demand for Arabian dates also created new demand for the back-breaking labor required to irrigate, tend, and harvest the annual date crops. Date plantations required a gigantic labor force, and in the nineteenth century much of this labor came from East Africa.

In the nineteenth century, the Arabian Gulf joined Egypt, the Ottoman Empire, and other regional powers in importing African slave labor to expand the production of cash crops for global markets. These slaves are an uncomfortable fit with prevailing perceptions of Middle Eastern slavery, which is conventionally seen as nonproductive and detached from economic processes.[2] Agricultural slavery, however, was far from exceptional in the Middle East. Although elite and domestic slavery were immensely important, a substantial proportion of enslaved Africans in the region worked in agriculture. In some ways, the forms of slavery found in the date gardens of eastern Arabia resembled forms of Atlantic slavery of a century before. This chapter demonstrates how globalization and expanding global markets influenced the demand for slave labor in the Gulf and how enslaved Africans contributed in vital ways to Arabian agricultural production and the Gulf economy. It also argues that even the most banal of commodities (for there could hardly be anything more humdrum than dried fruit) can illustrate the far-reaching social and economic effects of expanding global trade networks during this early period of globalization.

Muscat and the Origins of the American "Date Trade"

By one estimate, the world possessed some 90 million date palms at the start of the twentieth century. More than half of these trees were grown in the countries touching the Arabian Gulf, with an estimated 30 million palms grown in Iraq alone. Oman's share of the world's date palms was relatively small, estimated at around 4 million trees, with most of these palms grown on the Batinah Coast.[3] Yet it was Oman that contributed the most to the creation of global markets for dates in the nineteenth century, particularly the lucrative market in the United States. American ships carrying cotton cloth from Massachusetts mills visited Zanzibar and Arabian ports annually beginning in the first years of the nineteenth century and within a few decades became the leading foreign traders in the region.[4] Following the seasonal monsoon winds of the western Indian Ocean, American ships visited Arabia to exchange cotton cloth, piece goods, and specie for coffee, hides, and dates.[5] Muscat was the center for Arabian date exports, and Oman was home to particularly hardy varieties of dates that could survive lengthy sea voyages and ripened earlier than most dates on account of Oman's southern latitude and intense summer heat. The *fardh* variety of dates ripened in August, allowing American ships enough time to load dates at Muscat, catch the monsoon winds, trade at Zanzibar, and make the hundred-day journey home in time for the winter holidays. As American ships commonly returned from their voyages in the autumn, the arrival of Arabian dates in New York before Thanksgiving became an American tradition. Although *fardh* dates were not highly regarded in Arabia, Americans loved the sweet, sticky variety, and grocers stocked and sold millions of pounds of the fruit annually as a holiday confection. Grocers would use an ice pick to chisel off portions of blocks of sticky dates and sell them by the pound.[6] The annual autumn arrival of ships from Arabia catapulted dates into their unlikely role as an American holiday tradition. By the late nineteenth century, the United States had become Oman's best foreign customer, and Omani producers expanded their date output to meet growing American demand.

Long before the arrival of Americans, dates circulated widely within a regional market that stretched from the Red Sea to South Asia. In the largest date-producing areas of the Gulf—Basra, Al-Hasa (the east coast of today's Saudi Arabia), and Oman—date exports provided the basis for extensive regional trade and facilitated the importation of staples like rice from India. In the eighteenth century, tons of locally produced dates from the Ottoman *sanjaq* of Basra (a subdivision of the Baghdad *vilayet*) were annually exported each September by ships from Muscat that brought home coffee from Yemen and other goods in exchange. Basra dates found their largest outlet in India, which annually exported an estimated 30 *lakhs* of rupees' worth of cotton piece goods, rice, indigo, sugar, and metals to Basra in exchange (1 lakh [a numbering unit] = 100,000).[7] Oman too carried on an extensive trade in dates with India, largely in exchange for rice. Muscat trade statistics of date exports and rice imports between 1874 and 1904 are mirror images of each other on a graph—rice imports and date exports rose and fell in tandem.[8] Every part of Oman uses rice as the base for its local cuisine, although no part of the country can produce it in any quantity. Eastern Arabia had long depended on India for rice and offered dates in exchange. But the regional date trade would become globalized in the nineteenth century largely as a result of American intervention.

It is unclear exactly when the first shipment of dates arrived in the United States, but it must have been very early in the young republic's history. The brig *Fairy* brought a shipment of "Arabian dates" to New York and Baltimore in 1818, and it was advertised in newspapers in Charleston, Georgetown, and New York.[9] (If that early shipment of dates was America's first, it would be a fitting testament to the changing world of the nineteenth century: the *Fairy* was an Atlantic slave ship refitted for the Indian Ocean trade, and its captain would later sail the founding group of African

American settlers to Liberia.) Packages of Arabian dates may well have arrived in smaller loads at American ports earlier than 1818 as ships sailed from Aden and Mokha with loads of coffee. The famous trade between Salem and Zanzibar began essentially as a by-product of the coffee trade with Yemen. In 1826, the brig *Ann* became the first Salem ship to visit Zanzibar. It had come to Mokha for coffee, but its captain found the town short of provisions and went to Zanzibar to engage in some coasting trade.[10] In the decades that followed, Salem vessels made a habit of visiting Zanzibar and Arabia together, using the Indian Ocean's regular monsoon winds to gather the best products of both markets for Salem and sell their Massachusetts cottons.

By the 1850s, several American ships visited Muscat each year. They came by way of Zanzibar and Aden and brought back enormous loads of dates, in addition to the produce of those two ports. Atkins Hamerton, the British consul at Muscat, counted eleven American ships in Muscat harbor between 1851 and 1852, nearly all of them from Salem—the *Cherokee, Sophurnia, Tom Corwin, Lucia Maria, Iosco, Arthur Pickering, Lewis, Sacramento, Elizabeth Hall, Emily Wilder,* and *Said bin Sultan* (three of these visited twice in two years). Some of those ships paid only with cash, while others brought large shipments of American cloth from Salem mills to sell. The *Lucia Maria*, for example, sold 200 bales of cloth in Muscat in 1850 and 110 bales in 1851; the *Arthur Pickering* sold 114 bales in 1850 and 369 bales in 1851. Hamerton observed that Americans carried on a massive business in dates at Muscat, paying "from 20 to 25 dollars the Bahar of 1800 lbs . . . which yields, if they are of the proper sort and reach America in good condition, 100 percent profit." He estimated that the vessels on average carried away between 1,500 and 4,000 bags of dates.[11] The logbooks of American ships confirm these estimates: the bark *Warren White* from New York left Muscat harbor in January 1853 with 1,500 bags of dates, which accounted for the ship's primary cargo.[12] Hamerton explained that American ships would typically purchase wool with cash at the Pakistani ports of Gwadur or Karachi, then sell cloth or sugar at Muscat and pay for dates with cash before proceeding (sometimes via Bombay) to Zanzibar to fill up with cargo before returning to the United States.[13] A later British consul at Zanzibar, Christopher P. Rigby, lamented in 1860 that American merchants were "acquiring a monopoly of the carrying trade of coffee and grains from Aden, of dates, hides, etc. from Muscat, and of wool and hides from Mekran."[14]

American trade with Arabia boomed in the 1850s and 1860s, with dates and coffee at the fore. Sixteen-year-old Lawrence Pierson Ward kept an unusually careful diary on his first voyage from Salem to Arabia aboard the *Elizabeth Hall* in 1851, and his account attests to the centrality of dates in the trade between the United States and the Indian Ocean. The Salem bark was one of many Americans ships engaged in this lively trade. According to Ward's diary, the *Elizabeth Hall* left Salem in March and arrived in Zanzibar fourteen weeks later in June. The crew stayed for ten days in Zanzibar and unloaded a thousand kegs of gunpowder and several hundred bales of cotton cloth and took on firewood and lumber for Arabian markets. They then sailed for Aden on July 9 and arrived two weeks later. In Aden, they unloaded tobacco, sugar, and cloth; took in stone ballast; and sailed for Mokha on August 12. When they arrived at Mokha six days later, they unloaded more cotton cloth and "Zanzibar poles" (mangrove) and took on $2,000 in cash and several hundred bags of coffee, in addition to sheep and goat hides. They sailed from Mokha on September 6 by way of Aden, arriving in Muscat on October 12. At Muscat they discharged their stone ballast and took on bales of merino wool and several hundred frails of dates, most of the ship's cargo (1 frail = 200 pounds); more than eight hundred frails, or eighty tons, were loaded in just three days between November 3 and 5. The ship sailed from Muscat on November 8 and arrived twenty days later back in Zanzibar, where it loaded with a few hundred bags of gum copal and cloves and sailed back for Salem on December 5, arriving three months later. The voyage from Salem to Zanzibar by sail typically took 80–100 days in each direction across the Atlantic, and round-trip voyages to the Indian Ocean typically took 11–13 months.[15]

The diary of another young sailor, William H. Townsend, who visited Zanzibar and Muscat in 1858 aboard the Salem bark *Imaum* (named in honor of the ruler of Muscat and Zanzibar), indicates that ships' captains would go to great lengths to obtain Muscat dates. Although the captain of the *Imaum* secured a lucrative cargo of coffee, hides, ivory, chili peppers, gum copal, and cloves in exchange for cash, gunpowder, cotton cloth, soap, and copper wire in Aden and Zanzibar, he would not consider heading home without a month's detour to Muscat to obtain dates. The crew of the *Imaum* spent ten days in Muscat harbor unloading stone ballast and replacing it with bags of dates with the help of six African workers who were brought from shore. Dates served a dual purpose as both ballast and commodity. Heavy sacks of dates frequently replaced stone ballast in the holds of Indian Ocean trading vessels on their return to the United States.[16]

By the 1860s business between Oman and the United States was brisk enough for Salem merchant John Bertram to leave an agent behind at Muscat to help facilitate the date trade. William Hollingsworth Hathorne negotiated for the best possible prices and sent regular intelligence to Bertram about what their rival buyers from New York and Boston were shipping and how much they had paid. His letters reveal that American buyers did not dictate the terms of exchange but had to compete with buyers for markets in Calcutta, Mokha, and Singapore. Nor did Americans have a monopoly on information. Sellers in Muscat were in communication with other date-producing regions, and a bad harvest in another region could drive up prices for Muscat's crop, as happened in 1866 when Hathorne wrote to Bertram, "The reason why the Dates are so high is because the crop in Bussora has failed and the dows that always went there, have come to Muscat this year for their cargoes." As a result, Hathorne explained, he had recently been outbid by Arab buyers from Yemen. "The day before yesterday I tried to break down the price of the Dates by refusing to buy any more at $42.50 but it was 'no go'[;] the Mokha men bought them all at that price." Another American merchant from New York also arranged to have an American agent buy for him in Muscat. Captain Upton of the *Hellespont*, a rival of Bertram's *Glide*, bought several thousand frails of dates for the *Hellespont* and the *Ella Virginia* in 1866 (although the latter never arrived, having wrecked off the coast of Mozambique).[17] The same year, the W. J. Towell Company became the first American export company to open a formal office in Muscat, and its sole purpose was shipping Omani *fardh* dates to the United States.[18]

In the contemporary world of mass-manufactured sweets it is difficult to comprehend the popularity in the nineteenth century of sticky dried fruit imported from Arabia. However, it must be recalled that processed candies manufactured on a massive scale were virtually unknown before Milton Hershey marketed his first chocolate bars in 1900.[19] In the United

States, dates were considered a confectionary delicacy well into the twentieth century. Dates were a popular ingredient in cooked desserts and ordinary meals. One 1923 cookbook included forty-two recipes for dates, including stuffed dates, date custard pie, date corn bread, date and celery salad, date corn muffins, date mush, mocha date icing, date tea cakes, rich date muffins, date fruitcake, date soufflé with custard sauce, date sponge with lemon sauce, date cream pie, Old English date pie, date cream filling, date scones, date and nut bread, date marmalade, Newport date ice cream, and bacon and date sandwiches.[20] Dates grew more popular year after year through the first quarter of the twentieth century. American date imports grew from an average of 10–20 million pounds annually between 1893 and 1903 to an average of 20–30 million pounds between 1903 and 1913. Date imports soared from 32 million pounds in 1920 to 53 million pounds in 1922 and peaked at nearly 79 million pounds in 1925.[21] Such rapid growth led to repercussions in both Arabia and the United States.

The date trade involved networks of merchants, producers, and financiers. New York importers built relationships with Indian merchants in Mutrah, the terminus of Omani caravan routes, to arrange annual date exports each autumn. Mutrah, a short distance north of Muscat, separated by only one cove (Riyam) and some rocky outcrops, was the domestic trade center of Oman, home to large Sindi and Gujarati Indian merchant families, and the primary port for dhow exports to India, East Africa, south Arabia, and the Gulf. Muscat, with its superior protected harbor for larger, square-rigged sailing ships and later steamships, dominated Arabia's trade with the West. Mutrah and Muscat were connected by small seacraft that operated in constant communication between the two nearly adjacent walled port cities. Merchants from Mutrah would receive orders from New York syndicates by post (and later by telegraph) and would then arrange purchases from individual producers. Some large landowners resided in Mutrah, having purchased date farms or acquired them as collateral for loans, so some shipments could be arranged locally. Others had to be arranged in the areas of production.[22] Merchants preferred to arrange the purchase well before the harvest, when producers were in greatest need of cash.[23] In describing the annual harvest, Paul Popenoe, a date expert who visited Muscat and the Semail Valley of Oman in 1912, explained that once the first of September arrived, "the whole of Oman is affected," and the operation "takes place on a large scale." Merchants arranged purchases while the fruit was still on the tree, and growers were responsible for delivery to Mutrah, at a cost of about $6.00 for every *bihar* of about 1,800 pounds. Popenoe estimated that in 1911 growers received only 1–1.5 cents per pound, or $1.50–$2.00 (U.S.) for the fruit of each tree.[24]

In the 1860s, date packers in the Gulf began using wooden boxes, which had previously been used to import tea and dry goods for shipments to the West, in place of traditional woven palm frond bags. The switch to boxes greatly improved the appeal and profitability of Gulf dates in Western markets. Under the old system, many dates were lost or damaged when the bags were removed from the produce, and parts of the fruit were notoriously dirty. Just before the turn of the century, Count Albert Asfar, who oversaw packing for an American firm in Basra and later owned his own firm, introduced the seventy-pound standard wooden box, which was specially imported for packing dates. This transition made date packing a truly global affair. By the early twentieth century, New York agents routinely shipped prefabricated pieces of wooden crates (called "shooks") from Scandinavia to be assembled at Muscat and Basra in advance of each date season.[25] Carpenters nailed the boxes together at the packing sites or godowns, and date packers were hired seasonally to fill the boxes. In Oman, harvested dates were brought to Mutrah by camel caravan in palm frond sacks. In Iraq, dates were brought to Basra in small local craft in palm frond baskets.[26]

The business of packing dates provided seasonal work in the Gulf that benefitted many workers, particularly women. In both Oman and Iraq, date packers in the chief port cities were usually women. By the first decade of the twentieth century, date packers arranged dates by hand, one-by-one, in neat rows and even layers inside each wooden box, sometimes with a sheet of wax paper between layers. Then a board was placed on top of the dates, and someone would stand on the box, pressing the dates together. As the numbers of rows of dates in a box remained consistent throughout the boxes (13–14 in Basra, depending on the variety), the dates could be easily split into smaller portions to be resold once they arrived at their destinations. In New York, date importers staffed warehouses where employees would repack date shipments into smaller containers.[27] In Oman, date packing was one of the few available forms of wage labor, and women were eager to crowd the Mutrah godowns to earn cash. Calvin Allen has suggested that the money earned through the date trade with the United States "benefited many more people than any previous mercantile activity" and for part of its duration served as the only form of wage labor in the country. In Oman, the packing season ran from mid-August to early December—about one hundred days—and an experienced female employee could earn over MT$60 working in that period. Carpenters who assembled the wooden boxes could earn MT$75–$125 in that same time in 1912.[28] But the business of irrigating, maintaining, and harvesting date crops frequently fell to enslaved Africans.

Dates and African Labor

The dramatic growth of the date export industry sharply influenced labor demands in the Gulf. Date trees had to be planted, tended, and irrigated, and date crops had to be harvested, transported, and packed before they could reach their markets. The primary area of nineteenth-century date expansion in Oman was Batinah, the 150-mile stretch of coast on the Gulf of Oman north of Muscat beginning around Seeb and continuing north of Sohar. Consequently, Batinah became a leading center of the slave trade and home to one of the largest populations of enslaved Africans in the Gulf. As the densest area of vegetation in eastern Arabia, Batinah had a bigger population and more agricultural production than any other part of the Arabian Gulf south of Iraq. But Batinah differed from the other date-producing areas in the region in that it required intense human effort to irrigate its palms. Most date production in Oman uses the *falaj* system of irrigation: hand-crafted cement, gravity-flow channels that convey water from natural springs in the Hajar Mountains in the Oman ophlolite.[29] Although it has some of the richest soil in Oman, Batinah does not receive a consistent flow of water from the inland mountains and relies entirely on ground water for irrigation through the use of wells.[30] Batinah farmers during this period employed the *zijrah (zaygra)*, the elevated well system used throughout the Arabian Peninsula and in Mesopotamia. This system consisted of a massive wooden framework, usually constructed of palm trunks, and a crossbar holding a rotating pulley wheel called a *manjūr*, connected by rope to a bull (or in rare cases a mule) to lift water from

Reenactment of an Omani *zijrah* (elevated water well), Muscat. Photograph by the author (2005).

"Men Pollinating Date Palm," Oman, 1912. Courtesy American Heritage Center, University of Wyoming. Paul Popenoe Collection, Box 177, Folder 2.

twenty feet below the surface using leather bags, which poured into cement-coated holding tanks, which further drained into irrigation channels, *aflāj*, to water several acres of date palms. The labor-intensive process required a male laborer, called a *bidār*, to work in shifts around the clock in order to water approximately every one hundred trees. In Batinah, the work of irrigation frequently fell on the shoulders of enslaved Africans.

An American date expert visiting in 1927 estimated that there were at least fifteen thousand *zijrah* wells irrigating date palms in Batinah alone.[31] Bertram Thomas, who worked as *wazīr* (minister) of finance under Sultan Taimur bin Faisal in Oman between 1925 and 1930, had the opportunity to visit Batinah on a number of occasions and estimated that there were "tens of thousands of oxen daily" working these water wheels in 1929.[32] "The cacophony from many wells operating at one time is really not unmusical," he wrote. "The effect is that of a weird assortment of stringed instruments, the cellos seeming always to delight in drowning the violas and fiddles, and the ensemble is a sort of tuning up of an orchestra." Thomas added, " 'Oil the wretched thing,' says a European impatient of its creaking and whining, but the owner has another view, for every well has a different note and he, from the far end of his garden, may thus know whether all goes well with his own."[33] V. H. W. Dowson of the Agricultural Directorate of Mesopotamia echoed Thomas: "Throughout the Batinah, is heard the plaintive shrieking of the pullies. To a suggestion that the axles might be oiled, the reply comes that the noisy wheel was better, *Ahzain*."[34] Bertram Thomas added that runaway slaves were often punished with long hours in chains working in irrigation: "The metallic chink of ankle-chains, heard, perhaps, from the bull-pit of a well within the date grove, is an indication of some such ill-fated escapade."[35] For slave owners, the *manjūr* functioned as a method of surveillance: a silent wheel meant an idle slave.

In addition to irrigation, Batinah date plantations required constant maintenance. Date palms have to be pollinated by hand, offshoots (suckers) removed, dead branches cut off, extra date bunches removed, and stocks kept clean, and—when the fruit is ripe—there is the enormous task of harvesting. In addition, in the shade of the date palms, farmers grew lucerne and other animal feed, in addition to vegetables for domestic consumption. Large parties of workers were required to boil the *maseybili* and *khameyzi* varieties, common in Batinah, in large copper cauldrons and dry them in the sun, turning them frequently prior to shipping these popular varieties to India.[36] Dates also needed to be packed or pressed and conveyed overland or by sea to ports of export. Palm frond bags had to be woven to hold the dates, and once the dates were ready to export, they had to be loaded onto boats, conveyed to their destination, and unloaded. Much of this work was performed by enslaved Africans, particularly men and boys.

In the late nineteenth century, slave traders increasingly exported young boys from East Africa for work in the date and pearl industries. By the 1870s, the ratio of male to female slaves aboard captured slave dhows on the Arabian coast reversed previous trends, shifting overwhelmingly in favor of young males. In 1872 the HMS *Vulture* captured a large slave dhow off the coast of Ras al-Hadd at the entrance to the Gulf of Oman. That dhow was carrying 169 captives from Pemba to Sur and Batinah; 124 were males and 45 were females, and the majority were children.[37] On interrogation, the captain of that ship provided testimony indicating that the slaves aboard were to be landed first at Sur and from there transferred to coastal production centers in northern Oman like Suwaiq in Batinah.

> Q. When did you leave Zanzibar?
> A. About 22 days ago.
> Q. With what cargo?
> A. In ballast of sand.
> Q. Where did you go first?
> A. To Pemba
> Q. Did you ship slaves there?
> A. Yes about 200 slaves belonging to different persons. These were shipped at Bunder Chuk Chuk and Bunder Reyamee.
> Q. Who were the shippers?
> A. Arabs. Mostly of Soor and some of Batineh. I do not know their names. Some were people of Sohar.
> Q. Were there not Arab passengers on board your vessel?
> A. Yes. 21 or 22.
> Q. Were they the owners of the slaves?
> A. Six of them were.
> Q. Their names?
> A. I only remember the following[:] Ali and Salim and Saeed of

Sohar and Hamad and Sulliman and another of Soor. The rest were passengers not slave dealers.

Q. Where did you intend to land the slaves?

A. At Soor. All of them at Soor. Some of them were for other places. Some were for Mutrah and for Seeb and Soweyk, but they were all to be landed first at Soor and taken thence as opportunity occurred to their destinations.[38]

Other dhows captured indicated a similar pattern: vessels bound for northern Oman with a large portion of young men. The HMS *Philomel* captured a dhow in 1884 that had 77 men, 14 women, 51 boys, and 12 girls (128 males and 26 females) aboard.[39] In November 1885 the HMS *Osprey* captured a forty-two-ton dhow around Ras Madraka in Oman bound from Ngao in East Africa to Sur with 49 male and 24 female slaves (8 men, 12 women, 41 boys, and 12 girls).[40] In fact, in the last quarter of the nineteenth century, it is virtually impossible to find evidence of any dhow captured off the Arab coast carrying more female captives from East Africa than males.

With the extra labor required for date production, Batinah became the primary destination of slaves in the late nineteenth and early twentieth centuries and was home to the largest population of Africans and their descendants in eastern Arabia.[41] In 1885 S. B. Miles noted that in contrast to the interior behind Sur, where demand for slaves was limited, in Batinah slaves were "in high request," and consequently most slaves were eventually landed there.[42] The dhow captured by the HMS *Philomel* in 1884, which contained 154 captives (128 male and 26 female), was en route to Khaḍra' (near Suwaiq) on the Batinah Coast.[43] In 1930, the British consul at Muscat remarked that "apart from the Batinah Coast, the method of irrigation does not demand slave labour."[44] Batinah continued to be described by Western observers as a center of the slave trade as late as 1930.[45]

From the second half of the nineteenth century through the early 1920s, Batinah absorbed the majority of enslaved Africans sent to eastern Arabia.[46] Because of its high demand for agricultural labor, Batinah became what historians of Atlantic slavery have called a "seasoning ground" for newly imported slaves—a zone for socializing or "seasoning" captive peoples. The newly enslaved had to learn the language of the masters, be made to accept their new positions, and submit to the will of the masters in order to be valuable as slaves.[47] The testimonies of enslaved Africans who received manumission certificates at British consulates and agencies in the Gulf between 1907 and 1940 almost universally describe a period of at least three years in Batinah prior to being sold to final destinations elsewhere in the Gulf. For young African boys, who made up a considerable percentage of those imported in the late nineteenth century, the time between arrival in Batinah and eventual sale was often equal to the time required to mature to the age of a beginning pearl diver (early teens).

The testimonies of runaway slaves who sought British protection in the 1920s reveal the ubiquity of time in Batinah prior to enslavement elsewhere in the Gulf. Almas, a thirty-eight-year-old pearl diver in Umm al-Quwain (today in the UAE), recalled being kidnapped in East Africa by a man named Sa'id when he was eight years old (around 1895). Almas was taken to Khaḍra' in Batinah for three years before he was sold to a man named Maftūl in Umm al-Quwain, who engaged him as a pearl diver.[48] Another man, Almas bin Khamis, a forty-year-old slave of an Arab merchant named bin Safar of Abu Baqara in Batinah, came aboard the HMS *Lupin* to seek manumission in February 1925 and told the commanding officer that he had been kidnapped from East Africa when he was very young (around 1890) by robbers and had been taken to Batinah, where he was sold to Ali bin Husain, for whom he worked as a gardener and a pearl diver and accompanied him on his journeys. When Ali died, Almas ended up in the hands of Ali's son, Saqr, who abused him and caused him to run away.[49] Feroze, a forty-year-old man who had been kidnapped from Zanzibar as a boy by Ali bin Abdullah of Khaḍra', was sold at Sohar around the 1890s. He served Sa'id bin Hamid of Sohar for several years until Sa'id died, after which he was sold by Sa'id's son to Majid bin Rashid of Dubai, for whom he worked for ten years. Majid trusted Feroze and made him caretaker of his gardens in Sohar, but after Majid died, his sons mistreated Feroze and eventually decided to sell him and the date farm and split the inheritance. At that point Feroze ran away, hoping that a manumission certificate would allow him to stay in Sohar, where he had a wife, two daughters, and two sons.[50]

Demand for slave labor for date production was already high between the 1860s and 1880s, but two devastating cyclones that hit Oman in 1885 and 1890 created even greater demand, not just to maintain the date industry, but also to rebuild it.[51] Occurring so close together with nothing nearly equivalent for a hundred years either before or since, these storms caused significant damage to the region's agriculture, particularly its date plantations. Storms of the magnitude of the 1890 cyclone had not struck Oman in centuries and did not hit again until 2007. The cyclone Gonu, which arrived on June 5, 2007, killed fifty people and did $4.2 billion in damage in Oman. But Gonu was a "near miss" for Oman. By contrast, the 1885 and 1890 storms were "direct hits." The weather patterns in the Arabian Sea usually shield Arabia and the Gulf from tropical storms and cyclones, and only very rarely is Oman hit with a true cyclonic storm, yet these two storms hit only five years apart.[52] The cyclone of 1885 made landfall on the Batinah Coast, damaging much of the area's rich date crop and creating demand for labor to replant trees. The storm landed on March 30, 1885, causing flooding that destroyed thousands of date palms in the region as far inland as Rostaq and significantly decreasing the date crop exported to the United States.[53] The June 5, 1890, cyclone was even worse. It pummeled the entire coast of Oman, destroyed much of the country's date-producing capacity, and laid to waste much of the country's commercial capitals of Muscat and Mutrah. It also killed at least 50 people in Muscat, who were drowned or buried by debris. That storm struck the entire coastline between Sur and Suwaiq. It began about midnight on the morning of June 5 and lasted for twenty-four hours, subjecting the coast to torrential rains and severe winds. Muscat received more than eleven inches of rain, and Mutrah, which was not protected from the northeast winds, suffered tremendous wreckage. Large ships washed ashore, small local craft valuing at least $25,000 were destroyed, and houses collapsed and continued to collapse in the following weeks from weakened foundations. Within a week, the sultan had received reports of at least 727 people killed across the country, and there were undoubtedly many more. The date crop was severely hit, with more than one hundred thousand date palms destroyed around the country. The majority of palms destroyed were in Batinah, where several thousand were washed out to sea due to flooding in the Semail Valley, the largest producer of the valuable *fardh* date.[54] The storm destroyed trees valued at over $1.5 million at the time and eliminated much of the region's productive capacity.

Loss of this vital cash crop at a time of its surging demand threatened to cripple the region's economy. The storms thus created demand for even more slave labor. Six months after the storm, the British political resident declared that the slave trade was now being "briskly carried on all over Oman and during the past year to such an extent as to constitute a grievous scandal requiring serious notice."[55] The Royal Navy subsequently captured large shipments of slaves from East Africa en route to centers of Omani date production. The first capture after the 1885 cyclone was made in September by the HMS *Osprey*. That dhow carried seventy-three captives (forty-nine male and twenty-four female).[56] The same week, the HMS *Ranger* seized a dhow that had just landed ten slaves at Sur.[57] Despite a drastic drawdown in the British antislavery presence in the western Indian Ocean after 1884, additional captures continued to be made throughout the 1880s and 1890s, particularly around the island of Pemba in East Africa, a major transshipment point for slaves bound for Oman. In May 1896 three dhows were even seized in the immediate vicinity of Muscat. Peter Zwemer, the American missionary in Muscat, recalled, "They contained in all forty-four slaves, the majority of them being boys between the ages of six and twelve, as these bring the highest prices in the slave marts of Oman."[58]

British officials noted the increase in the slave trade from East Africa beginning around 1885 but largely attributed it to the discontinuation of the antislave-trade patrols of the HMS *London* around Zanzibar and drought and famine conditions on the coast of East Africa around the same time.[59] To be sure, the timing of the cyclones in Oman coincided precisely with climatic events in East Africa that contributed to the rise in the supply of slaves on the coast. Demand for labor to rebuild Oman's date plantations coincided with ecological disaster and an increase of available labor in Africa. Mike Davis has argued that such climatic changes in Arabia and Africa were more than coincidence. The mid-1880s was a period of famine in numerous places, including Russia, Bengal, Madras, and the Great Plains of North America.[60] Japan, Ethiopia, Mauritius, Sudan, and Texas all experienced similar phenomena.[61] Davis attributes the phenomena to climatic shifts associated with La Niña/El Niño cycles.[62] Frederick Cooper noted that in East Africa a substantial revival of the slave trade took place in 1884 in part because of an increase in supply of slaves brought about by a devastating famine on the mainland of Kenya and Tanzania. Cooper found that "people were desperate enough to sell their neighbors, their children, and even themselves in order to survive."[63] British consul John Kirk and other observers on Zanzibar noticed a marked increase in slave traffic from famine-stricken Tanganyika, particularly from Zaramo territory. Likewise, in Kenya, Cooper notes that in 1884 "large numbers of Mijikenda pawned themselves or their children for grain to the coastal plantation owners, who had been spared drought afflicting the immediate hinterland. Most likely the Mijikenda expected that such people could be redeemed, but this rarely happened."[64] Climate could influence the slave trade on both the supply and demand sides of the equation.

Globalization and the Basra Trade

James Gelvin and Nile Green have noted that the contraction of time and distance made possible by new, faster forms of transportation and communication had profound implications for Muslim societies. The period that the authors aptly name the "Age of Steam and Print"—between roughly 1850 and 1930—enabled the diffusion of ideas, technologies, and commodities with unprecedented speed and breadth. In this particular period of globalization, steamships and railroads moved migrants, pilgrims, and trade goods at previously unknown scales and speeds, as the telegraph and lithographic presses spread ideas as well as state power in new ways. Steam travel enabled Muslims to explore the world with unprecedented ease, empowering Muslim travelers to bring back European technologies and teachings that would set the stage for new forms of education, science, medicine, and religious practice in the Middle East and beyond. Record numbers of Muslim pilgrims could now perform the hajj. At the same time, steam and rail transit opened more of the region to economic exploitation and European exploration, missionary activity, and tourism and created unforeseen opportunities and crises for imperialism (for example, the specter of controlling cholera in an age of mass transit and unprecedented pilgrimage to Mecca). The increase of speed and the decrease of transport costs associated with the introduction of the screw propeller and the compound engine in the late nineteenth century unfettered trade from the rhythms of the monsoons. These factors enabled rapid intercontinental maritime trade as well as riverine transport, linking regional markets to one another and bringing isolated regions into contact with the expanding global economy. Likewise, the telegraph in the Middle East served as both a tool of state power, enabling the Ottoman Empire to rapidly maneuver its troops and officials, and a means of protest. Gelvin notes that telegraph stations were intermittently mobbed by crowds and used to submit petitions to Istanbul complaining of abuses by local officials and landlords, suggesting that the telegraph had come to symbolize a direct line to the sultan—a sign of the growing expectations of the populace on the nation-state. The "Age of Steam and Print" was thus distinct from prior eras of globalization by manner of degree as opposed to kind. Long a crossroads for global trade, the Middle East was no stranger to connectivity, but the nineteenth century ushered in an era of extroversion of unprecedented scale.[65]

For the Gulf specifically, faster forms of communication and transportation created new avenues for trade. The telegraph, the Suez Canal, and the steamship helped expand the date trade between Arabia and the United States and allowed Basra to join Muscat in supplying the growing American market. The Indian Mutiny of 1856 emphasized the need for London to have a direct telegraphic cable to India. The newly created Indo-European Telegraph Department oversaw the completion of cables linking London to Bombay by way of Suez and Aden, in addition to cables linking London to Calcutta by way of Karachi and Tehran. Muscat was first linked to Aden and Karachi by telegraph by 1860, and communication technology improved substantially over the following years.[66] By the last decade of the nineteenth century, merchants in the United States could communicate by telegraph to buyers in date-producing centers in the Gulf.[67]

When the Suez Canal opened in 1869, the voyage from New York to Muscat was cut by a third by steamers. By that time, New York had surpassed Salem in imports from the Indian Ocean to the United States. In fact, by 1860, New York's port had established dominance over all American ports, clearing more imports than all other major American ports combined.[68] The fruit docks of Brooklyn handled nearly all of the date imports along with most of the other fruit imported into the United States. In the 1880s, steamers would bring five hundred boxes of dates at a time to Brooklyn, each box weighing fifty pounds. Sailing barks were becoming a rare sight by the mid-1880s but would occasionally dock in Brooklyn with shipments of up to six thousand frails of dates. In 1885, the United States imported 10 million pounds of dates with an increasing portion of them from Basra.[69]

In spite of the new forms of transportation and communication, large traditional sailing vessels like the Salem barks remained profitable and continued to make the voyage to Muscat to bring back tons of dates annually. John Bertram's *Glide* made thirty voyages to the Indian Ocean before 1887, when it wrecked off the coast of Madagascar.[70] Bertram built several more ships for the Indian Ocean trade, the most famous of which was his *Taria Topan*, built in 1870 and named for one of the leading Indian merchants of Muscat and Zanzibar and one of the region's most successful creditors. The double-decked 631-ton bark made twenty-six voyages to the Indian Ocean before being sold in 1893. With its three masts and large hold, the *Taria Topan* could bring back exceptionally large loads very quickly (it broke existing records on its maiden voyage to Zanzibar—sixty-eight days from Salem around the cape) and almost always ran the same itinerary—Zanzibar-Aden-Muscat—usually in about nine months. When the ship completed its third journey in 1873, the *Boston Journal* reported, "She brings one of the most valuable cargoes ever received here from Arabia, consisting of ivory, ebony, dates, gum copal, etc. Among the leading items of her cargo are 6035 frails of dates [600 tons], 1600 bags of cloves, and 3539 blocks of ebony."[71]

The Omani *fardh* date remained the most popular variety imported into the United States throughout the nineteenth century and consistently sold at a higher price than all other varieties well into the twentieth century. Paul Popenoe attributed the popularity of the *fardh* date in America over its Iraqi competition to the fact that it was the only variety imported into the United States "which can be bought in fairly presentable condition." He explained: "Its tough, firm flesh allows it to come on the table intact, while the superior and *khadhrāwī* of Busreh have been so squeezed out of shape by the heavy feet of the Arab packer that they do not look presentable, no matter how good their flavor may be."[72] In Los Angeles, Newberry's grocery store sold "New Fard Dates" (from Muscat) for 15 cents a pound in November 1895 and "New Golden Dates" (from Iraq) for 10 cents per pound. In February 1917, Ralph's Grocery Company sold

"Fancy Fard Dates" at 19 cents per pound in its four Los Angeles locations, while "Golden Dates" (Iraqi varieties) were sold at 35 cents for two pounds.[73]

Yet in terms of volume, the Omani *fardh* variety was surpassed by Iraqi dates well before the turn of the century. Basra date exports roughly doubled with the opening of the Suez Canal, jumping from £67,000 in 1868 to £126,000 in 1869.[74] Although Omani dates had whetted America's appetite for dates, that appetite was increasingly satisfied by Iraqi produce. By 1911, *fardh* dates accounted for only 3,882,008 pounds out of the 29,504,592 pounds (or roughly 13 percent) of dates imported into the United States, although this amount still represented a quarter of the value of date imports. Five years earlier *fardh* dates had accounted for roughly 27 percent of the value of American imports.[75] By 1929, 83 percent of the dates imported into the United States came from Iraq.[76]

In the 1870s Basra date exports soared. Several foreign steam navigation companies facilitated the movement of freight down the Tigris and Euphrates to Basra and competed with each other for shipping between Baghdad and Basra and for export routes to Bombay, Karachi, and London.[77] A deal in 1878 among the owners of most of the major European companies against the backdrop of the heightened traffic on the Tigris during the Russo-Turkish War of 1877–1878 created a powerful partnership that merged the capital of major players, like Thomas Lynch and William Mackinnon, that dramatically increased trade volume in the region. The biggest beneficiary was the date industry. Gray Mackenzie and Company shipped 6,718 tons of dates from Basra in 1879 and 11,868 tons in 1882.[78] Americans imported a growing proportion of Basra dates to supplement the Muscat dates, but initially the trade with Basra ran through British steamers by way of London. This fact makes it challenging for the historian today to determine how much of Iraq's produce was actually bound to the United States and how great a factor the United States was in Iraq's economy. India and Persia undoubtedly continued to be major consumers of Iraqi dates, but the United States and Britain bought up more and more of the produce. India imported an average of around 30,000 tons of dates in the 1880s and nearly twice that amount by the 1920s. The main region in India importing dates at the turn of the twentieth century was Bombay (65 percent of total date imports), followed by

Gujarat (23 percent), Madras (6 percent), and Bengal (5 percent).[79] Most of India's dates came from Iraq (58 percent), followed by Oman and eastern Arabia (28 percent) and Persia (14 percent). Economic records from the British mandate of Mesopotamia are inconsistent, but if the 1926 date export statistics from the British mandatory government of Iraq are any indication, at the climax of the international date trade, the value of British and U.S. date exports totaled more than the value of India's and Persia's date exports combined. In 1926, the United States accounted for 26 percent of Iraq's date exports, and India accounted for 25 percent. It is unclear how much of Great Britain's share of the date exports (30 percent) was in fact destined for the United States, but the amount was certainly large. Persia received 19 percent of Iraq's date exports.[80]

The American trade undoubtedly contributed to the growing wealth of Basra. By the 1870s the transformation of the city was visible to visitors like Major R. M. Smith, director of Persian telegraphs, who wrote the following:

> Anyone acquainted with Bussorah only a few years ago could not fail to be struck with its altered and improved appearance. Instead of the unbroken line of Palm Groves which concealed the Town at some distance behind them and the river on which nothing but a few Buggalows were to be seen, the bank now presents an imposing line of substantial European-looking houses, offices and godowns, while the river itself is alive with boats and barges going to and from the steamers whence the rattle of the steam winch is heard incessantly. The general bustle and movement are in striking contrast with the still monotony of former years.[81]

One of the companies to establish new offices in Basra was the Hills Brothers Company of New York, which would become the largest importer of dates to the United States. It developed from a small fruit enterprise founded by John Hills in 1871. Originally an importer of green fruit, citrus, and grapes, Hills was forced to specialize in dried fruit by the 1890s because of the growth of the domestic fruit markets in Florida and California. In 1893, John Hills and his brother William joined forces and founded the corporation called the Hills Brothers Company, with a small warehouse in Brooklyn. As their date imports from the Gulf increased, they decided to send company vice president Frank H. White to Iraq to establish a branch office in Basra in order to end their reliance on London companies for their supply of Iraqi dates. In the last years of the nineteenth century, the first steamers filled with fresh dates were shipped directly to the company warehouse in Brooklyn, allowing the company to operate autonomously of London. In 1900, Hills Brothers opened a distribution office in Chicago to facilitate the marketing of produce to the Midwest.[82] By 1902, the Hills Brothers Company had a full-time agent in Basra, H. P. Chalk, who lived there year-round with his wife. The company owned a river-front building, which it called "Beit Hills," from which it oversaw its operations, including its own date farm. In Basra, the company worked through a date buyer named Haji Abdulla Negem, with whom it would annually entrust $10,000 in gold coins to procure dates for shipments to New York.[83]

John Hills served as company president until his death in 1902, after which a family feud resulted in his son-in-law's taking the helm of the company and William Hills leaving to start his own competing firm in 1905.[84] Both the Hills Brothers Company and the William Hills Jr. Company decided to focus increasingly on packaged goods instead of bulk goods in order to maximize profits. Both companies sent waxed cardboard packing material in bulk to the Gulf, where the boxes were assembled and filled with dates, generally in one- and two-pound packages. William Hills built a partnership with the Mutrah merchant Ratansi Purshotum and carried on a brisk business in Muscat dates. By 1910, Hills Brothers had decided to brand its Basra dates with the "Dromedary" name and a trademark camel on each box, and it embarked on an aggressive advertising campaign to market the name as a symbol of consistent quality and cleanliness.[85]

By the 1890s American business with Basra was so extensive that merchants launched several direct steamers annually to sail to New York loaded exclusively with Basra dates. Sharon Thoms of the American Mission in Basra described the scene in 1899: "The date packing season, which is now on, is the busy season of the year for Basrah. We have as many as fourteen vessels in the river at one time, including one Turkish and one English man of war. Then there are as many as one hundred sailing vessels in the river from the Gulf coast, India, the Red Sea, and the east coast of Africa."[86] In 1899, shipping companies began an annual "date race" from

Dromedary date advertisement, *Saturday Evening Post*, 1913. Courtesy Thomas Madsen, Pack Ryt, Inc.

Basra to New York—a competition to see who could land the first shipment of "golden dates" for the holiday season.[87] Once dates were harvested and packed in Basra, competing ships—usually German and British steamers—were quickly loaded and sent the 9,981 miles to New York, stopping over in Muscat to pick up a selection of *fardh* dates. Readers could follow the progress of the ships through wire reports in local papers, and the arrival of the first ship was heralded with dramatic fanfare. The winner of the "date race" received recognition, a monetary prize, and a bonus for the importing company, as the first shipments of dates sold at higher prices than subsequent shipments. In 1912, the winning ship earned $120,000 for the consignees of the dates.[88] The bonus by the 1930s averaged about $1.75 per ton.[89]

In time, the annual date race grew faster and more competitive. In 1907, the steamship *Gulistan* lost to the *Umzumbie* by twenty-four hours. In 1912, the race was won by Captain Charles Bliault and the *Turkistan* (owned by F. C. Strick and Company of Swansea), which beat out the *Stanhope*.[90] In the 1920s competition to import the first crop of dates had increased to the extent that for the thirty-first annual race in 1930, Hills Brothers abandoned its three-time champion charter, the *Shahristan*, in favor of a brand new oil-burner, the *Gorjistan* (F. C. Strick and Company), which broke all previous records, completing the Basra–New York journey in twenty-six days, beating its rival, the *Montauban*, and delivering a five-thousand-ton shipment of dates worth $1.5 million. The voyage was historic because it marked the first time a date ship had delivered such a fresh cargo—less than forty days from the dates having been picked off the trees. Ten years earlier, the voyage itself took forty-two days, but by 1927 it had been cut to thirty-one days. When a date ship arrived in the dockyards in Brooklyn, hundreds of longshoremen would work day and night to unload the cargo. In 1930 and 1932 more than two hundred stevedores unloaded the winning cargoes and filled trainloads of eighty cars with dates for the Midwest.[91] The "date race" was a masterful stroke of public relations spin that made for easy advertising for date-importing companies. But their main marketing technique was not selling dried fruit but selling Arabia and the Orient.

Purveyors of dates used images of Arabia and the Orient to exoticize an otherwise mundane product to attract American consumers. The technique was not unusual for the period. The early twentieth century was an era in which exoticism was commonplace. Brad Evans explains that in the late 1880s and 1890s old hierarchies in the United States (master/slave, savage/civilized) had been called into question by the ending of slavery and the Indian Wars, the closing of the American frontier, and large-scale immigration, while at the same time, a barrage of new forms of media converged with increased contact with other ways of life brought on by imperialism.[92] Representations of exotic cultures were on display at fairs and expositions and newly inexpensive books, newspapers, and magazines. By the turn of the century, American literature, art, and fashion regularly imported into urban centers images of the Other as "cultural commodities" in the forms of exotic things and people. In this awkward period of heightened awareness of difference, international exhibitions put exoticism on view; photographs and films provided new opportunities to reproduce difference as spectacle; folklore was revitalized; and literature embraced the local—writing in dialect, local color fiction, stories of immigrants and rural folk.[93] The period, not surprisingly, coincided with the pinnacle of orientalism in art in Europe and the United States and the emergence of Art Nouveau.[94] Holly Edwards has identified the "migration of Orientalist imagery from unique objects to mass-produced materials" as one of the hallmarks of the period between 1870 and 1930.[95]

As was also the case with pearls, cigarettes, and other commodities popular in the early twentieth century, the appeal of dates to the American consumer lay in the exoticism of the Orient. Advertisers played to preexisting stereotypes by emphasizing archetypal images associated with Arabia; camels, deserts, Arabs, and palm trees adorned the packaging and advertisements of all sorts of products. In a period in which exotic women featured regularly on the packages of cigarettes and cigars, date-manufacturing companies incorporated exotic symbols of Arabia—daggers, camels, sheikhs, palm trees—to market their imported fruit.[96] Likewise, R. J. Reynolds used a similar imagery to sell his Camel cigarettes. When the U.S. Supreme Court broke up the dominant American Tobacco Company for violation of the Sherman Antitrust Act in 1911, four major competitors emerged: Liggett and Meyers, R. J. Reynolds, Lorillard, and American. Those companies divided up the former trust's primary tobacco brands, including several "Turkish" cigarettes with oriental names like

Mecca, Fatima, Turkish Trophies, Murad, and Helmar. But Winston-Salem–based R. J. Reynolds inherited no brands of his own and so had to create them from scratch. In 1913, Reynolds test-marketed Osman, a Turkish blend, and Red Kamel, a straight Turkish cigarette, before finally settling on Camel, "a blend of burley and bright tobaccos with Turkish leaf for taste and aroma, sold in a pack of 20 for 10 cents."[97] Camel's flavor accounted for part of the new brand's success, but its oriental appeal, reinforced with a vigorous advertising campaign, probably accounted for the remainder. In its first year, the brand sold 425 million cigarettes; by 1915 R. J. Reynolds reported earnings of $4.7 million (and an advertising budget of $1.9 million), and by 1919 Camel was America's number one brand, representing about 40 percent of the nation's total cigarette market. Camel's distinctive packaging featured a camel in front of a backdrop of palm tree, sand, and two pyramids.

But date-importing companies had actually pioneered the use of camels and other Arabian imagery for mass-marketing, having used them long before the first Camel cigarettes. Reynolds may in fact have drawn inspiration from advertisements for Muscat and Basra dates. One of the most important importers of *fardh* dates from Muscat, the W. J. Towell Company, marketed its "Finest Muscat Dates" around the turn of the century in a one-pound waxed cardboard package bearing a reproduction of a photograph of Omani men walking beside camels laden with dates. The side panels bore the phrases "Delicious, tasteful, strengthening. Shall speak for itself" and "Specially packed for messes and clubs."[98] The Hills Brothers Company was the ultimate master of orientalist advertising. Hills Brothers trademarked the image of the dromedary camel in April 1911, applied it to its brand of golden dates (that is, Iraqi dates), and embarked on an aggressive advertising campaign that included print advertisements in newspapers and magazines, giveaways to public schools (2,900 teachers sent in for Dromedary date materials for their classes as a result of one advertisement), recipe contests, and cookbooks.[99] A Hills Brothers magazine advertisement for Dromedary dates ("from the Garden of Eden") in 1913 featured the bold-print phrase "A Gift from the Orient" and portrayed a tall, dark, and thin bearded Arab man wearing a flowing white robe, a head covering, and *khanjar* (dagger), with palm trees and a camel in the background, extending a dark-complexioned hand to an appreciative white woman in an archetypal American house dress as she prepares a table covered in white linen, china, and wine glasses. Above the Arab's outstretched hand (which remains a comfortable distance from the woman's slightly withdrawn hand) is a package of Dromedary Golden Dates, surrounded by an archetypal crescent moon, below which is found the following text: "FRESH, sweet and luscious just as they were when gathered on the banks of the Euphrates in far off Arabia, where grow the finest dates in the world. Packed in layers with waxed paper between, wrapped in parchment and enclosed in individual dust-proof packages. Such are Dromedary Dates. A Gift from the Orient."[100]

Muscat and Basra were not the only places in the Middle East to expand agricultural production in the late nineteenth century in response to global markets. Producers of silk and tobacco in Anatolia, grain in Iraq, olives in Tunisia, figs in Smyrna, oranges in Palestine, and cotton in Egypt and Sudan all responded in similar ways to the date producers of eastern Arabia.[101] The shift toward cash-crop production was once described in terms of dependency or incorporation—part of an inevitable process whereby Western countries gained economic hegemony over so-called peripheral peoples.[102] More recently, cultural historians have demonstrated the transformative potential of global markets for both producers and consumers.[103] The development of Arabian date production is a more complex story of dependency than world-systems analysis would allow. Dates transformed Americans' tastes and fueled their imaginations about Arabia just as American capital enriched Gulf producers and spurred demand for African labor. American merchants did not dictate the terms of trade in Arabia. They were dependent on networks of local traders, growers, and financiers. Arab producers took advantage of the new sources of foreign capital and expanded production in response to American demand. But the regional markets that predated American trade never lost their importance. At its peak, the American trade equaled, but never exceeded, Basra's long-standing trade with India. Globalization, in the form of new methods of communication and transportation, broadened the horizons of both Arabian produce and American commerce. Enslaved Africans made the expansion of the region's date production possible. Their labor would soon find even greater demand in the region's second global industry: pearling. But as will be seen in the coming chapters, the same forces that helped create Arabia's global markets helped destroy them. Globalization created new rivals—including Arabia's key customer, the United States, which transformed from date consumer to date producer in the 1930s, ending its century-long trade relationship with Muscat, Basra, and Baghdad when southern California developed a date industry of its own using offshoots of Arabia's own date palms (see chapter 6).

3

PEARLS, SLAVES, AND FASHION

At the turn of the twentieth century, a six-year-old boy named Ismail bin Mubarak was kidnapped from his hometown of Mkokotoni in Zanzibar and carried away to Arabia. Ismail's kidnapper took him to Batinah, a stretch of the coast of northern Oman, where he sold him to a man from Hamriya (near Dubai). Five years and two owners later, Ismail found himself the slave of Salim bin Sultan of Sharjah, who sent him to the pearl banks each season and forced him to dive for pearls. In March 1931, when Ismail was nearly forty years old and had spent two decades of grueling work as a pearl diver, he stole one of his master's boats and fled with four other enslaved divers to the British naval depot at Bassidu on Qishm Island off the coast of Persia.[1] There, Ismail and his companions were taken aboard the HMS *Hastings*, where sailors recorded their diverse stories: a twenty-six-year-old Zanzibari diver, who as a boy had served in the German East Africa campaign, was tricked by a dhow operator who promised to take him from Zanzibar to Mombasa but instead took him to Dubai and sold him as a slave; a twenty-year-old Swahili pearling crewman who was born to slave parents in Persian Mekran was sold at age ten to slave owners in Oman; and two pearl divers of mixed Swahili-Baluchi ancestry in their early twenties who had been kidnapped and sold to slave owners in Oman in the early 1920s. Ismail and his fellow runaways were a cross-section of the slave divers of the Arabian Gulf.[2]

Although they were not the only divers, Africans were essential to the massive Gulf pearling industry, which by 1900 produced more wealth from pearls than all other regions of the world combined. Pearls had long been a staple of the Gulf economy, feeding regional markets centered on India and the Middle East, but in the late nineteenth century, Gulf pearls, like dates, found new markets in Europe and North America. Changing fashion among wealthy elites in Europe and North America led to an exponential growth in pearl imports and a global pearl boom, which drove the expansion of pearl diving around the world. The rising value of pearls created fantastic wealth among leading pearl merchants. French pearl conglomerates used the fortunes they amassed from Gulf pearls to construct the new arcades of the Champs-Élysées in Paris as Gulf pearl merchants embarked on a building campaign of their own, constructing new luxury homes that are landmarks in Gulf cities today.

The increased demand for divers in the Gulf also led to a rise in the slave trade from East Africa. Slave divers worked alongside free divers during the annual pearling season in several months of grueling labor. Just as consumers today tend not to think much about the origins of their clothes or shoes or the components of their cellular phones, consumers in Western countries thought little about the conditions of workers in the pearl banks that produced the pearls they wore (even as they protested slavery in the Indian Ocean). This chapter describes the labor of pearl divers and the methods of controlling both slave and free labor in the Gulf pearling industry. Talented slave divers could fetch high prices if sold and could often negotiate benefits with their masters. But no diver was truly free. A complex system of debt and obligation kept free divers in perpetual indebtedness, ensuring their annual return to the pearl banks. Enslaved Africans, who accounted at times for perhaps as much as half of the Gulf's diving population, performed labor essential to the Gulf economy while facing the double bind of debt and slavery. The systems of debt obligation in the Gulf, which facilitated the massive pearl production in the late nineteenth century, sparked debate among British colonial officials as to whether all pearl divers were in some way enslaved. In the Gulf, slavery grew in importance as global markets for pearls surged. As was the case with dates, the globalization of markets for pearls sharply influenced labor demands and fueled an increase in the slave trade from East Africa.

Pearl Diving in the Arabian Gulf

In 1863, Sheikh Muhammad bin Thānī, ruler of Qatar, described the economic realities facing the population of coastal eastern Arabia to the traveling European scholar William Palgrave: "We are all, from the highest to the lowest, slaves of one master, [the] Pearl."[3] The sheikh's remark masks the very real disparity between slave and free in the Gulf, but it reveals his understanding of the growing demands of global markets, which were already being felt in the mid-nineteenth-century Gulf. Even before the Gulf's lucrative pearl export market reached its ultimate peak half a century later, Sheikh Muhammad and others could sense the growing regional dependence on global markets, particularly the growing market for pearls. But Sheikh Muhammad's comment also illustrates a wider global paradox of the late nineteenth century: the era of expanding global markets that followed the abolition of slavery in much of the world also created systems of labor that mirrored slavery or were in fact systems of slavery.

The Arabian Gulf had been a major site for pearl diving since antiquity and had been a leading producer for regional markets centered on India for centuries, but in the late nineteenth century soaring global demand for pearls sparked a worldwide surge in pearl production, and the Gulf became its epicenter. Pearl diving intensified at pearl banks from Mexico to Australia and from Malaysia to Tahiti, but the Gulf was by far the world's leading producer. Between 1873 and 1906, the value of pearl exports from Bahrain increased by more than 800 percent. By 1905, the value of pearls produced in the Gulf exceeded the production of all other parts of the world combined. At the peak of pearl production, the Gulf pearl banks were worked by more than three thousand boats that employed tens of thousands of men from Muscat to Kuwait. The pearling industry was the largest source of employment in the region, and chronic shortages in labor for diving created a demand for slaves. Enslaved divers from Africa became a common sight by the late nineteenth century and were universally regarded as the region's best and most valued divers. The rapid growth of the Gulf's pearl production accompanied the global boom in consumption of gems and precious stones beginning in the 1870s and the rise of a class of consumers who were willing and able to pay for them. Particularly in Europe and North America, diamonds, pearls, and other precious stones entered mainstream high fashion in the final decades of the nineteenth century and accompanied the rise of the modern fashion industry. The pearl industry expanded in tandem with the diamond industry, but pearls ultimately even surpassed diamonds as the gem of choice for fashionable women.[4]

The annual diving season in the nineteenth-century Gulf looked much like it had in previous centuries. The main difference was that in the nineteenth century diving became a truly massive enterprise. But as in the past, each diving boat consisted of an all-male crew, including one *nākhudha* (captain; plural *nawākhida*) and an equal number of *ghawāwīs* (divers; singular *ghawwās*) and *siyūb* (haulers; singular *saīb*), in addition to an assortment of *radhafa* (assistants or extra hands; singular *radhīf*) and *awlād* (boys or apprentices; singular *walid*).[5] The captain's responsibilities included gathering the crew members and paying them at the end of each season, selecting the pearl banks to be fished, leasing a boat if he did not own one, preparing the necessary provisions for the boat, maintaining order aboard, and selling the pearls for the best price possible at the end of the season. Diving began each morning and continued until sunset, with only an hour's break in the afternoon. Each diver wore only a loincloth and was equipped with only a pair of horn pincers (a clip similar in shape to a clothespin, made of bone, shell, or horn and worn on the nose to prevent water from entering), leather fingertips, and a knife. The pearling enterprise depended in large part on the relationship between the diver and hauler, who worked together in pairs. Divers descended to the sea floor with the aid of a heavy stone weight, of which several sizes were kept onboard. The stone weight was attached to a rope and fitted with a loop to the diver's foot. With the aid of the hauler, the diver would slip his foot into the loop, inhale, and descend rapidly to the sea floor.[6]

Typical dives would take a diver to depths of between fifty and eighty feet and would last between one and two minutes. When a diver reached the sea floor he kept his foot in the weight's loop, reached, and maneuvered himself as best he could to collect as many oysters as possible—rarely more than a few from each dive—using the knife to pry the shells from the rocky surface below. For as long as he could hold his breath, the diver put oysters he collected into a net basket tied to his waist with a second rope, which extended up to the boat and was closely monitored by the careful hands of the hauler above him. Before ascending, the diver released the weight, which the hauler pulled back onto the ship, and signaled to the hauler he was ready to resurface by tugging the second rope fastened around his waist. The hauler pulled the diver back to the surface as quickly as possible before his air expired. Divers would rest for only a few minutes before repeating the process.[7]

Diving crews heaped the oyster shells into a pile in the center of the boat and made no attempt to determine which divers had collected which oysters. The shells were allowed to sit through the heat of the day and then overnight. Each morning the crews would sit around the pile of shells and, under the supervision of the captain, pry open the oysters and search the smelly flesh inside for pearls. Only a small minority of oysters contained any type of pearl (one in five by one estimate), and most of those found

"The Pearl Fishery in the Persian Gulf," from *The Graphic*, Oct. 1, 1881. Used by permission. © Illustrated London News Ltd./Mary Evans.

were of the smallest variety, but as members of the crew found pearls, they passed them to the captain, who placed them in a cloth bag for safekeeping until the catch could be sold. The process continued in this way for 130 days until the end of the season.[8]

In the Gulf, diving was a seasonal occupation. The pearl-diving season lasted approximately five months of the year. As hard as it may be for contemporary observers to imagine given the region's notorious heat, the waters of the Gulf are too cold between October and April for anyone to tolerate being submerged in them long enough to make pearl diving possible without modern diving equipment. In the early nineteenth century, the first pearl-diving season, called the Ghaūs al-Bard (the Cold Dive), began around the middle of April each year, when the shallow waters warmed to a temperature to permit diving. It lasted about forty days. During the Ghaūs al-Bard, divers could tolerate the cold water for only half an hour at a time, so shifts were changed frequently, and divers stayed close to shore in shallow water. The main diving season each year, Ghaūs al-Kabīr (the Great Dive), began in June and lasted through September. During this season the ships of each locality departed and returned in unison according to local decree, and hundreds of boats and thousands of men participated. The main diving season was the primary source of income for coastal and insular Arabia in the nineteenth century and involved deepwater diving long distances from shore for weeks at a time. The third season, Mujannah, was much smaller in scale, duration, and production and involved wading in the shallow waters in the autumn.[9] By the end of the nineteenth century the Ghaūs al-Bard had been eliminated or merged into the Ghaūs al-Kabīr, which then began in the middle of May and continued for 130 days until the middle of September. An additional season, the Radda (Return) began a few days after the end of the Ghaūs al-Kabir and lasted for about three weeks. Some divers continued to participate in the Mujannah season during low tides near shore in the late nineteenth century as well. Some divers and diving captains also engaged in diving outside of the Gulf, either around Socotra Island near the Red Sea or in the Gulf of Manaar in Ceylon.[10]

Pearl banks were spread across the Gulf and varied annually in terms of yield, requiring pearl captains to move from place to place in order to find productive areas. Boats were accordingly kept away from towns for weeks at a time and were unable to return home for the duration of the season. Pearl boats would come ashore only in order to resupply, usually every three weeks. When within reach of a coastal town, they were provisioned by local entrepreneurs who specialized in delivering drinking water and supplies to pearling boats.[11]

African Labor and Pearl Diving

Enslaved Africans and free men of African ancestry accounted for a large number of the pearl divers in the late nineteenth and early twentieth centuries. Although the proportions cannot be determined with precision, the descriptions of several contemporary observers attest to a substantial proportion of African pearling crewmen. Captain E. L. Durand, filing a report in 1878, noted that while most haulers in the Gulf were Bedouins or Persians, the divers were generally "sedees" (Africans) and sometimes "sedee domestic slaves."[12] J. G. Lorimer, in his comprehensive gazetteer of the Gulf, stated that the divers were "mostly poor Arabs and free Negroes or Negro slaves; but Persians and Baluchis are also to be found among them, and in recent years, owing to the large profits made by divers, many respectable Arabs have joined their ranks."[13] Paul W. Harrison, who spent twelve years in the Gulf with the American Mission in the early twentieth century, recalled in 1924 that many divers on the Trucial Coast were slaves, but "they do not number over one-half the divers." "Most of these slaves are Negroes from Africa," he explained. "A few are Baluchees from the Makran coast between India and Persia."[14] Charles Belgrave, who spent the better part of three decades in Bahrain and the Gulf beginning in 1925, recalled that while most divers abstained from eating much during the dive season and were relatively gaunt, "the pullers were stalwart specimens; many of them were negroes with tremendous chest and arm development."[15] In 1929 the British senior naval officer in the Gulf estimated that there were twenty thousand slave divers (roughly a quarter of the total) diving in the Gulf in each season.[16] Bertram Thomas, in his report on slavery in Batinah in 1929, estimated that a fifth of the "army" of thousands of divers that Batinah sent to the diving banks each year were enslaved.[17] Allan Villiers also counted "the huge muscular slave" among the Gulf pearl divers following his visit to the pearl banks with a *tawwāsh* in the 1930s.[18]

African slaves also appear in letters received at the British Residency complaining of instances of piracy and listing slaves among "lost property." Raiders attacked the *bughala* (large dhow) of Ghaīnim bin ʿAli al-Mahairbī at Al-Bidda in the summer of 1876, killing two men and taking MT$400 worth of pearls and one "seedie slave" valued at MT$120.[19] Captain Mohammad bin Rāshid of Lingah, complained of being attacked at Khor Shajij in the summer of 1887 by men with guns and swords who wounded two members of his crew and stole pearls, gold, guns, dates, rice, one "black slave," and two (presumably free) "Cidi men."[20] African divers and haulers can also be seen in the photographs taken by twentieth-century photographers like Ronald Codrai, who documented life in Arabia. Photographs of pearling crews and notable pearling singers reveal a significant African presence throughout the industry.[21]

A great many slave divers who sought their manumission from British officials at Muscat, Sharjah, Bahrain, and Bushehr gave personal testimonies

Sir R. Hay, "Pearling Boat at Bahrain Pearling Banks," 1926. Used by permission. © Royal Geographical Society, UK (with IBG).

of being kidnapped from East Africa as young boys and being sent for diving as soon as they reached the proper age—usually their early teens. The following statement was recorded by Faraj bin Sulaiman in Sharjah in August 1938:

> My name is Faraj bin Sulaiman, born at Sawahil, aged about 40 years. I was kidnapped from my native place when I was young. I do not know the name of the kidnapper who brought me to Sur and sold me to one Abdur Rahman al Maghribi whom I served for about 15 years at Sur. Later he brought me to Dubai and sold me to Muhammad bin Rashid of Dubai. My master died 20 years ago and after his death I remained in the service of his uncle Rashid bin Ubaid who used to send me to diving every year and take over my earnings. Two years ago I married a free woman named Zahroh who is still living with me. Owing to the gross ill treatment of my master Rashid, I ran away from Dubai to Sharjah in order to take refuge at the British Agency and to request that I may be freed from slavery.[22]

Sa'ad bin Mubarak, another enslaved African in Dubai, was kidnapped from East Africa as a child and brought to Dubai, where he was sold to Nāsir bin Khalifah, who sent him diving each year and took his earnings, providing only the minimum for his upkeep. When Sa'ad was about forty years old in 1938, following the collapse of pearl prices, his master stopped giving him enough to survive, so he ran away and sought his manumission certificate in Sharjah.[23] Another man, Juma bin Fundi, originally from Mfenesini in Zanzibar, who as a boy had worked as an orderly to a British officer in the East African campaign, boarded a dhow from Zanzibar to Mombasa, where he hoped to find work, but the dhow never landed at Mombasa. Juma was kidnapped by the owner of the dhow, Hamid bin Salim of Batinah, and was sold at Dubai to Mohamad bin Ibrahim of Sharjah to work as a pearl diver around 1926.[24] In 1925, an eleven-year-old Ethiopian boy named Surūr was tending cattle in the Wallamo region of Ethiopia when he was seized by kidnappers. His captors took him to Tajura on the Somali coast and shipped him, along with fifty others, to Jeddah, where he was sold to a man who took him to Qatar and eventually sold him to a pearl merchant who engaged him as a diver. About five years later, he managed to escape from his master and boarded a boat bound for Basra. At Basra he met some Somali men who were working as stokers on a British steamer, and they assisted him in getting to Djibouti and home to Ethiopia by way of Muscat.[25]

Some divers of African descent worked as free divers, but many others were second-generation slaves—not brought directly from East Africa themselves but born into slavery from parents who had been brought previously. An old man named Bashir bin Farajullah appealed to the Political Agency in Bahrain for a manumission certificate in 1934. The agent's staffer estimated that he was about eighty years old and remarked that he "looks like a Negro and talks Arabic." He had been born a slave in Qatar to slave parents serving in the house of Sheikh Abdullah bin Qāsim al-Thāni, the ruler of Qatar. When he was about thirty years old, the sheikh sold him to a pearl-diving captain named Abdullah bin Jābur al-Musallamī of Gharayah (in Qatar), whom he served as pearl diver for fourteen years. Then, at the age of forty-four, his master took him to Hasa, where he sold him to a man who employed him for three years as a gardener. Realizing that Bashir was not fit for that type of work, the new owner set him out to earn his own keep. Bashir subsequently returned to Qatar, got engaged as a free diver, earned a few rupees—enough to get married—and returned to his old master in Hasa with his wife, where he remained into his old age.[26] Another man, Sadain bin Farhan, had been born in Hanjam (an island in the Gulf) around 1884, to slave parents who had been brought from Africa. Sadain and his father worked together as divers for their master until his father died.[27]

The lives of pearling crews were hard, and health problems abounded. Ruptured eardrums were almost universal, and some veterans claimed that one had not gained proficiency until this occurred. Blindness was not uncommon among seasoned divers, who sometimes continued to dive after losing their sight. Respiratory problems, particularly bronchitis, were common, as was scurvy, but most captains knew to carry enough lime juice to last for the entire season. Skin problems on account of the long hours in the water were widespread. Pearl diving was also dangerous because of sharks, stingrays, and (most commonly) jellyfish. By the early twentieth century many divers wore tight-fitting cotton suits that could partially shield the body from the painful stings.[28]

To combat the loneliness and monotony of life on the water and to promote steady work and group solidarity, many captains hired a professional singer, or *nihām*—often a diver who had retired due to age, blindness, or injury—to sing during the long journeys at sea. The music of the pearl divers has been preserved in the musical tradition known as *fijrī*, which takes its name from the Arabic word for dawn, representing the time when work and singing began during the diving season and when the musical sessions finished at the traditional gathering places *(dār sha'bīa)* during the off season. Pearling music was divided into five genres, each named for its rhythm and the specific purpose for which a song was sung. On pearling boats songs were sung *a cappella*, with a lead singer chanting and the crew echoing or the crew repeating a section and the lead singer improvising or singing new verses on top of the voices of the crew. Boats frequently had problems, and songs were especially useful during the lull before a boat could be repaired at sea. Singing was done with the permission of the captains. During the off season, songs were sung all night in homes or coffee houses using instruments including a small drum called the *marūās*, ceramic pots called *jahāl*, and small brass cymbals called *tawus*. The singing was often accompanied by dancing that incorporated giant leaps into the air.[29]

Most pearling songs focused on religion and love. Religious songs praising God, the Prophet, and sometimes Ali (as many divers were Shi'a) were especially popular as diving boats headed out to sea, praying for safety and a successful season. Some of the most popular themes were the beauty of a beloved woman and mourning the long absence from home. Many songs spoke of home, the smell of flowers, and the air of the desert, and they occasionally expressed one's sorrow at feeling stolen from one's homeland by the pearling life. Pearls themselves were the subject of numerous songs, usually in the context of bringing a diver back home to loved ones.[30]

When the boats returned to shore at the close of the annual season, the captain set about selling the boat's catch and paying off the crew. In the early twentieth century, as demand for pearls increased sharply and prices soared, middlemen *(tawāwīsh)* would visit the pearl banks themselves and offer captains cash for pearls on the spot, selling to larger merchants in the cities for profit. If a captain owned the boat he commanded, he had the option of selling the pearls to the pearl merchant of his choice. If the boat was rented, the captain was obligated to sell the pearls to the owner of the boat, usually at a deflated price for payment in kind rather than cash. This system maximized the lender's profits. If the captain owned the boat, he took a cut of 20 percent of the gross earnings. The remaining proceeds were split among the crew, with divers receiving three shares and haulers two shares of the remainder. If the boat was leased, the owner of the boat kept the 20 percent, and the captain received a diver's share. On the Trucial Coast, the sheikh of the town from which the boat sailed sometimes received a diver's share of the proceeds as well. If the boat was leased, the crew was forced to take payment in kind—most often in bags of rice. What could not be used by the crew was sold in the market for cash, which was then distributed among the crew.[31]

Pearls and Profits

Most of the profit generated by the pearl industry benefited the merchants and financiers, many of them Indians, who owned the boats and lent them at interest to the captains and in turn took half of the proceeds of the dives. For financiers, risk was comparatively low, and payback was consistently high. The pearls could be sold at high prices to agents with connections, and the rice used as payment for the crew could be acquired through connections for less than its local value in cash. The dual sources of income benefited the financiers. Likewise, the ruling families fared well. In the case of Bahrain, the rulers benefited indirectly from the pearl trade from duties levied on imports. The more successful the diving season and the more wealth that was created locally, the greater the number of imports in luxury and bulk goods and thus the greater revenue produced from import duties. Much of the money was used to build and furnish elaborate houses with modern conveniences.

The primary destination of Gulf pearls throughout the nineteenth century was Bombay, and business was handled largely through Arab and Indian merchants in Bahrain and, later, Dubai. For most of the industry's history, round pearls were almost universally exported to India, where they were sought by royalty and used throughout Hindu societies in weddings, where a pearl was often bored as part of marriage ceremonies.[32] In India, pearls were widely used to make long necklaces worn by women, ornamental jewelry worn on the top of the head, and elaborate earrings and nose rings. They were also incorporated into ornamental rose water sprinklers, incense burners, and works of religious art. The bulk of the Gulf pearl trade was thus always to India, and merchants from the major cities of Surat, Karachi, and (most prominently) Bombay sought pearls of all sizes in the Gulf markets. Within the Gulf, Muscat served as the pearl export center for much of the eighteenth century, but by the mid-nineteenth century it was overshadowed by Bahrain. While residents of Oman were not great consumers of pearls, sources tell of Seyyid Sa'id's impressive collection of rare pearls in the nineteenth century, and his wives were known to have possessed an assortment of marvelous pearls as ornaments. Bombay remained the center of Gulf pearl exports until 1907. Before that year European merchants from London, Vienna, and Paris purchased pearls from Indian middlemen in Bombay for their respective markets. But during the U.S. Panic of 1907, British creditors who normally extended credit to Gulf pearl traders in Bombay collected on their loans and created a temporary lapse in the Gulf pearl-purchasing system, severely limiting exports. One Parisian jewel firm saw the lapse as an opportunity to capture the Gulf's pearl catch and shift the center of the world pearl market to Paris, where it would remain for twenty-five years.

Like the global boom in ostrich feathers, or plumes, around roughly the same time, the global pearl boom was built in part on global networks of Jewish merchants and traders.[33] The owner of the Parisian firm that would dominate the world pearl market during its greatest period of growth was Leonard Rosenthal. Rosenthal was born in Vladikavkaz in the Caucasus region of Russia between the Black and Caspian Seas, about fifty miles west of Grozny, Chechnya, near the city of Beslan. He emigrated to Paris at the age of fourteen, learned French, and scraped together a living as a teenager by working as a petty trader in furniture, antiques, art, and anything else he could pick up cheaply in Paris auctions. After the death of Rosenthal's mother, his father emigrated to Paris and brought all of his children. Leonard, then seventeen, was entrusted with the welfare of two of his younger brothers, Victor and Drosia. Between 1890 and 1906, to make ends meet, Rosenthal sold an increasing number of small art objects to members of the Club des Marchands de Pierres Précieuses, a few of whom began asking him to find buyers for small lots of jewels. He spent the profits he earned on purchasing pearls and developed a local reputation as a small-time pearl dealer, forming with his brothers the small firm Rosenthal et Frères. In 1907 Paris was recovering from a long slump in trade that had devastated many of the firms that dealt in French luxuries. Rosenthal's firm had survived but was desperate for a financial boost. That desperation led Rosenthal to initiate a plan that would make his company the most successful pearl firm in the world.[34]

The value of pearl exports from the Gulf had more than quadrupled in the quarter century ending in 1904. At the close of the nineteenth century, Bahrain alone saw pearl exports rise in ten years from 3.7 million rupees in 1894 to 10.3 million rupees in 1904. Jewelers in Europe recognized the great potential of the pearl market, and a few firms contemplated bypassing the Bombay middlemen by traveling directly to the Arabian Gulf. In 1905, two Parisian merchants visited Bahrain to attempt direct purchases. Gastone Perrone, an amateur trader, did not fare well, but a competitor, Émile Nattan, who owned a large jewelry business in Paris, arrived later and purchased 400,000 francs' worth of pearls. Following her apparent success, Madame Nattan made plans to return the following year but failed to arrive in 1906. In her place, Victor Rosenthal of Rosenthal et Frères arrived and purchased 187,000 rupees' worth of pearls. The Rosenthal brothers had the advantage of a permanent agency in Bombay from which to deal with the major markets at Bahrain, Dubai, and Lingah. Victor already had substantial knowledge of the market from working with the Bombay office and learned Arabic. Following Victor's departure, rumors circulated in Bahrain that his firm had lost considerable money on the purchases. Victor Rosenthal nevertheless returned the following year and purchased 350,000 rupees' worth of pearls. Following the Panic of 1907 in the United States, a great opportunity presented itself, and Rosenthal et Frères took advantage. The value of total pearl exports from Bahrain, which had steadily risen since 1900, dropped from 12.4 million rupees in 1907–1908 to 5.5 million rupees in 1908–1909. The drop was mainly attributable to two factors. First, a plague outbreak, which killed nearly two thousand people, occurred in Bahrain from April to July 1907 (at a time when the island's population was estimated at just over one hundred thousand) and frightened a large portion of the working population away. Second, tighter markets in Europe meant fewer purchases in Bombay and a shortfall in returns for Bombay merchants, who in turn recalled advances they had lent to pearl traders. This situation created a temporary slump in the trade. Leonard and Victor proposed to return to Bahrain to buy the "entire stock" of pearls the following year at rates above the current prices in order to undercut the competition. The necessary cash for the scheme was well beyond the Rosenthals' means, but they convinced a prominent banker to lend them several million francs. In the following three years, the Rosenthals succeeded in cornering the European pearl market. As it happened, this maneuver was perfectly timed. Values of pearl exports from the Gulf were poised to increase exponentially and enter their peak years, 1910–1914.[35]

In his memoir, Leonard Rosenthal attributed his firm's virtual monopoly of Gulf pearl exports to Europe to his brother's on-the-spot research of the market over the previous three years and his local knowledge of the sellers. Victor determined that in order to convince local dealers to sell him their stock he would have to convince them that his firm was sufficiently wealthy to make major purchases and to continue returning to Bahrain indefinitely. To demonstrate he meant business, Victor returned to Bahrain in 1909 and made an ostentatious display of wealth. He converted his money and brought all of it in the form of 50-centime (half-franc) silver coins. Leonard Rosenthal recalled the story of his brother's reception in dramatic fashion: "On the day of the arrival of his funds, the astounded Arabs beheld fifty donkeys, heavily laden, transporting in an almost endless line boxes full of money from the ship to my brother's house. As they were unacquainted with any European money except pounds sterling in gold, the defile of donkeys aroused their admiration and respect. We became, in their imagination, the richest men in the world, and from then on the finest lots of pearls were offered to us without the least hesitation. We had won the battle."[36]

According to the British political agent at Bahrain, Victor Rosenthal stayed thirteen weeks in Bahrain and carried away an estimated 1.3 million rupees' worth of pearls in 1909 (about 25 percent of the total market that year) and 4 million rupees' worth of pearls in 1910 (about 36 percent of the total). In his annual trade report on Bahrain for the year 1909–1910, the political agent lamented the fact that no British firms had sent agents to Bahrain and that the Rosenthals were cornering the market and had in fact been so successful that they had sent another representative to Dubai that year: "He is able to get the best available direct information by weekly telegraph from [the] Paris market, which enables him to effect his transactions on much more substantial grounds than his rivals, and to such extent is this recognized that as far as his transactions become known, he is used by the other merchants as a weather-cock of the market."[37]

The success of Rosenthal et Frères continued in subsequent years. Victor reportedly purchased pearls valued at 6.4 million rupees in 1911.[38] The *New York Times* reported that Rosenthal's fortune in 1914 amounted to no less than 450 million francs (well over $1 billion in today's terms). Leonard's daughter, the accomplished playwright and performer Rachel Rosenthal, wryly recalled the opulence in which she was raised in Paris during one of her first major performances, titled *Charm*:

> The walls were embossed dull silver lacquer, strewn about with a few Chagalls, some Monets, a couple of Pissarros, even a little Guardi. In the middle was our dining-room table, which was a solid round slab of pink Carrara marble. As you went into the salon, you walked up three steps which were shiny, solid brass. The salon itself, walls decorated on both sides by Jean Dunant, presented monkeys in the trees, ducks in a pond, flamingoes on black ground, swans on gold ground. At the far end, nothing but glass and two huge aquariums filled with exotic fish, through which you could see our pretty little eighteenth-century garden at the end of which was a lovely stone fountain with a couple of little angels, and over it, lightly draped a weeping willow.[39]

By the start of World War I, Leonard Rosenthal had begun diversifying his investments by expanding into Paris real estate. These efforts expanded significantly in 1925, when he purchased the palatial Dufayel estate in the Champs-Élysées, which he demolished and erected in its place the Arcades des Champs-Élysées (Arcades du Lido), which stands today at Nos. 76–78 Champs-Élysées. The Arcades was the first of many residential-to-commercial conversions on the famous boulevard, and it started the movement to convert it to a posh shopping district. By 1928 Rosenthal's real estate company owned twenty-six buildings on the Champs-Élysées, all of them conversions from residential to commercial property, which annually netted Rosenthal over 30 million francs. Maurice de Waleffe estimated Rosenthal's net worth in 1928 at 300 million francs.[40] The same arcades of Paris that first inspired Walter Benjamin's *Arcades Project* in 1927 were built in part with the wealth from Gulf pearls.[41]

Making Pearls Popular (Again)

The meteoric rise of pearl consumption in Europe and North America between 1880 and 1930 was not an altogether new phenomenon. It was instead a revival of tastes that had predominated in European royal courts during an earlier "pearl age" between 1524 and 1658. Pearls had enjoyed wide popularity among European royalty following the introduction of cargos of pearls from the Spanish and Portuguese conquests of the sixteenth century. Caribbean pearls from the Venezuelan island of Margarita flowed into Europe following the Spanish conquest of the island and the enslavement of its local inhabitants to dive for pearls. Asian pearls from Ceylon and the Gulf also came into European possession following Portuguese conquests in the Indian Ocean and the occupation of Hormuz. Pearl fashion subsequently waned following the mid-seventeenth century upheavals in Europe and through the late-eighteenth-century age of revolutions, persisting in muted form until revived in the mid-nineteenth century with help from royal women like Queen Victoria in England and Empress Eugénie in France.[42]

In England, Queen Victoria was a leading force in women's fashion in the early decades of her reign and was in large part responsible for the revival of European pearl fashion. In her public appearances she was consistently seen wearing a pearl necklace and always wore a four-strand pearl portrait bracelet—a gift from Prince Consort Albert. During her reign, she spent £157,887 with the crown jeweler, Garrard. She retrieved several missing pieces of jewelry from the British treasury, including the famous Hanoverian pearls—the six long rows of pearls originally owned by Pope Clement VII, given to Catherine of Medici, and inherited by Mary, Queen of Scots, and Elizabeth I. The loss of the pearls to Victoria's cousin, the king of Hanover, in 1858 represented a loss to the nation in many English eyes and was reflected in the poetry of Tennyson. When Victoria regained the pearls, she made a point of wearing them in an official portrait so everyone could see they were back in British possession. The pearls she received following her coronation as empress of India in 1876 provided the supplies for future jewelry designs of the dynasty. Following the death of Prince Consort Albert in 1861, Victoria went into a semi-permanent state of mourning, limiting her public appearances and wearing black for the remainder of her life. But even in mourning she wore her trademark tasseled pearl sautoir and favorite pearl bracelets. Likewise, in Second Empire Paris (1851–1870), Empress Eugénie revived the opulence of the French court with royal attire privileging pearl necklaces. Her preference for black pearls created a trend in the middle of her reign that was mimicked around Europe and North America.[43]

Following the fall of the French monarchy in 1871, Empress Eugénie lost her already contested fashion preeminence in Paris, the Western fashion capital. In the late Victorian era, with their queen in mourning, English women lost their once leading fashion role model, and consumers looked increasingly to minor royalty, landed aristocracy, and a growing class of *nouveaux riches* for fashion trendsetting. Fashionable women in Europe and North America increasingly looked to actresses like Sarah Bernhardt and professional beauties like Lillie Langtry as role models. Sarah Bernhardt's costumes in Sardou's *La Tosca* in 1888, for example, influenced Western women's dress almost immediately. Following Victoria's death in 1901, her son, Edward VII, and his wife, Alexandra, Princess of Wales, set numerous fashion trends and helped intensify the growing pearl revival. Throughout her reign, Alexandra wore a trademark dog-collar necklace made of four rows of pearls, which she wore to hide a scar on her neck that was the result of a childhood disease. Her style of necklace nevertheless caught on as a popular fashion trend. Edward helped further popularize pearl pins among aristocratic men.[44]

In the last decades of the nineteenth century, as a by-product of the Industrial Revolution and the birth of big business, the *nouveaux riches*—commercial magnates, agricultural landowners, and the professional classes—joined the ranks of high society and eventually took it over in dictating fashion trends in Europe and North America. In the United States, the Carnegies, Vanderbilts, Morgans, and other multimillionaires sought to distinguish themselves as part of a new American aristocracy and used fashion to this end. As wealth began to replace lineage as the measure of respectability in Europe and the United States, the bodily display of wealth grew in importance, and pearls increasingly became the vehicle of this display. If America's new aristocrats could not be royalty, they could dress like royalty. William K. Vanderbilt emphasized this point when he bought a pearl necklace that had previously belonged to Catherine of Medici and followed the purchase with a more extravagant one of a necklace of five hundred pearls that had formerly belonged to Empress Eugénie as gifts for his wife.[45] Vanderbilt's daughter, Consuelo, who inherited the necklace from her mother, symbolized the rise of the new American elite in 1895, when she married Charles Spencer-Churchill, Duke of Marlborough, becoming the first member of the new American aristocracy

"Duchess of Marlborough." Bain News Service. George Grantham Bain Collection, Library of Congress Prints and Photographs Division, Washington, D.C. Call #LC-B2-3733-7 [P&P].

to marry into European royalty.⁴⁶ Consuelo Vanderbilt's portraits invariably depict her wearing pearls.

In the late-nineteenth-century age of copper, steel, oil, and railroad magnates, New York's Fifth Avenue became the epicenter of luxury consumption for the new class of American multimillionaires. Prior to the late 1880s, the record for individual jewelry sales in the United States stood around $25,000. In the late 1880s, members of the Vanderbilt family began a social campaign that left old sales records far behind. When Gertrude Vanderbilt became engaged to marry Harry Payne Whitney in 1896, Harry's uncle, Colonel Oliver Hazard Payne, a partner with John D. Rockefeller in Standard Oil, placed an order with a Fifth Avenue jeweler for a sixty-inch necklace of perfect sixteen-grain pearls, valued at over $150,000, as a wedding present. The jeweler searched Europe for six weeks for enough pearls to make the necklace before finally finding a necklace of that exact description in London: the necklace of the late duchess of Montrose. Gertrude Vanderbilt Whitney wore the royal pearls in numerous photographs following the wedding, which merged two great American aristocratic families.⁴⁷ The jeweler who negotiated the purchase described the event as a sign of a transformation in American luxury consumption. It was not only the largest jewelry sale in American history, but it also marked a "new era—the day of the dearest of all gems, the pearl." As the jeweler explained, "This had been a diamond country. Now the time of luxury had awaked, when diamond ornaments large enough were becoming too heavy to carry around. The pearl, four and five times as valuable by weight, was to take its place. The gem of European royalty was coming to America."⁴⁸

In the early decades of the twentieth century, pearls dominated mainstream women's fashion in the form of long pearl necklaces, pendants, earrings, and decorations on brooches. *Harper's Bazaar* announced in 1909 that jewelry had become "a necessary incident of the modern costume." That season's jewelry trends were "large pendants using Ancient and Oriental *motifs* and themes from nature such as insects, animals, leaves and vines, likewise with brooches. To accentuate the oriental pendants ... long pearl necklaces, and pearl hat pins."⁴⁹ Pearls, like dates, were deliberately marketed and consumed as an exotic oriental luxury. Like ostrich feathers, which were consciously worn by women as an emblem of African exoticism, pearls became an exotic must for "oriental" costume balls, theme parties, and "fancy dress" balls.[50]

Global Pearl Production

With the boom in pearl prices at the close of the nineteenth century, pearl production rose around the world. Pearl banks in Venezuela, Australia, Baja California, the South Pacific islands, Sri Lanka, and the Sulu Islands (between Borneo and Mindanao in the Philippines) dramatically expanded their production. The Gulf was by far the global leader in pearl production, with the pearl fisheries of Ceylon a distant second. In the early twentieth century, the Gulf was the source of roughly half of the entire value of pearls produced in the world and an estimated 80 percent of the fine pearls in demand in Western markets. In 1906, the Gulf accounted for 49 percent of global pearl production, Ceylon 15 percent, the rivers of the United States 8 percent, Australia 6 percent, East Asia 5 percent, the Sulu Islands 4 percent, Venezuela 3 percent, and Mexico 3 percent.[51] Fortune-seeking Europeans migrated to several centers of production, most notably Australia, to try their hands at mechanized pearl fishing. Many of these men reported on their experiences in books and magazines.[52] The seed pearls of Venezuela's Margarita Island had become so valuable at the turn of the century that the American consul at La Guayra, Louis Goldschmidt, estimated about four hundred boats and two thousand men were involved in the pearl industry there in 1901, and a French company recently began sending its own divers with mechanical diving apparatus.[53] In Australia, the Caribbean, and the Gulf of California, European divers in modern diving equipment or using mechanical dredges participated in global pearl production, but they never produced pearls in the quantity that the tens of thousands of divers of the Gulf annually produced using traditional diving methods.

Not even the United States was immune to the global pearl-diving craze of the turn of the twentieth century. By 1906, the rivers of the United States accounted for the third largest annual pearl production in the world. While rare pearl finds between the 1850s and 1870s caused temporary runs to local streams in places like New Jersey and Ohio, the freshwater pearl industry in the United States did not develop to a massive scale until the discovery of the upper Mississippi Valley pearl resources. More than $10,000 worth of pearls were found in the summer of 1889 in tributaries of the Mississippi River in southwestern Wisconsin. As the waters of these tributary rivers were shallow enough for a person to wade in to collect the pearl-producing freshwater mollusks, no special skill or experience was required, and thousands of Americans set up camps along the Mississippi's tributary rivers between Wisconsin and Arkansas. By the turn of the twentieth century, Americans in the Mississippi Valley were struck with a sort of "pearl fever." Local papers announced important pearl discoveries and sent off rushes of pearl hunters to local streams and rivers. Some of the biggest production took place in Arkansas, where the streams flowing from the Ozarks had especially productive mussels, and a significant number of freshwater pearls were found between 1897 and 1941.[54]

Debt and Slavery

The life of the pearl diver in the Gulf differed vastly from that of the most successful pearl merchants. Even the best of divers lived in poverty, and the position of the slave diver was considerably worse than that of the free diver, as slaves surrendered all or most of their income to their masters. For a typical crew member, earnings for a season were insufficient to provide subsistence for the remainder of the year, but captains and the capitalists who financed them encouraged the divers to accept additional wages on credit in anticipation of higher earnings the following year. The system of credit—offered at the beginning of the pearling season in order to maintain divers' families while they were away diving, at the end of the season, and during the off season—kept the divers constantly indebted to their captains, ensuring they would return to dive the following year. The debts were recorded on paper for each diver, but since nearly all divers were illiterate, they had little power to ensure the records were accurate. They also depended on their captains, who arranged the pearl sales in private, to report the proceeds accurately. There was undoubtedly much abuse, and many contemporary observers likened the system of indebtedness to slavery or serfdom. The situation was exacerbated on the Trucial Coast. There, merchants frequently delayed payments until sales could be secured in Bombay, a process that often meant months without payment and disappointment when sales of lots of pearls brought less than expected.[55]

If the lot of the typical diver was harsh, the situation was infinitely worse for divers who were, in fact, enslaved. As noted, unlike the earnings of other divers, the earnings of slaves went to their masters. Masters sent their slaves diving each year, often with a representative from the masters' tribes or localities to ensure the slaves did not abscond. While "free" divers brought bags of rice and cash home from the annual dive and could dream of one day possibly paying off their debts, slave divers had to surrender all or nearly all of their earnings, making it impossible to ever earn their freedom on their own. During the off season, many free divers from the Gulf returned home and lived on their earnings from the diving season without taking other employment. But some hard-working divers from the Batinah region of Oman were also known to join pearl ships in Sri Lanka in order to generate a second form of income, thus diving for the better part of the whole year. Slaves who were sent by their masters to dive during the summer months had to be maintained during the off season, but since skilled divers could yield high returns, they were in high demand outside the Gulf and could be induced to work for more months of the year.[56]

Even if a diver were free in the sense that he worked for himself and kept his own earnings, his perpetual indebtedness would require him to continue diving year after year, so his situation in many ways mirrored that of slaves. For most of the history of the pearling industry in the Gulf, a diver's debts could also be passed down to his sons after he died, so debt, like servility, could be inherited. Records of pearl divers' debts that survive in archives demonstrate that debts were nearly impossible to repay. The account of Bashir bin 'Umran bin Abdullah, a diver for one Matar bin Matar of Dubai for 1925, shows that Bashir started the year with a debt of 2,300 rupees. He earned 20 rupees in the winter and 152 rupees in the summer, sums that reduced his debt to 2,128 rupees. He then received an advance consisting of 50 rupees and two bags of rice valued at 25 rupees apiece, followed by a further advance of another bag of rice (25 rupees), a basket of dates (7 rupees), a maund of coffee (7 rupees), and 30 rupees in cash. He was also later debited for the cost of one cloak and one tablecloth (50 rupees total). The advances amounted to 219 rupees, bringing the total debt to 2,347. Thus, the amount he owed increased by 47 rupees for the year in spite of his earnings of 172 rupees from the pearling season. He was extended credit of about 27 percent beyond his annual earnings in order to ensure his continued indebtedness and hence his return the following season. Naturally, Matar bin Matar had access to the rice, dates, and cloth at wholesale prices and provided them to Bashir at retail prices, contributing to his profits.[57]

Like their enslaved counterparts, free divers could be purchased, in effect, from their employers by payment to the employers of the debt amount claimed against the diver. For example, a merchant named Rashid bin Abdullah effectively purchased a diver named Ismail bin Sanqah in 1923 when Rashid paid Ismail's former captain, Mohammad bin Ghanem, 1,100 rupees "being his claim from Ismail on account of diving." Ismail's debt record thus began with the sum of 1,100 rupees, and it quickly grew to 1,594 rupees by the beginning of his first diving season with Rashid when Ismail received 340 rupees in cash as an advance, plus installments of two bags of rice (40 rupees), a basket of dates (14 rupees), and a cloak and shawl (100 rupees). In the 1924 season he earned 233 rupees, which reduced his debt to 1,361 rupees, but he subsequently took 70 rupees in cash, plus a bag of rice (20 rupees), a cloak (40 rupees), and a basket of dates (16 rupees), bringing his debt back up to 1,507.[58]

The starting amount in a diver's debt book was often so high because slave owners actually wrote the purchase price of a slave as the slave's starting debt. A forty-year-old enslaved diver named Jumah Kanaidish, who appealed for manumission in Muscat in 1936, provided evidence that his master had been indebted to a merchant for 2,200 rupees and, being unable to pay, sold Jumah to the merchant in lieu of cash. Jumah's new master wrote his purchase price in his diving book as his debt. Three years later, Jumah still "owed" his new master 2,216 rupees.[59] Average prices for slave divers ranged by location, age, and skill level. Spotty evidence from 1910 to 1930 includes prices for divers as low as 600 rupees and as high as 2,000 rupees, with averages somewhere between 900 and 1,500 rupees.

The perpetual cycles of debt for both enslaved and free divers thus created relationships of dependency and entitlement that required divers to work for their captains year after year and therefore limited their mobility and freedom. Although many divers may not have been literally enslaved, they had to provide for themselves and their families in an economic environment that placed them in perpetual debt servitude. Enslaved divers were forced to hand over their earnings or advances to their masters, but the masters were, in theory, obligated to provide for their sustenance.

The British administration eventually came to recognize that the position of anyone of African ancestry in the Gulf was particularly difficult, even if he or she was legally free. The secretary to the political resident in the Persian Gulf noted in 1925 that "their earnings, in the majority of cases, are not paid to them entirely and whatever out of same is given them is valued at very low prices. These two are the reasons for which diving slaves run away from their Nakhudas."[60] The political agent in Bahrain in 1928 recognized that Africans were the worst off because of their risk of being kidnapped and enslaved. The agent wrote, "We know how easy it is for any black to be kidnapped and sold by Bedouins." He continued, "Less than three years ago, dark-skinned cousins of the sultan of Muscat were seized by Bedouins in close proximity to the Sultan's own territory. If this fate can befall near relatives of the Muscat house, what can the black diver expect?"[61]

Growing markets and changing fashions spurred a dramatic increase in pearl production around the world, nowhere more so than in the Gulf. Enslaved Africans were essential to the expansion of the Gulf pearling industry in the late nineteenth century. Their labor enabled the Gulf to tap into the new wealth created by new demand for pearls. However, within a few years the Gulf economy was in for a shock. As with the date industry, new competition and the onset of a global depression would ultimately spell the doom of the Gulf pearl industry. The global forces that had created new fortunes and driven the demand for slave labor would also help destroy the slave-based pearling economy.

4

SLAVERY AND AFRICAN LIFE IN ARABIA

In May 1907, Faraj bin Saʿid, an enslaved African pearl diver, entered the British political agency offices in Bahrain seeking manumission from his master. Unlike many other enslaved divers who sought British assistance in that era, Faraj did not appeal for manumission on the grounds of physical abuse. He explained that he had been kidnapped from his home in Ethiopia in 1894, when he was twelve years old, and taken to Mecca, where he was purchased and brought to Najd in eastern Arabia. After working three years there, following four years at Basra and two years at Kuwait for three different masters, he was bestowed as a gift upon Bazza bint Sultan, the wife of his most recent master, in 1905. Bazza sent Faraj pearl diving each season and took all of his earnings, but what made his condition unbearable was that Bazza failed to provide him a wife. When Faraj ran away to the British political agency to seek manumission, his master, Bazza, quickly followed to beg his return. In describing the occasion, the agent wrote that he expected that Faraj would "probably return to his mistress who has been kissing and stroking his cheeks and promising him a wife."[1]

Faraj's case is unique, but his experience illustrates the lives of other enslaved Africans in Arabia in his day. Africans worked at a wide variety of tasks in the Gulf, ranging from the elite to the mundane, from the maritime to the agricultural to the domestic. Their labor was not limited to the examples provided in the previous two chapters. They could be found among the slave soldiers and bodyguards of rulers, among the domestic servants of elite households, and also as the slaves working in the back-breaking pearl and date industries. Many pearl divers had, like Faraj, been kidnapped from Africa as boys and forced to labor in various occupations until in their teens they were enlisted as divers. During the peak of the Gulf pearl industry in the early twentieth century, enslaved pearl divers who brought consistent profits to their masters could expect their masters to arrange a marriage for them, conventionally around the age of twenty-five. As a twenty-five-year-old diver in Bahrain, the undisputed center of the Gulf pearl industry, Faraj was near the peak of his career and would have had grounds to expect his master to arrange a marriage for him. Bazza's failure to fulfill this obligation was grounds for Faraj's desertion.

This chapter addresses aspects of everyday life among enslaved Africans in the Gulf in the early twentieth century, particularly with respect to labor, abuse, resistance, family life, and mobility. The experience of each slave was unique, and it is impossible to re-create a complete picture of slave life in the Gulf over the course of more than a century from the sources of the few enslaved Africans whose stories have been preserved. But the sources—mostly manumission testimonies—do allow us to see some of the ways that enslaved Africans negotiated the bonds of slavery, asserted themselves, and experienced interdependence in the Gulf over a broad period. By examining the first decades of the twentieth century, we can learn something of this broader experience.

Enslaved Africans in the Gulf typically had little control over their lives, but during the economic boom centered on the date and pearl industries around the turn of the century, some were able to negotiate their terms of service. The bonds of enslavement affected every aspect of family life, from marriage and concubinage to childbirth. Masters in the Gulf could flout customary law, which demanded that the child of a female concubine and a free male have free status. Instead they sometimes sold and resold concubines until they were discovered to be pregnant, at which time they were hastily married to male slaves to conceal the child's paternity. Especially prized male slaves, particularly the most skilled pearl divers, could expect their masters to provide them with a bride when they reached their mid-twenties, and several slaves, such as Faraj, absconded or threatened flight when their masters failed to meet this obligation. Enslaved Africans often resisted enslavement through violence, refusal to work, slowdowns, and *petit marronage* (running away). At least one slave murdered his master, while many more endured beatings, shackles, and abuse. Runaways took advantage of British manumission policy to gain government certificates that allowed them to negotiate new terms of service as free laborers. British officials in turn struggled to balance the demands of local rulers with the claims of runaway slaves and debtors. While slave experiences varied widely in the Gulf, some general trends are detectable and worthy of examination.

Victimization and Agency

Madeline Zilfi has correctly recognized a tendency for scholarship on slavery in the Middle East (as elsewhere) to be framed in binary terms—as "victimization versus agency." The fact that some enslaved populations found ways to assert degrees of independence or dignity amid the horrors of slavery, she notes, has given rise to "polarity in the characterization of repressive systems," such that "the scars of victimization are weighed against evidences of indomitability and assertions of agency."[2] Taken to one extreme, conditions of slavery can be depicted as so severe as to be inhuman, while on the other extreme, slaves could become so autonomous that the system could be said to be benign or even beneficial. In the Middle East, abolitionists and apologists for slavery could present equally compelling cases using very different evidence. In the Ottoman Empire, Muslim intellectuals framed thoughtful defenses of slavery as part of a broader defensive response to Western critiques of Ottomans (and Muslims generally) and focused on the "benign" elements of slavery in the region. Abolitionists, by contrast, found sufficient examples of cruelty to paint Muslim societies as backward and retrograde and slaves so helpless and victimized as to require Western intervention. As the work of Ehud Toledano, Y. Hakan Erdem, Eve Troutt Powell, and Madeline Zilfi demonstrates, Muslim intellectuals were quick to point out both the ironies of European condemnation of slavery and the supposed "mildness" of slavery in the Middle East. For example, when Egyptian law student Ahmed Shafik heard French cardinal Lavigerie give a sermon attacking Muslim attitudes toward slavery, he responded with a presentation of his own at the Khadivial Geographic Society in Cairo in 1890; in it he condemned Christians for complicity in institutions of slavery and highlighted the capacity for slaves to be integrated into their masters' households in Egypt.³ European imperialists were frequently conflicted on the subject—John Hanning Speke, for example, lamented the trauma of the slave trade but argued that "the slave in his new position finds himself much better off than he ever was in life before."⁴

In recognizing the victimization-versus-agency debate in the literature on Middle Eastern slavery, Zilfi builds on a critique advanced by Stanley Elkins, who identified a "damage"-versus-"resistance" divide in literature on slavery in the American South that emerged between the 1950s and 1970s. Elkins noted a shift away from the long tradition in American history of highlighting the damaging effects of the brutality and exploitation of slavery (exemplified by his own book, *Slavery*, and Kenneth Stampp's *The Peculiar Institution*) to a new tradition by the mid-1960s that emphasized "resistance and culture" (exemplified by John Blassingame's *The Slave Community*, Herbert Gutman's *The Invisible Fact*, and Eugene Genovese's *Roll, Jordan, Roll*). Elkins attributed the ideological shift to diverse factors, including a shifting perspective of African Americans regarding their own history amid the civil rights movement, Vietnam, the 1965 Moynihan Report, campus uprisings, and the emergence of Black Studies programs. By focusing less on the stultifying effects of harsh treatment under slavery and more on slaves' preservation of individuality and dignity, the mid-1960s shift in focus to "resistance and culture" anticipated the rise of diaspora studies and ultimately the Black Atlantic paradigm and the explorations for "Africanisms" and African cultural retentions in the Americas. "The dilemma," wrote Elkins, "is how you can emphasize vitality and achievement while you are also emphasizing decline and degradation." The experience of enslaved and oppressed groups obviously involves both aspects of this dichotomy, but historians have tended to emphasize one element over the other for various reasons at various times.⁵

In literature on Atlantic slavery, the victimization-versus-agency debate is at least as old as Melville Herskovits's *The Myth of the Negro Past* (1941) and Raymond and Alice Bauer's "Day to Day Resistance to Slavery" (1942). These works argued that enslaved Africans used work slowdowns and poor work performance both as forms of indirect protest, day-to-day resistance, and sabotage against planters and to preserve their dignity and culture as agents of active resistance.⁶ But perhaps the best example of American scholarship exemplifying what Elkins identified as the post-1960s turn toward "culture and resistance," and one that provides a potential model for studies of slavery in the Middle East, is Eugene D. Genovese's *Roll, Jordan, Roll* (1974). Genovese invoked the writings of Italian Marxist philosopher Antonio Gramsci to argue that slaves in the American South developed a "contradictory consciousness"—at once "defending themselves effectively against the worst of their masters' aggression" and thereby retaining "their right to think and act as autonomous human beings," but at the same time "accepting" the paternalism and domination of white masters. Slaves in the American South possessed two opposing modes of consciousness—one urging activity and the other urging passivity—which allowed them to retain their moral integrity while also conceding to the necessity of submission to relations of paternalism for survival. "Master and slave had both 'agreed' on the paternalistic basis of their relationship, the one from reasons of self-aggrandizement and the other from lack of an alternative. But they understood very different things by their apparently common assent," wrote Genovese. Paternalism, he argued, "rested precisely on inequality." Masters "desperately needed the gratitude of their slaves," while slaves "turned the dependency relationship to their own limited advantage. Their version of paternalistic dependency stressed reciprocity."[7] In T. J. Jackson Lears's assessment, Genovese made it possible to understand how "powerlessness combined with paternalism to influence the slave's consciousness in ways that reinforced the master's hegemony." But slaves did not merely concede. On the contrary, their conduct "reveals a complex combination of accommodation and resistance."[8] Historians since Genovese have also invoked Gramsci to understand relations of reciprocity and paternalism that are inherently unequal but that nevertheless provide space for limited autonomy of enslaved or subordinate groups. One of the most well known of these scholars is James C. Scott, who argues that subordinate groups frequently assert autonomy while maintaining public appearances of subordination.[9]

The victimization-versus-agency debate for slavery in the Middle East is, as Zilfi acknowledges, still in its infancy, although the scholarship on slavery in the region is growing. The challenge for historians of slavery in the nineteenth- and twentieth-century Gulf is to allow for both "damage" and "culture" within the limitations of the sources, which are largely communicated through one or more mediating layers. In the following pages, I argue that slave life in the Gulf, insofar as it can be re-created through existing sources, involved both victimization and agency. Enslaved Africans carved out autonomous spaces for themselves and preserved their dignity and culture while at the same time suffering the alienation and abuse experienced by slave societies everywhere. Although on the whole slavery in the Gulf was presumably "milder" than the harshest forms of chattel or gang slavery in the Americas, examples of abuse abound. Likewise, Africans in the Gulf found ways to assert their independence and preserve elements of their culture, even if they embraced much of the culture of their masters. Examples of their agency differ from what scholars have found in much of the Atlantic world, but they share much in common with other branches of the global African diaspora.

Slave communities in the Gulf present additional challenges for historians. Examples of armed revolution and the creation of maroon communities are largely absent, and the preponderance of evidence suggests that slaves acquiesced to many aspects of paternalism. By employing the strategies of Genovese and Scott, we may yet gain some ground in understanding such paradoxes of slave life in the Gulf. Both authors offer perspectives on power relations that allow for interpretations of conduct under systems of power that oblige subordinate groups to "adopt a strategic pose in the presence of the powerful" and therefore to represent their critiques of power in the form of a "hidden transcript" or "backstage discourse consisting of what cannot be spoken in the face of power."[10] For Genovese, this conduct took the form of "simultaneous accommodation and resistance to slavery." Slave resistance found expression in "pre-political protest" (for example, theft, arson, destruction, work slowdowns) and also in culture, particularly autonomous religious expression. "The slaves of the Old South," wrote Genovese, "unlike those of the Caribbean and Brazil, did not take up arms often enough or in large enough numbers to forge a revolutionary tradition. The Southern slaves' role in shaping an organic master-slave relationship unfolded under objectively unfavorable military and political circumstances that compelled a different path."[11] Likewise, Scott's critique of Gramsci asserts that what may appear in public to affirm the hegemony of a dominant group over a subordinate one may in fact mask hidden forms of protest. These "hidden transcripts" may be present when all visible signs indicate subordinate groups are affirming their acquiescence to paternalism or domination: "Subordinate groups have typically learned . . . to clothe their resistance and defiance in ritualisms of subordination."[12] The suggestions of Genovese and Scott allow for the possibility of agency in the face of victimization or apparent domination if we look in the right places.

Identity and Consciousness

One pronounced aspect of African agency in the Gulf was self-assertion through self-identification. British imperial officials in the Gulf believed that enslaved Africans lost their former identities after a period of time due to the unique type of slavery that existed in the region. Officials understood enslaved Africans to be incorporated into their masters' households in such a way that their identities were intimately intertwined with those homes and families and all former affiliations were lost due to the slaves' acceptance into the household, but evidence suggests a more complex consciousness. In British official circles, slavery in Arabia was almost universally described as "mild," "gentle," or "benign." Indeed, British imperialism in the Gulf was premised on the notion that slavery in Arabia was fundamentally different from Atlantic slavery and could therefore be tolerated as a benign indigenous institution to be phased out gradually. This was the logic used to justify the Royal Navy's anti–slave trade campaign's efforts to limit only "fresh" importations of slaves to Arabia, never to limit the transit of "domestic slaves," who were assumed to be well cared for. Language was usually the test of whether an African captive was a "lawful prize" by a British cruiser. If a captive could understand Arabic, he or she was assumed to be a "domestic slave"; if not, he or she was considered a "raw" or "newly imported" slave, brought in violation of treaties with various Gulf sheikhdoms as an act of piracy. The report of the Fugitive Slave Commission of 1876 is filled with language that would have been familiar to all British officials in the Gulf in this period, as seen in the following dialogue between Sir George Campbell and Captain James Anthony Browne:

CAMPBELL—"Of what breed were those boys and girls? . . ."
BROWNE—". . . They were jet black Africans."

CAMPBELL—"Do you think that they were recent importations from Africa?"

BROWNE—". . . I am pretty well certain that they were brought over in a native craft. . . ."

CAMPBELL—"Did they seem to you to be fresh Africans? Could they speak any civilized language?"

BROWNE—"No, they were as wild as could be."[13]

Apologists for slavery in the British colonial administration in the Gulf (and elsewhere in the empire), even early in the nineteenth century, used similar language to describe slavery in Arabia as inherently benign and paternalistic. As mentioned, John Malcolm, who served as British emissary to the court of Persia from 1799 to 1801, visited Muscat in the course of his travels and described the slave population as far better treated than the slaves of the plantations of the Atlantic world. He observed that most slaves were married and became "in a manner, part of their master's family." Slaves in Muscat "not unfrequently (with the exception of the woolly-headed Caffree) lose . . . all trace of their origin." He remarked, "When we take a comparative view of the fate of the victims of this commerce, from the stain of which our own country is hardly yet purified . . . we shall be compelled to acknowledge the superior humanity of Asiatic nations."[14]

As was the case in Zanzibar and elsewhere, slavery in Arabia was assumed by colonial authorities to have a justified "civilizing" function that could not be suddenly eliminated.[15] Slavery was understood to be a natural and timeless feature of Arab society. Bertram Thomas, for example, noted that "It may be taken as a general principle that Arabs will not do any work of a 'laboring' kind and from time immemorial have had slaves to do it for them." But, he argued, slavery was far gentler in Arabia than in the Atlantic. In general, he explained, the lot of "the domestic slave is on the whole good and may be even better than that of many free men. Slaves are well fed and looked after because it pays their masters to treat them so and there is something of a tradition which checks a master in ill-treating a slave." Thomas believed that slavery was milder and also a natural state of affairs in Arabia. He remarked: "To attempt to compel Arabia, in its present state of development, to give up slavery could perhaps be compared with attempting to compel Glasgow to give up the use of mechanical apparatus and whisky."[16] However, despite the presumed gentleness of Gulf slavery and the apparent power of the master's household to eliminate a slave's former identity, evidence suggests that enslaved Africans represented themselves by constructing or retaining identities beyond their masters' households. Enslaved Africans and their descendants in the Gulf embraced different geographical, political, and religious identities at varying times and in creative ways. These identifications are particularly evident in manumission testimonies.

As chapters 2 and 3 demonstrated, the growing demand for labor in the date-farming and pearl-diving sectors of the Gulf economy kept the trade in enslaved men and women profitable well into the twentieth century. Slaves in these sectors joined those already in demand for their roles in Arab households as domestics, retainers, soldiers, concubines, manual laborers, and markers of prestige. Although official British policy tended to tolerate the institution of slavery in eastern Arabia, the Gulf administration took exception to cases of physical abuse and blatant neglect within its jurisdiction.[17] It thus maintained a policy, which became systematic from 1921 to 1941, of granting official manumission certificates at British consular offices to runaway slaves who could show evidence of abuse or neglect. Embossed with an official government seal (rendered in both English and Arabic) and modeled on Islamic manumission documents, government manumission certificates were highly valued by their holders and were one means to secure a degree of freedom and respectability in Gulf society—although there was no guarantee against re-enslavement by either the slave's original master or another party. Those who appear in the records are not a truly fair sample of the entire enslaved population in the Gulf. Men outnumber women, and slaves engaged in pearling far outnumber those in other vocations. The greater mobility required to get to a British consulate or agency also privileged men over women, and work conditions in the pearling industry incentivized greater rates of absconding. The testimonies are not exclusively from Africans; they include many Baluchis as well. Runaway slaves who presented themselves before a British consul or agent in the Gulf provided basic information about themselves in exchange for a manumission certificate and therefore provide some of the best information on slave life in the Gulf. The testimonies could vary in length and detail, depending on which officer recorded them, but they almost always began with a recounting of a slave's origins and method of arrival in Arabia. In many of these testimonies, individuals recount precise knowledge of the geography of their homelands, even when they were kidnapped decades before. They may have been members of their masters' households, but they identified themselves as something more.

Manumission testimonies were recorded in a first-person narrative account artificially created from an individual's responses to a series of standard questions. They are nevertheless revealing. Many runaways were born into slavery in Arabia and were *muwalid* slaves or, in British official circles, "domestic slaves." Many of these individuals recounted stories of kidnapping and sale within Arabia—from Yemen or the Hejaz to Qatar or Kuwait by way of Nejd or Hasa, from Oman to the Trucial Coast or Bahrain by way of Batinah or Buraimi, and so forth. But many of the manumission testimonies also contain narratives of capture and enslavement in Africa and transport to Arabia. These cases are of particular interest because they reveal the places where enslaved Africans originated, or at least the way they remembered their origins (or how the transcriber of the account understood those origins) and how they identified themselves.

Some applicants identified their origins in precise locations in Africa, while others recollected only vague geographies. At times this distinction is unclear. For example, Marzooq bin Saad, who was about thirty-five years old when he applied for a manumission certificate at Bahrain in 1927, recalled "when a child of 13 years I was stolen by Abdullah bin Saif of Sohar while I was in Marindi at Zanzibar and was taken to Batinah where I was kept for a year. After the period of one year Abdullah bin Saif took me to Debai and sold me to Khamis bin Said."[18] Marzooq may have remembered the specific district of Zanzibar Town to which he belonged, but depending on who was translating the account, he may instead have intended to refer to Malindi on the East African coast, which was also sometimes referred to as Zanzibar.

Some applicants who were born into slavery in the Gulf knew the origins of their parents. A few cases from Bahrain in 1928 attest to this fact. 'Abdullah bin Sa'id (age thirty) stated that he was from Yemen, but his father was a slave "Nubian by origin," while Mubarak bin Salim (age thirty-five) said he had been born at Mecca, but his father was a slave "Sudani by origin," and Marzuq bin Mubarak (age twenty-two) said he was born at Sharjah but his parents were slaves "Zanzibari by origin."[19] Others remembered specific details of their kidnappings, including the names of their captors. Mabrūk bin Ali (age thirty) gave testimony at Bahrain in 1928 as follows: "I was born in Abyssinia. My parents were free people, Abyssinian by origins. When about 7 years of age one Salman (father's name not known) stole me away to Jeddah, where I served him for about 2 years."[20] Individuals who were kidnapped while very young might have only vague memories about the experience. One man in his fifties who sought manumission at Bahrain in 1929, for example, recounted the following: "I was born in Swahil. I do not know who were my parents. I came to learn afterwards that my mother died when I was young and my father was killed, but I do not know by whom. When I was about 5 or 6 years old, I was brought to Soor by somebody I do not know. All I remember is that when I came to my senses I found myself in the service of Jasem bin Thani of Qatar."[21] In another account, however, a sixty-year-old man, who presented himself in 1931 at the same consulate, recalled being kidnapped at about the age of six by Bedouins and could remember not only being from Sudan, but also specifically being from Khartoum. His kidnappers sold him to a man named Ahmed before he was then sold to a slave broker at Jeddah.[22]

A large number of runaway slaves who sought manumission at stations in the Gulf identified themselves as being born in Zanzibar. It is unclear how precisely this geographical term was applied. It may have been used as a gloss for the islands of both Zanzibar and Pemba (curiously, almost no testimonies seem to recall shipment from Pemba, which Royal Navy reports identified as a major center for exporting slaves to Arabia) or possibly for the whole coast. Farhan bin Mubarak (age forty-five), who sought manumission at Bahrain in 1931, recounted, "I was born at Zanzibar. I was kidnapped at the age of seven and brought to Soor. There I was sold to one Muhammad bin Ali whom I served for about 18 years."[23] Some used the looser term "Sawahel," after which consular officers added "(African coasts)," referring to the Swahili coast of East Africa. Others cited specific locations in northeast Africa. Omar bin Ali Somali (age twenty-two) recounted, "I was born in Barbara. While I was in my tenth year of my age I was kidnapped by one Ahmed, a slave broker, who brought me to Waqra near Qatar and sold me to Rahid bin Hamad."[24] Likewise,

Bilal bin Rashid (age forty) recounted with a similar level of detail his kidnapping from Suwakin: "I was born in Sawakin in Africa. I was a baby when my mother and myself were kidnapped by certain unknown slave dealers and taken to Jedda. We stayed in Jedda for a period of 15 days during which my mother died and I was later taken to Mecca and sold to one of the Sherifs of Mecca named 'Ali bin Labbās in whose service I remained 6 years."[25]

Transcriptions of some testimonies demonstrate the bias or ignorance of the official who recorded the statements. Faraj bin Sulaiman (age thirty-four), whose testimony was taken at Sharjah by an agent who clearly had limited understanding of East Africa, has a record that states: "I was born at Maryimma of South West Africa [before being kidnapped and taken to Sur in Oman]." (His actual testimony likely described the *mrima* coast of East Africa.)[26] Other testimonies demonstrate the dedication of some officials and their eagerness to get the facts straight. An unusually lengthy batch of correspondence accompanies the investigation of a woman named Hadiyah bint 'Ali, who appealed to the political agent at Kuwait in 1921 on the basis of abuse from her master. Her case reveals the complexity of questions of nationality and subjectivity for British officials in the Gulf. The political agent recorded the following:

> The woman states that her name is Hadiyah bint 'Ali, and that her mother's name was Sa'īdah bint Tibn. She belonged to the Nubian (Nūbī) settlement just outside Sawakin town, the sheikh of which, at the time of her capture, was Abu 'Anjah. When she was about 20 years of age, their settlement was raided by the Hadandawā, whom she describes as a tribe living in the hills not far from Sawakin, and some two hundred women and children were carried off. There were no British in Sawakin at the time, but within a year of her capture she heard that we had occupied it. A few months after her capture she was taken to Qunfidah, and sold to one Ahmad bin 'Ali, a native of that town, with whom she remained until his death some twelve years later, and to whom she bore a son, named 'Atiyah. About a year after Ahmad bin 'Ali's death, his eldest son, Muhammad, sold her to Muhammad and Ahmad of the Subbān family. She was about a year with the Subbān in Jiddah, and was

then taken to Madinah and sold to 'Abdullah bin Fahad al-Ghanim of Hail, who took her with him to Hail, and, six months or so later, brought her to Kuwait, in May 1920, and sold her to her present master, Shahin bin Muhamad al-Ghanim.[27]

Subsequent correspondence in Hadiyah's file indicates that her case proved too complex to be actionable because it involved the intricacies of the Anglo-Egyptian Condominium and the timing of the Battle of Omdurman. Officials determined they could not intervene on her behalf.

In other cases claims to political subjectivity could have profound implications. Runaway slaves used political claims to bolster their efforts to receive a manumission certificate. Some runaways who had an African appearance were, in fact, second-generation slaves born in other parts of Arabia and were kidnapped into slavery in other parts of the Gulf. Such was the case with Khamis bin Mubarak (age thirty), whose statement was recorded in Bahrain in 1929. Khamis used both his primary language and his political allegiance to establish the merits of his request for manumission: "My mother tongue is Arabic. I am a subject of the Sultan of Mukallah. I was born at Mukallah (S. Arabian Coast). I was hardly 8 years old when I was kidnapped by Shaikh Salim bin Abbad of Mukallah, who brought me to Batinah and there sold me to Hamad bin Rashid of Wodam, Batinah."[28] Another runaway slave named Sarur gave testimony indicating that he was born in northeast Africa (possibly Djibouti) and was a French subject who was kidnapped and sold to a British subject. He would eventually be sold into slavery in Medina and then in Qatar before he ran away and provided his testimony to British officials in Bahrain. His statement began as follows:

> I am a slave by birth and was born in the desert of Habsh [Ethiopia/northeast Africa]. I am a French subject. I was only 7 years of age, when I was kidnapped from my Master, whose name I do not know. The kidnapper sold me to another fellow and this transaction went on for some time when at last I fell into the hands of one individual, who was a British subject and native of Hudandawa, a town on the coast of Africa. The last man brought me to Medina and there sold me to one Muhammad Toufique by name, resident of Medina. I served him for 9 years as an assistant in masonry work.[29]

Stating one's origins in political terms held the promise of improving one's ability to receive formal manumission. But this approach could also backfire. A runaway slave named Faraj bin Nasib (age fifty), who provided his testimony at Bahrain in 1929, testified that he was born into slavery to slave parents in Shehr on the southern coast of Yemen and was a subject of the ruler of Shehr and Mukalla. He was then kidnapped at about twelve years of age and taken to Sur in Oman and then to Hamriyya (near Dubai) in Trucial Oman (today's UAE), where he was forced to work as a pearl diver. In the margin of Faraj's testimony, a British official regretted that Britain had "no treaty with the Shaikh of Hamriyah." The appeal was denied.[30]

The manumission testimonies include a diverse assortment of places of origin and reveal the ambiguities and complexities of many geographic terms and the possibilities of political allegiances. A survey of ninety manumission testimonies given by enslaved Africans who specifically recalled being kidnapped from Africa demonstrates that sixty-two of them (69 percent) recalled being kidnapped from Zanzibar and the Swahili coast (East Africa) and twenty-eight (31 percent) recalled being kidnapped from northeast Africa (Ethiopia and Sudan in particular) between the years 1872 and 1927. Despite the diversity of geography, it is a challenge to know how much meaning these geographic designations held for those providing the testimony beyond the specific questions asked by the British officials. Since these are virtually the only words attributed to these individuals in the records, there is room for speculation. But what is clear from the record is that few manumitted slaves in the Gulf felt a strong enough connection with their ancestral home to seek to return there. Notes by the political resident in the Persian Gulf in 1900 indicate that few of the manumitted slaves expressed a desire to be relocated to Africa. The political resident noted: "My own experience shows that none of the slaves (at least those that I have come across) is keen on going to Zanzibar. If they have come from Lingah or Bahrain, they wish to return there after being manumitted. Local slaves prefer to stay on in Bushehr. Any that wishes to go away prefer Muscat, Bussorah or Jeddah to Zanzibar. At the most 5% will like to go to Zanzibar unless we sent the slaves without consulting their wishes."[31] When the sheikh of Dubai captured a Qatari slave trader in 1925 and handed five captive Ethiopian slave women over to the British government, the statements of the women confirm that none had a desire to go back to

Ethiopia because they feared they would be re-enslaved. One testimony stated the following: "I was living with my sister Medinah in my native place Selali in Abyssinia. The Bedouin slave traders kidnapped and took me to a village named Midi. Here they sold me to a man called Abdur Rahman of Qatar who took me by land route to Qatar and from there he took me in a boat to Debai for sale. At Debai I was taken by Shaih Said bin Maktu's men who handed me to K.B. Isa the Residency Agent, Shargah. I have no intention of returning to my own country as I fear the slave traders will enslave me a second time."[32] Fear of re-enslavement appears to have trumped what were likely strong connections to kin and homeland. This is not to say a symbolic connection was not maintained, just not one strong enough to motivate a slave's efforts to return given circumstances that could lead to re-enslavement. From the Atlantic-centered paradigm of diaspora studies, this perspective may seem unusual, but it appears to have been widespread in the Gulf.

Labor, Abuse, and Resistance

Enslaved Africans in Arabia also asserted their agency in the difficult and often abusive realm of labor. As mentioned, Africans in the Gulf labored at a variety of tasks, ranging from the maritime (diving, sailing, fishing, steeving, and crewing) to the agricultural (irrigating; pollinating; harvesting and maintaining orchards, date groves, and fields of various crops; and working in animal husbandry). African men worked in pearling crews and on date plantations, although many also worked in construction and in the gathering and porterage of construction materials. Still others worked in elite households and as the soldiers, bodyguards, or retainers of rulers. Many women hauled water, prepared meals, produced handicrafts, and worked in child care and as attendants and domestics for households. Enslaved Africans could work at a variety of tasks over the course of a year and a lifetime. As mentioned, many African boys worked in date gardens when they were first imported to the region and were then moved into pearl diving when they reached their early teens. Outside the main pearling season (April through September), some pearl divers and pearling crewmen in the Gulf worked at other tasks such as fishing, hauling, or construction.

For enslaved pearl divers, off-season labor varied greatly by age, experience, and owner. A fifty-year-old enslaved Abyssinian man in Darīn, Hasa, was a pearl diver during the summer and house builder in the winter from the late 1880s to the late 1920s.[33] One slave of Sudanese ancestry who had been born in Mecca around 1893 served his master in Qatar from about 1909 to 1928 as a diver in the summer and herding sheep, collecting firewood, and drawing water during the winter.[34] A fourteen-year-old boy who was an enslaved diver at Darīn dived for pearls in the summer and cut grass for his master's cattle and sheep in the off season.[35] One thirty-four-year-old *muwalid* slave reported in 1930 that he had worked at a variety of positions for his master in Qatar "for nine years as a hauler, for one year as a cook, for four years as a diver, for three years in the custom house and for one year as a Launch Engineer."[36] Another enslaved diver in Jubail listed among his off-season duties bringing drinking water to his master's house, working in his cultivated lands, and preparing coffee.[37]

Many masters did not provide food or clothing to their enslaved pearl divers in the off season, so slaves had to earn their own subsistence. A twenty-four-year-old *muwalid* slave in Hirah worked for his master as a diver for fifteen years but never received any of his earnings for his own use for clothing and other needs. In the off season, he fished and used his meager earnings from fishing to supply his needs.[38] Mubarak bin Abdullah, an enslaved Swahili diver at Hamriyya, who had been kidnapped from East Africa around 1901 when he was ten years old, worked as a diver for his master during the pearling season but had to provide for himself during the off season. He quarried stones to support himself in the winter.[39] Another enslaved diver, Sa'id bin Ismail, who had been kidnapped from Zanzibar in the 1890s, explained that he had to work in the winter in order to provide for his wife and two daughters because his master refused to support him in the off season.[40] Juma' bin Marzūk, another enslaved Zanzibari man, expressed similar grief about his experiences at Ras al-Khaimah. He had been kidnapped from Zanzibar by Suris when he was a child in the 1870s or 1880s and brought to Sur and then to Batinah. He was sold to a pearl merchant in Sharjah, who kept him until he was about thirty; he was then sold to a man in Umm al-Quwain and eventually sold to a dhow owner in Ras al-Khaimah, for whom he worked as a diver for about seven years. Juma''s master gave him a few rupees from his earnings at the end of each diving season, but it was not enough to support him and his wife. When he sought manumission from the British political agent at Muscat in 1934, he complained, "If I was free I could have worked and supported her, but being a slave I had to work also for my master after the closing of the diving season."[41]

Although many enslaved Africans in the Gulf were well treated in the workplace, slave life in the region presented unique challenges, and physical abuse was common, particularly in the regions surrounding the Gulf pearl banks. Punishment for uncooperative slaves most often took the form of beatings with sticks and imprisonment in shackles.[42] The story of one enslaved African pearl diver is revealing. Mubarak bin Nār was five years old when he was kidnapped from Zanzibar around 1895, brought to Sur, and sold at Dubai, where he became an enslaved pearl diver. Many years later, at the start of the 1930 season, Mubarak proved too ill to dive. His master, who was heavily indebted to some of Dubai's Arab and Persian merchants on account of falling earnings, became desperate. He beat Mubarak for refusing to dive even when he was lying in his sickbed. When Mubarak told his story at the Muscat consulate, officials noted marks of abuse on his back.[43] Another man, Hubaish bin Rashid, who had been kidnapped along with his mother and sold to a pearling captain in Dubai, worked as a diver for his master while his mother worked in the house. When Hubaish's mother became too old to be of service, the master turned her out of his house, and Hubaish had to provide for her from work he did on the side. In 1937, Hubaish asked his master for five rupees to help with his mother's upkeep. His master beat him severely. Hubaish testified that his master "trampled me and broke the bones of my hips."[44] Further effects of physical abuse were evident in the broken bones, scars, and broken teeth of fugitives who sought manumission at British agency offices.[45]

Other enslaved divers were burned with hot irons as a form of punishment. Branding with hot irons was also a popular form of traditional medicine in eastern Arabia in the early twentieth century, and the scorching of skin was believed to have curative properties. Thus not all of those who showed burn marks had been victims of punishment. But in some cases, the branding of enslaved men appears to have been used to "cure" insubordination or their inability to dive for pearls. A diver named Musaʿad bin

Zayed was born to free African parents in Yemen around 1900 and was kidnapped while out tending flocks when he was about fourteen years old. He was taken on an eleven-day journey to Doha, where he was sold to someone who quickly sold him again to Salim bin Bakhit of Dalma. At first Salim employed Musa'ad to quarry stones and do other odd jobs, but when the diving season approached, he told him to go pearl diving. Musa'ad told Salim he did not know how to dive and would not be able to do it. He recalled that his protests "offended him and he burnt me with a red hot iron near each of my ears. The following year again the same mishap befell and I was burnt in three places on my chest and in one place on the left ribs."[46]

A related story is preserved in the records of the British Royal Navy. At sunrise on October 26, 1921, the HMS *Crocus* was near Abu Musa Island (located in the middle of the Gulf, roughly halfway between Sharjah and Lingah) when it was hailed by a man in distress on the eastern side of the island. Khamīs bin Halais, a twenty-two-year-old *muwalid* slave of African ancestry who was originally from the Sharqiyya region of Oman, had been kidnapped from his home the previous year and was sold at Dubai to Rashid bin Afra, who took him to the island.[47] The commander sent a boat from the gunship to pick up Khamīs, "his pursuers being only 100 yards behind him at the moment of his stepping into the boat." The commander reported that "Upon examination on board, it was found he had received three severe burns with some hot implement which he stated that his owner had given him because he had not (or would not) learn to dive for pearls. He had also received several thrashings, the marks of which were visible. One leg required medical dressing on account of a poisoned abrasion."[48]

Women also experienced abuse. Stories from the Trucial Coast and Qatar reveal that jealous wives of masters could be especially harsh toward enslaved women. A woman named Khadia bint Mabrook, who as a young girl had been kidnapped from East Africa in the 1890s along with her parents, served in the house of a man in Qatar named Abdul Azīz al-Ma'na and was married to one of his male slaves when she was about twenty years old. After her husband died at the pearl banks around 1926, her master's wife began treating her cruelly. Khadia reported that "As my master's wife treated me with harshness and often beat me with sticks, and as her big daughter hit me on the head with a stone and struck me in the eye, I managed to escape."⁴⁹ Another woman complained that when her work slacked a little while she was ill, her masters beat her severely.⁵⁰

In spite of the ever-present threat of beatings, kidnapping, and general abuse, many of the enslaved Africans in the Gulf demanded to be treated with dignity and acted assertively, even if punished for their behavior. At least one slave killed his master. Although the details of the event are difficult to sort out, Hamad bin Ibrahim, the ruler of Umm al-Quwain, was killed by one of his slaves in February 1929. (He was succeeded by Sheikh Ahmad bin Rashid al-Mu'alla, who ruled the emirate through independence in 1971 and until his death in 1981.)⁵¹ More frequently, slaves would confront their masters with a grievance or run away. A frequently asserted grievance was the lack of proper food and clothing. In general in the Gulf, tradition demanded that slave owners provide their slaves with enough food for their subsistence and at least one new item of clothing annually. As the Gulf date and pearl industries began floundering after the late 1920s, masters pressed for greater work from their slaves, even though they simultaneously failed to meet their obligations to their enslaved workers. In consequence and despite the threats against them, many slaves asserted themselves, demanding that their masters meet their obligations. The case of an African *muwalid* slave named Muhammad bin Sa'ad exemplifies this struggle. Born into slavery in Qaṭīf around 1908, Muhammad was employed by his master to provide grass for his camels in town in summer and in winter to graze his camels in the territory outside of town with other shepherds. In the winter of 1938, Muhammad's master told him to graze his camels in the desert alone. Muhammad refused, not because the job was uncomfortable or dangerous but because, in his words, "My master was giving me food but not proper clothing." Muhammad explained, "I told him that I would not accept this job if he was not going to provide me with proper clothing." Muhammad reported that his master then "fell angry with me and tried to beat me with a stick saying that I had to obey all his orders as I was his slave." Muhammad made up his mind that he could no longer serve his master and fled three days later to Dammam and boarded a fishing boat for Bahrain.⁵²

Slaves in the Gulf were required to go barefoot, but they were highly conscious of dress, so the failure of a master to provide an annual *khamīs* or other item of clothing was a frequent point of conflict. In 1930, an enslaved diver in Hirah named Walaid confronted his master Ahmad bin Salim and complained that the only clothing he received came from his meager earnings as a fisherman in the off season: "I told my master that I have benefited him much from the earnings of my diving, could he not afford to pay me something?" Instead of complying, Walaid recalls that his master "shouted and Arabs came up and arrested me and placed me in irons for two months." Once released, Walaid fled to Sharjah.[53] Similarly, in 1938, a forty-year-old enslaved diver of Ras al-Khaimah named Bilāl bin Marzuq confronted his master for consistently taking all of his earnings and asked him to provide some clothes for him. The two began to quarrel. Bilāl recalled, "As I insisted on him to get me some clothes he took me to Ras al-Khaimah in order to purchase some for me, but on the contrary he complained against me to the Ruler of Ras al-Khaimah, who imprisoned me for four days and then released me. I returned to Ras al-Khaimah with my master who handed me over to three Bedouins of Khawatir tribe to sell me at Buraimi." Bilāl managed to escape when his captors took him with them to 'Ajmān to buy supplies, and he eventually traveled to Sharjah to seek manumission.[54]

Evidence of organized resistance on a large scale is limited. One possible case of attempted organizing among enslaved pearl divers appeared in 1931. Mubarak bin Wadnar, a Zanzibar-born diver about thirty-three years old, appeared at the political agency in Bahrain in April 1931 seeking a manumission certificate. He alleged that he had been kidnapped ten years earlier by a man from Sur, who brought him to Dubai and sold him to a man there who died after three years. The man's wife sold him to Muhammad Bashir, a Dubai pearling captain, whom Mubarak served for seven years as a diver. Mubarak alleged that his master treated him cruelly, and he showed marks on his back from being beaten with sticks. When the political resident inquired of the Sharjah agent about the man's scars, the agent investigated his case and learned that his captain had beaten him because Mubarak "wanted to induce the divers to stop diving."[55] What success Mubarak had at organizing the divers is unknown, but the thrashing he received may have been meant as both punishment for insubordination and a deterrent to other would-be leaders.

Slaves in the Gulf also resisted by slowing their production or reducing their productivity, thus inflicting financial harm on their captors. Paul

Harrison, an American missionary who worked in the Gulf between 1909 and 1954 and witnessed pearl diving on the Trucial Coast firsthand, remarked in 1924 that "Unquestionably it is the slaves who have reduced the standards of what a day's and a season's work ought to be to its present level on the Pirate Coast. Most of these slaves are negroes from Africa."[56] Harrison believed that the slave divers' "attitude of listlessness and indifference" tended to "pull all the rest down to their level." He explained that their complete indifference to their duties would be clear to anyone "who has watched them work, or rather their very successful efforts to avoid doing any work."[57] Harrison was certain that this lack of productivity was not laziness but a form of passive resistance. "As passive resisters," he wrote, "these slaves are superb. I have seen one of them, disgruntled by some mistreatment or insult, simply lie down on the job and no expostulation or threat seemed to stir him."[58]

By far the most frequent form of resistance to slavery in the Gulf was flight. Farhan bin Bilal, a Swahili enslaved diver in ʿAjmān who had been kidnapped from East Africa as a child and had been diving for several years, asked his master in the summer of 1939 for his portion of the annual diving advance. His master gave him only five rupees. Farhan found the amount unacceptable: "I refused to take it and told him that the amount was insufficient. He replied that on my return from diving he would give me any amount I required out of my earnings, but I did not accept his promise." Instead, Farhan took an opportunity to escape and fled for Sharjah to seek British manumission.[59] Another man, Jumaʿh bin Ibrahīm, was kidnapped from Mombasa in the 1910s and brought to Sur by sea and to Mudhaibi by camel and then sold at Sharjah a month later to a pearl merchant named ʿAdbullah bin ʿAli As-Sārī, who made him a pearl diver in his boat. In 1938, after Jumaʿh had been diving for many years, his master gave him a meager eight rupees at the start of the diving season. When Jumaʿh refused to take them, his master put him in chains and locked him in his godown. When ʿAbdullah was away at sea, Jumaʿh broke the door to the godown and found some neighbors who were willing to help him break his chains. He then fled Sharjah for Batinah and eventually landed at Muscat to seek British assistance.[60]

Slavery and Family Life

Enslaved African men and women in the Gulf faced difficult lives of hard work and strictly governed sexuality, but they often found ways to resist their conditions and negotiate some degree of sexual freedom.[61] Enslaved men, but not women, sometimes arranged their own nuptials, though rarely their first wedding. Take the case of Sa'id bin Sanqur, born into his master's household in Sharjah around 1913. When Sa'id turned fifteen, his master sent him out for diving and took his earnings, although Sa'id was allowed to retain some of his diving advances. Sa'id's master also married him to one of his female slaves, named Kaniyah, whom Sa'id divorced after two years. Sa'id then arranged his own marriage to Lattuf, a female slave of another master, with whom he had two daughters. When Sa'id was twenty-three, he divorced Lattuf and after a few months expressed a desire to marry Salluah, the female slave of another master. However, as he lacked the money to do so, he borrowed some gold ornaments from his master's wife, which he mortgaged to a Hyderabadi merchant in Sharjah for about one hundred rupees, enabling him to afford the marriage.[62] Such were the options of some *muwalid* slave men.

Nevertheless, such cases were rare. Marriage contracts of enslaved men and women in the Gulf were usually arranged by their owners or by other masters.[63] Arranged marriages served the dual purpose of placating valued slaves and producing offspring that could potentially work for the master or be sold for profit. Male slaves were traditionally first married when they reached the age of twenty-five, female slaves around age fifteen. Not all arrangements were agreeable to everyone involved. For example, one unfortunate man named Mubarak bin Salmīn was sold around 1920 to Hamad bin Saif al-Suwaidi of Dubai, who married him to one of his female slaves named Zuhru, who, according to Mubarak, preferred his master.[64] Indeed, as such contracts were arranged without consultation with the slaves involved, many slave marriages were unhappy, and divorce was common throughout the first half of the twentieth century. Divorces initiated by enslaved males were frequent; those initiated by female slaves were less common.[65]

A slave's marriage was no guarantee against sale, and enslaved men and women were frequently sold away from their families. This was the case with Sadullah bin Sālem, who was born a slave in Yemen, kidnapped by men from 'Asīr, brought to Qatar via Hasa in the late nineteenth century, and then made the slave of Sheikh Qāsim bin Muhammad al-Thānī, the ruler of Qatar. When Sadullah reached maturity, he was married to Mabruka, one of the sheikh's female slaves. The couple had three sons and two daughters, but only the daughters survived childhood. At the time of Sadullah's manumission, one of them was married to the slave of another member of the royal family, and the other was fifteen and unmarried. When Sheikh Qāsim died in 1913, Sadullah and his family passed to 'Abd al-'Azīz bin Qāsim, but 'Abd al-'Azīz subsequently sold Sadullah away from his family to a man in Sharjah who sent him diving.[66] In some cases, masters of male slaves paid dowries to the owners of female slaves in order to contract a slave marriage, although the slave couple often continued to work for their respective masters.[67]

A slave could also marry a free person, though most of these arrangements were between enslaved men and free women. For example, Sulaiman bin 'Abdullah, born in Sudan, kidnapped around 1903 when about five years old, and sold via Jeddah and Hasa to Qatar and later Darīn, was married to a free woman of Yemeni ancestry when he was twenty-five.[68] Another enslaved diver named Mabrūk bin 'Ali, born to free parents in Ethiopia and kidnapped at the age of seven around 1905, was similarly married to a freeborn woman of Yemeni ancestry when he was about twenty-five.[69] However, these mixed marriages were subject to special pressures, as the story of Zahra bint Mubarak indicates. Zahra, a *muwalid* slave born of Swahili slave parents at Sharjah around 1900, was manumitted by her elderly female master. Zahra subsequently married Habush, an enslaved pearling crewman from Batinah. One day the two got into an argument over a debt Habush had accrued. The disagreement turned into a fistfight; Habush fell to the ground and ten days later died from his injuries. Zahra ran away when she perceived local jurists contemplated enslaving her and selling her as repayment for her late husband's debts.[70]

Although polygyny was common in the Gulf, available evidence suggests that male slaves rarely, if ever, had more than one wife, and it is clear from manumission testimonies that enslaved men frequently remarried shortly after divorcing a previously assigned wife. For women, however, being divorced by an enslaved husband could mean the potential of being sold. One thirty-five-year-old enslaved woman named Salhuh bint Ahmad had been married by her master in Umm al-Quwain to a male slave named Mabrūk. When Mabrūk divorced her in 1937, her master prepared to sell her, and she ran away to Sharjah.[71]

Infant mortality among enslaved Africans in eastern Arabia appears to have been very high in the late nineteenth and early twentieth centuries. Many married couples who were enslaved never had children, few appear to have had more than five children, and rarely did all of a couple's children survive to adulthood. Walaid, who had been kidnapped in East Africa when he was five or six years old, brought to Sur, and sold as a slave to Qatar around 1885, was married when he was about thirty years old to a female slave of one of his master's relatives. Of the couple's two daughters and four sons, all died except a son named Sālim, who became the slave of Walaid's wife's master's son. The marriage may not have been particularly happy: when Walaid's master died around 1923, Walaid passed to his wife's master, who manumitted his wife but kept Walaid as a slave. Seizing her freedom, Walaid's wife left him.[72]

In general, masters controlled the bodies and reproductive lives of their slaves. When a female slave born in the household came of age, her master was entitled to take her as his concubine or marry her to one of his male slaves or the slave of someone else. In some cases masters availed themselves of all these options. Hilaweh bint Rashid, who was born in her master's house on Za'ab Island around 1907, was married at the age of fifteen to Nubi, one of her master's male slaves. She gave birth to a son and a daughter, but in 1938, when her daughter was a year old, her husband died. Her master then took Hilaweh as his concubine for two years before marrying her to a man from Batinah.[73] Masters could sell away a slave's spouse as easily as marrying slaves to one another. Faraj bin Sulaiman, born on the Mrima coast of East Africa around 1905, was kidnapped as a child by a man who took him to Sur and after a year sold him to 'Isā bin 'Ali on Za'ab Island. 'Isā worked Faraj as a diver for four years before marrying him to a slave woman named Latīfah. Three years later, despite the fact that Latīfah had given birth to a child, 'Isā sold her to Bedouins.[74]

As mentioned in chapter 2, in the late nineteenth century, slave traders imported such numbers of young boys from East Africa to work in the growing date and pearl industries that by the 1870s the ratio of male to female slaves among captured slave dhows on the Arabian coast reversed previous trends, shifting overwhelmingly in favor of males. In the last quarter of the nineteenth century, the evidence from dhows captured by British cruisers off the Arabian coast overwhelmingly demonstrates that by then the traffic from East Africa comprised mostly male slaves. In such an environment, not all male slaves were permitted to have socially accepted sexual relations within legally sanctioned marriages. It is perhaps through this lens that we should view evidence of homosexuality and pederasty among some male descendants of enslaved Africans in the Gulf—although the extent to which either was practiced is extremely difficult to gauge from the written record, especially as both were officially prohibited and severely punished when proven by jurists.

Given the unique conditions created by the lopsided ratio of males to females, homosexual relationships may have been common among unmarried men, as suggested by Unni Wikan for the region of Batinah in Oman, particularly on a short-term basis.[75] One record notes that in August 1936, Yūsuf bin Khamīs, "a negro from Basra" (probably an ex-slave or descendant of a slave) working as a teacher of boys in Dubai, was convicted of pederasty and punished accordingly. Yūsuf "was seen from adjacent houses to commit an unnatural offense on a young boy in his room with a friend," and people from the area "rushed on them and caught Yūsuf and his friend." Yūsuf's friend, who tried to escape, "jumped over the wall to the ground with the result that his buttock was fractured." As for Yūsuf, "he was caught by Said bin Bati and was taken to the sheikh. The sheikh sent him to the *qāḍhi*. When the offense was proved, he was given a very severe beating which caused a wound on his head." The sheikh resolved to send Yūsuf back to Basra as soon as his wound healed. His friend received no further punishment. After some investigation, it became known that Yūsuf had formerly been sent away from Bahrain, Qatar, and Sharjah for "making mischief."[76]

In the early twentieth century Arab men in the Gulf frequently took secondary wives or concubines, who held a lower legal status than a legitimate wife and were generally taken for short periods of time ranging from a week to a few years. In theory, under Islamic law children of female concubines had a legally recognized status as free descendants of their fathers. In practice, this was often not the case. Masters regularly exchanged female concubines, often for periods as brief as seven to ten days. In a number of cases, when the woman was discovered to be pregnant, she was given in marriage to a male slave, and her child was treated as the child of slaves. In other cases, the pregnant concubine was sold far away where the child would not interfere with the father's personal life.

In one case, Sa'id bin Hazim of Dubai purchased Maryami bint Mubarak, a Sudanese woman, and made her a concubine. When (around 1903) he found Maryami to be pregnant, he married her to Johar, his African slave, and her son took the name Khamīs bin Johar rather than Khamīs bin Sa'id. When Khamīs was twelve years old, Sa'id manumitted the boy along with his mother. But in 1924, Sa'id and Khamīs's parents were all killed when plague hit Dubai. The following year Sa'id's daughter and her husband decided to re-enslave Khamīs, either to sell him or send him to work for profit. Fearing an unknown fate, he ran away to Sharjah to seek manumission.[77]

Around the turn of the century, Sa'id bin Bilal al-Gharāhal of Ras al-Khaimah purchased an East African woman named Saluhah and married her to his Swahili male slave. Saluhah and her husband had a daughter named Maryami, and when Maryami was seventeen years old, Sa'id made her his concubine. Maryami became pregnant and gave birth to a son, named Juma', who legally should have been considered the free son of Sa'id. However, when Juma' was seven years old, Sa'id died, and his relatives divided his estate. Sa'id's son 'Ali inherited Maryami and attempted to sell Juma' as a slave, in spite of the fact he was his half-brother. In May 1931, Maryami took her son and fled.[78]

Zainab bint Mubarak, another young woman of African ancestry, was born in Yemen, orphaned when she was seven years old (around 1904), and subsequently raised by her uncle. One day, while grazing sheep, she was kidnapped and taken first to Jeddah and then to Mecca, where she was purchased by a hajj pilgrim named Muhammad bin 'Ali bin Kamil, who took her back by steamer to his home town of Sharjah. She recalled in 1927 that Muhammad "had sexual intercourse with me for some time and then he married me to a slave named Selim." It is unclear from her account whether she was pregnant at the time she was married to Selim. Zainab subsequently gave birth to five children, three of whom survived infancy. It is possible that Zainab's master was the father of her first born, although Zainab asserted that Selim was the father of the three surviving children. One of the three surviving children was kidnapped, and the other two remained in the service of her master through at least the late 1920s.⁷⁹

Such cases were not limited to enslaved Africans. A Baluchi woman who was kidnapped from Mekran was sold to a man from Khan, a dependency of Sharjah near Dubai. Her master, Rashid bin 'Ali, took her as his concubine until she became pregnant. He then married her to a Baluchi slave named Marzūq, and she gave birth to a daughter who took the name Rafia'h bint Marzūq Baluchi. When Rafia'h was six years old, Rashid sold her mother to a man in another town and gave Rafia'h as a present to his brother Abdullah bin 'Ali in Jumairah. Abdullah raised Rafia'h until she was fifteen and then married her to one of his Baluchi slaves named Sorūr. Rafia'h and Sorūr continued serving Abdullah for ten years. Then Rashid got into a fight with his brother, came to Jumairah, and took Rafia'h from Abdullah's house by force. Rafia'h subsequently escaped and fled to the British agency in Sharjah to seek a manumission certificate.⁸⁰ It is surprising that although paternal lineage was a vital part of identity in the Gulf, it was in many ambiguous cases uncontested. In the late 1890s 'Abd ar-Rahman bin Khalfan al-Mutawwa' of Dubai took as a concubine a *muwalid* African woman, the daughter of one of his slaves. Around 1899, she gave birth to a son who took the name Khamīs bin 'Abd ar-Rahman and was treated, according to his own account, as 'Abd ar-Rahman's legal son. Sometime later, 'Abd ar-Rahman turned Khamīs's mother out of his house but kept Khamīs with him. Around 1925 (possibly during the Dubai plague of 1924–1925) 'Abd ar-Rahman died, leaving in the household Khamīs, his three sisters, and three of his father's slaves. Around 1930, Shamsah, one of Khamīs's sisters, began to treat him as if he were a slave, insisting that he go diving with a captain she had selected. Khamīs protested and even asked the British-appointed residency agent at Sharjah to help him, without success. He eventually became so despondent that, fearing enslavement, he traveled to Muscat to request a government manumission certificate.⁸¹

When the British resident asked the Sharjah agent about Khamīs's case, he replied that after some investigation he concluded that Khamīs was not 'Abd ur-Rahman's son but actually the son of a slave. The details were fuzzy, but the agent alleged that Khamīs's mother had been married thrice before 'Abd ur-Rahman took her as his concubine and was pregnant from her last marriage before 'Abd ur-Rahman slept with her. Although he slept with her several times before Khamīs was born, Khamīs was not his child. Rather, he was the child of his mother's former husband. 'Abd ur-Rahman's slaves called Khamīs his son, but 'Abd ur-Rahman "reprimanded the slaves for saying so and so they stopped so doing." Khamīs was thus not 'Abd ur-Rahman's son but his slave. Furthermore, the agent reported, 'Abd ur-Rahman's daughter had, after her father's death, manumitted Khamīs, who had not only gone diving of his own accord, but had also acquired a considerable amount of debt. His flight to Muscat was thus an attempt to escape his debts rather than an effort to regain his paternal rights of freedom.[82] In such cases, paternity was difficult to prove, and in this case we unfortunately do not know the outcome. Some *muwalid* slaves never knew their real fathers because their mothers had been concubines who were sold away once they became pregnant. Zamzam bint Wadh, a woman from Dhofar of probable African ancestry, was as a child kidnapped from her home by Bedouins who sold her to Muhammad bin Sa'id of the Bani Bu 'Ali tribe from Sur. Muhammad kept Zamzam as his concubine for ten years. When she then became pregnant, he sold her to Mohanna bin Sa'id of Wudam, who after a month took her to Abu Dhabi and sold her to a man named Khalaf bin Ataibah. In Khalaf's house, she gave birth to a girl named Safi and married a Kuwaiti man named 'Abd ur-Rahman bin Mohanna. Safi's paternal name is not recorded, but it is highly unlikely that she took the name of her biological father or ever met him.[83]

One final story perhaps best illustrates both the limitations and possibilities for negotiating degrees of sexual freedom in the Gulf in this period. Letters intercepted en route to Bahrain from Doha attest to the sale of some women in Qatar in April 1935. 'Abd al-'Azīz and 'Abd ar-Rahmān bin 'Abd al-Latīf Al-Mana' wrote to Nāsir bin Muhammad Al-Mani' to verify the sale of his slave women to Juma' al-Somali. Juma', the men explained, made the best offer for the women and proved more reliable than other interested parties. Juma' paid 1,000 rupees and $135 all together for them, which was less than Nāsir expected, but they felt they had to accept his price because the women were causing problems. As the men explained, "If they were taken by some other person he would have kept them with him and then returned them as being unfit (for service). The reason was that whenever anyone wanted to buy them they used to show themselves to be unfit, which made the purchasers refrain from buying them. When Ibrahim Islam heard about them he asked us to send them to him and after seeing them he returned them without making any offer whatsoever."[84] 'Abd al-'Azīz and 'Abd ar-Rahmān did not want to lose the opportunity to sell to Juma' al-Somali since he wanted to take the women with him by car right after he purchased them. How the women showed themselves to be "unfit" to their potential buyers is unknown, but the record allows for the possibility that they somehow found a way to negotiate their situation, perhaps by deliberately acting in a manner designed to discourage undesirable purchasers or reduce their sale price in order to, at the very least, harm their seller.

Manumission and Mobility

Africans also exercised agency by seizing opportunities for manumission and mobility. As Sean Hanretta reminds us, the traditional "triumphalist" narrative of abolition, which holds that Europeans introduced freedom through colonial emancipation, tends to reify the notion that manumission was alien to African and Islamic societies, denying African and Muslim agency.[85] In fact, manumission was common in the Gulf prior to and beyond the scope of British colonial rule. In particular, it was not uncommon for a master to manumit his or her slaves before death or before going on hajj. In such cases slaves were provided a document, usually prepared by a local *qādhi*, attesting to the former slave's freedom and prohibiting his or her re-enslavement. In practice, the document had value only where it was respected by others. If the freed person were far away from the family of the person who had authorized the manumission, the paper was less likely to be respected. Beyond coastal towns, anyone who appeared to have a servile lineage could be instantly enslaved regardless of any documentation that person might carry. Even in the metropolitan Gulf, re-enslavement was not uncommon. During difficult financial times, the children of people who had manumitted slaves sometimes re-enslaved their parents' former slaves after the parents' death. For example, a thirty-year-old pearl diver named Belal bin Khamīs, a *muwalid* slave belonging to a woman in 'Ajmān, was freed by his master when she wanted to go on hajj in the early 1920s. A local imam came and wrote out a certificate of manumission, which was subsequently certified by the *qādhi* of Dubai and some witnesses. After the woman returned from her pilgrimage, the man continued to dive for pearls and live on her property, in exchange for which he gave her a portion of his earnings. He reported being well treated by the woman and satisfied with the new relationship. However, in 1925, while Belal was away at the diving banks, his master died, and one of her relatives from Qatar came and claimed him as part of her property. Belal complained that he was no longer a slave and showed the man his manumission certificate, but the Qatari took the paper and put him in chains.[86]

On the Trucial Coast, members of the royal families of local sheikhdoms were not above re-enslaving manumitted slaves. In 1921, Ayeshah bint Khalifa, sister of the late sheikh, Zaid bin Khalifa, who ruled Abu Dhabi from 1855 to 1909, manumitted her slaves upon her death, and her son, Saif bin Mohammad, endorsed their manumission papers. Sheikh Zaid's son, Sultan bin Zaid, who succeeded his father and ruled Abu Dhabi from 1922 to 1926, did not approve of his aunt's act of manumission and re-enslaved her former slaves, reportedly tearing up their manumission papers. One of her former slaves, a diver who had been kidnapped from Zanzibar as a child, ran away to Muscat seeking a British manumission certificate.[87] Sheikh Rāshid bin Ahmed, the brother of Sheikh Khālid bin Ahmed, ruler of Sharjah from 1914 to 1924, enslaved a woman of East African ancestry along with her three daughters and carried them off to Dubai, claiming that the woman's mother, Salamah, had been the slave of one of his relatives, even though Salamah had been manumitted by her master in 1885 prior to his death.[88]

Yet the rulers of the Trucial Coast sheikhdoms could also be magnanimous. In one case, Sheikh Saqr bin Khālid, who ruled Sharjah from 1883 to 1914, prevented a relative, Sheikh Rāshid bin Ahmad, from re-enslaving a family of Swahili ancestry who possessed manumission certificates. When Rāshid placed the teenage son in chains and tried to send him to the diving banks, Saqr prevented him on the basis of his mother's manumission document. But when Khālid bin Ahmad succeeded Saqr, Ahmad re-enslaved the whole family and imprisoned them for twenty days.[89]

An alternative to desertion, traditional manumission, or the British manumission certificate system was for an outside party to purchase the freedom of an enslaved person. Mesoud, an enslaved East African pearl diver in Bahrain, had his freedom purchased by the Reformed Church in

America's Arabian Mission at Bahrain after he had worked for several years in the off season in domestic work. In 1940, Mrs. Harold Storm of the Arabian Mission recalled a conversation with him in her garden in Bahrain.

> "In my country," says Mesoud, gazing sorrowfully at the prostrate branches, "we have trees, and grass, and flowers everywhere."
>
> "Where is your country, Mesoud?"
>
> "Mombassa," and his eyes gaze into the past. "Arabs stole me when I was a boy. I've been a slave all my life until I came to the Mission. I'd be a slave diving for pearls now if the Doctor didn't pay."[90]

Most of the enslaved men and women who received manumission from British authorities did not express a desire to return to their home countries in Africa. Some were one or two generations removed from their African homes. Others had been kidnapped when they were so young that they had little or no connection to their former homes. As mentioned above, several of those who were old enough to recall the details of their former homes expressed a fear of being re-enslaved if they were to be repatriated.[91] Still, among the enslaved community, there is evidence that many people retained a fondness for their former homes in Africa and a longing for home or at least a curiosity about the prospect of returning to Africa.[92] When British officials granted manumission certificates, they commonly encouraged freed men and women to settle in Muscat or Bahrain, where they believed they would find the safest homes. Although few former slaves made the journey back to their home countries, there is evidence that some did. Juma' bin Raihan, who was born in Bagamoyo around 1871, kidnapped when he was fifteen, and brought to Wudam in Batinah, worked as a hauler in the pearling industry for forty years. In 1926 he was about fifty-five years old and was too old to continue working as a hauler. He had a wife and three daughters and decided that he wanted to return to East Africa. He fled to Muscat, seeking a British manumission certificate with the hopes of bringing his family with him to Africa.[93]

Some of the most remarkable stories of mobility come from the RCA's Industrial School for Freed Slaves at Muscat. Recall that the school had begun when Peter Zwemer received his sixteen boys from the British consul in 1896. An illness led to Zwemer's premature death in 1898, and his replacement, the missionary George Stone, died as well shortly after taking over the school. RCA missionary James Cantine took over the mission in 1899 and oversaw the boys' instruction in the manual arts. Just as Cantine was preparing to sail to Basra one day, another slave dhow was captured and brought into Muscat harbor. According to Cantine, the boys of the Freed Slave School "were quite excited at the news, and wanted me to go at once to the English Consulate to see about getting others. On my telling them that I had no extra food, they said that each would share his plate of rice with a new boy!"[94]

By late 1899 the school had become more than Cantine could handle, and he began to find positions for them outside of the mission home. Two of the oldest boys were employed at the British consulate, and three others had asked to be allowed to graduate "into active life," so Cantine wrote that he was "now looking for suitable persons to whom they may be bound until they are eighteen." After three years of schooling, many of the boys had "gained as much book-learning as they are capable of using to advantage, while their growing bodies and tough muscles need more exercise and manual labor than we in our little house and garden can give them."[95] By the end of 1899, Cantine had found new homes for all but one of the boys. The school was removed from the mission budget in spring 1901.

In 1906, Cantine updated supporters on the Freed Slave School boys' whereabouts and activities in a special report in the mission's newsletter, *Neglected Arabia*. He regretted to report that four of the original eighteen boys were dead. Mark, who broke house rules and slept on the roof of the mission house to escape the intense Muscat summer heat one night, fell from the roof and later died from injuries in July 1899. Andrew died of cholera during an outbreak in November of the same year. Two other boys died aboard British gunboats: Samuel at Colombo and Peter on a troop ship in South Africa. Most of the boys were either hired onto British naval vessels or handed over to British consuls or RCA mission stations in the Gulf. John was sent onto the HMS *Sphinx* in August 1899 and in 1905 was last heard of in a letter sent during shore leave on Zanzibar. Thomas was given to the care of Percy Cox in October 1899, just as Cox was taking over as the new consul in Muscat. (It is unclear whether Thomas remained in Muscat or followed Cox to Bushehr when Cox became acting political resident in the Persian Gulf in 1903. Cantine provided no specifics but implied Thomas was aboard a British gunboat in 1906.) Solomon was sent to Bahrain, where he served in the house of Peter Zwemer's brother, Samuel, and his family for two years.[96] At Bahrain, one missionary attested that "his anxiety to please, his cheerfulness and honesty soon endeared him to our missionaries there."[97] Solomon was put in charge of babysitting the Zwemer children, and for years afterward he kept in regular correspondence with Cantine and Zwemer and donated a tenth of his earnings to the RCA board.[98] His personal and financial devotion to the ministry was complemented by his embrace of an oppositional worldview that perceived British military and imperial efforts as an extension of Christianity. Solomon later found his way onto the flagship of the East India Squadron and then onto the HMS *Fox* during World War I. In a letter to James Cantine, Solomon wrote, "Don't you think I have forget the Christian religion, but I am still with the Christians. I have got my Bible with me and the song book, too, so you need not be afraid of me, I with Jesus and Jesus with me." Elsewhere he wrote, "I am still your own boy William H. Solomon of the Arabian Mission on the mission field, only pray for me that I may grow up to be a faithful in Christ and in the Christian navy."[99]

James, whom Cantine described as once "wild and unruly," had been influenced by a "family of excellent Christians in Bombay" and wrote to tell Cantine that he still prayed to God every day. Cantine saw him during his shore leave at Muscat in 1905 and exclaimed that he "scarcely recognized him with his manly stature and neat blue uniform." James had been hired as a deckhand on a British gunboat. Later, in a letter from Bombay, James wrote to reassure Cantine that "Here in Bombay some of our boys come every day to have a pray to God at my house according to Bible which you taught us at mission house, Muscat." Years later Cantine learned that James had found work at an industrial school in India. "Here he discovered that one name was not sufficient, so added to the James 'Cantine.' A year or two later, a missionary friend in India sent me a newspaper clipping telling of my arrest for chicken stealing or some equivalent crime!"[100]

Philip was sent to live with Dr. Sharon Thoms at Bahrain in November 1899. When Philip passed through Muscat in 1905 on his way to India, Cantine noted that he had saved up a considerable sum of money from his earnings and determined that he would do well wherever he was headed. Stephen was sent to work at the government dispensary in Muscat and was still there in 1906, having earned himself a reputation as a faithful and competent worker. Alfred was sent to work with Samuel Zwemer in Bahrain and eventually ended up on a merchant steamer running between India and England. A picture in Zwemer's papers at the RCA archives in New Brunswick depicts an African boy in October 1902 accompanying the colporter, Ameen of Amarna, "on his way to Kuweit with a box of bibles and books." The boy carrying a heavy trunk over his shoulders in the photograph may be Alfred, who would have been thirteen and living in Zwemer's house at the time. Adrian, the youngest of the boys, was sent to Ahmeduagar to the industrial school of the American board in India, where he studied carpentry. Henry, who was always considered "somewhat deaf," had not found a suitable home by 1906 and was still living at the mission station in Muscat. Henry's deafness had been apparent from the time of his arrival at the mission. His birth name appears on the original transfer manifest as "Hajiboo," a response presumably provided by his compatriots. In Swahili, *hajibu* literally means "He doesn't answer."[101]

Nathan was sent to Bombay in 1899. Isaac was sent to the Reverend Fred Barny, the RCA missionary in Basra, in December 1899, but by 1905 he had found his way to Bombay. Cantine had heard disturbing rumors that they had become Muslim but hoped it was not true. David and Joseph were sent to live with a family in Bombay. Joseph was still there in 1905, but David was on his way to Australia in some capacity. David eventually found employment with the Mesopotamia Persia Corporation, Bushehr, and subsequently obtained a position in the British residency offices at Bushehr. Correspondence in the India Office records indicates that decades later David was working in the residency office. Marginalia on letters reveal that David was described as "our peon" and "our porter" by residency staff.

Perhaps the most dramatic story of any of the boys was that of Solomon, the first of the younger boys to leave the mission house. When Solomon was brought to Muscat in 1896, he was approximately eleven years old. Following his work for Zwemer in Bahrain and his stint with the British Royal Navy on the HMS *Fox*, Solomon subsequently migrated to New York City, where he found work as a janitor in an apartment house. Solomon appears in the 1920 U.S. Census as "William H. Solomon," living as a single lodger, age forty, at "251 West 133rd Street, Manhattan," and working as a telephone operator. His place of birth is listed as Africa, and his parents are both listed as born in Africa.[102] Solomon's address places him in the heart of 1920s Harlem, only a few short blocks from Marcus Garvey's Universal Negro Improvement Association (UNIA) headquarters and Liberty Hall.

In August 1925, Solomon attended Dr. Samuel Zwemer's daughter Elizabeth's wedding to Claude Pickens (the American missionary to China) at Mt. Vernon, New York,[103] and he remained in correspondence with

"Solomon." From *Neglected Arabia* 2, no. 5 (1906): 16. Courtesy Reformed Church in America Archives, New Brunswick, NJ.

Zwemer into the 1930s, by which time he had taken the name W. King Solomon. In January 1934, Solomon used his friendship with Samuel Zwemer, then a professor at Princeton Theological Seminary, to make an appeal to the British government. Zwemer wrote to the British political resident at Muscat on Solomon's behalf seeking to establish documentation of Solomon's manumission and his status as a British subject. Solomon, Zwemer explained, had lost any documentation he used to have and wanted to establish his British status because he was "anxious to return to his native country, East Africa."[104] The efforts were fruitless because the boys of the Freed Slave School had never been issued formal government manumission certificates. Not defeated by the Gulf administration's inability to help him, two years later, with Zwemer's assistance, Solomon tried to trace some documentation of his manumission through the political resident in the Gulf, this time writing his own appeal. His letter reads as follows:

> Dear Sir:
>
> Many years ago (in 1896) I was rescued by the Consul of the British Government at Muscat from a slave dhow, and with seventeen other boys put under charge of Rev. Peter J. Zwemer, an American Missionary at Muscat. During the period of the World War I served on a British ship, and after the war came to New York. But I lost all papers that I had, and am now unable to establish the fact that I was released from slavery at Muscat, and am a British subject.
>
> One of the other boys who was with us is now at Bushire. His name is David, and he can corroborate what I am writing to you. My former master is Dr. Samuel M. Zwemer, who lived on the Persian Gulf, and is now a professor at Princeton, USA.
>
> Can you trace any record of my liberation and secure me a statement to that effect?
>
> Very respectfully yours,
> W. King[105]

The Muscat vice consul replied in March 1937 that no documentation could be found and suggested Solomon contact the British Admiralty through the consulate-general in New York.[106] Solomon may have shied away from pursuing the issue further because he may not have been officially discharged from the navy. He was also reportedly in poor health. The correspondence preserved in the India Office records nevertheless indicates that David and Solomon corresponded regularly until approximately 1928.[107] An intriguing detail comes from their correspondence: one of the marginal notes by the consular staff refers to David as "David Feruz," indicating that David, like Solomon, had taken his Christian name as his forename but added a surname of his own choosing. But in David's case, he had elected to use his original birth name (preserved in the manifest from Peter Zwemer's original bond with the British consul in 1896), "Ferooz," to serve as his surname.

Whether Solomon ever managed to return to East Africa is a conclusion not obtainable from available records. Since many African sailors jumped ship in desirable ports and did not receive formal discharge papers, Solomon may not have wanted to contact the Admiralty. However, his expressed desire to return to East Africa in his late forties, after more than thirty years away from his childhood home, could indicate a strong connection to his roots or perhaps a connection to New York's Pan-African political movements. The last known documentation of Solomon is his World War II draft card, dated April 26, 1942. It lists Solomon's age as fifty-two, his place of birth as "Center East Africa," his place of residence as "102 W. 119 St., Apt. 4E, New York City," and his occupation as "unemployed." "Race: Negro; Height: 5-5; Weight: 130; Hair: grey."[108] He does not appear to have made it back to Zanzibar.

For most enslaved Africans in the Gulf in the late nineteenth and early twentieth centuries, work, sexuality, marriage, and reproduction were affairs controlled by others. Still, many enslaved men and women succeeded in dictating some of the terms of their family life and labor. Some freed slaves such as Solomon made their way to the other side of the world. Some enslaved pearl divers such as Faraj bin Sa'id, whose story opened this chapter, negotiated certain aspects of the terms of their enslavement from a strong position. However, as will be seen below, with the collapse of the Gulf date and pearl industries in the 1920s, even the most accomplished divers faced an uncertain future.[109]

5

ANTISLAVERY AND EMPIRE: PARADOXES OF LIBERATION IN THE WESTERN INDIAN OCEAN

During the pearling season of 1873, an enslaved pearl diver named Joah swam from his boat and climbed aboard a British cruiser.[1] The slave of a Dubai pearling captain, Joah had been brought by his master to dive at pearl banks near Zairku, an uninhabited sandy island in the Persian Gulf halfway between Abu Dhabi and Doha. It was nearly the end of the pearling season, and Joah's boat was one of seventy-three pearling vessels anchored near the island waiting out a passing storm when the HMS *May Frere*, a British "despatch vessel" en route to Bahrain, happened to anchor nearby. Around eleven o'clock at night, Joah swam off from his master's boat and climbed aboard the *May Frere*, begging British protection from his master. The commanding officer, Captain Guthrie, deferred the request to his passenger, Major Grant, the first assistant resident, the ranking officer aboard. Following what he thought to be protocol, Major Grant granted Joah asylum, determining that once he had been admitted on board, he was on British soil and entitled to protection. As soon as word reached the captains of the pearling boats that Major Grant refused to surrender Joah to his master, all seventy-three pearling boats weighed anchor in spite of the rough weather and departed out of fear that other slaves might flee or that the boats might face retribution from the Royal Navy for having slaves among their crews.[2]

In the weeks that followed, Grant's actions led to a diplomatic hailstorm. Captain Guthrie worried the action would set a dangerous precedent for British naval vessels that might encounter pearling boats in the Gulf. "It would be rather awkward if the cruiser found out that one-third of the boat's crews were slaves," Guthrie noted. An unscrupulous commander might seize the pearling boats as "slave dhows" and lawful prizes "on account of the head money he would be entitled to for them, quoting as precedent '*May Frere.*'"[3] Edward C. Ross, the political resident, conjectured that if commanders made a habit of accepting runaway slaves at the pearl banks, "where the diving is carried on almost entirely by domestic slaves," they might all run off to British vessels and cause "a general feeling of consternation and disgust. . . . We should no longer be looked on as the friendly protectors of the maritime Arabs."[4] Grant himself recognized that "if domestic slaves are allowed to receive protection on board every English ship they come across, the owners will be great losers, and the pearl fishing will come to a standstill, as nearly all the divers belong to that class."[5] The Home Government agreed that if runaway slaves found refuge on British ships, then "their masters would be entirely ruined," a situation that would destroy British material interests "by the mistrust and hatred which would be occasioned."[6]

The ensuing legal debate ultimately led the Admiralty Office to distribute its infamous "Circular No. 33" of July 31, 1875, which ordered "all Commanders-in-Chief, Captains, Commanders and Commanding Officers of Her Majesty's ships and vessels" around the world to deny refuge to runaway slaves except in extreme, life-threatening cases. "The broad rule to be observed," the order stated, "is that a fugitive slave should not be permanently received onboard any description of ship under the British flag, unless his life would be endangered unless he were not allowed to come aboard." The justification for the strict new policy came from the experience of the Gulf and directly quoted the correspondence surrounding Joah's case: "For it might happen, to take an extreme instance, that the whole slave portion of the crews of vessel engaged in the pearl fishery in the Persian Gulf, might take refuge on board British ships, and if free there, their masters would be entirely ruined, and the mistrust and hatred caused in their minds would be greatly prejudicial to British interests."[7]

The circular elicited an enormous public outcry in Great Britain. The order was immediately condemned in the British press as a moral outrage. *The Times*, the *Post*, the *Daily News*, and the *Standard* each issued scathing denunciations of the Admiralty. The *New York Times* ran an article that

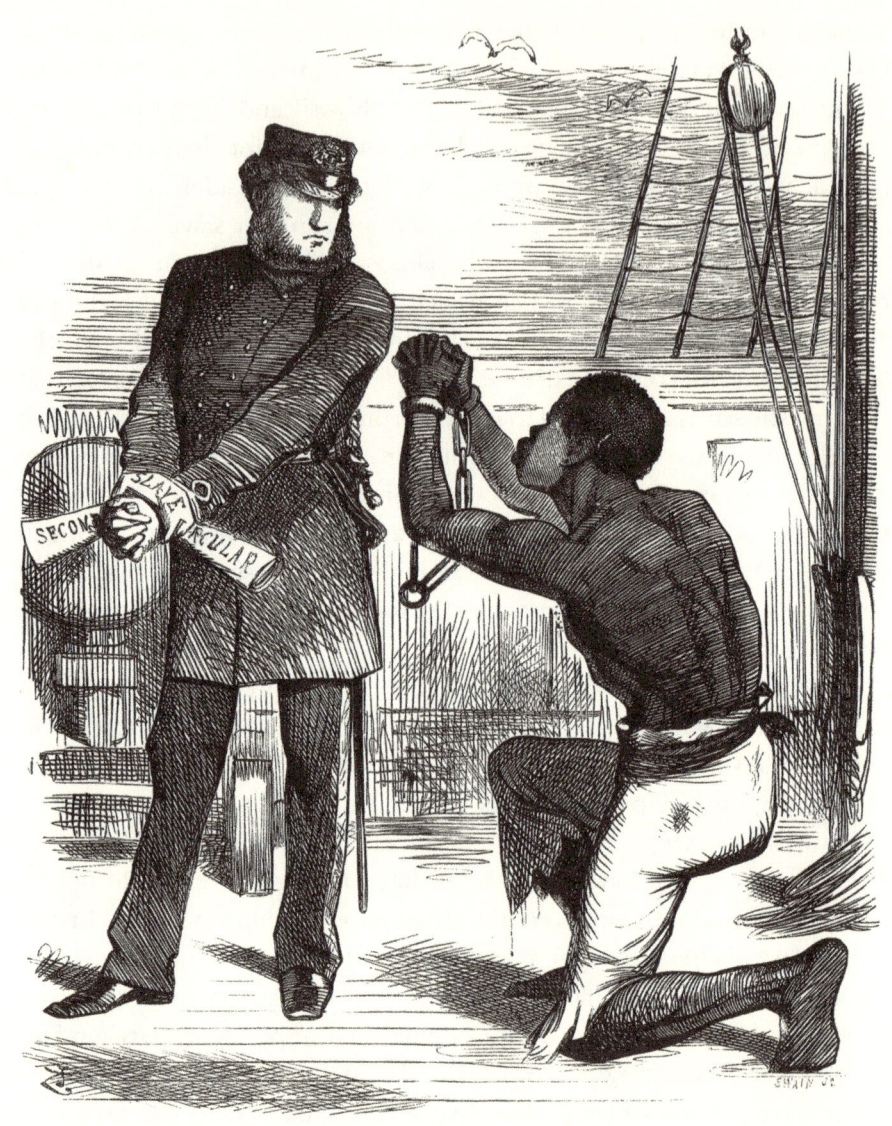

MEN AND BROTHERS!!

Fugitive Slave. "TAKE THESE OFF!"
Captain, R.N. "HOW CAN I?—WITH *THIS* ON?"

John Tenniel cartoon, "Men and Brothers!!" *Punch*, March 4, 1876. Used by Permission. © Punch Limited. Image #1876.03.04.79.

began, "Some idiot in the Admiralty a short time since took into his head to send out instructions to the Navy with regard to the treatment of fugitive slaves." The criticism concluded, "It is probable that the person who drew it up had not the faintest idea of the great principle he was bringing into jeopardy, but only went on heaping up verbiage, as a fool does, without knowing exactly either what he meant to say or what was the meaning of what he did say."[8] Popular uproar against the circular emerged in every major city in Great Britain. Popular gatherings denounced the government, and petitions poured into Parliament. The government ultimately had to call a special commission, the Royal Commission on Fugitive Slaves, which subpoenaed experts from British colonial administrations around the Indian Ocean to testify about the extent of the slave trade between East Africa and Arabia and the means that could be employed in suppressing it. The proceedings of the hearings filled a massive, 350-page volume and included famous antislavery activists and renowned explorers, missionaries, and colonial officials. Caroline Shaw argues convincingly that the controversy of the Admiralty's Circular No. 33 sparked a grassroots movement that would come to shape Britain's (and the world's) conceptualizations of asylum and refuge.[9] Enslaved pearl divers like Joah were vital to the Gulf pearling industry at a moment when the world was entering a pearl craze. British officials recognized the Gulf's dependence on slave divers and built colonial policy in the region around it. As with other parts of the British Empire, economics and political expediency took precedence over abolitionism.[10]

In this chapter, I argue that in both East Africa and the Gulf, British antislavery efforts were frequently contradictory or half-hearted because British statesmen recognized that slave labor was vital to the economies of these regions. Officials often turned a blind eye to slavery because enforcing antislavery policy jeopardized British hegemony. In the Western Indian Ocean, antislavery measures were chronically underfunded; fraught with inconstancies, graft, and fraud; and frequently conducted with callous disregard for those whom their efforts were intended to help. Antislavery was a tool of expediency applied where and when needed for imperial ends but, as a policy goal, frequently forgotten. Slavery and the slave trade drifted variously from foreground to background in British priorities in the second half of the nineteenth century and through the first half of the twentieth century. As elsewhere in the empire, an antislavery ethic could be invoked to justify policies of conquest or occupation, yet slavery could just as easily be ignored or justified within areas under British control. The indifference with which enslaved Africans were treated by British officials and the inconsistencies in the enforcement of antislavery treaties may seem out of place to twenty-first-century observers, but the cases of East Africa and eastern Arabia are far from unusual. In this chapter I support an argument advanced by Richard Huzzey, Suzanne Miers, Fredrick Cooper, and others who have shown that British antislavery efforts frequently underpinned Victorian territorial expansion, reinforced racist attitudes toward Africans, favored the transition to other forms of coerced labor, and helped develop commercial interests and translate them into national interests. British antislavery policy in Africa was not consistent, purely altruistic, or exclusively humanitarian.[11] As Miers has noted, "The slavery issue was used by the colonial powers during the partition of Africa to further their own ends, but, once their rule was established, they took only minimal action to end the institution and sometimes even supported it."[12] Historians of Africa have documented the paradoxical nature of antislavery justifications for actions like the occupation of Lagos, Nyassaland, Uganda, and Zanzibar; the blockade of East Africa; and the construction of the Uganda railway and as the pretext for the Brussels Conference, which gave legal justification to both the occupation of African territory and the suppression of African resistance. The contradictory nature of antislavery in the Indian Ocean is not entirely surprising, and the examples from East Africa and the Gulf provide further evidence of what was, in fact, the rule rather than the exception.

A widely popular adage holds that the Persian Gulf in the nineteenth and early twentieth century was a "British lake."[13] It may therefore seem surprising that the slave trade persisted in the Gulf in spite of treaties and efforts to suppress it. Great Britain, after all, possessed the world's most powerful navy at the close of the nineteenth century and had been at the forefront of global antislavery since the opening of the century. Britain negotiated a series of treaties with local rulers and had embarked on a naval crusade for the express purpose of ending the slave trade from East Africa to the Gulf. Viscount Palmerston, when foreign secretary in 1846, pledged that Great Britain would be "the main instrument in the Hands of

Providence" to "put an end to the African Slave Trade," and he urged the political agent for Muscat and Zanzibar to impress upon "these Arabs" that it was "in vain [for them] to endeavour to resist the consummation of that which is written in the Book of Fate" and that they "ought to bow to Superior Power, to leave off a pursuit which is doomed to annihilation."[14] But in spite of such hyperbole, the suppression of the slave trade had by the end of the century yielded to other priorities.

Despite the fiery antislavery rhetoric of the nineteenth century and the aggressive, highly publicized antislavery patrols of the Royal Navy in the western Indian Ocean, slavery remained alive and well in eastern Arabia well into the twentieth century. The slave trade from East Africa to the Gulf persisted, as evidenced by the Gulf political resident's discovery in 1900 that at least one thousand enslaved Africans were still annually imported to the Omani port of Sur. In 1902, Portuguese forces caught more than one hundred men from Sur in the process of shipping more than seven hundred enslaved Africans (mostly Makua) from the Mozambique coast. And newly imported slaves intermittently presented themselves at British agencies and aboard navy ships seeking manumission well into the twentieth century. The slave trade from East Africa to the Gulf persisted, but the British administration in the region turned a blind eye to it because slavery was vital to the Gulf economy.[15] Put succinctly, the aims of liberal politics clashed with the aims of liberal economics. Likewise in Zanzibar, fighting the slave trade and abolishing slavery diminished remarkably in importance once the territory became a British protectorate in 1890. Almost overnight, slavery ceased to be a scourge and came to be seen instead as a mild institution to be phased out gradually so as not to disrupt the coastal economy and the positions of Arab elites. But even in its heyday, the British antislavery campaign in the Indian Ocean was fraught with inefficiency, underfunding, fraud, and callousness. A great many of the "freed slaves" captured in the Indian Ocean died shortly after being rescued. Those who survived were often farmed out to local elites to work as domestics or put to work in the ports. When deposited at mission stations or in port cities in Kenya, Mauritius, Zanzibar, and the Seychelles, "freed slaves" were frequently renamed; introduced to new clothing, religion, and language; and required to perform labor similar to slaves in Arabia. In reality, the lives of so-called "freed slaves" were remarkably similar to those of slaves in the Gulf. Those tasked with "freeing slaves" were often unsympathetic and sometimes even abusive toward their wards. Moreover, many free African sailors were mistaken for slaves during the campaign. Some wealthy Zanzibari merchants were even sent to South Africa as "prize negroes" and forced to perform menial agricultural labor after being "rescued" by the Royal Navy. The antislavery campaign disrupted legitimate trade, destroyed trade vessels with no ties to the slave trade, and failed to check a trade that continued well into the twentieth century. For all its bluster, the British antislavery campaign in the Indian Ocean was more about appearances than actual suppression. Antislavery efforts advanced the interests of imperialists but failed to stop the slave trade. Slavery was simply too economically important.

Diplomatic and Naval Efforts in the Indian Ocean, 1808–1873

British antislavery efforts in the Indian Ocean began as an extension of endeavors in the Atlantic Ocean, and, like actions in the Atlantic, centered on diplomatic attempts to secure antislave-trade treaties and naval pursuits to enforce them. Great Britain had outlawed the trading in slaves by its citizens in 1807.[16] By the time Atkins Hamerton, agent of the British East India Company at Muscat, arrived at Zanzibar in 1840, the Royal Navy had been involved in the suppression of the slave trade in West Africa for more than three decades, beginning with the arrival of the first naval vessels off the coast of West Africa to enforce the new law in 1808. Until 1825, the navy annually captured and freed about 1,000 Africans in the Atlantic who were being carried to slavery in the Americas. Between 1825 and 1840 the annual captures averaged between 4,000 and 5,000.[17] The Royal Navy's involvement in East Africa, on the other hand, had been minimal up until that time. Captain Fairfax Moresby visited the western Indian Ocean in the HMS *Menai* in 1820 and acted as the senior naval officer at Mauritius from 1821 to 1823, during which time he made some efforts for suppression of the slave trade, including the capture of the French slaver *Camilla* in Zanzibar harbor with 140 slaves. Moresby also succeeded in securing the first antislavery treaty in the Indian Ocean when the sultan of Muscat agreed to prohibit the transportation of slaves from

East Africa to India and the Mascarene Islands and to submit to naval searches at sea.[18] While technically in force from 1822, the treaty had little effect. Captain William Owen's tour of East Africa and south Arabia to chart the coastline of the western Indian Ocean between 1822 and 1825 produced further information on the extent of the slave trade, but little effort was made to stop European and Arab slave traders. No British man-of-war visited Zanzibar again until 1843, when Commander Wyvill arrived in the *Cleopatra* at the invitation of Hamerton.[19] Although Viscount Palmerston wrote in 1846 that the British would be used as the hands of Providence for the ending of the slave trade, the Foreign Office was content to pursue treaties and did not request formal antislavery patrols from the Board of Admiralty for well over a decade.[20]

Meanwhile, the Government of India, which oversaw early British affairs in the Gulf, likewise made little serious effort to suppress the slave trade. Its primary goal remained protecting the route to India, and this goal required the maintenance of the political and economic status quo in Arabia and the Gulf. Any efforts to disrupt the slave trade were deemed likely to breed discontent. The Government of India proclaimed in 1842 that "the Governor General in council entertains the strongest doubt of the permanent success of any sudden or violent effort to suppress this trade, as at present carried on." Such a course, the statement continued, "can hardly fail to excite the ill will of the people, and the jealousy of the chiefs will lead them to counteract our measures."[21] Seizures in the 1840s and 1850s were thus few and far between.

In 1840, Colonel Hamerton began negotiations with the Omani sultan, Seyyid Sa'id, that concluded five years later in a formal treaty with the British government that would take effect in 1847, limiting the slave trade to what were considered to be the borders of the sultan's territory. In the intervening years, Sa'id agreed to a series of restrictions on slave trading aimed at limiting the public sale of slaves and the ability of Qawāsim and other Arabs from the Trucial Coast to rent houses in town in which to gather slaves or anchor their ships in harbors he controlled.[22] Sa'id had his own reasons for implementing these measures. The public slave market was a growing source of embarrassment in the presence of European visitors (Hamerton observed that Sa'id "dislikes white people to see the slave market"), and the Qawāsim were notorious for evading his taxes.[23] In 1839,

Seyyid Sa'id complained to the political resident at Bushehr that slave traders from the Trucial Coast were stealing three to four times the number of Africans they were paying for in the slave market, thus undercutting a significant portion of his tax revenue.[24] This loss of revenue was compounded by the sultan's inability since the 1820s to profit from the formerly lucrative slave market to the Mascarenes. Sa'id repeatedly complained that the Moresby Treaty cost him $100,000 annually.[25]

When the Hamerton Treaty went into effect in 1847, the transport of slaves was officially limited to the coast between Kilwa in the south and Lamu in the north. It was still permissible to transport slaves from Kilwa to Zanzibar and Pemba and to ports on the coast as far north as Lamu, but beyond those limits vessels could be searched and seized at sea. The British government considered the treaty a major step forward in the suppression of the slave trade, but for Sa'id it represented success in gaining formal recognition by a major European power of his claims to territories in coastal East Africa, which in many places were tenuous at best, as the loss of the island of Nosy Bé to the French demonstrated.[26] Sa'id's control over the coast was contingent on his navy, which, while extensive for the region in that period, held mainly symbolic power. The sultan's ships were old and frequently lacked adequate sailors to work them. Hamerton described Sa'id's navy as decrepit, ill-equipped, and maintained by young slave boys. He claimed that at Muscat, the young sailors of the sultan's ships were so poorly trained that three to five of them would be killed each time they fired the cannons for salutes.[27] When Sa'id sent an expedition of 1,600 men to put down a rebellion in Siwa in 1848, it suffered a complete defeat.[28] With the enforcement of Hamerton's treaty in the hands of Sa'id's navy, the slave trade was allowed to continue without hindrance for most of the next decade. The treaty served Sa'id's purpose of validating his expansionist dreams but was otherwise window dressing.

In 1858, Captain R. B. Oldfield of the Royal Navy arrived at Zanzibar in the HMS *Lyra* with orders to begin actually enforcing the antislavery treaties produced by the diplomatic efforts of the four preceding decades. Between 1858 and 1873, the Liberal Party, which controlled Parliament in Britain with the exception of three years (1866–1868), made ending slavery a priority. Following the few captures by Moresby and Owen between 1820 and 1825, Zanzibar's slave trade had gone unchecked until the *Cleopatra* arrived in 1843. Its departure was followed by a seven-year lapse before the visit of the *Castor* and *Bee* in 1850–1851. These ships destroyed baracoons—structures constructed for holding slaves until they could be shipped—at Tanga and Kilwa and provided some temporary enforcement of the antislavery treaty with limited effect.[29] But it would be another seven years before formal naval patrols of Zanzibar territory would begin. The arrival of the HMS *Lyra* in 1858 formally inaugurated a three-decade-long antislavery campaign in East Africa that would have some, albeit limited, impact.[30]

The arrival of the HMS *Lyra* coincided with the beginning of an ineffectual effort by the Indian Navy in the Gulf, as well as the presence of antislavery activist officials in the British residency in the Gulf. Felix Jones, who was political resident in the Persian Gulf from 1856 to 1862, was determined to "strike a blow at slavery" in the Gulf by intercepting and searching Qāsimī vessels returning from East Africa. In a break with previous policy, Jones requested Commodore Griffith Jenkins, commanding the Indian naval squadron in the Gulf, to search dhows returning from East Africa during the spring season of 1859. Jones imagined that Qāsimī ships sailed together as a fleet and that the dhows would be easily spotted and inspected as a group by a diligent squadron. With the HMS *Falkland* and the brig *Tigris*, Jenkins and his men patrolled the entrance to the Gulf during the hottest months of the year and, using the *Falkland*'s tenders, rowed after and boarded between forty and fifty dhows, finding only one slave. Jones and Jenkins considered the mission a disaster. Jones was furious with the "meager results," as he had hoped the mission would succeed in "convincing slave dealers and all maritime Arabs engaged in this inhuman traffic that their acts would at length receive a signal check."[31] Jenkins became enraged at Jones's lack of appreciation for the sacrifice his men had made. He replied that rowing in the open sun for twelve to twenty hours a day, chasing dhows in "that fearful hot climate, was the most trying that any officers or seamen could be employed in." Jenkins informed Jones that there was no such thing as a Qāsimī fleet, as vessels traveled alone or with a single ship as a companion. He suggested that steamers be employed in the future in place of galleys and attributed the lack of success to the countervailing winds, the unhealthy climate, and the likelihood of slaves being landed further south on the coast around Masira Island and marched inland to avoid naval patrols.[32] From information Jones gathered in Gulf slave markets, the trade had increased in 1859 in spite of all efforts.[33]

British antislavery efforts in the western Indian Ocean between 1858 and 1865 were characterized by inefficiency. Early efforts to suppress the East African slave trade were based on British antislavery experience in the Atlantic, but conditions in East Africa differed significantly from West Africa. While the Atlantic slave trade had been dominated by bulky, square-rigged ships of European build, the East African slave trade was conducted via smaller, lateen-rigged ships (incorrectly all referred to as dhows) of lighter draught that could move more easily against the wind and outrun British men-of-war. The geography of the East African coast and islands, with numerous creeks, thick vegetation close to shore, reefs, and shallow inlets, favored smugglers in light vessels over bulky naval patrols.

Different conditions of the East African slave trade required many adjustments, but these changes were slow in coming, partly on account of the lower priority Britain placed on antislavery duties even under Liberal Party rule. Viscount Palmerston, leader of Britain's reunited Liberal Party, complained in 1860 that successive Boards of Admiralty had "never cared a farthing about the suppression of the Slave Trade," considering it "a sort of penal duty," and had "sent to it all the old tubs that were fit in their opinion for nothing else."[34] Many of the vessels sent to patrol the East African coast were indeed antiques unsuited for antislavery duty. The HMS *Gorgon*, which was sent to patrol the coast of East Africa in 1859, was near the end of its lifespan and was destroyed when it returned to England at the end of its tour in 1863. The *Gorgon* was a 1,613-ton paddle steamer built back in 1837. It could get only up to nine knots and burned twenty-six tons of coal per day. The smaller boats sent off of the ships for patrolling and boarding dhows were ineffective against the wind and often had to be rowed long distances by exhausted crews in rough water. Most of these boats did not have sufficient storage or cover for the crews that were sent off on lengthy journeys with only limited supplies, much less the facilities for any rescued slaves.[35]

As W. Cope Devereux's *A Cruise in the "Gorgon"* (1869) makes clear, the HMS *Gorgon* made few captures. Devereux's description of a typical chase of a dhow on the east coast of Zanzibar in September 1861 illustrates the ship's sad record. Spotting an *mtepe* (a type of small dhow) hugging the shore, the commander sent his fastest boarding boat in pursuit and ordered the ship's rocket tubes readied to fire. Devereux describes the results as follows: "Unfortunately, the *munition de guerre* is damp and out of order, so that the pirate escapes. A fresh breeze springs up, and away goes the gig's mast. The *matape [mtepe]* runs her nose into the bush, most likely disposes of her slaves, and then continues to run along the coast with the speed of the wind, leaving our boat miles behind. So we lose her, but hope for better luck next time."[36]

As British antislavery efforts in the Indian Ocean continued in subsequent decades, the Royal Navy's actions were severely limited by a shortage of ships and resources. In the 1860s the Royal Navy regrouped its foreign stations, and the East Indies Station took over antislavery duties in East Africa. As of February 1864, China had become its own foreign naval station, and it took with it the bulk of the East Indies fleet (thirty-nine ships) to patrol the whole of East Asia from Malaysia to Japan. The East Indies Station, which now covered the entire Indian Ocean from Mozambique to Rangoon, consisted of between seven and eleven ships between 1865 and 1875, but it could never afford to have more than four ships at a time patrol East Africa. Centered at Trincomalee, Ceylon, the East Indies Station was required to keep most of its ships around India and the Arabian Gulf and could maintain only limited communication with its East Africa division.[37] The antislavery squadron rarely consisted of more than three regular ships to patrol 4,000 kilometers (2,500 miles) of coastline.[38] For the next quarter century, the East Indies Station directed a half-hearted effort to patrol for slave ships in the western Indian Ocean but without much success.

The Royal Navy's celebrated antislavery efforts in the western Indian Ocean in the 1860s were ineffective and chronically underfunded. When Admiral Cockburn entreated the Admiralty board in 1871 for more ships and resources for antislavery duties in the Indian Ocean, the Admiralty replied that "the Treasury have positively decided not to sanction any increased charge for suppression of the slave trade at present, consequently no object appears gained by discussing what might be done with an increased force."[39] And although much credit is often given to the antislavery patrols for suppressing the slave trade, the results of the Royal Navy's campaign were actually modest.[40] When statistics are adjusted to remove the more dubious cases of vessels that were captured without any enslaved Africans aboard or fewer than ten Africans aboard (who may well have been passengers or crew), the numbers of captured slaves are relatively small. The results from the antislavery patrols between 1865 and 1873 indicate that the largest number of captures made in that period were made along the coast of Somalia (43 percent) and that the majority of enslaved men and women captured (55 percent) were found north of the sultan of Zanzibar's jurisdiction, either on their way up the Somali coast or having already arrived off the coast of Arabia. Furthermore, despite rhetoric calling for an end to the slave trade to Arabia, more than a third of the slave captures (34 percent) were made in the Mozambique Channel and were most likely not part of the trade to Arabia. The brisk trade in enslaved Africans carried on between Mozambique and Madagascar and the Mascarene Islands operated largely independently of the slave trade to Arabia,[41] so the inclusion of these captures in annual figures padded the annual count of freed captives, improving the image of the antislavery squadron's performance against the trade "to Arabia."

The commanders and admirals who supervised the antislavery squadron were under no illusions that their patrols were effective. In 1868, Admiral Leopold G. Heath estimated that British ships had seized "less than 5 percent of the slaves exported" from East Africa in that year.[42] Admiral Heath's words were echoed by nearly every naval commander, admiral, and consul involved in Indian Ocean antislavery efforts between 1858 and 1873. In 1860, C. P. Rigby estimated that 3,000–5,000 slaves were taken north from Zanzibar each year.[43] He later estimated that "not even one per cent of the slaves taken north every year is captured by British cruisers."[44] Brigadier W. M. Coghlan in a personal note to Consul Robert Lambert Playfair in 1863 wrote that he thought that the Royal Navy squadron on the East Indies Station was "absolutely useless" and the slave traffic in the Red Sea and Arabian Gulf were "uncontrolled."[45] The ineffectiveness of British antislave-trade efforts was not lost on foreign observers. One American merchant mocked the efforts in a letter to his parents in 1883: "This is a noble work they are doing out here. Three thousand men—ten great men of war iron clad with rifled cannon, yachts, steam-launches, hulks, stations—all work for a year and catch a 7 ton dhow and one little slave! Alla-hum-de-le-la!"[46]

The Persistence of the Slave Trade after 1873

The year 1873 is frequently given as the beginning of the end of the East African slave trade. As mentioned above, most published estimates of the East African slave trade assume a sharply declining curve following that date. In that year, Sir Bartle Frere made his acclaimed visits to the sultan of Zanzibar, Seyyid Bargash, and the sultan of Muscat, Turkī bin Saʻīd, and negotiated a treaty with the latter to prohibit the importation of slaves on the Arabian coast. Frere's negotiations with Bargash were unsuccessful, but Sir John Kirk followed Frere's visit with a more forceful approach. Bargash was told to sign a treaty prohibiting the slave trade or face a naval blockade around the island of Zanzibar. As Kirk explained to Bargash, he had "not come to discuss but to dictate" the new antislavery treaty. Under threat of blockade, the sultan acquiesced and signed a treaty on June 5, 1873, prohibiting the transport of slaves from anywhere on the coast of East Africa (even to the islands of Zanzibar and Pemba), authorizing the closure of the slave markets, and forbidding Indian subjects from owning slaves.[47] The treaty between Kirk and Bargash was signed with much pomp and circumstance in the sultan's palace, followed by salutes from the cannons of the naval vessels in the harbor. G. K. Gordon described the occasion as follows: "An Arab standing by the Sultan read the treaty in Arabic, and placed it in front of the Sultan, who signed it with his usual flourishing signature. Dr. Kirk added his signature, and instantly we heard the booming of the ship's guns, firing a salute of 21 guns, to announce the great paper had been signed. There were no further ceremonies, and we left to return to the ship to shed our hot dress uniforms. The next day the sultan closed the slave market."[48] But in spite of the new treaty and a British naval presence in the western Indian Ocean, the slave trade persisted for another half century.

In the months immediately following the declaration of the new treaty, shipments of enslaved Africans by sea indeed ceased. But they were to resume shortly after, using modified methods and alternative routes. The most important of the new routes to emerge in the post–1873 period were inland routes from Kilwa to the north to the closest points on the coast to Pemba, the region around Dar es Salaam, Bagamoyo, Pangani, and further north to Mombasa, Malindi, and Lamu. Kirk heard the first reports of the land route to Mombasa and Malindi when he arrived at Malindi in 1873 to manumit the slaves of Indian subjects.[49] The following year, Rear Admiral Arthur Cumming reported hearing that Arab slave dealers were "grateful to the English" for imposing the latest antislavery treaty on the sultan, as the new land routes worked more efficiently for them.[50] One British commander lamented that the new land routes were "negating the work on the sea." While a fairly effective antislavery blockade had been imposed on Zanzibar at sea, he estimated that twelve thousand slaves had been marched up the coast in 1874. According to customs records, the legal imports to Zanzibar by sea the previous year had been fifteen thousand.[51] Reports on the land route led to a formal investigation by J. Fredric Elton in 1875. Elton determined that there was indeed an inland "slave track" that headed northward out of Kilwa. Elton determined that the land route now superseded the sea route and that slaves were being sent for sale on the Somali coast, where they were sent by sea in large numbers.[52] In spite of the new treaties and increased efforts, the Kilwa trade was reported to be going strong in 1876, with an estimated fifteen hundred new slaves arriving each month, about two-thirds of whom were sent to Zanzibar and Pemba after being marched north via overland routes.[53] In 1877, a local trading party came upon and attacked what was described as a party of Arab slave traders en route to Malindi.[54] Further reports stated that slaves were marched north to the Somali coast, where they were embarked for the Gulf, and to the south there were rumors of slaves being run directly to Oman from Madagascar.[55] Kirk found further evidence of the caravans to Somaliland during his visit to the Benadir Coast in 1875.[56]

Enforcing the new treaty with existing naval resources proved to be an immediate problem. In 1873, only two ships were available to patrol the entire coast of East Africa.[57] Given the new responsibilities under the treaty of 1873, Captain Malcolm recommended significant changes to the antislavery fleet in East Africa. He recommended that a depot ship be stationed at Zanzibar to be used as a base for launching smaller vessels; he suggested yachts, preferably American yachts, which could compete with dhows when heading into the wind. Malcolm named several suitable depot ships that were currently sitting unused in British ports, among them the HMS *London*. In addition, the new patrols should be equipped with Hale's war rockets, which were ineffective as weapons but powerful as psychological tools.[58]

"Steam-Pinnace of the HMS *London* Chasing a Slave Dhow." *Illustrated London News*, December 17, 1881. Used by permission. © Illustrated London News Ltd./ Mary Evans. Reference #10015376.

When the HMS *London* arrived at Zanzibar in 1875, it was clear the slave trade had not diminished in spite of the new treaty. In 1874 the antislavery squadron captured fifteen dhows and 695 slaves.[59] In 1875 the captures included thirty-five dhows and 426 slaves.[60] E. D. Young, who visited Lake Nyasa in 1875, described extensive devastation caused by slave raiding and described multiple slave dhows plying Lake Nyasa.[61] The land route was known to be thriving, and authorities in the Gulf saw no signs of a decline in slave imports. Shortly after the arrival of the *London*, however, antislavery prospects improved significantly. As Captain Malcolm suggested, having the HMS *London* serving as a depot ship for smaller patrol craft proved to be far more efficient for antislavery duties than previous systems.

The renewed efforts by the HMS *London* had many successes. By 1876, Elton could report that slave collecting at Tugula was at an end,[62] and Kirk reported in 1877 that the slave trade around Cape Delgado was now totally extinct and that everyone formerly involved in the slave trade was reportedly now involved in legitimate trade.[63] In 1879, the commander-in-chief of the East Indies Station reported that he believed the Gulf slave trade to be extinct.[64] By 1884 admirals who led the antislavery crusade reversed the pessimism of their predecessors. The celebrated treaty between the sultan of Zanzibar and the British government signed under pressure from Bartle Frere and John Kirk in 1873, combined with the diligent work of the Royal Navy, appeared to have finally succeeded. In his classic history of the Royal Navy and the slave trade, Christopher Lloyd places the date for "the end of the Arab slave trade" in 1883.[65] Other historians place the termination date in 1880 or even earlier.[66] Given the evidence from 1876 to 1883, Lloyd's conclusion appears logical. By 1883, the navy had witnessed diminishing shipments of slaves from East Africa for seven straight years. Unlike their counterparts in the preceding two decades, naval commanders now regularly reported that the slave trade was steadily declining, and Captain Luxmore of the HMS *London* wrote in 1882 that "the slave trade appears to be paralyzed."[67] The HMS *London* was broken up and sold, and a new system of vice consulates along the coast was put in place to supplement and replace regular naval patrols.[68] Admiral Heath had suggested the establishment of vice consulates on the coast as early as 1869, when he had lamented that the navy was capturing at most only 5 percent of the slaves being transported north.[69] Under the vice consular system, British agents would be stationed at four key ports on the coast—Kilwa, Lindi, Mombasa, and Lamu—and they would cooperate with local representatives of the sultan to report on the movements of local inhabitants and prevent the revival of the slave trade. Kirk escorted the new vice consuls to Lamu and Mombasa, John G. ("Jack") Haggard and Charles E. Gissing, to their stations in December 1883.[70]

The vice consulates failed completely by 1886.[71] John Haggard's letters home vividly reveal the reasons for the failure of the system. To begin with, Haggard's power was limited by the weakness of the sultan's governor at Lamu, on whose authority Haggard relied. Local authorities permitted the governor to raise his flag—the symbol of the sultan's authority—only on Fridays, and Haggard was obliged to do the same.[72] Haggard could roam about the town only when escorted by an armed guard.[73] For several months when the threat of Somali incursions was high, he was essentially a prisoner in his own home. Haggard and the sultan's governor were equally fearful of Somalis. Haggard's authority was also undermined by the fact that no British men-of-war visited Lamu for months at a time, and Haggard was far removed from the comforts of home. He confessed to his brother as he approached the end of his first year in Lamu that after such "solitude and confinement," a man "would probably go mad or commit some other insanity."[74] The extent to which John G. Haggard's letters from Lamu to his family may have influenced the literary work of his brother, Rider Haggard, including his novels *King Solomon's Mines* and *She*, is a subject worthy of further study.[75]

In spite of the establishment of vice consulates and the navy's continued antislavery patrols, the slave trade persisted in modified form and was reinvigorated almost immediately after the destruction of the HMS *London* in 1884. The HMS *Philomel* captured two dhows near Sur carrying large shipments of slaves. The first, caught near Ras al-Hadd on October 13, 1884, was carrying 154 slaves (128 males and 26 females). Clearly by 1884 the slave trade had resurged.[76] The expansion of the use of dhows for the slave trade on Lake Nyasa indicates a growth of the slave trade between the interior to the coast in the final decades of the nineteenth century.[77] Gwyn Campbell has also shown a corresponding increase in the slave trade in the Mozambique Channel.[78]

Testimonies of enslaved Africans who sought manumission certificates from the British government at its consulates and agencies at Bahrain, Sharjah, and Muscat between 1907 and 1943 attest to a continued slave trade to the Gulf after 1873 as well. Of the ninety manumission testimonies described in chapter 4 that were given by enslaved Africans who specifically recalled being kidnapped from Africa (the same records include additional testimonies from *muwalid* slaves—born in Arabia—in addition to free Arabs of African descent who were kidnapped from other parts of Arabia, as well as Baluchi slaves) sixty-two petitioners (69 percent) recalled being kidnapped from Zanzibar and the Swahili Coast (East Africa) and twenty-eight (31 percent) recalled being kidnapped from northeast Africa (Ethiopia and Sudan in particular) between the years 1872 and 1927. While this sample size is too small for any generalizations about the dates of importations of all Africans to the Gulf, it does provide evidence that the slave trade continued into the twentieth century.[79] Of the sixty-two Africans who recalled being kidnapped from East Africa, thirty-two (more than half) were kidnapped between 1895 and 1910. About half of the Africans who recalled being kidnapped from northeast Africa (fifteen out of twenty-eight) were kidnapped between 1900 and 1919. If these limited figures provide even a rough guide, it may be supposed that the slave trade between East Africa and the Gulf persisted into the twentieth century and perhaps grew stronger after 1885, particularly between 1895 and 1910.[80] This increase also paralleled climatic events in Oman and East Africa (chapter 2) that influenced both supply and demand.

British naval patrols and diplomatic maneuverings may have reduced slave trafficking to eastern Arabia, but they did not eliminate it. Slave trading from East Africa to eastern Arabia continued and came to an end only decades later as a result of factors that were largely beyond Great Britain's control. As the previous chapters demonstrate, the growth of the slave trade to the Gulf was intimately connected with globalization and expanding markets for Gulf commodities. So long as these markets remained profitable, powerful incentives to import slaves persisted. Arab slave traders also quickly found ways to avoid detection by the Royal Navy. In response to the increased antislavery patrols in the Indian Ocean, slave traders resorted to various forms of evasion. The most observable immediate measures were forms of violent resistance to the boarding vessels employed by the British Navy. Some dhows returned fire on approaching British patrol boats. Others feigned surrender and waited for the boat to pull alongside before dropping heavy rocks and smashing holes in their hulls. Others cleared their decks and allowed marines to board while lying in wait and then ambushed them, spearing the marines through the sail.[81] A more popular form of evasion was running the dhows ashore. Often when dhow captains sighted British cruisers and it was clear that they could not outrun them, they would run their ships into shoals where the British craft could not go, or they would run aground, destroying the hulls of their own ships but buying sufficient time to disembark the slaves and hide inland, where the navy had no authority. In these cases, when possible, a small naval landing party would row ashore to measure the dhow in order to complete the necessary certificate for the crew to be paid its bounty. One dhow captured by the navy and sold as a prize fetched MT$200 in Muscat in 1852.[82] If the delivery of more than fifty slaves to Oman could be arranged later, the voyage could still be profitable for a dhow owner

"Encounter with Slave Dhow: HMS *London* off Zanzibar." *The Graphic*, December 17, 1881. Used by permission. © Illustrated London News Ltd./Mary Evans. Reference #10690948.

charging MT$4 per slave in freight. With cargoes of up to two hundred, the choice of running a dhow ashore was simple.[83]

Slave traders also took advantage of international law. Since it was forbidden for British cruisers to board French ships except to inspect papers, any dhow flying a French flag could transport slaves with impunity. Many dhow owners obtained French passes and flags at Nosy Bé, other ports in Madagascar, and later at Djibouti to transport legitimate cargo and then used the cover of the flag to transport slaves. Some dhow owners kept multiple flags and hoisted the French flag as a matter of convenience.[84] Yet another form of evasion was the use of false intelligence, which was employed at various times by Arab dhow captains and British naval captains alike. In 1861 the crew of the HMS *Lyra* was tricked by a faulty report by local residents about a departing slave dhow, only to learn that an actual shipment of slaves had occurred elsewhere immediately after the *Lyra*'s departure.[85] One ingenious use of false intelligence occurred in 1865 when "reliable reports" circulated that the HMS *Penguin* had foundered on a reef between

Marka and Brava. Consul Playfair sent another man-of-war to investigate, and when no report was heard, sent yet another man-of-war to look into its prolonged absence. With all three antislavery patrols up north, Zanzibar was left unguarded, and houses in town filled up with kidnapped and purchased slaves to be shipped. Playfair lamented that the slave trade was carried on in "the most open manner," and prices skyrocketed in the following days from $14 to $30–$40 (and even $70 temporarily) per slave in accordance with increased demand.[86] In fact, the *Penguin* had not been stuck on a reef but had captured two large dhows and had been forced to carry the large captures of slaves up to Aden. As the other two ships were in search of the *Penguin*, it was the only ship to make captures that season.[87]

Problems of Identity

In addition to its struggles with resources and resistance, the Royal Navy faced serious problems throughout its antislavery campaign in the Indian Ocean—namely, problems of identity, problems of perspective, and problems of "disposal." The first of these involved internal struggles with poor understanding of local conditions and populations: distinguishing who was enslaved in a world in which masters and slaves could share common traits and appearances. One particularly striking example from South Africa is illustrative. On August 24, 1864, a Muslim man named Mohammad 'Ali appealed to the consul general of the Ottoman Empire in Cape Town with a simple request. He sought the Ottoman consul's assistance in returning, along with about twenty of his compatriots, to his home in Zanzibar. As Mohammad 'Ali explained, he and twenty-seven others had been on a routine journey from Mombasa to Zanzibar five years earlier when their ship had been stopped by a British man-of-war on suspicion of involvement in the slave trade. They had, in fact, been trading commercial goods between Zanzibar, Muscat, the Comoro Islands, and other places on the East African coast for the Arab firm of Jamal bin Nasser and 'Abdullah bin Salem and had been on their way home to Zanzibar on October 9, 1859, when they were stopped and searched by the HMS *Lyra*. The British officers mistakenly assumed that the passengers and crew of the dhow were slaves. The passengers attempted in vain to explain that the eight women aboard were, in fact, the wives of eight of the merchants. In spite of their appeals, the crew of the *Lyra* transferred everyone onto the man-of-war, condemned the dhow as a slave trader, and burned it, as was the standard practice for suspected slave vessels deemed "unseaworthy" and incapable of being sailed or towed to port.[88]

Three months later, the *Lyra* conveyed the men and women to Cape Town, where they were officially determined to be slaves in the Vice Admiralty Court on January 23, 1860. They were then given to the collector of customs, W. S. Field, who, in accordance with his auxiliary function as the curator of liberated Africans for Cape Town, secured work for them with a local employer. Field recalled that "on landing they appeared to be more intelligent than most others here, and were able to earn a livelihood at once."[89] Mohammad 'Ali recalled that Field looked into their case and "was satisfied that we were not slaves," but "no provision was however made for us, and we were obliged to go and work for our daily bread." In his letter to the Turkish consul, Mohammad noted that since he and his companions were unacquainted with the languages of the Cape Colony, they were largely dependent on the charity of other Muslims for their survival. In 1864, they were employed by a Dutch man, J. A. H. Hecht, Esq., in Cape Town.[90]

The five-year delay in Mohammad 'Ali's appeal for his return to Zanzibar can partly be attributed to his lack of recourse. Field remained the curator of liberated Africans until his death in 1865. The presence of an Ottoman consul in Cape Town was something new in 1861—a legacy of bilateral treaties Britain had made with the Ottoman Empire following the Crimean War. The Treaty of Paris (1856) granted the British certain capitulations, including authority to protect the interests of Christian minorities and foreign merchants in Turkey, but it also allowed the Ottomans to act as protectors of Muslim minorities in certain British colonies such as the Cape. Petrus Roubaix's position as interim honorary consul for the Ottoman Empire between 1861 and 1889 marked an important turning point for Cape Muslims. Almost immediately after Roubaix's appointment, Malay Muslims appealed to the Ottoman sultan to provide them with a Muslim scholar to teach them Islamic theology and law. Sultan Abdülaziz appointed the Kurdish Iraqi jurist Abu Bakr Effendi to the Cape of Good Hope in 1862, and he became a leading figure in the development of the Muslim *ummah* (community of the faithful) in the colony. Whether Abu

Bakr Effendi had any direct association with Mohammad 'Ali and his Zanzibari companions is unclear, but Roubaix's reputation for serving the interests of the Muslim community at the Cape would certainly have been well known to the Zanzibaris.

The mistakenly captured Zanzibaris became a source of embarrassment for British authorities. The colonial secretary and the governor of Cape Colony appear to have initially buried the complaint and taken no action. A year later, seeing no resolution to the problem, Roubaix wrote twice to the governor of Cape Colony, stating that the Zanzibaris' claims were "of a painful and distressing nature" and that he considered it his "duty to use the best of my endeavors to obtain some kind of redress for the sufferers."[91] By late November 1865, Roubaix wrote to inform the governor that he had taken it upon himself to pay Mohammad 'Ali's way to Zanzibar to appeal to Sultan Mājid himself.[92] This message apparently got the attention of the governor. The following day he dispatched a letter to the political agent at Zanzibar, forwarding the details of the Zanzibaris' case in the following terms: "I have the honor to submit for your consideration copies of correspondence on the case of certain Arabs, who were brought here in one of Her Majesty's ships of war and condemned as slaves in 1860, but who assert that they were perfectly free when captured."[93] Yet when Sultan Mājid received news of the case, he drafted a letter to the Cape governor, requesting him to send the captives to Zanzibar, debit him the expenses, and punish the captain who had sent them there as the government saw fit.[94] As late as May 1866, Roubaix wrote to Mājid lamenting that nothing yet had been done, and the record of the case unfortunately ends here. Whether the group eventually managed to return to Zanzibar cannot be determined from the archival record.

Mohammad 'Ali and his colleagues were not the only "liberated" Africans to be taken to Cape Town in the nineteenth century. Many more "prize negroes"—as they were commonly known—preceded and followed this group of Zanzibaris.[95] They were also not the only free people to have wrongly been captured by the Royal Navy and "liberated" as slaves. What makes the case of Mohammad 'Ali and his compatriots such a compelling story is the fact that they asserted their freedom and their identity as Arabs at the same time that British authorities involved in the antislavery campaign considered them to be enslaved Africans.

Within a few years of the incident involving Mohammad 'Ali, many more cases of people wrongly captured came to light. In January 1869 at Aden— the most convenient port of adjudication for captures made off of the East African coast north of the Equator—General Edward Russell heard evidence from the officers of the HMS *Star* about captures made near Brava on the Somali coast. John G. Lynch, boatswain of the *Star*, recalled that after he presented his evidence on four of the dhows that his crew had captured the previous November, one of the supposed slaves among the captives declared himself not only to be free, but also to have been the captain and part owner of one of the destroyed dhows. He told the Vice Admiralty Court that the interpreter had intimidated him into silence and had even visited the other captives the day before the trial to warn them that "if any of them said they were free they would all be put in the sun and left to die."[96] In all, thirty-six free sailors were wrongly captured by the HMS *Star* that month. These individuals were eventually sent to Zanzibar, leading John Kirk, consul at Zanzibar, to remark that "such a mingling of slaves and freemen as has taken place in this instance, which is certainly no exception, could only occur through inefficient or dishonest interpreting." He added that "as a set, those who embark in our cruisers as interpreters are an illiterate and worthless set."[97]

Cases in the Vice Admiralty Court in Zanzibar supported Kirk's claims. Many interpreters lacked the language skills to fulfill their duties and therefore relied on guesswork or operated as "yes men" for officers already intent on taking prizes in order to take advantage of bounties awarded for rescued slaves and captured slave ships. Between 1866 and 1869 prize money for captured dhows was 30 shillings per ton plus £5 per slave landed alive.[98] John Kirk adjudicated a case in May 1869 in which the HMS *Nymphe* had destroyed a fishing boat captained by an Arab man named Hamad bin Sahel on the basis that the interpreter had found the captain's shipping pass to be out of date, it having been issued by the sultan of Zanzibar's authorities more than a year earlier. The captain had pleaded with the *Nymphe*'s crew, offering his fish, nets, and all of the dates he had aboard if he could keep his boat, but the commanding officer refused, considering the boat a fair prize since its pass had expired. Kirk examined the pass and found that it had in fact not expired, and he summoned the interpreter to explain himself. Kirk found that the interpreter was unable to read Arabic

"The East African Slave Trade: Examination of Captured Slaves in the British Consul General's Court at Zanzibar." *Illustrated London News*, December 17, 1881. Used by permission. © Illustrated London News Ltd./Mary Evans. Reference #10690947.

and had no knowledge of the Arabic months.[99] The prospects of a share in the antislavery bounties evidently proved too attractive for some translators, and graft abounded.

In 1870, when Consul Churchill was hearing a case against the captain of a boat seized near Brava by the HMS *Teazer*, it became clear to him that the interpreter in that case could not distinguish between the Swahili (and Arabic) words for thirty, fifty, sixty, or ninety and had condemned the vessel on the basis of his assumption that the ship had a cargo of fifty slaves instead of a combined crew and passenger list of around thirty people. The interpreter was himself a freedman who had been brought into service from the Seychelles and had little knowledge of Arabic or Swahili.[100] A case heard by John Kirk in the Vice Admiralty Court in Zanzibar in 1872 echoed this problem. Baraka, an enslaved man from Pemba of *mzalia* (or *muwalid*) status, had been seized by the HMS *Wolverine* from a dhow that was traveling from Zanzibar to Pemba because, when interrogated, he told the interpreter that he was going to *sell* cassava, and the interpreter understood him to say he was going to *be sold*. Kirk, who interviewed Baraka himself in Swahili, summoned the interpreter, a Somali man, and found that he was unable to speak Swahili and had in fact never been asked whether he could at the time he was recruited. He had been selected by the assistant political resident in Aden as an interpreter for the HMS *Forte* sometime earlier on the basis that he could speak Somali and Arabic, but he could neither speak Swahili nor read Arabic.[101] Erik Gilbert has demonstrated that many of these problems were linked to the Royal Navy's policy of granting cash bounties to sailors for the number of heads of slaves freed, as well as the size of the slaving vessels seized. The temptation for exaggerating the measurements of ships, destroying evidence, and "freeing" non-slaves was, therefore, great.[102]

Problems of Perspective

Another tragic element of the antislavery campaign was that many of the officials tasked with liberating slaves and caring for them were unsympathetic and sometimes even abusive toward their charges. The focus of such officials tended to be on earning bounties rather than improving the lives of captives. In his memoir, *Slave-Catching in the Indian Ocean*, Captain Philip Colomb likened the rescued Africans brought aboard his ship to animals such as dogs and sheep. Recalling the recently rescued Africans conveyed from Aden to Bombay under his command aboard the HMS *Dryad* in 1868, Colomb wrote, "I sometimes think I see in my dog's wistful eye something more of apprehension of surrounding circumstances than I could detect when I looked for it in the face of the ordinary rescued slave." Further, Colomb was not convinced that slavery was any worse for Africans than their being left alone in the interior. In his opinion, "Almost any change from the interior of Africa is a change for the better."[103] Captain G. J. Sullivan in his memoir, *Dhow Chasing in Zanzibar Waters*, used similar comparisons to animals and in some cases animal names. Sullivan called one heavyset Yao woman "the elephant" as "there was not a man or woman in the ship to be compared with this monster." Another freed slave was nicknamed "the toad." Sullivan also recalled that Consul Churchill, commissioned with manumitting slaves aboard Sullivan's ship, described Ngindo women, who were known for their use of decorative facial scarring, as not a tribe but "a new species altogether until then undiscovered; and for the benefit of natural historians he would call it 'Lumpy Kiboko' (Lumpy Hippo)."[104]

Both Colomb and Sullivan believed in a hierarchy of races aboard their ships, with Ethiopians and Oromos representing the most civilized and intelligent and with declining states of intelligence and beauty from groups from further south and further inland. Sullivan found that "the Galla language [was] the only one that appeared anything like completed and interesting." The languages of the "inferior tribes" of the interior seemed to him "but very limited in their words; broken ejaculations and oft repeated syllables produced monotony in the sounds."[105] (Repeated syllables, common in Bantu languages and other Niger-Congo languages, were also commonly seen as evidence of inferiority by those who associated such sounds in English with baby talk.) More familiar-sounding Afro-Asiatic languages sounded more sophisticated to Sullivan than the Niger-Congo languages. Likewise, Sullivan thought that Swahili, which he recognized to have been influenced by Arabic, had "more than probably become an improved language, owing to the intermingling of the Arabic with it." Crew aboard both men's ships had a habit of giving more attention and extra allotments of food to the Oromo women they found most attractive, creating feelings of resentment among other groups aboard and fueling divisions. Captain Sullivan also freely used the word "nigger" to describe East Africans and encouraged its use among his interpreters. Sullivan was struck by the way his African wards had "no special regard for anything on board" and the way they treated the first lieutenant, who had been charged with their care, "in their simple negro view of it [as if] he possessed a supernatural power, so that they had only to speak to him to get all they wanted in life." Sullivan recalled one instance in particular:

> On one occasion I came out and found him surrounded by negroes from every tribe talking away in their respective jargons to him, some wanting to have their disputes settled, rattling away as if they fully expected they were understood, others asking questions apparently about food, and some recounting with an air of the greatest mystery and importance something that had taken place between their tribe and another. "Huaga Yastakili, Kutiva, Katika, fumba," or some such words, were replied to with, "Oh! yes, of course, I perfectly agree with you." "Now suppose you and Marlborough and Sally, and Jim and Peggy, go grindum cornum

and boilum in the potum you have dinner, if not you have none."[106]

Problems of "Disposal"

A serious problem that dogged British officials in the Indian Ocean was the question of "disposal" of liberated Africans. The unfortunate term applied to the resettlement of freed slaves betrays an element of the expendability of liberated Africans in the official mind of civil servants tasked with liberation. Unlike the Atlantic, the Indian Ocean lacked an East African equivalent to Liberia or Sierra Leone, where "freed slaves" could be reliably disembarked. Officials had a very real fear that if African captives who were freed from slave dhows were simply put on shore they would immediately be re-enslaved. Disembarking captives anywhere other than a British port was frowned upon. But the nearest ports with courts of adjudication were Aden (1,300 miles away), Port Elizabeth (2,100 miles away), and Bombay, a distant 2,800 miles away—a journey of twenty days in 1860.[107] Until the opening of the Vice Admiralty Court at Zanzibar in 1868, all Africans captured aboard dhows off the northern coast of East Africa had to be kept on the decks of the British vessel until they could be disembarked at Aden. The limited deck space on most British men-of-war dictated the number of slaves that could be taken healthily on board, and in many cases cruisers had to make the lengthy return to Aden instead of making additional captures. In 1865 the HMS *Penguin* had to sit out most of the slaving season when it made two large captures of 120 and 140 slaves respectively and had to return to Aden both times, allowing many other ships carrying slaves to pass freely.[108]

In the 1860s, most captives were taken to Aden and Bombay, where a great many of them died shortly after arrival. In 1871, Bishop Tozer of Zanzibar determined that of the nearly 3,000 Africans captured from dhows and brought to Aden between 1865 and 1869, 35 percent (over 1,000) had died within five years. According to Bishop Tozer, Colonel Robert Lambert Playfair at Aden confirmed that in his experience, freed slaves landed at Aden were decimated within a year of landing there—"all from the same cause—disease of the lungs."[109] At Bombay the situation was similar. Between 1865 and 1869, nearly 2,500 freed Africans were received, and of these 31 percent (more than 750) died within five years.[110] In other words, a third of the Africans "liberated" by British cruisers and sent to Aden and Bombay died shortly after their "rescue."[111]

Whether aboard slaving vessels or antislavery ships, mortality rates among captive Africans were high. Evidence of mortality aboard the slaving vessels that traveled between East Africa and Arabia is sparse because in the quarter century that the East Indies Station patrolled the western Indian Ocean for slavers (between 1865 and 1889), the Royal Navy made only thirteen captures of large slave vessels anywhere near the Persian Gulf. The best documented of these captures was the case of the *Yasmeen*, caught off of Ras al-Hadd by the HMS *Vulture* in September 1872. Lt. Col. Edward C. Ross, in his role as consul and political agent at Muscat, examined the captain of the *Yasmeen* and learned that the ship had left Pemba sixteen days prior to reaching the shores of Oman. At Pemba, the ship had boarded 184 slaves, and 15 had died on the voyage. When picked up by the *Vulture*, the ship was found to have 169 aboard, and another 4 died by the time the *Vulture* arrived at Muscat four days later. Among the survivors, "a great many cases of small pox" were found.[112] If the case of the *Yasmeen* is any indication, the mortality rate among enslaved Africans shipped between East Africa and Arabia may be estimated at around 10 percent.

Mortality was also high among captives taken aboard British ships. Probably the most famous case of disease ravaging the population of recaptured Africans was that of the *Progresso*, a Portuguese/Brazilian slaving ship bound from Mozambique to Rio de Janeiro on April 13, 1843. Captured at sea by the HMS *Cleopatra*, the 140-ton *Progresso* was escorted to Port Natal. It had 447 Africans (189 men, 45 women, and 213 boys) crammed aboard in a hold 37 feet by 21.5 feet and only 3.5 feet high. It was decided to put 50 of the captives aboard the *Cleopatra* and leave the remainder on the *Progresso*. When the ships finally arrived at Port Natal fifty days later, 1 of the 50 captives placed on the *Cleopatra* had died, but fully 175 of the 397 who were left aboard the *Progresso* had died, most from disease.[113]

Smallpox was one of the most serious problems aboard antislavery cruisers. In 1868, Admiral Heath praised Commander De Kantzsow for his "most judicious arrangements," which prevented the spread of the disease to the crew of the *Star*.[114] In ten days, between November 4 and 13, 1868, the HMS *Star* had destroyed twenty-four dhows and had taken captive 134 presumed slaves off the coast of Somalia. Two days en route to Aden, smallpox was discovered among 2 of the captives. Two more cases were found the next day, and on November 20, 2 captives died. Two days later, another died, followed by another on December 2. By the time the *Star* arrived at Aden on December 17, 7 of the 134 captives had died and a stoker among the ship's crew had been diagnosed with smallpox. De Kantzsow limited the spread of the disease by placing those diagnosed in two cutters that were dragged behind the ship and then destroyed upon arrival in Aden.[115]

The same year, the HMS *Daphne* captured seventeen dhows and took 305 captives, several of whom were diagnosed with smallpox. The records state that a total of 291 captives landed at the Seychelles that year, indicating that perhaps 14 died of smallpox before arrival.[116] Sullivan himself put the number of dead at 16, with another 14 diagnosed with smallpox by the time they arrived. When Sullivan returned to the island in the *Daphne* four months later, he heard that 50 of those landed had died of smallpox. If accurate, this would put the number of dead from smallpox among the 305 captives at 66 (more than 20 percent).[117]

Naval instructions as of 1869 required that officers take captured slave vessels to the closest port of adjudication, where the cases could be heard by an admiralty or vice admiralty court. An exception could be made if a captured vessel was deemed to be "unseaworthy" or would endanger the lives of the crew if it were attempted to be towed to port.[118] The following year, Admiral Heath argued that making "a depot of freed slaves at Zanzibar, the very centre of the slave trade" was a "bold" but "in many respects wise proposal" because it would save cruisers the trouble of sailing to the Seychelles or Aden. "It is of the greatest advantage to our cruisers," he explained, "that their condemned cargoes should at once be taken out of them."[119] In the second half of the nineteenth century, British cruisers had several options for disembarking their captives: Aden, Bombay, the Seychelles, Mauritius, Natal, Cape Town, Zanzibar (where liberated Africans were sent to the Church Missionary Society [CMS] mission, the Universities' Mission to Central Africa [UMCA] mission, the Roman Catholic mission, the sultan, or "in town"), and, later, the mainland of East Africa (the CMS missions at Frere Town and Rabai and the Spiritan mission at Bagamoyo, where Stanley observed 170 freed slaves deposited

"Slaves Rescued from Arab Dhow near Zanzibar" [HMS *Philomel*, April 1893]. Courtesy Beinecke Rare Book and Manuscript Library, Yale University. The Land of Zenj Photograph Collection. General Collection, Box 6, Folder 41, Image #4.

from British cruisers in 1874).[120] But each of these points of "disposal" had its problems.

By the late 1880s, with very few exceptions, captures were made in the immediate vicinity of Zanzibar, and liberated Africans were "disposed of" at one of four nearby locations: the UMCA mission at Zanzibar, the French mission at Zanzibar, the CMS Frere Town mission in Mombasa, and in Zanzibar Town. The HMS *Garnet*, for example, captured eleven dhows on suspicion of slave trading between November 1887 and June 1888, and from these eleven dhows, 231 captives were liberated, 4 of whom died before they could be disembarked. Of the remaining 227 captives, 24 went to the UMCA mission, 56 went to Frere Town, 42 went to the French mission at Zanzibar, and 105 were placed "in town."[121] Some of the liberated Africans who were placed "in town" in the 1880s were recruited into the sultan of Zanzibar's military. An account that was undoubtedly influenced by personal recollections of naval crews at Zanzibar provides a glimpse into local perceptions of placement "in town."

"What becomes of the slaves that are liberated when the dhows are captured?" said I.

"Oh, the boys are sent to the Boys' Mission Schools at Zanzibar, and the girls to the Female Mission there also; while the men folk, at least all the able-bodied and strong ones that are not too old, are enlisted into the sultan's army—the Sultan of Zanzibar, I mean, the Seyyid Burgash that was. When I was there, the commander of his army was a lieutenant of our navy who had been 'lent' by government for the purpose for three years, and now he has left the service altogether and is known as 'General Matthews' on the east coast. A right smart chap he is too, for he drilled the niggers as well as if he were a born sojer instead of a sailor!"

"Do the slaves like this business?" I asked, thinking that their "freedom" seemed rather questionable; and then, too, consider the cost both in men and money it is to England every year.

"Well, I don't believe they do," answered the ex-man-o'-war's man—"I've heard some of them say that they were quite contented to work on the clove plantations, and preferred that to loafing about the streets of Zanzibar, where hundreds of them are to be seen every day, with nothing to do and very little to eat, unless they take to thieving!"[122]

A potential breakthrough in the problem of "disposal" came with the new CMS mission at Frere Town, established near Mombasa in 1875. The future of the Frere Town mission was presaged by an interview before the Royal Commission on Fugitive Slaves the same year:

> SIR LEOPOLD HEATH—What I have suggested would be, I suppose, a sort of centre from which civilization would radiate into the interior?
>
> CAPTAIN SULLIVAN—Yes, but a great guard must be put against the Arabs, and the Indian population, bringing their habits and their customs, their religion, their vices, and their influences into such a place.
>
> HEATH—It would be different from Liberia in that it would be under English rule, whereas Liberia, I think, is under the rule of these uneducated blacks, is it not?

SULLIVAN—It would be entirely under the rule of an English staff.
HEATH—That is the difference between what you are suggesting, and the state of things at Liberia. Liberia is ruled by blacks themselves?
SULLIVAN—Yes.[123]

With the first large influx of captives at the CMS mission at Frere Town in 1875, Reverend William Price "collected all the adult freed slaves—more than 200—and George David (the 'native catechist') [who had been brought from the CMS Nasik mission near Bombay] endeavoured to impress upon their minds two truths which are at the foundation of all true religion—the being and omnipotence of God." Price observed that George David, after stating that there is a God and that He is everywhere present, began teaching his pupils through rote memorization:

> He expressed the substance of his teaching in the following formula:—"Muungu Killa pahali yupa, jun na thun" ("God is in every place, above and below"); and then, dividing his audience into several groups, he patiently persevered with each group, till they could not only repeat the words after him, but utter them without his assistance. I am within the mark when I say that he repeated the words at least 300 times. The exercise lasted an hour and a half, and the patient teacher was rewarded at last by imprinting on the minds of his rather obtuse pupils. This may seem a small result; but it was worth the labor. Minds full of darkness do not easily open to the first rays of spiritual light.[124]

Initially the Frere Town mission was widely hailed as a success. According to a census taken by Reverend Price in 1876, the mission had 115 men in residence (52 of whom were baptized), 84 women (32 baptized), and 143 children (111 baptized), for a total of 342 liberated Africans. Nearby Rabai station had 31 men (30 baptized), 24 women (23 baptized), and 37 children (15 baptized), for a total of 92 residents.[125] But Frere Town soon developed some problems. In July 1881 reports received at the consul's office in Zanzibar about abuses of liberated Africans by CMS missionaries at Frere Town prompted an investigation by Frederick Holmwood and Commander Mather Byles of the HMS *Seagull*. Byles reported that he observed evidence of severe beatings among some of the liberated Africans at Frere Town and that the presiding lay superintendent of the mission, J. R. Streeter, did not deny that he had beaten nearly every African in residence at one time or another, arguing that the discipline of the place required corporal punishment. Byles wrote that he had freed numerous fugitive slaves in his duties with the East Indies Station, "but none of them had been beaten as severely as the two men I saw at the mission." The stick with which they were beaten, he explained, was "one with the most punishing nature that can be found in any part of the globe." The two men, he considered, "had their constitutions quite shattered by the flogging. Another man still showed scars of a beating more than two years before." What horrified him most, Byles said, "was when I saw the number of young, well dressed, and decent looking married Christian women that presented themselves before the consul and stated they had been flogged." Mr. Streeter informed the investigators that he flogged supposed culprits as it was the only way to make them confess to their crimes. Byles found Streeter's practices revolting and an embarrassment to both the CMS and England.[126] Streeter was recalled and Reverend Price was sent from England to Frere Town to sort out the mess.[127]

One of the great ironies of British antislavery efforts in the Indian Ocean was that similar fates met both enslaved Africans in Arabia and those liberated slaves placed by cruisers at the various depots around the Indian Ocean. Both were forced to provide labor for their overseers. Both were given new names and new clothes. Around the Indian Ocean, on Christian missions at which Africans captured on the high seas by British cruisers were deposited, liberated Africans were made to labor on plantations producing both the food they ate and cash crops to subsidize the costs of the missions. This irony was not lost on local populations. On Zanzibar, freed slaves at British mission stations were known as *watumwa wa Wangereza*, "slaves of the British."[128] Reverend William Bartlett Chancellor closed an April 1877 letter from the CMS mission in the Seychelles by boasting that the cash crops at Venn's Town (vanilla, cocoa, coffee, and cloves), which liberated Africans and support staff at the mission were cultivating under his direction, were "coming on well, especially the cocoa which is really beautiful." Then in the next sentence, he wrote: "Please send me out a book on the cultivation of the above plants and their preparation for the market." That part of the operation had not been planned. Liberated Africans were to be taught a work ethic even if the fruits of their labor had no immediate outlet and their wardens had no real training to offer.[129]

Liberated Africans who were delivered to Bombay were sent to work in railway construction, apprenticed in workshops of the railway company, or employed in the port or by the police. Others were sent to the India government's model farms at Khandesh and Badgaon Farm.[130] At Aden, according to Brigadier Coghlan, the former resident, there was little difficulty finding work for liberated Africans while their numbers were few. "I released the men, and let them take their chance as free labourers, and the women I apportioned amongst the respectable families."[131] By 1868, however, Coghlan's successor, Edward Russell, when confronted by a series of large deliveries of freed slaves, complained that he could not "yet find suitable employment and protection for the slaves landed in March last." He had too many freed slaves already on hand and stated, "I am of the opinion that the landing of slaves at this port to be kept a considerable time under surveillance is, to the unfortunate beings, a state of slavery."[132]

As Christopher Saunders has shown, "prize negroes" were in high demand in Cape Town and Natal for their work in urban centers and on plantations. "Prize negroes" were assigned to indentured contracts of three to five years. Planters petitioned the government for more when supplies of "freed slave" labor ran out.[133] When sugar prices soared in the 1870s, sugar planters in Natal requested that the government supply them with "freed slaves" to work on their plantations. According to Patrick Harries, between 1873 and 1880 almost six hundred "Makua" or "Zanzibari" recaptives were "freed" in Durban, "where they were immediately bound to serve labour contracts ranging from three to five years in length."[134] In 1876, Admiral Cummings testified that Natal had become a more convenient depot for freed slaves. "For instance, in the colony of Natal they agree to pay the expenses of liberated slaves." A monthly ship that passed from Aden to Natal stopped off at Zanzibar and could take liberated slaves to the colony at its expense. It had thus become more convenient to land captives at the Vice Admiralty Court at Zanzibar and send them on to Natal from there.[135]

Most disconcerting to observers back in Great Britain, however, were reports that British officials were "selling" the labor of freed Africans to planters in the Seychelles and Mauritius. Such a claim was made by Henry Morton Stanley in a public meeting in 1872 and reported in *The Times* of London.[136] In testimony before the Royal Commission on Fugitive Slaves in March 1876, Francis Fleming, a former acting magistrate in the Seychelles, recalled that during his tenure in 1874 he observed British men-of-war landing freed slaves three or four times. Fleming testified that after a short time in government care, liberated Africans were indentured into five-year contracts "like the Coolies." He stated that "they are in want of labour in the Seychelles and when a cargo of slaves arrives the applications are very numerous for them."[137] Likewise Captain Sullivan stated that the problem with landing freed slaves at the Seychelles was that "although they are very welcome there, they fall into the hands of the French creoles or half castes; and at one time the miserable pittance which they received from their employers made their condition worse than slavery, but afterwards they increased the allowance." As late as 1870, he said, liberated Africans sent to the Seychelles were put to work cultivating the land for creole farmers producing coconuts and manufacturing coconut oil. He thought that even though they were technically set free after two or three years of indenture, "by that time their condition has become second nature, and although they are set free I do not suppose that they look much above it; they can never get back to the mainland again." Their only option for survival if not working for a planter was fishing.[138]

In matters of family life, Africans who were enslaved in Arabia and those who were liberated by British cruisers had similar experiences. The marriages at the various depots for freed slaves around the Indian Ocean were arranged by missionaries just as marriage contracts of enslaved men and women in the Gulf were arranged by their masters. Missionaries often paired their charges with one another and oversaw their marriages. Reverend Chancellor reported how he had arranged the marriages for some of his first pupils at Venn's Town in the Seychelles: "Last Saturday I paired off our big boys and girls for marriage. It was an amusing but somewhat difficult task. Billy loved Dolly and Omen was smitten with Anna but Dolly fancied Omen and Anna wanted Billy. At last after a little maneuvering I, at least I fancy I did, succeeded in inducing the boys to love the girls who loved them."[139] At Aden, Sister Mary explained to Bartle Frere that girls at the convent "remain with us until we can have them married or placed in service."[140] At Frere Town, Reverend Price married off his charges in a manner similar to Chancellor's at the Seychelles:

> *December 21st*—Went to Frere Town and married fourteen couples of the freed slaves. It was an occasion of some little excitement and amusement. The men and women were grouped apart, and then the men, as their names came up, were asked to name the objects of their choice. This, in most cases, they were unable to do, and there was nothing for it but for the would-be husband to enter the charmed circle and lead off the object of his affection. Generally there seemed to be a preconcerted arrangement between the parties, but not always. One unfortunate wight came forward, and, on looking round on the galaxy of black beauties, was so bewildered, that he was unable to fix his choice on any one in particular. With a peculiar nervous shrug and a crimson blush which was all but visible through his black skin, he said, 'I should be very happy to marry them, but don't know who will have me.' He subsided amidst a roar of laughter from his companions, and his case was of course postponed. Another no sooner pointed out the lady of his selection than she coquettishly turned her back upon him, and began to stare vacantly in an opposite direction. I said, 'Very well, no compulsion; let him stand aside.' This was more than she expected; she only wanted to be wooed and won like others of her sex, and seeing that under the circumstances this process was inadmissible, she quickly relented, and gladly suffered herself to be led away to the group of selected brides. The number being completed, I took each couple separately, and, joining their hands, required them 'to pledge their troth either to other.' It is a pleasant thing to feel that one has made twenty-eight people happy; for though in one sense their happiness is sublunary, it is according to God's ordinance. The number was only limited by the number of cottages ready for married couples. By next week we hope to have as many more.[141]

Although some attention was paid to the preferences of both the men and women at Frere Town, the pairing of couples was largely a matter of convenience and, as was the custom with enslaved Africans in the Gulf, conducted at the behest of the masters.

Africans caught up in the vicious conditions of slavery in the western Indian Ocean faced similar prospects whether enslaved or "liberated" by British cruisers along the way. Whether landed in Arabia or caught at sea, their chances of survival were limited by the risks of disease and conditions upon arrival at their ultimate destinations. As Prestholdt has shown, both enslavers and redeemers sought to remake these individuals in their own images, beginning with removing their birth names and replacing them with new ones and providing them with new languages and religions. Both enslavers and redeemers used African labor freely and controlled elements of the Africans' personal lives, including their marriage partners and their livelihoods. Whether they remained enslaved or were "freed" as part of the western Indian Ocean antislavery campaign, many of these individuals lived parallel lives.

Although it may seem to us today as paradoxical, British antislavery did not promote notions of racial equality but rather applied, albeit unevenly, efforts that sought to end the slave trade without acknowledging Africans as equal to Europeans. As Richard Huzzey has demonstrated, British antislavery did not develop a radical anti-racist or anti-imperial perspective. Instead, "the triumph of antislavery ideas, ironically, gave a new life to British racial prejudice."[142] British antislavery action in the Indian Ocean reached its apex in the decades surrounding the 1865 Morant Bay Rebellion in Jamaica, which was taken as "an explicit demonstration of the failure of British emancipation policy and as evidence of the former slaves' incapacity for responsible citizenship."[143] The violence of Morant Bay confirmed for many mid-Victorians that blacks were unsuited to freedom. The decline in sugar production in Jamaica in the twenty years following abolition was popularly seen as "the direct result of the indolence of free black labour." In the aftermath of the rebellion, British public intellectuals, including Thomas Carlyle, John Tyndale, and Joseph Hooker, and leading newspapers such as *The Times* and the *Standard* described Africans as a uniquely savage and indolent race "unsuited for freedom."[144] If British antislavery efforts appear in retrospect to have been haphazard and uneven, that was at least partially because Africans were increasingly deemed to neither understand nor deserve the freedom British officials were working to provide. And slavery, after all, was vital to the Gulf economy. But as the next chapter explains, that fact was about to change.

6

GLOBALIZATION AND THE END OF THE EAST AFRICAN SLAVE TRADE

In 1902, the United States Department of Agriculture (USDA) sent a plant explorer to bring back offshoots of date palms from Iraq, Baluchistan, and Muscat, and another explorer obtained further selections from Algeria and Tunisia in 1905.[1] The USDA had previously arranged through correspondence the import of sixty-eight young palms, mostly seedlings, and distributed them among experimental stations in Yuma, Arizona; Las Cruces, New Mexico; and four stations in California back in 1890. But it was David Fairchild, an agricultural explorer for the USDA Bureau of Plant Industry, who initiated the first site visit to the Gulf that would secure the best offshoots for propagation in California. He visited Muscat in February 1902 in a steamer full of Shi'a pilgrims on their way to Karbala. In Muscat he arranged for the American consul to secure offshoots of *fardh* dates from the Semail Valley and send them to Bombay, where he would pick them up and ship them to California.[2] He then visited Bahrain, where he arranged to have some offshoots of the *khalāsa* date from Hofūf in Hasa (now in Saudi Arabia) sent to Bombay as well. At Basra, he collected samples of several date palms, including the popular *halāwī* variety. He subsequently steamed up the Tigris to Baghdad, collecting samples of dates from the largest date growers around Baghdad, and packed the offshoots in mud-filled burlap sacks, boxed them, and transported them on a nine-week passage to Washington, DC. Three decades later, Fairchild was pleased to report that several of the varieties he had brought from the Gulf were being grown in the Coachella Valley in California around Mecca.[3] Fairchild encountered Africans on every length of his voyage in the Gulf. His diaries indicate that he was fascinated by the persistence of slavery in the region and the presence of African slaves. He photographed several of them, and he appears to have asked local authorities about them. From one of his notebooks, it appears that he was told by someone that *halwa*, the Omani sweetmeat, was made from the breast milk of African slave women, although he subsequently discovered the hoax and crossed out the entry and wrote "not true" in the margin. He photographed the enslaved Africans who carried passengers ashore in Muscat and the African porters and rowers aboard rowboats in Bahrain. When he photographed the African servant of the Bahrain political agent, he took care to identify him as a slave but not the slave of the British officer (who had hired the man and paid him a daily wage). Enslaved Africans were still ubiquitous in the Gulf during Fairchild's visit in 1902, as demand for their labor was still high. But that demand was about to diminish. Fairchild was a harbinger of new economic realities that would confront the Gulf in the following decades and would reduce the demand for African labor and eventually help eliminate the East African slave trade.[4]

This chapter describes how global economic forces drove the catastrophic collapse of the Gulf's two leading industries in the 1920s and 1930s and how this collapse affected the slave trade and the lives of enslaved Africans in the Gulf. This chapter introduces some of the men who helped to unmake the Gulf economy and unwittingly eradicate demand for slave labor in the Gulf. These men include David Fairchild, the plant explorer best known for importing the famous cherry blossoms of Washington, DC; Mikimoto, the Japanese cultured pearl magnate; and Paul Popenoe, a California horticulturalist best known for championing eugenics. Mikimoto, the son of a noodle maker, perfected the process of culturing pearls and used industrial technology to mass-produce and market cultured pearls at the peak of the gem's popularity. At the same time, Paul Popenoe brought offshoots of the best varieties of Gulf date palms back to propagate in California. Popenoe followed the trail first blazed by Fairchild. The more developed economies of Japan and the United States replaced the Gulf's exotic exports with products of their own, and in only a few years the Gulf's date and pearl industries declined sharply and, with the onset of the Great Depression, ultimately collapsed. At the same time, pearls and dates transformed Japan and California. Japan's Tatoku Island earned fame from Mikimoto's female pearl divers, while the Coachella Valley in southern California sprouted towns like Mecca, Arabia, and Biskra (and even a high school with "Arabs" as its mascot). With the date and pearl industries in tatters, African labor declined in importance in the Gulf. This decline in demand was the greatest contributor to the decline in the slave trade to the Gulf from East Africa. There were two other factors influencing this decline: the unlikely intervention by the Portuguese on the coast of Mozambique and catastrophic economic conditions in Baluchistan, which led the Baluchi slave trade to replace the East African slave trade as the primary source for slaves in the Gulf.

The Decline of the Date Export Industry

Just as quickly as globalization had created vibrant export industries in the Gulf, it ushered in their demise. The Gulf's key date market in North America dwindled as soon as the United States developed a date industry of its own in California. There were no palms in Palm Springs until the twentieth century, when plant explorers like Popenoe, sponsored by the USDA, engaged in what Londa Scheibinger calls "biopiracy," a profession as old as the Columbian Exchange.[5]

Fairchild's visit to the Gulf in 1902 was not accidental. The USDA had long recognized the value of date imports from the Gulf and the potential to undercut those imports by developing an American date industry. After extensive study, the USDA determined that the best soil and climate for date production in the United States was in the Salton Basin in California. In 1905, water from the Colorado River, which was being diverted to the Imperial Valley for irrigation, broke through its canal system and produced a rush of water into the Salton Basin. Before the canal system was finally restored, the Colorado flowed for two years into the basin and formed the Salton Sea, now a permanent feature of California's landscape. The accidental flooding and the addition of a new system of canals from the Colorado River to the Coachella Valley created the perfect environment for growing date palms.[6] Soon after, Popenoe, who had a stake in a farm in Thermal, California, visited the Gulf in 1912 and purchased offshoots of the most desirable varieties and brought back nine thousand young palm trees, including the beloved *fardh* variety.[7] Together the visits by Fairchild and Popenoe would spell the beginning of the end for Gulf date exports to the United States.

Paul Popenoe and the End of the Gulf's American Date Market

Years before he became known as the leading proponent for eugenics in the United States, Paul Popenoe was a date farmer. Popenoe would ultimately come to edit the *Journal of Heredity*, head the Human Betterment Foundation, and advocate publicly for eugenic sterilization of individuals with physical and mental handicaps, but he discovered his interest in heredity while propagating dates in the desert of southern California. Popenoe also unintentionally became an agent behind the steep decline in the Gulf date export market to the United States in the 1920s and indirectly to the decline in demand for African labor in the Gulf.

Popenoe visited the Gulf in order to bring back offshoots of the best varieties of dates for propagation in California. He was ostensibly traveling on behalf of his father's horticulture business, West India Gardens of Altadena, but he also carried letters of introduction from the USDA and had a standing job offer from the USDA's Bureau of Plant Propagation. Popenoe had visited Algeria and brought back North African varieties of dates for his father's experimental farm in the Coachella Valley. After some initial success with these palms, Popenoe went to the source of the American imports to bring back the varieties that were already popular in the United States. His voyage to Arabia in 1912–1913 demonstrates how the technologies that made possible the extension of Gulf products to global markets could also lead to their downfall. Popenoe successfully used steamships, telegraphs, river freighters, international lines of credit, and a network of American diplomats, merchants, and missionaries to successfully negotiate a foreign business environment and bring back the key to creating California's date industry.

The twenty-five-year-old horticulturalist arrived in Muscat on October 21, 1912, aboard the S.S. *Kasara* from Karachi in the company of his younger brother, Wilson. In their letters home, both professed amazement at what "a fine clean little town" Muscat was, with its vibrant market, a population of thirty or forty thousand, and twin refurbished Portuguese forts overlooking the harbor with cannons on display and watchmen calling out the all-clear at regular intervals between the towers. The weather was much like what the men were accustomed to in southern California: "decidedly comfortable." Wilson likened the city to Avalon on Catalina Island and marveled that the sultan had electric lights and a telephone in his palace and that the town now had a functioning hospital. The British consulate's tennis court was busy with sailors from the five British gunboats in the harbor, and the sailors also found cheap entertainment from boys who would dive from rocks for pennies.[8] The Popenoes found ten Europeans and Americans in residence in Muscat. Among them, Homer Brett, the American consul, a southern gentleman from Mississippi who Paul reckoned to be about fifty years old, made all of their local arrangements. In response to an inquiry from Paul earlier in the year and a USDA letter of introduction, Brett secured the sultan's permission for himself and Paul Popenoe to travel into the Semail Valley. The sultan, Faisal bin Tūrkī, also offered to provide camels, letters of introduction to seven allied sheikhs in the area, and an armed escort.[9]

Popenoe interpreted the sultan's gesture as one of mutual benefit: "He likes to send out an occasional party under his protection that possesses some importance, just to show the upcountry chiefs that he still has friends."[10] In fact, the sultan's authority in the interior of Oman was considerably weak, and even his control over the city of Muscat was occasionally threatened by raids from rival sheikhs. But if sponsoring an American explorer's trip into the country's richest date-producing region for the purpose of creating a rival market in California was the sultan's idea of a self-strengthening measure, the plan backfired. Popenoe's sojourn to the Semail Valley was twice met by ambush, and the sultan was obliged to send a force of 3,500 men the following month to avenge the insult.[11] Within months the Imamate Rebellion was under way, and the interior of Oman elected its own imam in opposition to the sultan and waged a civil war that effectively divided Oman for decades. Then, of course, Popenoe would ultimately make things much worse by bringing Muscat's prized commodity to California to undercut a major portion of Oman's economy.

After paying a visit to Wells Thoms, the American missionary doctor at the Mutrah hospital, Popenoe and Brett followed the coast to the Semail

Valley and then followed the valley seventy miles into the interior, traveling in the mornings and evenings in order to avoid the heat of the day and staying with the sultan's cousins and allies along the way. All together they were gone about a week. Popenoe found about forty varieties of dates growing in the valley, although he estimated that about two-thirds of the palms under cultivation were the *fardh* variety, a testament to the importance of the American market. He noted that the fort overlooking the valley was armed with ten cannons (one of which worked) and a garrison of fourteen guards. The working cannon fired a shot each night at 9 p.m., when the gates to the fort closed. Popenoe had been studying Arabic for about a year and had visited date-producing parts of North Africa so he could hold his own in discussions about dates, but Brett knew no Arabic and, according to Popenoe, had "absolutely no knowledge of Arab ways," although he had been in Muscat for a year. The two Americans were entirely dependent on their translator and guide. Popenoe wore a pith helmet.[12]

When they returned to Muscat, Popenoe set about arranging to ship five hundred offshoots, including two hundred of the popular *fardh* variety

Paul Popenoe with his shipment of date offshoots, Basra, 1913. Courtesy American Heritage Center, University of Wyoming. Paul Popenoe Collection, Box 175, Folder 6.

and an anticipated one hundred of the prized *khalāsa* variety, widely regarded as the best variety in Arabia and native to Hofūf but grown in limited quantities in the Semail Valley. On Brett's recommendation, Popenoe commissioned a local merchant named Muhammad Fazel, who Brett considered "the honestest man in Masqat," to secure and pack the offshoots and prepare them for export. He doubted whether he could actually manage to get any more than fifty offshoots of *khalāsa* dates since the British government had just bought up two hundred of them and sent them to Zanzibar. Popenoe left Muscat and headed on to Basra on a passenger steamer.[13]

Popenoe arrived to find Basra bustling with activity. The date-packing season was in high gear, and the whole Shat al-Arab north of Mohammerah was crammed with "innumerable" date-packing sheds and workers loading piles of boxes into lighters. Popenoe found Basra harbor full of at least "a dozen big ocean steamers," in addition to "any number of smaller craft, making it look much busier than lots of big ports I have seen."[14] His first order of business was to meet with H. P. Chalk, the manager of the Hills Brothers Company's operations at Basra, whom David Fairchild of the USDA had written to request aid for Popenoe. Fairchild had visited Basra in 1902 and had relied on Chalk to secure a few offshoots of Basra varieties, which he sent to the USDA research station in Yuma, Arizona. Fairchild took care to acknowledge Chalk in an article he wrote for *National Geographic*, appreciation that could not have pleased Chalk's employers in New York.[15]

Chalk realized that helping Popenoe could jeopardize his own career. A new, rival date-production center in California was the last thing Hills Brothers could have wanted. Chalk evidently hoped to drag his feet long enough that Popenoe would leave in frustration, but Popenoe was determined. "Every day he says, 'tomorrow,'" Popenoe complained. "He is a pin-headed Britisher who has got the idea that we are going to ruin his business by competition, he is too lazy to improve his own scandalously slack methods by which he might hold his own with us, so he is down on us."[16] Popenoe recalled their first meeting:

> When I met him he exclaimed, "So you are one of the men who is going to take the bread out of our mouths, are you?" "On the

contrary," I replied. "We Californians are going to make you richer by increasing your sales." Then I went on to point out how ridiculously small the total consumption of dates in America was at present, how it was certain to jump as the public became acquainted with fresh, clean, attractive dates, and how, as California would be unable to supply more than a fraction of the demand for many years to come, the public would buy Busreh dates because they could not get the California product. "Dates of some kind they must and will have," I concluded, "and the demand is going to grow twice as fast as the supply that either you or we can turn out."[17]

However disingenuous, Popenoe nevertheless managed to secure offshoots of the most popular Basra varieties: *khadhrāwī, barhi, halāwī*. Chalk eventually gave in to Popenoe's requests and introduced him to a prominent date grower in Basra named Yusef bin Ahmed.[18] Despite Chalk's initial protests, the Hills Brothers Company was an essential part of Popenoe's success in Basra. But Popenoe would never have succeeded in his efforts without a global support network, and in particular the help of the American missionaries in the Gulf. As mentioned in the introduction, the Reformed Church in America (or Dutch Reformed denomination) had established a series of mission hospitals in the Gulf through the church's Arabian Mission. The Cantine, Bennett, and Van Vlack families took pity on the Popenoe brothers, who were attempting to maintain their vegetarian diet living in an international guest house. The missionaries allowed the Popenoes to stay in the mission house and allowed them to pay only the lowest possible missionary rates for their room and board. Then when Paul came down with typhoid and suffered for several weeks from high fevers and delirium, the missionary doctors nursed him back to health.[19] Ultimately, the American connections paid off, and the Hills Brothers Company agreed to a contract to secure date offshoots from Basra for a commission of 450 rupees plus expenses.[20]

Popenoe then took advantage of the regular steamer service on the Tigris River to travel north to Baghdad aboard the *Julnar*, one of three steamers operated by the Euphrates and Tigris Steam Navigation Company, a British firm whose business was limited by Ottoman regulations to three ships in order to privilege its rival Turkish company, Jaafer. (In retaliation for the restrictions, the *Julnar* carried a large barge on each side to treble its carrying capacity.)[21] At Baghdad, Popenoe settled into the British club and hired a young mixed-race assistant, Nasuri bin Anton al-Baghdadī, from his hotel in Basra to accompany him as he met important date growers of the region. His first appointments were with the growers Hajji Abdul-Rahmān and Mullah Naji al-Hajj.[22] One of his most important connections in Baghdad was a Kurdish sheikh named Peshaga ibn Sagakia. According to Popenoe, he had been driven out of Persia in a quarrel and had immigrated to Baghdad with most of his community. Popenoe was startled to learn that the workers who assembled his order of offshoots were unpaid. After inquiry, he reported: "The sheikh and his tribesmen formed a sort of feudal community in Baghdad: he provided them with what money they needed for the necessities of life, and in return they worked for him on the various porterage and packing jobs that he had undertaken. All the money from the contracts went to him, and they worked at his bidding. . . . The chief handled an immense amount of business with two or three hundred men always at his call. . . . But that such a system of feudal organization could be extended into the modern business world was rather startling."[23]

Popenoe engaged Peshaga in a contract to procure five hundred offshoots from Bedra and transship them to Kūt. (The contract listed Popenoe as "Paul ibn Bobno.")[24] Popenoe's main business partner in Baghdad was a merchant named Seyd Rawf, whose full name is unfortunately not preserved in Popenoe's records but who likely secured more than two thousand offshoots.

Popenoe sent his brother, Wilson, down to Basra to oversee the packing of the dates from Basra and Muscat, while Paul wrapped up his sales in Baghdad and steamed down the Tigris by way of Kūt to pick up his order of 450 offshoots from Peshaga.[25] Wilson arrived in Basra to find the packing well under way, although not to his satisfaction. Wilson thought that it was "a mighty good thing I came down here, with particular emphasis on the mighty." Tomlinson of Hills Brothers had turned the packing of the palms over to a subcontractor who was not using sufficient burlap to protect the offshoots on their journey to the United States. "I tell you the way that nigger was doing the job actually made me sick," Wilson wrote, explaining how he tore open all of the palms that had been packed and

Paul Popenoe and Mullah Najji, Iraq, 1913. Courtesy American Heritage Center, University of Wyoming. Paul Popenoe Collection, Box 175, Folder 4.

made the worker repack them under his supervision. The Basra dates were complemented by the arrival of the Muscat dates and about 400 *khalāsa* dates from Hofūf procured by an American missionary at Bahrain.[26] After several hours in customs and haggling with the laborers who loaded the palms in Basra, the Popenoes finally left Basra aboard the S.S. *Mokta* (Strick Line) on February 24, 1913, and arrived in London on April 17 by way of Suez. From London the offshoots traveled to New York, where they were inspected and transshipped to Galveston and then sent by rail in refrigerator cars to Thermal, California. The total shipment amounted to more than 9,000 date palms.

When the trees procured from the Gulf and several varieties from North Africa reached maturity a decade later, California began to replace the Gulf as America's primary source of dates. An Australian visitor in 1914 calculated that two hundred thousand palms had been planted in the Coachella Valley in California.[27] With an additional injection of cash from the Gillette Company in the 1920s and a flurry of speculation among southern California land owners, the California date industry took off. For the Gulf, the development of California's date industry meant the loss of the region's largest export market. The decline in date exports to the United States after 1925 was precipitous and can in large part be attributed to the development of the domestic date industry in California.

In the years that followed, Fairchild's and Popenoe's investments paid big dividends. California's date industry grew exponentially and replaced the dates imported to the fruit docks of Brooklyn from Basra and Muscat. Popenoe's offshoots helped ensure that California farmers would have a sufficient supply of young date palms to create successful farms in southern California. As it turns out, his timing was perfect. World War I eliminated any chance of importing any additional offshoots from the region for several years. By the late 1920s, California dates were being harvested and brought immediately to markets around the country. Date importations to the United States fell sharply. Popenoe, Fairchild, and others like them had used the tools of global trade to undercut a major world market.

The Collapse of the Gulf Pearl Industry

In 1894, a Japanese noodle-shop owner named Kokichi Mikimoto perfected the ancient Chinese practice of producing cultured pearls by inserting a spherical piece of mother-of-pearl into oyster shells and inducing the oyster to produce a pearl. Mikimoto leased a small island named Tatoku and began producing cultured pearls from oysters grown in cages. He received a ten-year patent on the process in 1896 and set a goal of producing 1 million pearls by 1902. His first crop of 4,200 semi-round pearls was harvested in 1900 by a group of exclusively female employees, and he set out to market his new product to the world. Mikimoto proved to be a master of publicity. He invited Emperor Meiji's popular cousin, Prince Komatsu, to visit his pearl-growing operation in 1900, and when the prince was selected by the emperor to represent the Japanese royal family at the coronation of King Edward VII in 1902, he presented some of Mikimoto's pearls to the royal family, generating headlines in London and Paris. By 1905 Mikimoto had 1 million oysters planted in his pearl beds, but four-fifths of them were destroyed by red tide. Among the saved oysters was an experimental basket in which the first perfectly round cultured pearls were produced, a method that he patented in 1908. His perfect cultured pearls began to enter the global pearl market between 1908 and 1911, when his representative, Rikiya Kobayashi, began marketing the cultured pearls abroad. Mikimoto soon opened a store in London and appointed agents in Paris and New York.[28]

By 1913, Mikimoto had perfected the cultured pearl to the point that it could not be distinguished from natural pearls, and he offered his product at a quarter of the market price for natural pearls. Applying the latest in assembly-line technology, he constantly increased production. He was known to say, "I want to live long enough to see the day when we have

Kokichi Mikimoto. Photograph by Edward Porter Henderson, 1945. Courtesy Smithsonian Institution Archives. Image #85-11399.

so many pearls we can sell necklaces for two dollars to every woman who can afford one and give them away free to every woman who can't."[29]

By the end of World War I, cultured pearls made inexpensive pearl necklaces available to working-class women in Western countries. By that time, women had entered the Western workplace in massive numbers and had come to embrace a leaner ideal figure, slimmer lines, and more masculine fashions. In the United States, the look of the 1920s came to symbolize the growing independence of women. That look involved the simple black dress popularized by Coco Channel, the bobbed hair popularized by dance sensation Irene Castle, and the long pearl necklace popular in wealthy circles for more than a quarter century and that was now available at a fraction of the cost. Pearl consumption rose, but demand for more expensive natural pearls declined. The decline devastated the Gulf in addition to European dealers in natural ("oriental") pearls.

Even the European pearl king's, Leonard Rosenthal's, fortunes changed with the arrival of the Japanese cultured pearl, which he called his "worst enemy." Between 1920 and 1935 Paris was the site of an intense debate among jewelers, scientists, journalists, and the courts about the legitimacy of Japanese cultured pearls. Leonard Rosenthal first encountered cultured pearls in 1913 and became concerned that the new pearls, which were being passed off as natural pearls, could have a devastating effect on Paris merchants. In 1920 Rosenthal and René Bloch brought suit in the French court system on behalf of the Chambre Syndicale des Négociants en Diamants et Pierres Fines. In the defense of cultured pearls, Lucien Pohl, the Paris commercial representative of Mikimoto, enlisted the authority of French naturalist and professor Louis Marie-Auguste Boutan of the Université de Paris and other scientists to testify to the authenticity of cultured pearls. In the end, Rosenthal succeeded in forcing dealers in cultured pearls to distinguish their products as "cultured" rather than "natural" or "oriental" pearls, and the label remains today, although the two varieties are indistinguishable to the naked eye.[30]

In 1930, the Banque Nationale de Crédit ceased lending to jewelry firms dealing in pearls because of the increased risk of devaluation brought about by cultured pearls. The bank's files attest to the fact that several of the leading dealers in pearls and fine stones entered liquidation in the early 1930s. Rodolphe Caesar Perles et Pierres Fines, worth 21 million francs, was liquidated in February 1931; Bourdier, worth 2.8 million francs, was liquidated in 1933; and Dunès, worth 1.2 million francs, was liquidated in 1934. Both of the leading pearl dealers, Rosenthal et Frères and Jacques Bienenfeld, entered special agreements with their creditors in the mid–1930s.[31]

When the Nazis invaded Paris in 1940, Rosenthal fled to Portugal and then Brazil before eventually settling in New York City in 1941.[32] Leonard's brother, Adolphe, who remained in Paris, was murdered in 1941, when men posing as police officers who claimed to be taking him to a concentration camp shot him in the temple and threw him from a moving car.[33] In the United States, Rosenthal attempted to continue dealing in natural pearls but found that by then Americans had little taste for them. He was eventually forced into trading in the same Japanese cultured pearls that had ruined his business in Paris. He revived many of his old business relationships and built a successful jewelry business at 610 Fifth Avenue, New York, and eventually retired in Beverly Hills, California, where he died at the age of eighty-three. Because his French citizenship had been revoked by the government of Philippe Pétain, Rosenthal was unable to reclaim his real estate holdings in Paris until two years before his death and then realized only a fraction of their original value.[34]

While the Gulf pearl industry persevered through the rise of cultured pearls well into the 1920s, the value of pearl production declined steadily from 1919 to 1929. Then, with the onset of the Great Depression in 1929, the pearl industry collapsed. After 1929, revenues from pearl exports were reduced to levels below even those of the mid-nineteenth century, and they never recovered. Pearls thus followed the same boom-and-bust cycle as ostrich feathers or plumes the decade before.[35]

By the 1920s, cheap cultured pearls had infiltrated the Gulf, where enterprising pearl merchants began to mix them with locally produced pearls in order to inflate their profits. Recognizing the potential disaster the trend posed for the local industry in the Gulf, the British Persian Gulf administration worked quickly to stop the flood, encouraging local sheikhs to make examples of corrupt merchants who would knowingly sell cultured pearls as natural pearls. In July 1935 two merchants in Bahrain were sentenced to seven years in prison for selling cultured pearls, but the rules were difficult to enforce.[36]

Additionally, the British Persian Gulf administration recognized the potential disaster the development of modern machinery and diving equipment posed to the industry. With the vast majority of the male workforce engaged in pearling and ancillary industries, the elimination of labor-intensive methods could spell catastrophe for the economy and create potential rebellion against the administration. The administration thus attempted to preserve stability in the region by maintaining the older, although comparatively inefficient, diving methods. In 1908 a Connecticut company tried to market inboard motors for pearling boats that could do the work of more than twenty men, thus replacing the oarsmen who eked out a living in the pearl-diving industry. The administration immediately buried the proposal and prohibited the import of any form of machinery that could save labor in the pearl banks. When a Persian man attempted to use a professional dive suit off the Persian coast, there was a loud outcry across the Gulf, and the use of suits was expressly prohibited by local rulers. It is likely that European fortune seekers would have gone to the Gulf in the late nineteenth century and mechanized production, just as they had done in South Africa, Australia, and California, had they not been repeatedly prevented by the British Persian Gulf administration.

In the aftermath of the collapse of the pearl market and in response to pressures from Parliament and the League of Nations,[37] the British Persian Gulf administration instituted a series of labor reforms in the pearl industry in the early 1930s, including the following: the formal introduction of personal account books for each diver, in which the diver had to approve of each deduction; a diving court to which divers could take complaints against their captains; orders that at least one diver was to be present at the time of the sale of pearls; prohibitions against a captain's pressing a man's debts onto the man's sons after his death; the institution of a fixed minimum wage, required to be paid to each diver and crewmember; and the creation of permission slips, called *barwahs*, allowing divers to pass freely from one diving center to another without being forced to dive for a captain to whom the diver had no legitimate debts. These permission slips were particularly helpful to newly manumitted African slaves, who were often susceptible to re-enslavement or conditions of virtual slavery after manumission.[38]

Although well intentioned, reforms were unpopular on many levels. The captains rejected the reforms as being too pro-diver and protested to the administration, requesting a return to the old system. The merchants and financiers resented the inconvenience caused by the reforms and their loss of already reduced profits. The mass production of cultured pearls in Japan had already destroyed much of the pearl industry of the Gulf. In Bahrain, the annual revenue from pearl exports in 1906 was over 12 million rupees, and the industry employed over 17,000 men and 900 boats. By 1931, pearl revenue was below 2 million rupees with roughly the same number of men employed but only 500 boats. By 1936, however, pearl revenue was below 700,000 rupees with 9,800 men from the island employed in the industry and just 364 boats. Pearl captains and merchants who had formerly benefited from the labor of slave divers now found them burdens.

The divers may have initially appreciated the efforts on their behalf, but when in 1932 an increase in wages could not be guaranteed on account of a worsening pearl market, a riot broke out in Muharraq that was quelled only by the deployment of armed British troops from India and local guards. Several people were killed and many others injured. During the disturbances, the Bahrain ruler's brother was humiliated when a passing boatful of angry pearl divers conferred on him the greatest possible insult— they picked up their loincloths and exposed themselves to him in defiance.[39]

The End of the East African Slave Trade

The end of the slave trade to eastern Arabia resulted less from British intervention than from exogenous factors, chief among them the decline in demand for slave labor following the collapse of the two biggest export industries in the region, which had both operated with the extensive use of slave labor. Other factors included intervention by the Portuguese in Mozambique in 1902 and the development of new sources of labor in the 1910s from Baluchistan and from locally kidnapped domestic slaves. The first of these additional factors was a surprising shift in policy by Portugal in Mozambique, resulting in the destruction of a significant number of dhows involved in the slave trade and the manumission in a single day of over seven hundred enslaved Africans on the coast of Mozambique who had been shackled and destined for Arabia.

The transport of enslaved Africans to the Gulf was still extensive at the turn of the twentieth century. In 1901, nearly one thousand slaves were still imported to Sur annually, and it was estimated that more than half of these were transported in dhows flying the French flag.[40] However, a major turning point in the history of the slave trade from East Africa to the Gulf occurred in 1902. The Portuguese colonial government in Mozambique, which had long tolerated extensive slave trading in its jurisdiction, sent a military expedition to Moma and the coastal district of Nampula and arrested over one hundred Omanis who were preparing to ship several hundred African captives.

In the middle of February 1902, a Portuguese engineer named Paes d'Almeida reported to the district governor of Mozambique that "a flotilla of suspicious looking Arab vessels" was anchored in the Bay of Samuco (Swahili: Simuku), hidden from the view of passing vessels. Samuco Bay, also known as Sangone Bay, is located about seventy miles north of Mozambique Island, between the Lurio and Mkubure Rivers, and was described by the British consul at Mozambique, H. E. O'Neill, in 1882 as a regional trade center for amendoim (groundnuts), calumba (a root used as medicine and dye), wax, and rubber in the "district of the Makua chief Nampwita."[41]

In response to Almeida's report, the district governor dispatched Captain Antonio d'Almeida Leima, the acting commandant of the naval division, to Samuco to investigate and sent Paes d'Almeida by land with an armed detachment of Mozambican troops to reinforce the navy. Captain Leima left Mozambique Island on March 6, 1902, aboard the *São Raphael*, the most modern ship in the Portuguese Navy, and rendezvoused at Samuco Bay two days later with two other ships sent from Almeida Bay. Some inhabitants of Samuco came aboard the *São Raphael* and told Captain Leima that a party of Arabs had fortified themselves in the area and was engaged in large-scale slaving operations in cooperation with the sheikh of Samuco, Nampuito Muno. On March 9 Captain Leima sent a large armed detachment ashore, which met up with Almeida's troops and attacked the Omani camp. The Omanis fought back with modern rifles and expanding bullets and, when finally overwhelmed, fled into the interior with many of their weapons and the Portuguese troops close behind. A

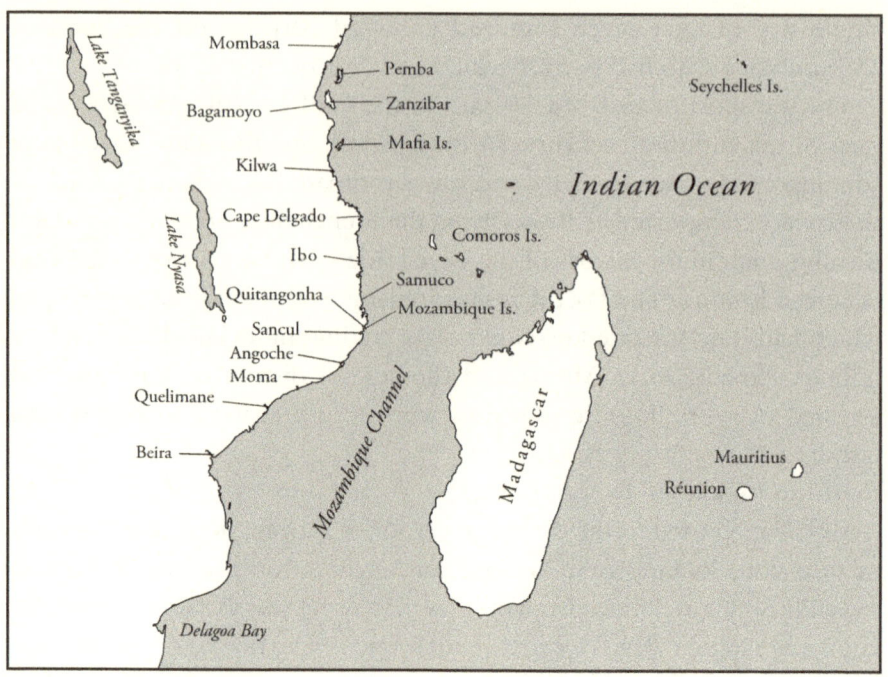

Mozambique Channel

total of 114 men were captured in the chase, but several escaped in the direction of the Lurio River. In addition, 55 men were reportedly killed in the fighting.[42]

When the Portuguese troops returned to search the Omani camp, they found 725 African prisoners with their necks in the bolted and forked sticks commonly used in the East African slave trade. When the prisoners were freed and interviewed, the Portuguese officers discovered that they had been taken from the interior by agents of Nampuito Muno and the vast majority had come from various branches of the Makua, with a few Yao from the Lujenda and Namuli districts. The sheikh of Samuco reportedly received an average of £3 for each enslaved person purchased by the Omani traders. When Portuguese troops searched the Omani dhows anchored in the bay, they found a number of letters written in Swahili in the Arabic script attesting to the long-standing relationship the traders had with the sheikh of Samuco. Some letters inquired about the dates on which slaves would be prepared to embark, and others complained of dissatisfaction with the physical condition of slaves purchased on prior occasions. Additional letters inquiring into intimate family matters were sufficient to convince the Portuguese authorities that Nampuito Muno had been associated with the Omani traders for a long time.[43]

Around the same time, the commandant of the district of Moma (south of Mozambique Island and Angoche) captured the crew of an Omani dhow named *Fatah Salam*, anchored in Moma Bay, on suspicion of slave trading. Although there were no captives aboard the ship at the time, it was found to contain incriminating correspondence in addition to a shipment of arms and ammunition and was alleged to be part of the same group of traders seized at Samuco. Seventeen Omanis were seized in connection with this ship, of whom two were set free.[44]

The Omani men seized in the raids at Samuco and Moma were imprisoned at Mozambique Island for nearly a year before being tried, and at least thirty of these men died in the Portuguese prisons before trial. Portuguese authorities attributed the long delay to the temporary absence of a qualified judge and the length of time required to translate the correspondence seized from the dhows and interview the extensive number of witnesses. The men seized at Samuco Bay were sentenced to be shipped to Angola for twenty-five years' exile, and those caught at Moma Bay were sentenced to seventeen years.[45]

The Portuguese attack on the Omanis is curious because it followed decades of collusion with and accommodation of slave traders on the coast of Mozambique.[46] As Nancy Hafkin has convincingly argued, in northern Mozambique, particularly in the region between Quelimane and Cape Delgado, administered from Mozambique Island, the Portuguese held only nominal authority, and the slave trade was allowed to thrive essentially unchecked for almost the entire nineteenth century. Coastal communities were ruled by independent sheikhdoms and sultanates, while the largely Makua populations of the immediate hinterland were governed by independent Makua monarchs. Successive governors at Mozambique Island discovered that they had no ability to force Portuguese will over the sheikhs of Quitangonha, Sancul, and Sangage or the sultan of Angoche. Instead, Portuguese authorities were forced into a "politics of survival." They were essentially dependent on the goodwill of the Swahili sheikhs and sultans of the surrounding territory in order to remain on Mozambique Island at all. Portuguese governors recognized the sheikhs in ceremonies, provided them with salaries, appointed a *capitão-mor* (captain-major) as representative to each, and attempted at various times to intervene in their succession, but they were completely beyond Portuguese control. Portuguese authorities could try to launch military expeditions against them, install replacement sheikhs, or withhold recognition of their authority, but these efforts were invariably thwarted or made meaningless. Portuguese forces were always outnumbered and outsupplied. Their control over the hinterland was essentially nonexistent, and they scarcely possessed maps or knowledge of the interior as close as eight miles away even at the end of the century.[47] This part of Mozambique was a Portuguese colony in name only.

Despite token antislave-trade treaties in 1836 and 1842 (which went unpublicized in northern Mozambique), Portuguese governors openly sanctioned slave trading or turned a blind eye to it until the end of the nineteenth century. Their low salaries required supplementation by various business dealings, including accepting bribes from surrounding sheikhs or receiving a commission on exported slaves. One sheikh of Quitangonha in 1856 even had a signed agreement with the Portuguese governor at Mozambique Island whereby the governor essentially received a 15 percent commission on each slave sold. Recognized sheikhs were supposed to trade exclusively with the Portuguese. Instead they did the opposite, trading with everyone else and attacking Portuguese merchants who came near their territory. Throughout the nineteenth century, the independent sheikh of Quitangonha—a scant ten miles from the governor's fort—"freely engaged in the slave trade with Brazilian, French, American, Arab and Swahili dealers, acting either with Portuguese complicity, or at least Portuguese knowledge."[48] The coastal sheiks were still exporting slaves to Madagascar and Arabia as late as the first decade of the twentieth century.

The decisive moment of change for Portuguese imperialism came in 1890. In that year, British ships sailed into Lourenço Marques harbor with the ultimatum that the Portuguese stay out of British-claimed territory in central Africa. Five years earlier, European powers had signed on to the principle of "effective occupation" at the Berlin Conference (1884–1885), agreeing to honor each other's territorial claims where those claims were clearly established by actual occupation. Published Portuguese maps claiming all of central Africa between Angola and Mozambique conflicted with Cecil Rhodes's dreams for expansion and British efforts at "protection" of the Shire River region around Lake Nyasa. Portugal's capitulation to the British ultimatum, as Hafkin explains, "sent great waves of anger and humiliation through the empire, ultimately resulting in the fall of the Portuguese monarchy in 1910." Portugal's response was to send in a new generation of colonial administrators to establish Portuguese rule in northern Mozambique as a matter of fact. The days of appeasement were over. The new officials would be hell-bent on establishing actual military control over the territory. From this point on, Portuguese authorities would be supplied with the weapons, soldiers (mostly from Angola and southern Mozambique), and ships required to bring the coastal sheikdoms at last into the empire in more than just name.[49]

By 1896, the Portuguese were fighting against a coordinated alliance of coastal sheikhs and Makua leaders determined to maintain the independence of the region and preserve the still lucrative slave trade. By 1902, the sheikh of Sancul, Suali bin Ali Ibrahimu, better known as "Marave," and the sultan of Angoche, Muha-Muheva Farallahi, better known as "Farelay," had formed a powerful union and were in open rebellion against the Portuguese, attacking their outposts, troops, and traders. The rebellion was ostensibly a reaction to the imposition of a hut tax in 1896, but it was also a fight to preserve the wealth derived from the slave trade that was still thriving along the coast between Moma and Memba. Marave and Farelay were joined by the leaders of the Imbamella and Namarral factions of the Makua, as well as the sheiks of Quitangonha and Moma in a relentless guerrilla war against the Portuguese.

Of particular interest to the Portuguese was control over the island state of Angoche, which by the late nineteenth century had ascended to a position of regional power and had become a center of Islamic expansion as well as the arms trade. Expansionist raids into the interior from the 1850s through the 1870s, led by Musa Mohammad Sahib Quanto, brother of the sultan of Angoche, Hassani Yussuf, helped Angoche supplant the ports of Mozambique Island and Quelimane as the primary destination of slave trade routes to Lake Nyasa. Musa Quanto, who in his youth had accompanied his uncle (an Islamic proselytizer and hajji) to Zanzibar, Madagascar, the Comoros, and up the Zambezi River, had become convinced that with the power of firearms Angoche could become a regional power. Through a series of raids into the interior he managed to make Angoche a vital destination for slave caravans led by Yao and people of Marave from the interior. Subsequently, Musa's nephew, Omar bin Cacogo Farallahi, furthered Angoche's interests in the hinterland through negotiations with local chiefs.[50]

By the 1890s the threat posed to Portuguese authority by Farelay and the independent and expansionist sultanate of Angoche could no longer be tolerated. A new Portuguese elite had arisen in Mozambique in the late nineteenth century that was less willing to adapt to local systems of social organization and eager to assert its control over the entire coast of Mozambique and the hinterland in order to effect the Portuguese claim to territorial occupation of the region. This new generation of Portuguese colonialists, as Liazzat Bonate has shown, was characterized by inexperience and unfamiliarity with established practices of local authority. The clash between "new" and "old" Portuguese elites in Mozambique led to such levels of political strife that the governor-general of Mozambique, Mousinho de Albuquerque, asked to be relieved of his post in 1898. He ultimately committed suicide in 1902 in the midst of extensive opposition to his policies. The days of toleration and collaboration with slave traders were coming to an end but not without fierce resistance from the local rulers who profited from the trade and the Portuguese elites who depended on the slave labor for their plantations or the indirect revenues of the trade for their livelihoods. In an ironic twist, Paes d'Almeida, who had originally reported the slave dhows in Samuco Bay and made possible their capture, was murdered within months of the capture of the Omani slave traders, one of the first victims of a fresh Farelay-Makua joint offensive in Imbamella Makua territory.[51]

The Portuguese crackdown in Mozambique had eliminated a large part of Oman's capacity to import African labor in the early twentieth century. Reports reached British officials that Sur entered a prolonged period of mourning once news of the attack reached the port. Weeping reportedly continued for many weeks. In addition to losing many of its beloved, Sur also suffered a tremendous loss of revenue as the historic chief importing city for East African slaves. Sur's diminished capacity and the declining demand for slave labor after the collapse of the pearl and date industries two decades later explain much of the decline in the importation of enslaved Africans into the Gulf. But the rise of an alternative source of servile labor was the final factor in the eventual collapse of the East African slave trade to the Gulf.

Alternative Labor Sources: Baluchistan and Arabia

New sources of labor from Baluchistan and Persian Mekran emerged in the first quarter of the twentieth century that proved to be a cheaper, more logistically convenient, and less risky option than importing slaves through the East African slave trade to the Gulf. In the first decade of the twentieth century, as Suri capacity for importing slave labor from East Africa declined sharply following Portuguese intervention in Mozambique, global demand for Gulf pearls and dates continued to grow, and demand for labor for these sectors remained high. Date exports to the United States were at this time higher than they had been for the past twenty-five years and continued to grow through the mid–1920s. The value of Gulf pearl exports had more than doubled in the two decades ending in 1904, and in the following decade, it would quadruple from there. At this time, producers on the eastern coast of Arabia increasingly looked across the Gulf to Baluchistan (Persian Mekran and parts of what is today coastal Pakistan) and to kidnapping members of the free African population already resident in Arabia to fill their labor needs. An important trend influencing the decline of the African slave trade during this period was the development of the Baluchi slave trade.

Although a significant number of enslaved Baluchis had been introduced to the eastern Arabian coast prior to World War I, Baluchistan went on to export a great many more people and by the 1920s had replaced East Africa as the main source of new labor for eastern Arabian markets. A number of factors contributed to this shift. First, several consecutive years of drought and locust invasion in Baluchistan and Mekran in the early twentieth century devastated agriculture and led to widespread desperation and famine in the region. Although officially neutral in World War I, Persia suffered severely during the conflict, losing a quarter to a third of the population of some districts, mainly to famine and disease. Agricultural production did not reach prewar levels until 1925.[52] Percy Sykes described the decimation of Shiraz in 1918 and explained that a fifth of the population was killed in a single month, dropping from fifty thousand to forty thousand in October 1918, mainly due to influenza.[53] Mohammad Ali Jamalzadeh, an eye witness to the famine in Fars, wrote that residents were so desperate for food that they were forced to eat cats, dogs, mice, crows, sticks, leaves, roots, and eventually even the human dead.[54] The famine conditions in Sistān, Baluchistan, and Hormozgān pressured many of the poorest people in the region to resort to debt pawnage to merchants and local elites. Children who were offered in pawn were sometimes sold by creditors across the Gulf to traders in Batinah. The desperate times in Baluchistan, which coincided with much better economic times across the Gulf, spurred a contraband kidnapping trade, through which women, children, and young men were captured and sold across the Gulf to Batinah or the Trucial Coast. The extent of poverty in Baluchistan was so severe in the early 1920s that A. P. Trevor, the British political resident in the Persian Gulf, lamented that many women who had been manumitted by British efforts and sent back to their homelands later returned to their old masters on the Arab side of the Gulf on their own accord.[55]

The fact that an apparatus for receiving and redistributing enslaved Africans had long been established on the Batinah Coast made the Baluchi slave trade even more appealing for those running it. The proximity of Baluchistan to the historic import centers of African labor on the Batinah coast, such as Wudam, Khaḍra', and Suwaiq, meant the transition to importation and distribution of Baluchi labor would not be difficult. From ports on the Batinah Coast, enslaved Baluchis were conveyed overland by camel to destinations on the Batinah plain, through valleys into Dhahirah and Buraimi or, commonly, through mountain passages to the northwest to Dubai and the Trucial Coast, most frequently through Wadi Ham. Batinah was such a center of Baluchi slave imports that the town of Khaḍra' was shelled by the HMS *Espiegle* in 1922 in an effort to dissuade residents of the town from harboring enslaved Baluchis.[56] Moreover, the rise of the Baluchi slave trade coincided with the rise of the lucrative contraband arms trade to Persia and Afghanistan, of which Muscat was the center.[57]

The traffic in enslaved Baluchis to eastern Arabia followed two routes. The first ran to the north from the Baluchi ports of Bunjī and Sīrīk (north of Jask, today in Iran in the province of Hormozgān) to Qatar and the Trucial Coast. The second ran south to the Batinah Coast, especially the port towns of Khaḍra', Wudam, and Shirs, from the Baluchi ports of Sudaich, Challaq, Gohurt, Pārak, Puzim, and Konārak.[58] The trade was generally widespread between Chahbar Bay and Puzim Bay and along the coast from those places as far as Jask. The Baluchi port of Gwadur was also used as a re-export center for the slave trade, especially for Indian youths who were kidnapped or lured into captivity under the promise of employment. Many boys were lured from Karachi to Gwadur by agents posing as employers, only to be captured on arrival and sold into slavery to work as pearl divers in eastern Arabia.[59]

In the Biyaban district of Persian Mekran, a local notable named Birkat Khan became notorious as a slave dealer in the first decades of the twentieth century. He lent money to local clients and took children as collateral for loans. When clients defaulted on their loans, he arranged to have their children sold into slavery in Batinah or the Trucial Coast and reportedly had three dhows that he used for this purpose. In the 1920s Birkat Khan was well known to Trucial notables for his eagerness to exchange enslaved Baluchis for firearms and ammunition. He was known to repay gifts of firearms generously.[60]

By all reports, the actual slave trading, from capture to sale, was conducted by Baluchi merchants rather than Arab Omanis. Traders brought enslaved Baluchis, usually children, to ports on the Trucial Coast or the Batinah Coast, where further sales and shipments were made, but the leading traders in the Omani markets were Baluchis as well. There are no records of any large shipments of enslaved Baluchis arriving at ports in eastern Arabia. Instead, the trade appears to have continued through small shipments of two or three people at a time in small vessels.[61]

By 1925, Baluchi slave boys could be acquired from across the Gulf for MT$400–$600. A pair of teenage Baluchi boys fled from a plantation near Suwaiq in 1929 claiming that they had been mistreated by their master, who had purchased them for watering his date plantations. They took shelter with the *wali* (governor) of Barka, sixty kilometers down the coast, and when their master sent seven men on camels to recover them, the *wali* pretended to not know their whereabouts and sent the boys to safety in Muscat.[62]

A number of Baluchi men sought to cash in on slave exchanges and used trickery to persuade unsuspecting teens into accompanying them to points of sale. In 1926, a fifteen-year-old Indian boy who had a job washing motor cars for a company in Karachi was approached by a Baluchi driver of the same company. The driver asked the boy to accompany him on a steamer leaving for Bombay, where he said they could get higher wages for their work. The boy agreed and followed the man, but when the steamer called at Gwadur, he told the boy they should take the rest of the journey by camel. They stayed overnight with two men at a village in the interior, and then the driver disappeared. The two men ordered the boy to take their sheep out for grazing, and when he told them he was not a slave, they tied his hands, beat him, and told him that they had bought him. They soon sold him across the Gulf to Batinah, and he ended up diving for pearls at Dubai.[63] A few years earlier, two Baluchis in Mutrah had tricked a young man into coming with them on pilgrimage to Baghdad but, on arrival at Abu Dhabi, sold him to a resident there who sent him to Dalma Island for pearl diving.[64]

In addition, a rise of domestic kidnapping in Arabia contributed to the decrease in the slave trade from East Africa to the Gulf in the twentieth century. In the beginning of the twentieth century, enslaved Africans, as well as free Africans and their descendants, became the subjects of widespread kidnapping throughout southeast Arabia. As mentioned above, a continued rise in demand for labor, particularly young male labor, combined with a decline in slave imports from Africa, created lucrative markets for human traffickers. By the 1920s, no one of African descent living in Arabia, whether slave or free, was safe from kidnappers. In 1925, two cousins of the sultan of Muscat who, according to British reports, were "negroes," were kidnapped in the sultan's territories and sold into slavery. They were also beaten for protesting their capture on the grounds that they were relatives of the sultan.[65] More typical cases of kidnapping in Oman resembled that of a boy named Gharib bin Sayeed. Born in servitude in Shinas on the Batinah Coast around 1886, the boy was kidnapped from Shinas at the age of about thirteen and taken to Abu Dhabi, where he was sold to a family to work as a domestic and later a pearl diver.[66]

A major factor contributing to the rise in kidnapping in Oman was the lack of any effective central government to suppress it outside of a limited area. While sheikhs and local authorities protected both enslaved and free Africans living within their jurisdictions, they had little power to coordinate the return of individuals once they were kidnapped and taken far away. The sultan of Muscat received numerous appeals from local notables seeking help in securing the return of people kidnapped from their towns. These were often appeals made on behalf of relatives of enslaved Africans or Baluchis who had been kidnapped, but they were also made for free men and women. In 1927, two leading sheikhs of Musilmat in Wadi Muawal in Oman, Abdul 'Aziz Ar Ruwaihi and Hamad bin Sa'id bin Ahmed Ma'awli, wrote a letter on behalf of a free man of African descent from their town named Taaib bin Bilal, whose fifteen-year-old son had been kidnapped and sold into slavery. Taaib had been manumitted at the age of four and had worked as a cultivator in Wadi Muawal as a free man ever since. Around 1924, he went to Zanzibar in hopes of earning more money and stayed for over a year. In 1926 he received word that his son, Aqīl, had been kidnapped by a renegade member of the Muscat royal family, 'Abdullah bin Saif al-Busaidi, and sold into slavery near Dubai. The leading elders of Taaib's hometown wrote a letter of recommendation to the sultan's council of ministers, and Taaib carried the letter to Muscat and presented it to the council; the case was eventually forwarded to the British political resident in the Persian Gulf at Bushehr.[67]

The political disruption in Arabia caused by World War I and the expansion of the Kingdom of Nejd also contributed to the rise in domestic kidnapping. Sulaiman bin Yusuf, a Nigerian born in Kano, went on pilgrimage to Mecca with his father in 1919. While in Arabia, they were attacked by robbers who murdered his father and took him prisoner. He was sold into slavery for about seven years and finally managed to escape to Bahrain in 1927 to appeal to the British political agent for manumission and passage home.[68]

During the period of Saudi expansion, many children of African heritage were carried away from Mecca, Medina, and Jeddah and sent to Nejd, and some of them were later sent for diving in the Gulf. In the following testimony, Bahkit, an Iraqi boy who had accompanied his uncle to Jeddah on business, was captured in the 1915 war between Sheikh Hussain and Ibn Sa'ud:

> I was ten years old when I accompanied my uncle to Jeddah for the purpose of trade. My father had died already. There took place a war at Jeddah soon after our arrival there. During these disturbances my uncle severed from me and I never heard of him afterwards. I was taken to Riadh from Jeddah as prisoner by Bedouins. I served a Bedouin at Riadh for seven years and was not given enough food to maintain myself equivalent to the work I used to do.
>
> A Bedouin of Riadh took me from there and brought me to Dammam, where he sold me to Ahmad bin Khamis Dowasir. I used to serve as diver for him in the sea. My master never gave me enough food and clothings and used to keep all my earning with himself. He always used to handle me very severely and to take labor from me by force. After being disgusted of my life with him, I managed to run away from him and came down to Bahrain.[69]

Bahkit's story is similar to those of many African ex-slaves and African slave descendants in the early twentieth century. A sample set of sixty-five enslaved men and women who told stories of being kidnapped from their homes in Arabia when they applied for manumission from British agencies and consulates in the Gulf between 1907 and 1943 demonstrates that kidnapping was very common in the first quarter of the twentieth century: thirty-seven of these sixty-five cases involved kidnappings that occurred between 1910 and 1924.[70]

The End of Slavery in the Gulf

The growth of the oil industry led to the improvement of the economy of the Gulf, creating the means for Gulf sheikhdoms to compensate slave owners for manumitting their slaves. In addition, under pressure from the League of Nations, the British administration in the Gulf began to press for formal declarations of abolition, particularly in view of the prospects of oil concessions after 1937, the rising power of Persia, and the shift of the seat of the British residency from Bushehr to Bahrain in 1947. The ruler of Bahrain issued a formal proclamation against slave owning in

1937, and the ruler of Qatar legally abolished slavery and provided compensation to slave owners for manumitting their slaves in 1952. In 1951, Britain formed the Trucial Oman Levies, which patrolled against slave trading in Trucial Oman. Saudi Arabia formally abolished slavery in 1963, and Oman followed in 1971. The path of formal abolition largely followed the development of the oil industry, which provided a source of revenue for compensation for slave owners as in the case of Qatar, as well as new occupations for newly manumitted slaves.

Manumitted slaves in the Gulf sheikhdoms frequently took the clan or tribal names of their masters and were incorporated into the existing social structure with the full rights of citizens in the newly independent states. Some freed slaves continued to hand over their incomes to their masters, and historical patterns of dependency endured. A remarkable story relayed to anthropologist Fredrik Barth at Sohar in the mid–1970s by a former slave named Miki exemplifies this pattern. Miki had been kidnapped and sold at Buraimi to a Bedouin family who forced him to herd their sheep and camels in the desert. He often had to endure days at a time with no food or drink except camel's milk. The family had a large number of slaves who performed all sorts of labor. When Miki turned thirteen, they sent him to Dubai to dive for pearls and kept his earnings, providing him with only simple food and clothes. After the British built a military base at Sharjah (around 1951), he obtained the permission of his masters to work there. For eight years, Miki worked at the base and handed over all of his wages from the British government to his masters without ever apparently raising the suspicion of his employers before eventually making his escape.[71]

The destitution of many former slaves forced them to become dependent on their former masters. In 1936, the British political agent at Bahrain reported the following story:

> An old man in Hidd was talking to the Agency Medical Officer and mentioned that he was a slave. The Medical Officer said that this was quite impossible, so the old man went off and brought—his manumission certificate! The Medical Officer said that this document did not show that he was a slave at all, but on the contrary that he had been freed by the order of the Government whereupon

the old man flew into a towering rage—"You lie! I know that it really says that I am the slave of so and so and it is proof that he must feed me—and no one shall cast doubt upon it!"[72]

Relationships of dependency in the aftermath of the collapse of the date and pearl industries endured for many years. In the 1970s Fredrik Barth recorded numerous examples of the ways in which ex-slave families continued to serve in a clientele capacity for the families of their former masters. In particular, at times of weddings, musical performances, dancing, and the preparation of the bride continued to be functions of descendants of former slaves for decades after slavery. Tradition formerly obligated slaves to call their masters *habib*, but Barth noted that by the 1970s the practice had been administratively prohibited. However, the descendants of ex-slaves continued to call the descendants of their former masters *'am* (paternal uncle) and were referred to by descendants of masters as *khal* (maternal uncle), terms denoting superiority and submissiveness respectively.[73]

The forces of globalization that helped create global markets for Arabian commodities also helped destroy them. Steamships, telegraphs, global lines of credit, and networks of merchants, missionaries, and diplomats helped facilitate the global trade in Arabian dates and pearls. But those same tools were just as easily used against Arab producers when agents from industrialized states used them to create rival production centers. The collapse of the date export market to the United States in the wake of competition from California coincided with the collapse of the pearl export market. Japanese cultured pearls, like California dates, undercut a major portion of Gulf exports and had disastrous consequences for the pre-oil Gulf economy.

The slave trade from East Africa to Arabia collapsed primarily as a result of the decline of Arabia's date and pearl markets. The Portuguese aboutface on slavery in northern Mozambique and the rise of new sources of labor, particularly in Baluchistan after World War I, contributed as well. Eventually, when rising oil wealth created a new economic boom in the Gulf, the region found new sources of cheap labor from South Asia that some have argued replaced or revived traditions of servitude in the Gulf. With the diminishing demand for African labor, many enslaved Africans were freed, while others were cast out to fend for themselves. Others continued to live in their masters' or former masters' households and work independently or as clients. Some found work within the growing oil industry, with the British imperial government, or in the Gulf's expanding cities. Although slavery was no longer acknowledged as an institution by the 1960s and slavery was abolished everywhere in the Gulf by 1970, old patterns of dependency and clientelism endured.

CONCLUSION: SILENCING AND FORGETTING

Tourists and visitors to the popular Al-Satwa quarter of Dubai today are frequently treated to Laiwa performances by local musical and dance troupes. Most of the Laiwa performers, who have a clearly identifiable African appearance, do not identify themselves as African. Ethnomusicologists agree that Laiwa is an African import, but French ethnomusicologist Maho Sebiane's interviews with members of the quarter's performers' association indicate that most identify themselves as Baluchi rather than African, and most share the same last name, Al-Baluchi. Sebiane calls the performers an "enigma"—their appearance is African, but their surname implies an Asiatic origin. Language provides little assistance, as the performers are as likely to speak some Baluchi, Hindi, and Urdu in addition to their first language of Arabic, and they tend to know only the few Swahili words included in the songs they perform. He hypothesizes that freed slaves may have taken the surnames of their masters, who may have been Baluchi or *'ajam* immigrants from across the Gulf. Alternatively, he speculates that the ancestors of these performers may have settled first on the Irano-Pakistani coast before making a second migration to the Arab coast and valuing their Baluchi migration experience more highly than their African origins.[1] Still another possibility is that the performers have chosen to call themselves Baluchi in an effort to deliberately obscure their African ancestry. Sebiane's research highlights a major challenge facing historians of the African diaspora in the Gulf: unlike many other branches of the global African diaspora, identification with Africa is not a common feature among the descendants of enslaved Africans in Arabia. Today, many of the characteristics associated with diasporic identity, including "a collective memory and myth about the homeland ... an idealization of the supposed ancestral home" and "the presence of a return movement or intermittent visits to home" are absent among many members of the African diaspora in Arabia.[2]

African heritage is likewise often obscured in public history and public memory in the Gulf today. The Muscat Gate Museum, located between Muscat and Mutrah in Oman, features an array of historical artifacts and cultural displays. In the center of the museum is a scale model of a working well system used extensively in the Batinah region of Oman. The laborer working the well is depicted as an Arab man with fair skin in a white *dishdasha* rather than an African, who typically performed such labor in Batinah. Up the hill in Qurum, the Museum of Omani Culture features enlarged photographs of Omanis engaged in representative forms of traditional labor. The photograph illustrating the date industry features an obviously posed light-skinned Arab man wearing a shimmering white *dishdasha*, *muzzar*, and *khanjar*, smiling at the camera, with brightly colored ripening dates over his shoulder, while he is tending a date tree. These two public displays provide visitors with the impression that the work that was often associated with the enslaved African workers who were prominent in the date industry—particularly the labor-intensive work of irrigation—was in fact done by others. Visitors to these museums are presented with versions of history that more comfortably fit nationalist narratives and gloss over the untidy subject of slavery. Likewise, the photographs that make up the pearl-diving exhibits of the Bahrain National Museum feature a scant few African divers.

It is unclear whether the omission of slavery and the slave trade in official scholarship and publications is a result of oversight, self-censorship, or state action, although there are occasional hints of deliberate censorship. Issam El-Mallah's classic account of Omani music is an excellent example. The liner notes for his *Music of an Ancient Civilization: The Sultanate of Oman*, which introduce the English section on Al-Laiwa, the variety of music and dance widely regarded as African in origin, begin as follows: "The aforementioned contacts with East Africa resulted in a certain degree of amalgamation of Omani and African arts, songs, and dances."[3] He goes on to describe the African origins of the drums, instruments, and style of performance. However, no previous mention of Africa is contained in the liner notes except in the context of "merchant trading voyages with sailing vessels," which the author informs us were "undertaken not only to East Africa but also to India and even to China." These vessels are mentioned only briefly in an earlier note introducing the dance song "Shubbaniyya," from Salalah.[4] The reader is left to conclude either that Al-Laiwa contains African influences as an indirect result of trade contacts or that some details provided by the author about the substantial population of enslaved Africans in the Batinah region of Oman were subsequently removed by a government censor. Either way, the African progenitors of the music and dance mode are elided from its history.

The Gulf Cooperation Council Folklore Centre's collection titled *Laiwa Music of the Gulf* is equally vague on the origins of the musical style.[5] Although the author, Waheed Al-Khan, identifies Laiwa as a "migrant music type" that retains features that "betray its African origins" (namely "its general basic rhythm and a resilient presence of some Sawahili phrases in the texts of its songs"), the author remains vague with regard to the type of migration this "migrant music" has made. Did the music travel alone, or did it migrate along with forced migrants from Africa? Nevertheless, both El-Mallah and Al-Khan agree that Laiwa spread around the Gulf by way of Oman.

The Oman Ministry of Heritage and Culture's third volume of its Contemporary Forms of Omani Folk Arts series covers the Batinah region and also discusses Laiwa and other forms of song and dance with origins in East Africa. The official volume is equally vague about the ways in which these traditions came to Oman. The volume says variously that Omanis who traveled, traded, and settled in East Africa "carried back" these traditions to Oman from Omani territory in East Africa, along with African indigenous religious traditions from "ancient times." Although the text describes the songs and dances in detail and gives several possible meanings for the word "Laiwa," it says little else about the process by which the musical form came to Oman. Readers are left with the impression that Omani traders witnessed the dances from the safe distance of their ships rather than the truth—that they carried back thousands of young Africans to labor on their own shores.[6] More recently, in July 2011, the Smithsonian Institution's National Museum of African Art in Washington, DC, partnered with the Sultan Qaboos Cultural Center (SQCC) to host Al Najoom, a traditional Omani dance group. Following a live performance featuring Afro-Omani musicians and dancers, a member of the audience inquired about the origins of the troupe's music and dance. In response, a representative from the SQCC explained: "Oman is an Arab country. It's not an African country. But Oman, throughout its history, was a crossroads to many cultures because it was on the eastern corner of the Arabian Peninsula. It is a seafaring country, and so a lot of people traveled back and forth and traveled through Oman. So, of course, we have taken a lot of different cultures and we have intertwined them with our own and that's why you can feel some of the African rhythms in our music. However, this is very particular to Oman."[7]

Michel-Rolf Trouillot describes "silencing" as "an active and transitive process: one 'silences' a fact or an individual as a silencer silences a gun. One engages in the practice of silencing." Trouillot argues that "Mentions and silences are . . . active, dialectical counterparts of which history is the synthesis." In his analysis of the "three faces" of Sans Souci (at once the name of independent Haiti's royal palace, Haitian King Henry's military nemesis, and a palace of Frederick I in Potsdam), Trouillot explains that "silences are inherent in history because any single event enters history with some of its constituting parts missing. Something is always left out while something else is recorded. . . . Thus whatever becomes fact does so with its own inborn absences."[8] He argues that the silencing of the history of the Haitian Revolution is partly attributable to omission. But it is also attributable to the treatment of the revolution in written history, which, he argues, reveals two tropes—formulas of "erasure" and formulas of "banalization." The former tends to "erase directly the fact of a revolution," while the latter tends to "empty a number of singular events of their revolutionary content so that the entire string of facts, gnawed from all sides, becomes trivialized." The general silence that Western historiography produced around the Haitian Revolution, he argues, stemmed initially from "the incapacity to express the unthinkable," but it later grew as Haiti became increasing marginalized. The Haitian Revolution could not be fit into prevailing nationalist narratives, and it engaged issues of racism, slavery, and colonialism—themes that the historical guild for so long considered irrelevant. The revolution thus "became a nonevent."[9]

Trouillot's analysis of Haiti provides a useful lens through which to explore the legacy of slavery in the Gulf. To say the history of slavery in the Gulf has been "silenced" is not simply to complain of a lack of attention in scholarly literature. Instead, the acts of silencing are, in Trouillot's words, "active and transitive." Among states, these acts take the form of deliberate omissions, sanitized accounts, and convenient (if awkward) editing. Among historians, silencing has hitherto involved a lack of space in the existing historiography to allow for a meaningful presence of enslaved Africans in the Gulf. And among the descendants of enslaved Africans themselves, this silencing has involved a mutability of identity and sometimes intentional "forgetting."

Observers from the Atlantic world are frequently puzzled by perceptions of race in the Gulf, where one may have an African appearance but self-identify and be identified by others as Arab. One source of this confusion is that in the Indian Ocean world, race has tended to be reckoned by paternal descent rather than by phenotype, a method that contrasts sharply with that in the Atlantic world, where race tends generally to be reckoned by the color of one's skin, exemplified by the "one-drop rule" of the North American experience. Many residents of the Gulf and scholars of the Indian Ocean attribute this difference to the homogenizing influence of Islam or the race-blind tolerance produced by the region's cosmopolitanism. For example, to illustrate the traditions of cosmopolitanism and tolerance in the Indian Ocean, Abdul Sheriff recounts the story of his visit to a mariner's family home in Sur, in which portraits of a man's relatives and a former African slave hung side by side on the wall and all them were identified as Arab.[10]

Despite cosmopolitan ideals, there remain strong factors influencing the exclusion of and discrimination against the descendants of enslaved Africans in the Gulf. During his fieldwork in Batinah in the 1970s, Fredrik Barth identified descendants of African slaves in Sohar as a "stigmatized" group that experienced "strong social pressures to isolate them as an endogamous unit" and that functioned as "a kind of de facto ethnic group."[11] Marc Valeri notes that today descendants of African slaves are often kept both geographically and symbolically distinct in Oman with some districts of Salalah, Suwaiq, Sur, and Sohar exclusively populated by slave descendants.[12] Certain stigmatized labor has also been associated with Africans. Barth noted that the descendants of slaves in Batinah commonly engaged in playing music in public for money and singing as public entertainment at weddings, two occupations popularly regarded as dishonorable in Oman.[13] Barth found descendants of slaves still popularly called *khadim* (slave), and Valeri notes that the term is still used today, and slave descendants are "also called '*abid* (slaves) or *zunuj* (black; sing. *zinj*) in Sur and the Dhofar region."[14]

While it is true that in the Gulf today one's racial identity is most often determined by that of one's father and grandfather rather than one's skin color, skin color *does* matter (or there would not be so many skin-lightening clinics in Dubai). Put simply, in the Gulf race matters alongside genealogy. Arabs in the Gulf who espouse notions of racial equality under Islam can also have strong social expectations and feelings related to race at particular times, including the selection of marriage partners. Because many Arab males from the Gulf enjoyed widespread mobility around the Indian Ocean world and frequently married into families beyond the shores of the Gulf, their descendants have often retained Arab identities whether their mothers were African, Baluchi, or Indonesian. But this Arab identity contains an internal hierarchy that influences perceptions of acceptable marriage arrangements. Jane Bristol-Rhys has identified numerous barriers between marriages of Arabs and various minority groups in the UAE.[15] Likewise, Israeli filmmaker Uri Rosenwaks has documented experiences among the descendants of enslaved Africans in Rahat, a town in Israel's Negev Desert, where few Afro-Arab Israelis knew of their slave lineage, although they experienced forms of racism in their communities, especially when seeking marriage partners from other groups.[16]

Some of the most important anthropological work on identity in the Gulf has been pioneered by Mandana Limbert, who sensitively explores the delicate subjects of marriage and social hierarchies in Oman among other themes in her book *In the Time of Oil*. Limbert notes that despite religious admonitions that race does not "officially" matter, real barriers remain for marriages between Arabs and the descendants of ex-slaves.[17] She tells the story of a young Arab woman in the 1990s who, by family accounts, "almost 'accidentally' married a man of a servant family." The man had originally come from another town, and despite the initial blessing of the young woman's grandfather, the approval of neighbors, and the man's reputation as an educated, good, and hardworking person, the wedding was called off after someone from the groom's hometown informed the bride's family that the man was in fact from slave lineage. Limbert explains that while official discourses "maintain that rigid class and race separations are antithetical to Omani history and Ibadism, in practice, some notion of race, especially in reference to color, mattered."[18] Limbert argues convincingly that race and paternal genealogy have been in tension in Oman since at least the 1970s and that old notions of "Arabness," defined as a class or caste category inherited through paternal descent, have recently begun to be overtaken by notions of "Arabness" defined as a racial or ethnic category, particularly as Oman has defined itself as an Arab nation with growing connections to the rest of the Arabian Peninsula and the Gulf Cooperation Council in particular.[19] Limbert explains that Oman's official interpretations of its history in Zanzibar emphasize relationships between Arab-Omanis and Africans as peaceful and part of a "civilizing process" through which Arabs and Africans remained distinct. "The relationship between the two groups is conceived as brotherly, and 'neighborly,' yet clearly hierarchical. Through the paternalizing and patronizing care of the Arab-Omanis, the 'Zinjis' could become brothers; brothers, however, who would never be allowed to forget that they had been slaves, that they had known nothing, and that they had had to be cultured."[20]

In a similar vein, Jonathon Glassman, in his recent incisive analysis of creolism and cosmopolitanism, highlights one of the most significant reasons for the obscuring of ancestral lineages in the western Indian Ocean. In his study of revolutionary Zanzibar, Glassman notes that islanders invoked real or imagined claims to foreign (Arab or Shirazi) origins in order to distinguish themselves from the more recent arrivals from the mainland, many of whom were slaves. By invoking a heritage of Arabness or *ustaarabu* (Swahili: civilization), islanders invoked a conscious sense of difference from the *ushenzi* (barbarism or unbelief) of the mainland interior. *Ushenzi* imparted a certain "slavish" quality on individuals that could be inherited and that was associated with lower social rank. Arab families who settled in East Africa reckoned their descent along the patriline and also, in theory, followed the principle of *kafa'a*, or female hypergamy, such that "so long as women married only at their rank or above, Arab families would not lose children to families of lesser ranks." The twin principles of patrilineal descent and *kafa'a* marriage allowed Arab men in the Indian Ocean diaspora to "have children with non-Arab wives without endangering the Arab status of their 'creole' children" or being tainted by *ushenzi*, which was increasingly "understood in racialized or quasi-racialized ways."[21] Glassman's argument is convincing. If he is correct about Zanzibar, his argument might also be applied to Arabia to understand the obfuscation of African lineage in the Gulf today as an effort to disassociate with the *ushenzi* or "slavishness" of the African interior and the legacy of the slave trade. In his study of Batinah, Fredrik Barth likewise identified something he referred to as "the taint of slave admixture."[22]

There are also more recent social, political, and economic factors at work. Racial relations in the Gulf are complicated by the fact that many of the descendants of Oman's most successful families who had settled over generations in Zanzibar and East Africa fled to the Gulf during the racial turmoil in Zanzibar and East Africa in the 1960s and 1970s. Descendants of the Swahili-speaking branches of elite Omani families today live alongside descendants of enslaved Africans who may not seem to outsiders considerably different in appearance. Add to this complex diversity of populations the recent trends of urbanization, dislocation, internal migration, and the tradition of homogeneity promoted by national dress, and there remains little incentive for those with servile ancestry to highlight this part of their family history.

Politically, descendants of slaves have been extended citizenship and have been coopted into the national identities of monarchial states, which concentrate political power in ways that exclude the majority rather than a minority of the population. Descendants of slaves can receive financial benefits of citizenship in a rentier state that are withheld from the region's newer and largely South Asian underclass of guest workers who today perform many of the tasks formerly performed by slaves for low wages and in often coercive circumstances. Descendants of slaves may experience forms of discrimination, but economic opportunities in Gulf monarchies are disproportionally skewed in favor of members of the ruling families and their allies, so they are not alone. Economic dynamics are further complicated by the contemporary poverty of Africa relative to the Gulf states. These combined factors may contribute to the development of a kind of "contradictory consciousness," described by Gramsci, that can produce the state of moral and political passivity identified by Genovese.[23]

When seen in the broadest context of the global African diaspora, the fact that diasporic Africans in the Indian Ocean have not always identified themselves through a continental (if anachronistic) concept of an African homeland, joined pan-African intellectual currents, identified as part of a global dispersed community, or formulated a return movement should not be surprising. These are features distinct to the American branch of the global African diaspora but are not normative features of the diaspora in its entirety. Pier Larson has cogently argued that "experiences of enslavement . . . are not universal sites for historical memory and identity formation in the diaspora." Although "experiences and memories of enslavement and racial oppression are key to African identities in the Americas, similar trauma has been purposefully forgotten or differently remembered in many other parts of the diaspora." In other branches of the African diaspora, including much of the Middle East and the Indian Ocean world, there have been good reasons for descendants of enslaved Africans—as well as their enslavers—to employ what Larson calls "countervailing forces of historical amnesia." Although commemorating enslavement is characteristic of the Atlantic branch of the diaspora, we must be careful not to expect to find that characteristic universally throughout the global African diaspora.[24] In fact, even the Atlantic experience of the African diaspora cannot be taken as static and monolithic. Experiences in parts of South America display similarities to the Gulf. Tanya Maria Golash-Boza's recent work on Afro-Peruvian communities in Ingenio indicates that "blackness" there is primarily a discourse on skin color rather than slavery. Her work challenges scholarship on the black diaspora that points to the "centrality of slavery for defining blackness in the diaspora."[25]

Furthermore, the shared experience of poverty in the twentieth century, when former slaves and former masters were forced to live side by side through decades of depression following the collapse of the date and pearling industries, may have reduced the significance of differences between African and Arab identities. It is perhaps this common experience of poverty—the families of former masters and slaves scratching out a living in the decades before oil—that most profoundly differentiates the legacy of Gulf and Atlantic slavery for the lives of their descendants today. The two regions that imported the greatest numbers of enslaved Africans— Oman and the Trucial States —were also the last two in the Gulf to develop significant oil industries. In the decades between the collapse of the date and pearl industries and the rise of the oil industry, the descendants of former slaves and former masters shared a common experience of destitution that must certainly have shaped the relationships between the region's ethnic majority and minorities. And it is perhaps this experience—more than religion, race, or culture—that best explains the seeming difference between the Gulf and the Atlantic with respect to race relations. The distinctiveness of slavery in the Gulf may not be either the type of labor or the religious context but the shared experience in the region as a result of global economic forces and subsequent transformations in Gulf slavery.

NOTES

Preface

1. Colomb, *Slave Catching in the Indian Ocean*, 30.
2. For example, one particularly promising document I examined in Zanzibar was a slave trader's account book with a cloth cover; it had been captured aboard a slaving vessel in the Mozambique Channel in 1868. The book had been bound into an archival volume with its pages sewn shut, and it had been sealed from view for a century. An archivist graciously cut through some of the threads to allow me to see the document. Although fascinating, the book mostly consisted of records such as, "And follows, one female slave for eleven and a half dollars. And follows, one male slave for eleven dollars. And follows, one female slave for ten dollars. And follows, two males slaves and one female slave for 23 and a half dollars." See annex to cases of HMS *Nymphe* (August 1868) in Vice Admiralty Court Proceedings 1867-68; ZNA AA 7/3.
3. Spivak, "Can the Subaltern Speak?," 297. See also Busia, "Silencing Sycorax"; Gyan Prakash: "Writing Post-Orientalist Histories of the Third World," and "Subaltern Studies as Postcolonial Criticism."
4. Troutt Powell, "Will That Subaltern Ever Speak?"
5. Toledano, *As If Silent and Absent*, 34–35.
6. McKnight, "'En su tierra lo aprendió'"; cited in Toledano, *As If Silent and Absent*, 34.

Introduction

1. Lieutenant Philip Francklin to Lieutenant-Commander R. H. Story, HMS *Lapwing*, May 23, 1896; PRO FO 881/6797. (One enslaved captive may have been an adult woman.)
2. Lieutenant-Commander R. H. Story to Rear-Admiral Drummond, Admiralty, May 25, 1896; PRO FO 881/6797.

3. Major Fagan (consul at Muscat) to British consul-general at Bushehr, January 20, 1898; in *Muscat Dhows Arbitration*, 41, and J. G. Lorimer, *Gazetteer of the Persian Gulf*, vol. 4, 2498.

4. Lansing penned a hymn about Arabia in 1889 that would serve as the mission's theme song; it contained a prescient verse: "To the host of Islam's leading/For the slave in bondage bleeding/To the desert dweller pleading/Bring His love to them" (cited in Scudder, *The Arabian Mission's Story*, 137–138).

5. P. J. Zwemer, "A School for Slave Boys," *The Mission Field* 9, no. 6 (October 1896): 194–195.

6. Reformed Church in America Archives, New Brunswick, NJ (RCA), Scudder Files–Muscat School 8/18, 6/49, 99.06, 1-0-08-0-04, "List of (16) sixteen liberated slave boys mentioned in the bond passed by Rev'd James Cantine representative of the American Arabian Mission, Maskat (July 14, 1899)," in No. 336 of 1899, Major C. G. F. Fagan, Political Agent & HBM's Consul, Muskat, to Rev'd James Cantine, American Arabian Mission, Muskat, 11 July 1899.

7. P. J. Zwemer, "Arabian Mission Notes," *The Mission Field* 9, no. 11 (March 1897): 163–164.

8. "At Home and Abroad," *The Mission Field* 10, no. 3 (July 1897): 71.

9. P. J. Zwemer, "Muscat," *Arabian Mission Field Report* 18 (April 1–June 30, 1896): 9–10.

10. The formative studies on the African diaspora in the Indian Ocean—Harris, *The African Presence in Asia*, and Shepperson, "The African Abroad"—have been supplemented by several important studies, including the following: Alpers: "The African Diaspora in the Northwestern Indian Ocean," and "Recollecting Africa"; Jayasuriya and Pankhurst, eds., *The African Diaspora in the Indian Ocean;* Catlin-Jairazbhoy and Alpers, *Sidis and Scholars;* Mirzai, "Slavery, the Abolition of the Slave Trade, and the Emancipation of Slaves in Iran, 1828–1928"; Larson: "Horrid Journeying," and *Ocean of Letters;* Campbell, ed., *The Structure of Slavery in Indian Ocean Africa and Asia*.

11. Lloyd, *The Navy and the Slave Trade*, 271; Gilbert, *Dhows and the Colonial Economy of Zanzibar*, 63.

12. For conventional narratives, see M. Gordon, *Slavery in the Arab World*, and B. Lewis, *Race and Slavery in the Middle East*. Notable exceptions include Y. Hakan Erdem's account of agricultural and industrial slavery in the Ottoman Empire, especially in textile production in Bursa and sharecropping near Istanbul in the sixteenth and seventeenth centuries in *Slavery in the Ottoman Empire*, 1–17.

13. Sheriff, *Slaves, Spices and Ivory*, 37–41; Landen, *Oman since 1856*.

14. Hawley, *Oman and Its Renaissance;* Al-Fahim, *From Rags to Riches;* Clements, *Oman;* Plekhanov, *A Reformer on the Throne*.

15. Cooper, *Plantation Slavery on the East Coast of Africa;* Allen, *Slaves, Freedmen, and Indentured Laborers;* Alpers, *Ivory and Slaves;* Sheriff, *Slaves, Spices and Ivory;* Campbell, *An Economic History of Imperial Madagascar;* Glassman, *Feasts and Riot*.

16. Sheriff, *Slaves, Spices and Ivory*, 35.

17. Gordon, *Slavery in the Arab World*; B. Lewis: *Race and Slavery in the Middle East*, and "Other People's History." Murray Gordon theorized that slavery in Arab countries was linked to a natural Arab disinclination for work. "Household slavery," he wrote, "was an indispensable form of labor in Arab society, where the people were ill-disposed to doing menial work." Arabs, he explained, were "too proud" to work as servants or "too independent in spirit to serve a master" (58). Ronald Segal explained, "Slaves in Islam were directed mainly at the service sector—concubines and cooks, porters and soldiers—with slavery itself primarily a form of consumption rather than a factor of production" (*Islam's Black Slaves*, 3–4). Bernard Lewis stated that "the most important slaves" were "domestic and commercial, and it is they who were the characteristic slave of the Muslim world" (*Race and Slavery in the Middle East*, 13–14).

18. Blackburn, *The Making of New World Slavery*; Solow, ed., *Slavery and the Rise of the Atlantic System*; Williams, *Capitalism and Slavery*.

19. Said, *Orientalism*, 262.

20. Austen, "From the Atlantic to the Indian Ocean."

21. Brunschvig, "'Abd"; Clarence-Smith, *Islam and the Abolition of Slavery*; Zilfi, *Women and Slavery*, 96–152.

22. For an excellent overview of the development of this historiography, see Toledano: "The Concept of Slavery in Ottoman and Other Muslim Societies," and *Slavery and Abolition in the Ottoman Middle East*, 135–168.

23. Zilfi, *Women and Slavery*, 96–152; Toledano, *As If Silent and Absent* and *Slavery and Abolition*; Erdem, *Slavery in the Ottoman Empire*; Troutt Powell, "Will That Subaltern Ever Speak?; Walz and Cuno, eds., *Race and Slavery in the Middle East*.

24. Campbell: "Introduction," xix–xx, and "Slavery in the Indian Ocean World."

25. Gelvin, *The Modern Middle East*, 35–46, 73–87; Wallerstein et al., "The Incorporation of the Ottoman Empire into the World Economy," 88–97; Owen, *The Middle East in the World Economy*, 180–188.

26. Hopper, "The African Presence in Arabia," 101–161.

27. Cited in Palgrave, *Personal Narrative*, 387.

28. Vernet, "Le commerce"; R. B. Allen, *Slaves, Freedmen, and Indentured Laborers*; Sheriff, *Slaves, Spices and Ivory*, 48–49, 64–69.

29. See, for example, Mignan, *A Winter Journey*, vol. 2, 240–245; Keppel, *Personal Narrative*, 19–23.

30. J. G. Lorimer, *Gazeteer of the Persian Gulf*, vol. 2, 238–241, 489–490, 1058–1077, 1382–1451. Campbell Gibson and Kay Jung, "Historical Census Statistics on Population Totals by Race, 1790 to 1990," U.S. Census Bureau Population Division Working Paper Series No. 56 (September 2002). By contrast, African Americans accounted for 10–12 percent of the U.S. population in the censuses of 1900 and 1910. Available at http://www.census.gov/population/www/documentation/twps0056/twps0056.html (accessed October 8, 2008).

31. W. Johnson, *River of Dark Dreams*.

32. See a helpful discussion on this point in Clarence-Smith, *Islam and the Abolition of Slavery*, 16–17.

33. Walz and Cuno, eds., *Race and Slavery in the Middle East*, 1.
34. R. Cohen, *Global Diasporas*, 162–167.
35. Alpers, "Recollecting Africa," 83–99.
36. Larson, *Ocean of Letters*, 350.
37. Larson, "Horrid Journeying."
38. Klein, Sheriff, and Austen cited in Larson, "Horrid Journeying," 439.
39. Larson, "Horrid Journeying," 442.
40. Chakrabarty, *Provincializing Europe*, 3–4.
41. Larson, "Reconsidering Trauma, Identity, and the African Diaspora."
42. Campbell, "Slavery in the Indian Ocean World," 60–61.
43. J. C. Miller, "A Theme in Variations."
44. Cooper, *Plantation Slavery on the East Coast of Africa*.
45. Alpers, "Slave Trade: Eastern Africa," 95–96; Campbell, "Slavery in the Indian Ocean World," 57.
46. Mintz, *Sweetness and Power*; Kurlansky, *Salt*; Stein, *Plumes*; Glahn, *Fountain of Fortune*; Wong, *China Transformed*; Manning, *Navigating World History*; Pomeranz, *The Great Divergence*; Prestholdt, *Domesticating the World*; Ho, *The Graves of Tarim*; Andrade, "A Chinese Farmer, Two African Boys, and a Warlord"; Trivellato, "Is There a Future for Italian Microhistory in the Age of Global History?"

Chapter 1. The East African Slave Trade and the Making of the African Diaspora in Arabia

1. "Where Slaves Are Slaves," *The Bystander*, November 27, 1907, 431. See also K. Hamilton and Salmon, eds., *Slavery, Diplomacy and Empire*, 114–115; "Chasing Freedom: The Royal Navy and the Suppression of the Transatlantic Slave Trade," Exhibition at National Museum of the Royal Navy, Portsmouth, UK, 2007.
2. J. S. Saldanha, "Précis on the Slave Trade in the Gulf of Oman and the Persian Gulf, 1873–1905 (With a Retrospect into Previous History from 1852) [Secret]" (1906), 50–52, 69; IOR L/PS/20/C246.
3. In making this argument, I am building on the ideas advanced by Gwyn Campbell in "Slavery in the Indian Ocean World," 52–63.
4. See the excellent discussions on this subject in Clarence-Smith, *Islam and the Abolition of Slavery*, 16–17, and Sheriff, *Dhow Cultures*, 217–237.
5. See, for example, the correspondence of Atkins Hamerton, agent of the British East India Company and British consul at Zanzibar. Hamerton wrote: "Each and every one the subjects of His Highness the Omam of Muskat are concerned in the slave trade. . . . The meanest of the Imam's subjects in Oman, Zanzibar and the Coast of Africa, whether an Arab, a half caste Arab, or a freedman, such freeman being a Mussulman, never dreams of doing any sort of labor. . . . Slavery is in the opinion of all Arabs a right guaranteed to them by their religion." Hamerton to Sec. Gov. Bombay, January 2, 1842; ZNA AA 12/29.
6. Sheriff, *Slaves, Spices and Ivory*.
7. Coupland, *East Africa and Its Invaders*, 4.

8. M. Gordon, *Slavery in the Arab World*, 58. Gordon linked the institution of slavery in the Middle East over several centuries to the legacy of early Muslim conquests and the Arab practice of secluding and veiling women. "Secluded within the confines of her own home and obliged to veil her face wherever she went in public, the Arab woman was turned into a sex object." According to Gordon, the thousands of military captives who were enslaved and taken back to Arabia after the early Muslim conquests had a profound impact on Arab society, implanting the institution of slavery into the Arab character: "This cheap, servile form of labor was quickly substituted in place of free women whose interest in work was dulled by the confining dicta of Islamic law. What purpose was there for a wife to take on the daily time-consuming and laborious chores of the household when obedient hands could be directed to do them in her place? The household work ethic could scarcely survive in these circumstances, particularly when free women were forced to while away much of their time in their sexually segregated quarters. This set the stage for use of imported slaves around the house" (60–61).

9. J. J. Miller, "The Unknown Slavery." "Judging by the sheer volume of material, one might come away with the mistaken impression that nowhere was the vile institution of slavery more entrenched than among the American hypocrites who declared that all men are created equal. And yet throughout Muslim history, starting with Mohammed himself, slavery was a vigorous and central part of Islamic civilization," Miller wrote. "Going back to Islam's birth in the 7th century," he explained, "14 million black slaves have been sold to Muslims" in contrast to "10 to 11 million Africans shipped in chains to the Western Hemisphere between 1650 and 1900," 41 and 42.

10. Sheriff, *Dhow Cultures*, 219.

11. In 1876, for example, the resident British government surgeon in Muscat estimated that a quarter of Muscat and Mutrah's forty thousand residents were "Negroes" and half of the remaining population was of "mixed race," consisting of "different degrees of admixture between the Arab and the Negro, and the Arab and the Abyssinian." See A. S. G. Jayakar, "Medical Topography of Muscat," Administrative Report of the Persian Gulf Political Residency and Muscat Political Agency for the Year 1876–77; CDR ND 1/H.

12. See chapter 2.
13. See chapter 3.
14. J. G. Lorimer, *Gazetteer of the Persian Gulf*, vol. 2.
15. *A Handbook of Arabia*, April 1919; IOR L/P&S/20/E 84, 239–260.
16. Ibid.
17. Ibid., 335–339.
18. *Ibid.*, 286–296.
19. Ovington, *A Voyage to Suratt*, 420–445.
20. A. Hamilton, *A New Account of the East Indies*, 64–66.
21. Ibid., 78.
22. Parsons, *Travels in Asia and Africa*, 154–161, 202–211.

23. Porter, *Remarks on the Bloachee, Brodia and Arabian Coasts, by Lieutenant John Porter in the Dolphin Brigg.*

24. D. Saunders, *A Journal of the Travels and Sufferings of Daniel Saunders.*

25. Niebuhr, *Travels through Arabia*, 113–124.

26. Razik, *Al-fath al-mubin al-mubarhim sirat al-sadat Al bu Sa'idiyin;* cited in Sheriff, *Slaves, Spices and Ivory*, 35.

27. Sheriff, *Slaves, Spices and Ivory*, 37.

28. Malcolm, *Sketches of Persia*, 17–21.

29. Ibid. 18.

30. J. Johnson, *A Journey from India to England*, 9–12. "In passing through the Bazar at Muscat, we saw an Arab with a stick in his hand, walking to and fro between two lots of boys and girls whom he was offering for sale, proclaiming aloud successively the price fixed on each," Johnson recalled. "They were ill clothed, and looked as if not at all concerned as to the event, having perhaps but few human comforts the loss of which to regret."

31. Buckingham, *Travels in Assyria, Media, and Persia*, 484.

32. Heude, *A Voyage up the Persian Gulf*, 24–25. Heude remarked that "most of the inhabitants who could afford it," including the sultan, migrated out of the city to "date plantations inland."

33. Mignan, *A Winter Journey*, 240–245.

34. Keppel, *Personal Narrative*, 19–23. Keppel stated his opinion of the appearance of the women as follows: "They are not handsome, as they partake too much of the flat noses and thick lips of their mothers." He described the slave auction as follows: "The market was held in an open space near the landing-place. Some twenty or thirty fat little negresses, from twelve to fourteen years of age, having their woolly locks neatly plaited, and their bodies well oiled, to give them a sleek appearance, were arranged in two rows, on some logs of timber. Too young to trouble themselves with their degraded state, they sat giggling and chattering with the utmost nonchalance. . . . In the meantime, the slave merchant was leading by the hand one of the party, and calling out her price. As for herself, she seemed more intent to catch the joke of her companion, than to ascertain any thing respecting her future destiny."

35. Ibid., 23.

36. D. Wilson, Resident, Persian Gulf, to Secretary Williamson, January 28, 1931; reprinted in *Returns: Slave Trade, East India and Ceylon* (House of Commons, July 31, 1838), 89–93.

37. Sheriff, *Slaves, Spices and Ivory*, 38.

38. Bhacker, *Trade and Empire*, 131.

39. See A. S. G. Jayakar, "Medical Topography of Muscat," Administrative Report of the Persian Gulf Political Residency and Muscat Political Agency for the Year 1876–77; CDR ND 1/H.

40. In fact, evidence for this trade is scant. See, for example, Talhami, "The Zanj Rebellion Reconsidered." See also Dunn, *The Adventures of Ibn Battuta*, and Bradley and Cartledge, eds., *The Cambridge World History of Slavery*, vol. 1, 75, and Pouwels, "Eastern Africa and the Indian Ocean to 1800."

41. Sheriff, *Dhow Cultures*, 217–237.

42. On this period see Kennedy, *The Prophet and the Age of the Caliphates*, 179–187.

43. Vernet argues that it is not possible to estimate the trade in the sixteenth century ("Slave Trade," 59). Lovejoy, *Transformations in Slavery*, 25; Larson, *Ocean of Letters*, 41. For simplicity's sake, for the purposes of these estimates I am including Madagascar but excluding the northeast African (or Red Sea) slave trade, although there was certainly considerable overlap between both of these regions and the East African trade to Arabia.

44. Vernet, "Le commerce."

45. Ibid.; Lovejoy, *Transformations in Slavery*, 60; Larson, *Ocean of Letters*, 41; Hooper and Eltis, "The Indian Ocean in Transatlantic Slavery," 17.

46. Sheriff, *Slaves, Spices and Ivory*, 43.

47. Hooper and Eltis, "The Indian Ocean in Transatlantic Slavery," 6. The authors argue that "the French route from the Indian Ocean to the Caribbean would probably not have existed without the Mascerenes," which provided an essential "bulking" function.

48. See R. B. Allen: *Slaves, Freedmen, and Indentured Laborers*; "The Mascarene Slave Trade," 38–41, and "The Constant Demand of the French"; and Sheriff, *Slaves, Spices and Ivory*, 64–69. Maria Theresa dollars, a silver currency, were popular in the Indian Ocean in the nineteenth century.

49. Sheriff, *Slaves, Spices and Ivory*, 68.

50. Ibid., 48–49.

51. Vernet, "East Africa: Slave Migrations," 2–3.

52. Cooper, *Plantation Slavery on the East Coast of Africa*; R. B. Allen, *Slaves, Freedmen, and Indentured Laborers*; Alpers, *Ivory and Slaves*; Sheriff, *Slaves, Spices and Ivory*; Campbell, *An Economic History of Imperial Madagascar*; Glassman, *Feasts and Riot*.

53. Hooper and Eltis, "The Indian Ocean in Transatlantic Slavery," 7–10.

54. Ewald, "Africa," 41.

55. Alpers, *Ivory and Slaves*, 215.

56. Hafkin, "Trade, Society, and Politics," 256; Sheriff, *Slaves, Spices and Ivory*, 226.

57. Hooper and Eltis, "The Indian Ocean in Transatlantic Slavery," 17.

58. Earlier estimates can be found in a variety of sources, including Baur, *Voyage dans l'Oudoe et l'Ouzigua*, 91; Beachey, *The African Diaspora and East Africa*, 14; Reusch, *History of East Africa*, 318; all cited in Martin and Ryan, "A Quantitative Assessment of the Arab Slave Trade of East Africa," 72; Ricks, "Slaves and Slave Traders in the Persian Gulf"; Austen: "The Islamic Slave Trade out of Africa," and "The 19th-Century Islamic Slave Trade from East Africa"; and Manning, *Slavery and African Life*, 79–81. For an excellent discussion on the challenges of retrieving quantitative data for Indian Ocean slavery, see Alpers, "Introduction," and "Mozambique and 'Mozambiques.'"

59. Lovejoy, *Transformations in Slavery*, 151; Larson, *Ocean of Letters*, 41; Campbell, *An Economic History of Imperial Madagascar*, 238.

60. Sheriff, *Dhow Cultures*, 218.

61. Baur, *Voyage dans l'Oudoe et l'Ouzigua*, 91; Beachey, *The African Diaspora and East Africa*, 14; Reusch, *History of East Africa*, 318; all cited in Martin and Ryan, "A Quantitative Assessment of the Arab Slave Trade of East Africa," 72; Coupland, *East Africa and Its Invaders*; Nicholls, *The Swahili Coast*.

62. Leopold G. Heath, to Secretary of Admiralty, Whitehall, "Annual Report on the Slave Trade," March 1, 1869; PRO ADM 1/6093.

63. Ibid.

64. The results from the antislavery patrols between 1865 and 1873 indicate that the largest number of captures made in that period were made along the coast of Somalia (43 percent) and that the majority of enslaved men and women captured (55 percent) were found north of the sultan of Zanzibar's jurisdiction, either on their way up the Somali coast or having already arrived off the coast of Arabia. Well over three-quarters of the Africans captured by the Royal Navy in 1866, 1868, 1869, and 1872 were caught on the coasts of Arabia or Somalia near or to the north of Brava, so clearly bound toward Arabia.

65. C. P. Rigby to Anderson, "Report on the Zanzibar Dominions" (No. 39 of 1860, n.d., ca. June 1860); ZNA AA 3/19.

66. C. P. Rigby to Brigadier Coghlan, Secret Department, October 5, 1860; ZNA AA 12/2.

67. C. P. Rigby to Wilson, April 2, 1861; ZNA AA 3/20.

68. C. P. Rigby to Anderson, Secretary to Government of India, April 18, 1861; ZNA AA 12/2.

69. C. P. Rigby to Secretary to Government of Bombay, May 14, 1861; ZNA AA 12/2.

70. Martin and Ryan, "A Quantitative Assessment of the Arab Slave Trade of East Africa," 79–86. (Martin and Ryan's figure is based on an estimated 2,500 per year from the 1810s and 1820s, 3,500 in the 1830s, 4,000 in the 1840s, 6,500 from 1850 to 1873, and 400 from 1874 to 1896.)

71. Lovejoy, *Transformations in Slavery*, 150–151. (Lovejoy's figure is based on 2,500 per year shipped in the 1810s, 3,500 per year in the 1830s, 4,000 per year in the 1840s, 6,500 per year in the 1850s and 1860s, and a sharp decline to less than 500 per year after 1873.)

72. Sheriff, *Slaves, Spices and Ivory*, 37–41, 226–231. (However, Sheriff's reasons for citing low numbers were based on the problematic assumption of a declining economy in the Gulf.)

73. Austen, "The 19th-Century Islamic Slave Trade from East Africa," 29, 33.

74. The main exception can be found in Sheriff, *Slaves, Spices and Ivory*, 35–41, 223–235, which suggests an improbable declining curve for exports in the second half of the nineteenth century. See also Sheriff, "The Slave Trade and Its Fallout in the Persian Gulf," 106.

75. Alpers, "The Other Middle Passage."

76. The evidence available to historians for recovering the details of the slave trade in the Indian Ocean differs from that of the Atlantic context. Unlike the slave trade to

the Americas in the eighteenth century, slave shipments in the Indian Ocean were not carried out by trading companies in registered ships with careful records and insurance policies. Documentation is limited; occasional Arabic documents seized aboard a slave dhow appeared in the Vice Admiralty courts, but most of these were subsequently destroyed in the name of efficiency. Many surviving documents offer less helpful details and appear designed to serve more as *aide-mémoire* than formal transactions. For example, some Arabic documents in the Vice Admiralty records at Zanzibar list the prices paid for slaves but no other identifying features about them such as embarkation and disembarkation locations. Documents that have been preserved in Arabia itself are generally not in public archives or available to researchers. Therefore, much of what we know about the slave trade in East Africa comes from naval court records and observations made by European traders, colonial officials, and sailors and the testimonies of the slaves themselves. This final source can be the most valuable, although slave testimonies have been preserved in limited quantities and present their own challenges. Taken together, these sources can provide a fairly clear picture of the world of the East African slave trade. See Kirk, No. 12 of 1872: "On 14 May 1873 by Order of Dr. J. Kirk HBM's Agent and Consul at Zanzibar, these Papers have been destroyed, they being thought to be no longer required"; ZNA AA 7/4; Alpers and Hopper, "Parler en son nom?"

77. The distinguishing feature of slavery in East Africa, as elsewhere, was alienation. Enslavement meant separation from kin, removal from one's homeland, and—in Orlando Patterson's words—"natal alienation." See Patterson, *Slavery and Social Death*, 6–7. See also Cooper, *Plantation Slavery on the East Coast of Africa*, 1–20.

78. Alpers, "The Other Middle Passage," 33.

79. David Livingstone described the situation around Lake Nyasa in a letter to his young son in 1861: "Passing up a beautiful valley came out in sight of the heel of Lake Nyassa. We went along the shores occasionally having a bath in its waters till we came to two Arabs building a dhow or ship of the same shape I suppose as Abram built of old for King Solomon. They were transporting slaves across the Lake as fast as two boats could carry them and the dhow was intended to do it faster. They were civil and presented meat, rice, sugar cane and a bit of Malachite. They were buying boys like you for two yards of calico or a shilling and girls for 4 yards or 2 shillings each. A sort of war had driven down thousands of poor people to the Lake for the sake of hiding in the reeds or hoping the Arabs would shield them. Now they have to sell each other for food." David Livingstone to Thomas S. Livingstone, December 16, 1863; NLS MS 1071.

80. See, for example, White, *Magomero*, 1–70; Maxon, *East Africa*, 143–144.

81. See Alpers, *Ivory and Slaves*, 240–242; Larson, "Horrid Journeying," 441; Kilekwa, *Slave Boy to Priest*.

82. "1st Witness called: Named Sanga, Marenga of the Ziraha tribe near Ugogo, was captured in war by the Maviti, sold to traders and brought to the coast to Bueni near Dar Salam. Slept at Bueni five nights was then shipped in dhow, there were eight of us originally, some are not yet shipped./2nd Witness, Funga-Funga of Khuta, was caught in war and sold to people coming to the Coast, slept two days at Coast and was

then shipped./3rd Witness, Meta, [I] am of Ziraha, was taken by the Mariti and sold by them to people who brought me to the Coast, slept near the Coast five nights. Was shipped in dhow." Note of Proceedings, No. 2 of 1872, in the Vice Admiralty Court at Zanzibar, 20 January 1872; ZNA AA 7/4.

83. Livingstone, *Last Journals*, 75. But, in fact, Livingstone himself unintentionally contributed to the slave raiding and disruption of some of the places he visited. In the eastern Congo, for instance, the horrible massacre that Livingstone witnessed at Nyangue in July 1871 now appears to have been partly the result of his interference in Manyema. Livingstone's published diaries minimize his role in the events that led up to the massacre. But a newly revealed source in the form of Livingstone's 1871 field notebook, reconstructed by a transatlantic team of researchers and made public in November 2011, demonstrates that it was Livingstone's own insistence on procuring a canoe to explore the Lualaba River that led directly to the exchanges that caused the conflict. See Wisnicki et al., *Livingstone's 1871 Field Diary*.

84. Livingstone, *Last Journals*, 64.

85. Médard and Doyle, eds., *Slavery in the Great Lakes Region of East Africa*.

86. See Sheriff, "Localisation and Social Composition," and Suzuki, "Enslaved Population."

87. Edwin Seward to Government of Bombay, October 25, 1866; ZNA AA 3/26.

88. James Augustus Grant, Journal on Voyage with Thompson, August 28, 1890; NLS MS 17918.

89. Livingstone, *Last Journals*, 116.

90. See Waller, *Paths into the Slave Preserves of East Africa*, 36.

91. Alpers, "The Other Middle Passage," 22.

92. Alpers, "The Story of Swema," 212.

93. Atkins Hamerton to Secretary to Bombay Government, January 3, 1842; ZNA AA 12/29. See also Hamerton to Secretary of Bombay Government, July 13, 1841: "I fancy in no part of the world is the misery and human suffering these wretched slaves undergo, while being brought here, and until they are sold, exceeded in any part of the universe. They are in such a wretched state from starvation and disease that they are sometimes not considered worth landing and are allowed to expire in the boats to save the duty of a dollar a head, and [are eaten] by the dogs. None are buried."

94. Sheriff, *Slaves, Spices and Ivory*, 231.

95. Suzuki, "Enslaved Population."

96. David Livingstone to Agnes Livingstone, February 8, 1866; MS 10704 Livingstone Correspondence, National Library of Scotland (NLS), Edinburgh, Scotland.

97. Cooper, *Plantation Slavery on the East Coast of Africa*, 153–212.

98. Prestholdt, *Domesticating the World*, 117–146.

99. "At midday yesterday, I was again called by this man, and went. The Banian said, 'I want bread.' He stood before the door. Then when I came near, he drew me into his shop. (Here the witness hesitates long before she can be induced to continue

her disclosure.) When the Banian got me inside he shut my eyes and mouth. I cried out once when he shut the door. He then lifted my clothes, put clothes over my face and tied them around my head. He knelt before me and laid upon me. He had taken off my clothes and tied them around my head. I struggled with him. He laid upon me. He then did with me as a man with a woman. He pushed me (ashamed to make further revelation). I was in great pain and cried out once. I tore off the cloth from my face and mouth. Then we got up and I saw blood and I began to cry." Dr. Edwin Seward, Evidence in Record of Case of Kehonja, aged 10 or 12 years, April 25–26, 1866; Outward Political Department, ZNA AA 3/26.

100. Atkins Hamerton to Commr. William Smyth HMS *Grecian*, December 5, 1841; ZNA AA 12/29.

101. S. Hennell, Resident, Persian Gulf, to Chief Sec to Govt of Bombay, from Muscat Cove, December 17, 1839; ZNA AA 12/29; Correspondence of Atkins Hamerton, British Consul at Zanzibar, 1841–1857.

102. A Report from (Moollam Houssain) Native Agent at Shargah, October 21, 1846; ZNA AA 12/29; Correspondence of Atkins Hamerton, British Consul at Zanzibar, 1841–1857.

103. Rigby to Secretary of Bombay Gov't, March 30, 1860; ZNA AA 12/2.

104. Ibid.

105. C. P. Rigby to Gov of India, April 18, 1861; ZNA AA 12/2.

106. "HMS *Wolverine* v. Zanzibar Dhow, Seized 9 Jan. 1872, Condemned Jan. 11, 1872"; Proceedings of Vice Admiralty Court, Zanzibar, January 11, 1872; No. 1 of 1872, ZNA AA 7/4.

107. Hamis bin Seyed bin Nasr to Sheikh Hamood bin Abdullah Mussarifi (20 Rabia il [Awwal] 1282) in Latham to Seward, September 23, 1865; ZNA AA 3/25. (Later, a captain captured en route from Pemba to Oman estimated his profits from delivering seventy-five slaves and other cargo would amount to MT$400; 1865 AA 3/25.)

108. "Examination of the Nakhoda of the slaver dhow *Yasmeen* captured by HMS *Vulture* and destroyed near Ras el Hadd, before Lt. Col. E. C. Ross, Political Agent and Consul, Muscat, 12 September 1972"; IOR R/15/6/5. (Letters seized aboard the *Yasmeen* in 1872 also verify that many passengers looking for passage to Oman preferred not to travel on ships carrying slaves.) In most of the literature on the slave trade in East Africa, slave traders are described in generic terms, simply as "Arab." In practice, Arab slave traders came from a small number of ports and represented only a fraction of the Arab tribes resident or trading in East Africa. In the testimonies of manumitted slaves, Arab slave traders are almost universally described as Suri Arabs, and there is little doubt that Suris made up a large proportion of dealers of slaves from East Africa. However, the name "Suri" applied to residents of the Sharqīya region of Oman generally and may have equally referred to residents of Jalān, Al-Kāmil, Al-Ashkara, Ras al-Hadd, or any village between them. While Sur was the primary entry point for most slaves entering the Gulf, it was not uncommon for dealers to come from inland towns and hire dhows from Sur, a custom that explains in part how, if a British patrol were sighted, captains could routinely put in at Al-Ashkara or smaller points to the south

and travel by land to the interior. As late as 1900, Sur was known to annually import nearly one thousand slaves, who were sent to destinations in the Gulf in small coasting craft or sent overland to the north. "Qāsimī" (pl. Qawāsim) is regrettably imprecise in nineteenth-century colonial documents and may refer to Arabs from the Gulf, although the centers of this particular tribe were Sharjah and Ras al-Khaimah. The British associated these Arabs with piracy and were quick to link anyone involved in the slave trade to piracy and their nemesis from the earlier nineteenth century. See also Marques of Lansdowne to Sir E. Monson, April 16, 1902; IOR R/15/1/552.

109. Letters addressed to buyers consistently show a significant representation of women among purchasers in Arabia. Letters seized by the HMS *Vigilant* in 1865 included slave trade correspondence to and from women, including a letter from [Azīza] bint Abdullah Misherafi that accompanied ten slaves she was sending to Hamood bin Abdullah Misherafi in the dhow of Omar bin Ali bin Ahmed. "Letters found in dhow taken by HMS *Vigilant*, 22nd September 1865"; ZNA AA 3/25. Another letter seized by the HMS *Vigilant* indicated that slaves of certain ethnicities were identified to be sent to purchasers in Oman, presumably by request. The letter included the following details:

The names of the slaves are these:

1. Sweil, a big one, he speaks Arabic and knows all the slaves.
2. A little boy named Songolo for Hamud bin Bedran bin Ahmed, of the slave tribe Myao.
3. A little boy named Jaisir, an Mgindo for Hamūd bin Bedran, his price was $14 1/2.
4. A girl who knows Arabic named Huda, a Myao for Hamud bin Bedran, $23 without customs duties.
5. A girl named Warada an Mnyasa belonging to Bint Ahmed bin Sayf. . . . The slaves are marked by shaving on the top of the head.

(April 1861; AA 12/2; Hamis bin Seyed bin Nasr to Sheikh Hamood bin Abdullah Mussarifi [20 Rabia il Akher (Thani) 1282]; ZNA AA 3/25).

Chapter 2. Slavery, Dates, and Globalization

1. Journal of Charles A. Benson, Barque *Glide* 1862–63, Charles Benson Papers (MSS 15), Peabody Essex Museum (PEM); Putnam, *Salem Vessels*, 62–105; Atwood, "Memorial of John Bertram." See also Sokolow, *Charles Benson*. An expanded version of this chapter appears as Hopper, "The Globalization of Dried Fruit."
2. See, for example, M. Gordon, *Slavery in the Arab World*, and Segal, *Islam's Black Slaves*. More recently, Walz and Cuno have argued that "Although slavery was an integral feature of Middle Eastern societies in the past, its history was different" (*Race and Slavery in the Middle East*, 1).
3. Popenoe, "The Distribution of the Date Palm."
4. Gilbert, *Dhows and the Colonial Economy of Zanzibar*, 33–36; Bennett, *New England Merchants in Africa*; Sheriff, *Slaves, Spices and Ivory*; Prestholdt, "On the Global Repercussions of East African Consumerism."

5. Bhacker, *Trade and Empire*, 109–113, 136–137.
6. C. H. Allen, "Sayyids, Shets and Sultāns," 140–156.
7. Kelly, *Britain and the Persian Gulf, 1795–1880*, 36–37. For a regional perspective, see Alpers, "The Western Indian Ocean."
8. *Persian Gulf Administration Annual Reports, 1873–1905.*
9. *Charleston City Gazette*, November 7, 1818; *Georgetown National Messenger*, December 16, 1818; *New York Daily Advertiser*, October 10, 1918; *New York Evening Post*, September 14, 1818.
10. Putnam, *Salem Vessels*, 62–63.
11. Atkins Hamerton to Malet, Government of India, August 26, 1852; Zanzibar National Archives (ZNA), AA 3/11. Cloth included twenty-five pieces of thirty-one yards in each bale.
12. "Journal kept on Board the Bark *Warren White* of New York, Benjamin Creamer Master, for a Transatlantic Trading Voyage. Carried Cargo of Dates" (Log 325), *Warren White* (Bark) Journal 1852–53, G. W. Blunt White Library, Mystic Seaport Museum (MSM).
13. Atkins Hamerton to Malet, Secretary to Government of India, June 30, 1853; ZNA AA 3/11.
14. C. P. Rigby to W. M. Coghlan, October 15, 1860; ZNA AA 3/19.
15. "Journal of Lawrence Pierson Ward Kept aboard the Bark *Elizabeth Hall* 1851–52" (Log 1851E2 Elizabeth Hall, Bark), Peabody Essex Museum (PEM).
16. "Journal Kept by William H. Townsend on Board the Bark *Imaum* of Salem, Mass., Stanford Perkins Master, 1858–59" (Log 579), G. W. Blunt White Library, Mystic Seaport Museum (MSM).
17. W. H. Hathorne to John Bertram, October 20, 1866; W. H. Hathorne to John Bertram, November 4, 1866; John Bertram Papers (MSS 104), Box 5, f. 5, Peabody Essex Museum (PEM).
18. C. H. Allen, "Sayyids, Shets and Sultāns," 140–153.
19. D'Antonio, *Hershey*, 106–126. Per capita candy consumption in the United States jumped from thirteen pounds in 1932 to nineteen pounds in 1941. See Hadary, "The Candy-Consumer."
20. Hills Brothers Company, *One Hundred Delights*, 5–13.
21. U.S. Department of Agriculture, *Yearbook of the United States Department of Agriculture*, 1894–1935.
22. C. H. Allen, "Sayyids, Shets and Sultāns," 140–156; Speece, "Aspects of Economic Dualism in Oman."
23. Popenoe, "The Home of the Fardh Date," 11.
24. Popenoe: *Date Growing*, 232–234, and "The Home of the Fardh Date," 11.
25. Each date-importing syndicate had its own logo on its boxes to distinguish it from its competitors. The Hills Brothers Company used the symbol "A1" on one side and a crown on the opposite side; Asfar and Company used "A. & Co.," etc.
26. Dowson and Aten, *Dates*, 261–262; Dowson, *Dates and Date Cultivation*, 43–57.
27. Dowson and Aten, *Dates*, 262.

28. C. H. Allen, "Sayyids, Shets and Sultāns,"151–155.

29. Wilkinson, *Water and Tribal Settlement*, 28–32, 36–47.

30. Ibid., 47–51; Graf, "The Batinah Hydrologic Area"; Dale, "The Water Resources of Oman."

31. "Report of Mr. Dawson, American Manager of the Iraq Date Company Following a Visit to the Batina in 1927"; IOR R/15/1/460. For an excellent discussion of social and cultural aspects of the *zijrah (zaygra)* and *manjūr* in Oman, see Limbert, "The Senses of Water in an Omani Town."

32. "The Word of Sultan Sa'id bin Taimur, Sultan of Muscat and Oman, about the History of the Financial Position of the Sultanate in the Past and the Hopes for the Future, after the Export of Oil, January 1968"; reprinted in Whitehead Consulting Group, *Sultanate of Oman Economic Survey, 1972*, appendix 2.

33. Thomas, *Alarms and Excursions*, 125–126, 142.

34. "Report of Mr. Dawson, American Manager of the Iraq Date Company Following a Visit to the Batina in 1927"; IOR R/15/1/460.

35. Thomas, *Alarms and Excursions*, 238.

36. *Administration Report of the Political Agency, Muscat, for the Year 1876–77*, 79–82; CDR ND1/H.

37. Senior Naval Officer in Persian Gulf (and Commander HMS *Vulture*) to Rear Admiral Arthur Cumming, Commander in Chief, East Indies, September 10, 1872; PRO ADM 1/6230; Lt. C. M. Gilbert-Cooper, "Capture of a Slave Dhow: Or the Vulture and Its Prey," n.d.; Lt. C. M. Gilbert-Cooper Papers, BGY/G/5; National Maritime Museum, London (NMM).

38. "Examination of the Nakhoda of the slaver dhow *Yasmeen* captured by HMS *Vulture* and destroyed near Ras el Hadd before Lt. Col. E. C. Ross, Political Agent and Consul, Muscat, 12 September 1872"; IOR R/15/6/5.

39. Commander HMS *Philomel* to Commander in Chief, East Indies, October 15, 1884; PRO ADM 1/6714.

40. Herbert W. Dowding, Commander HMS *Osprey*, to Rear Admiral Frederick W. Richards, Commander in Chief, East Indies, September 19, 1885; PRO ADM 1/6758.

41. Secretary to Government of Bombay to Political Resident, Persian Gulf, October 31, 1889; IOR R/15/1/200. "Few [slaves] seem to be sent inland to the Sharkeyyeh and Jaalan, as owing to the system of irrigation in those parts, there is not the same demand for labor on the date plantations as there is in the Batinah, where the date trees have to be watered from wells"; Maj. Saddler, "Report on visit to Sur," April 1895, no. 5–11; cited in J. A. Saldanha, "Précis of Maskat Affairs, 1892–1905," Part I, p. 53; IOR L/PS/20/C245.

42. S. B. Miles to E. C. Ross, December 7, 1885; IOR L/PS/20/C246.

43. S. B. Miles to E. C. Ross, October 31, 1884; IOR L/PS/20/C246.

44. Political Agent, Muscat, to Political Resident, Persian Gulf, January 21, 1930; IOR R/15/1/230.

45. PRPG to Foreign Secretary to the Government of India, New Delhi, March 18, 1930; IOR R/15/1/230.

46. G. P. Murphy, P. A. Muscat, to PRPG, n.d., No. 69 of 1929; IOR R/15/1/225.
47. Meillassoux, *The Anthropology of Slavery;* Manning, *Slavery and African Life,* 114–115.
48. "Statement made by Almas of Swahil, aged 38 years, recorded on 27th Shaban 1343," March 23, 1925; IOR R/15/1/208.
49. "Statement of Almas bin Khamis, aged about 40, of Swahil, recorded in Sabzabad," April 13, 1925; Commanding Officer HMS *Lupin* to Senior Naval Officer, Persian Gulf, HMS *Triad*, February 24, 1925; IOR R/15/1/208.
50. "Statement of Feroze (father not known), negro, slave of Hamad bin Majid of Dubai (Trucial Oman), aged about 40," October 13, 1926; IOR R/15/1/216.
51. "Cyclone" is the meteorological term used for a "hurricane" in the Indian Ocean, just as "typhoon" is the name for the same phenomenon in the Pacific. The term "hurricane" is technically only used in the Atlantic. All of these terms refer to the same phenomenon: a "cyclonic storm."
52. Fisher and Membery, "Climate."
53. *Administration Report of the Muscat Political Agency for 1884–85;* IOR R/15/6/17.
54. Surgeon Major A. S. G. Jayakar (in charge Pol. Agency Muscat) to Col. E. C. Ross (Pol Res in the Persian Gulf and Consul Gen for Fars, etc.), Muscat, September 21, 1890; IOR R/15/6/20.
55. E. C. Ross, Political Resident in the Persian Gulf and Consul General for Fars to W. J. Cuningham, Sect to Govt of India Foreign Dept, Calcutta, December 29, 1890; IOR R/15/6/20.
56. Herbert W. Dowding, HMS *Osprey,* to Rear Admiral Sir Fred'k W. Richards, Commander in Chief, September 19, 1885; National Archives, UK, Admiralty Records, ADM 1/6758.
57. Commander Ripon, HMS *Ranger,* to H. W. Dowding, HMS *Osprey,* Senior Naval Officer, Persian Gulf Division, October 19, 1885; National Archives, UK, Admiralty Records, ADM 1/6758.
58. Peter Zwemer, "A Plea for the Support of a Few Rescued Slaves at Muscat," *Arabian Mission Field Report* 19 (July–September 1896): 9–11.
59. J. S. Saldanha, "Précis on the Slave Trade in the Gulf of Oman and the Persian Gulf, 1873–1905 (With a Retrospect into Previous History from 1852) [Secret]" (1906), 37–41; IOR L/PS/20/C246.
60. M. Davis, *Late Victorian Holocausts.*
61. Hourwich, "The Crisis in Russian Agriculture"; Hane, *Peasants, Rebels, Women, and Outcastes,* 27; Barton, *The Red Cross,* 136–142.
62. M. Davis, *Late Victorian Holocausts.* Steven Serels notes that the regional famine in Sudan that lasted from 1887 to 1891 was only partly attributable to climate. Mahdist military strategy and Anglo-Egyptian responses contributed as well. Mahdist commander 'Abd al-Rahman Al-Nujumi's efforts to expand and provision his forces in 1888 and British destruction of crops along the Nile to prevent this provisioning contributed to food shortages and famine. See Serels: "Watering Slaves and Growing Grain," and

"Famines of War." For more on the famines in northeast Africa in this period, see Pankhurst and Johnson, "The Great Drought and Famine," and de Waal, *Famine That Kills*.

63. Cooper, *Plantation Slavery on the East Coast of Africa*, 126.
64. Ibid., 128.
65. Gelvin and Green, "Introduction," in Gelvin and Green, eds., *Global Muslims*; Gelvin, "Modernity, Tradition."
66. Winseck and Pike, *Communication and Empire*, 1–42.
67. J. H. Wilson, *United States Telegraphic Cipher*, 12.
68. Albion, *The Rise of New York Port*.
69. Riggs, "The Fruit-Ships at New York."
70. Putnam, *Salem Vessels*, 103.
71. Cited in ibid., 108.
72. Popenoe, *Date Growing*, 233.
73. *Los Angeles Times*, February 16, 1917.
74. Owen, *The Middle East in the World Economy*, 182.
75. Popenoe, *Date Growing*, 233; U.S. Department of Agriculture, *Yearbook of the United States Department of Agriculture*, 1912.
76. Ibid., 1930, 958.
77. These companies included Gray Dawes and Company, Lynch Brothers, D. Sassoon and Company, the Oman-Ottoman Company, and the Euphrates and Tigris Steam Navigation Company. For more on the role of British shipping on the Tigris and Euphrates, see Fattah, *The Politics of Regional Trade*, 123–158.
78. Munro, *Maritime Enterprise and Empire*, 178.
79. India, Commercial Intelligence Department, *Annual Statement*. Statistics, 1885–1930.
80. H. M. Government to the Council of the League of Nations, *Annual Reports*, 1920–1931. For more on Iraq in the mandate period, see Sluglett, *Britain in Iraq*, and Dodge, *Inventing Iraq*.
81. Major R. M. Smith to Major Bateman Champion, June 1, 1878; FO 60/414; cited in Munro, *Maritime Enterprise*, 178.
82. *The Story of a Pantry Shelf*, 130–132.
83. Fairchild, *The World Was My Garden*, 235–236.
84. William Hills to Ratansi Purshotum, October 27, 1905; Ratansi Purshotum Papers, private collection, Muscat, Sultanate of Oman; The *Story of a Pantry Shelf*, 133.
85. *The Story of a Pantry Shelf*, 133–136.
86. Sharon Thoms, "The Date Season," *Arabian Mission: Quarterly Letters from the Field* 31 (July–September 1899): 14–15.
87. Fairchild, "Persian Gulf Dates," 24.
88. "Turkistan Wins Date Race," *New York Times*, November 10, 1912, 6.
89. "Nostalgic Note," *Time*, December 8, 1941.
90. "Turkistan Wins Date Race," *New York Times*, November 10, 1912, 6.
91. "Date-Laden Ships Racing from Iraq," *New York Times*, October 3, 1930, 55.

92. Brad Evans, *Before Cultures*, 4. Evans demonstrates that distinctions formerly expressed in racial terms awaited a conceptualization for expressing difference in the United States. The anthropological notion of "cultures" that had circulated in Europe for half a century took additional time to catch on in the United States and only became popular with the work of early anthropologists like Franz Boas around 1910. Kroeber and Kluckhohn, in *Culture*, posit the existence of a "cultural lag" of about fifty years between the emergence of the culture concept in Germany in the works of Herder and Tylor in the late nineteenth century and the penetration of the term into British and American parlance through the work of early anthropologists.

93. Evans, *Before Cultures*, 4.

94. Silverman, *Art Nouveau in Fin-de-Siècle France*.

95. Edwards, ed., *Noble Dreams*.

96. Mitchell, "Images of Exotic Women."

97. R. J. Reynolds Tobacco Company, *Golden Leaves*, 34–46; Sobel, *They Satisfy*, 59–63, 72–82.

98. W. J. Towell date package, private collection of Vimal Purecha, Mutrah, Sultanate of Oman.

99. Palmer and Schlink, "Education and the Consumer," 189; Hills Brothers Company, *Dromedary Cook Book*, Hills Brothers Company, Department of Food Research, *Dates in the Healthful Diet*.

100. "A Gift from the Orient," Dromedary date advertisement from Hills Brothers Company in *Saturday Evening Post*, 1913.

101. Owen: *Cotton and the Egyptian Economy* and *The Middle East in the World Economy*; Issawi, "Middle East Economic Development"; Bernal, "Cotton and Colonial Order in Sudan"; Critz, Olmstead, and Rhode, "'Horn of Plenty.'"

102. Wallerstein et al., "The Incorporation of the Ottoman Empire into the World Economy."

103. See, for example, Prestholdt, *Domesticating the World*.

Chapter 3. Pearls, Slaves, and Fashion

1. Statement of Ismail bin Mubarak, Swahili, aged 40 years, recorded at the Political Agency, Bahrain, May 23, 1931; IOR R/15/1/209.

2. Telegram from HMS *Hastings*, Henjam Radio, to Political Resident in the Persian Gulf, No. 1501, March 30, 1931; "Summaries of Declarations of Refugee Slaves," April 1931; IOR R/15/1/209.

3. Cited in Palgrave, *Personal Narrative*, 387.

4. Kunz and Stevenson, *The Book of the Pearl*, 80; L. Rosenthal, *The Pearl Hunter*, 66.

5. J. G. Lorimer, *Gazetteer of the Persian Gulf*, vol. 1, part 2, 2227.

6. Villiers, *Sons of Sinbad*, 393–396. See also Al-Shamlan, *Pearling in the Arabian Gulf*.

7. E. L. Durand, *Administration Report of the Persian Gulf Political Residency and Muscat Political Agent for the Year 1877–78*, 32; PRO FO 78/5108; J. G. Lorimer, *Gazetteer of the Persian Gulf*, vol. 1; Villiers, *Sons of Sinbad*.

8. Belgrave, *Personal Column*, 43.

9. Captain E. L. Durand, "Notes on the Pearl Fisheries of the Persian Gulf," Appendix A to Part II, *Administration Report of the Persian Gulf Political Residency and Muscat Political Agency for the Year 1877–78* (Calcutta: Superintendent Government Printing, 1879), 34; CDR ND1/I.

10. J. G. Lorimer, *Gazetteer of the Persian Gulf*, vol. 1, part 2, 2228–2229.

11. For an excellent discussion of the operation of the pearling industry, see Al-Hijji, *Kuwait and the Sea*, 25–50.

12. E. L. Durand, *Administration Report of the Persian Gulf Political Residency and Muscat Political Agent for the Year 1877–78*, 32; PRO FO 78/5108. The term *sidi* (also rendered variously as "sedee," "seedee," and "seedie") was a term originating in northern India to describe people of African descent, many of whom were employed in maritime trade. In the wider Indian Ocean context, British officials applied the term to descendants of East Africans, enslaved and free, outside of East Africa. See Ewald, "Crossers of the Sea, 83.

13. J. G. Lorimer, *Gazetteer of the Persian Gulf*, vol. 1, 2228.

14. Harrison, *The Arab at Home*, 88.

15. Belgrave, *Personal Column*, 44.

16. Senior Naval Officer, Persian Gulf Division, HMS *Triad*, to Commander in Chief, East Indies Station, September 12, 1929; No. 27G/56/1, IOR L/PS/12/4091.

17. "Notes on Slave Trade by Wazir Thomas, August 1929"; P. 7418/29, IOR L/PS/12/4091.

18. Villiers, *Sons of Sinbad*, 375.

19. *Fatwa* of Khalīfa bin Yūsuf bin 'Ali al-Khamīrī, Qādhi of Abu Dhabi, dated 27th Rajab 1293; cited in W. F. Preideaux to T. H. Thornton, August 31, 1876; enclosure no. 5 in H. W. Norman (et al.) to Marquis of Salisbury (Secretary of State for India), November 9, 1876; copied in Burdett, ed., *Records of the Persian Gulf Pearl Fisheries*, vol. 1, 97–110.

20. "Statement of Mohammad bin Rāshid Al Bu Samat, resident of Lingah," August 9, 1887; reprinted in Burdett, ed., *Records of the Persian Gulf Pearl Fisheries*, vol. 1, 103.

21. Codrai, *The Emirates of Yesteryear*, 50–65.

22. Statement of Faraj bin Sulaiman born at Sawahil (Zanzibar) aged about 40 years. Recorded at Sharjah August 12, 1938; IOR R/15/1/211.

23. Statement made by Sa'ad bin Mubarak, aged about 40 years, recorded at Sharjah, January 31, 1938; IOR R/15/1/210.

24. Summary of Declaration of Juma bin Fundi, Swahili, Native of Mfenesini District of Zanzibar. Age unknown (recorded April 1931); IOR R/15/1/209.

25. W. L. Bond to Colonel G. Loch, December 27, 1933; IOR R/15/1/209. When Surūr arrived in Djibouti, he was interrogated by officers, and his story was passed on to the British consul at Addis Ababa, who in turn forwarded the details to the political agent at Muscat. For an excellent discussion of free Somali and other African free laborers in western Indian Ocean maritime work, see Ewald, "Crossers of the Sea," 69–91.

26. Statement of Bashir bin Farajullah, aged about 80 years, recorded at the Political Agency, Bahrain, in Political Agent, Bahrain, to Secretary to Political Resident in Persian Gulf, March 11, 1934; IOR R/15/1/209.

27. Statement made by Sadain bin Farhan, aged about 50 years, April 4, 1934; IOR R/15/1/209.

28. Al-Shamlan, *Pearling in the Arabian Gulf.*

29. Al-Khān, *Aghānī al-Ghaūs fī al-Baḥrayn.* For an excellent analysis of pearling and other maritime music in the Gulf, see Ulaby, "Performing the Past."

30. Harbān, *Al-Fijri*, 3–41.

31. Durand, "Notes on the Pearl Fisheries," 30; Al-Zayyani, *Al-Ghaūs wa at-Tawāsha.*

32. *Encyclopedia of Islam*, vol. 3, 78–82; Hansman, *Julfar, An Arabian Port*, 94.

33. See Stein, *Plumes.*

34. L. Rosenthal, *The Pearl Hunter*, 21–60.

35. L. Rosenthal: *The Pearl and I*, 112–115, and *The Pearl Hunter*, 66–67.

36. L. Rosenthal, *The Pearl Hunter*, 68.

37. C. F. Mackenzie (Political Agent Bahrain), *Report on the Trade of the Bahrain Islands for the Year 1909–10*, p. 2; in Tucson, ed., *Persian Gulf Trade Reports*, vol. 5.

38. D. L. R. Lorimer (Political Agent Bahrain), *Report on the Trade of the Bahrain Islands Together with Statements of Imports, Exports and Shipping Returns for the Year 1910–11*, p. 3; in Tucson, ed., *Persian Gulf Trade Reports*, vol. 5.

39. R. Rosenthal and Chaudhuri, *Rachel's Brain and Other Storms*, 20–21. Charm was performed one time only before an audience at Mt. St. Mary's College Art Gallery in Los Angeles on January 28, 1977.

40. L. Rosenthal, *The Pearl Hunter*, 163–170; de Waleffe, *Quand Paris était un paradis.*

41. See Benjamin, *The Arcades Project.*

42. Donkin, *Beyond Price;* Joyce and Addison, *Pearls*, 81, 104. For an excellent discussion of this era of pearl consumption, see Warsh, "Adorning Empire."

43. Hackney and Edkins, *People and Pearls*, 73; Hancock, "The Stones in the Sword," 14; Thieme, "The Art of Dress in the Victorian and Edwardian Eras," 21; E. Wilson, *Adorned in Dreams*, 32; Fischel and von Boehn, *Modes and Manners of the Nineteenth Century*, vol. 4, 80–174.

44. Thieme, "The Art of Dress in the Victorian and Edwardian Eras," 21; Hackney and Edkins, *People and Pearls*, 73; Worsley-Gough, *Fashion in London*, 14–17.

45. Hackney and Edkins, *People and Pearls*, 68.

46. Balsan, *The Glitter and the Gold;* Stuart, *Consuelo and Alva.*

47. A. Howard, "Selling Jewels to Multimillionaires"; Hackney and Edkins, *People and Pearls*, 104–105.

48. A. Howard, "Selling Jewels to Multimillionaires," 62.

49. L. Walker, "Fashions in Jewelry," 489.

50. Stein, *Plumes*, 18–26.

51. Kunz and Stevenson, *The Book of the Pearl*, 80; L. Rosenthal, *The Pearl Hunter*, 66.
52. Whitmarsh, "Fishing for Pearls in Australia"; Bligh, *Golden Quest*.
53. Goldschmidt, "Pearl Fisheries in Venezuela," 26.
54. Hull, "River Pearls," 1; McGinnis, "Pearl Search Began in 1897"; Sutton, *Arkansas Wildlife*.
55. Villiers, *Sons of Sinbad*, 376–378.
56. Clarence-Smith, ed., *The Economics of the Indian Ocean Slave Trade*, 8.
57. Statement of account showing the debts of Bashir bin 'Umran bin Abdullah as copied from the Account Book of Matar bin Matar resident of Dubai, attachment to Bashir bin 'Umran bin Abdullah to Family of Bin Ali, October 7, 1925; IOR R/15/1/208.
58. Statement of account showing the debts of Ismail bin Sanqah to Rashid bin Abdullah, May 26, 1924; IOR R/15/1/208.
59. Case of Jumah bin Sanqur, known as Jumah Kanaidish, aged 40 years, October 27, 1936; IOR R/15/1/219.
60. Secretary to PRPG Bushehr, September 27, 1925; IOR R/15/1/208.
61. Agency Bahrain to HRP Dickson, Secretary to PRPG Bushehr, November 16, 1928; IOR R/15/1/204. See also Secretary's notes, Office of Political Resident in the Persian Gulf, August 5, 1931; IOR R/15/1/205.

Chapter 4. Slavery and African Life in Arabia

1. Statement of Faraj bin Sa'id, slave of Bahrain lady, Bazza bint Sultan, wife of Khalifa bin Zaid al Jalahima, aged about 25 years, May 16, 1907; IOR R/15/1/213.
2. Zilfi, *Women and Slavery*, 96.
3. Ahmed Shafik, "L'esclavage au point de vue musulmane," *Bulletin de la Société de Géographie de l'Égypte* 5 (1982); cited in Troutt Powell, "Slaves or Siblings?," 221; Toledano, *Slavery and Abolition*.
4. Cited in Troutt Powell, "Slaves or Siblings?," 219.
5. Elkins, "The Slavery Debate," 40. On Africanisms, see Holloway, ed., *Africanisms in American Culture*; Hall, *Africans in Colonial Louisiana*; Lemelle and Kelley, *Imagining Home*.
6. See also Stampp, *The Peculiar Institution*; Elkins, *Slavery*; Blassingame, *The Slave Community*; Genovese, *Roll, Jordan, Roll*; Gutman, *The Black Family in Slavery and Freedom*; and Fogel, "Cliometrics and Culture."
7. Genovese, *Roll, Jordan, Roll*, 146–149.
8. Lears, "The Concept of Cultural Hegemony," 574.
9. Scott, *Domination and the Arts of Resistance*. See also Glassman, *Feasts and Riot*, 12–25, and Guha, *Dominance without Hegemony*, esp. 13–23.
10. Scott, *Domination and the Arts of Resistance*, xi–xii.
11. Genovese, *Roll, Jordan, Roll*, 598 and 587.
12. Scott, *Domination and the Arts of Resistance*, 96.
13. Testimony of Captain James Anthony Browne, examined April 4, 1876; in Great Britain, Royal Commission on Fugitive Slaves, *Report of the Commissioners, Minutes of the Evidence, and Appendix* [C-1516-L], 58–60.

14. Malcolm, *Sketches of Persia*, 9–11.

15. See, for example, Report by Commissioner J. T. Last on the Working of the Decree for the Abolition of the Legal Status of Slavery (January 25, 1898) in Sir A. Hardinge to the Marquess of Salisbury, March 23, 1989; reprinted in Irish University Press, *British Parliamentary Papers, Slave Trade*, vol. 95, *Correspondence and Other Papers Relating to the Abolition of Slavery, 1890–1899*; and Rennell Rodd to Earl of Rosebery, December 31, 1893; *C. 7707. Africa No. 6 (1895), Correspondence Respecting Slavery in Zanzibar* (London, 1895), 12–18. On missionary and colonial perspectives on the "civilizing" effects of slavery, see Prestholdt, *Domesticating the World*, 117–146.

16. "Notes on Slave Trade by Wazir Thomas," August 1929; P. 7418/29, IOR L/PS/12/4091.

17. Hopper, "Imperialism and the Dilemma of Slavery."

18. Statement of Marzooq bin Saad aged about 35 years, May 3, 1927; IOR R/15/1/204.

19. Statement of a slave 'Abdullah bin Sa'id aged about 30 years, recorded at the PA Bahrain, March 3, 1928; Statement of slave Mubarak bin Salim, aged about 35 years, recorded at the PA Bahrain, March 3, 1928; Statement of slave Marzuq bin Mubarak aged about 22 years recorded at the Pol Agency, Bahrain, July 20, 1928; IOR R/15/1/204.

20. Statement of Mabrūk bin Ali, aged about 30 years, October 29, 1928; IOR R/15/1/204,

21. Statement of slave Walaid (father's name unknown) aged about 50 years recorded at the Political Agency, Bahrain, May 15, 1929; IOR R/15/1/204. The phrase "when I came to my senses" was used at the Bahrain agency regularly to indicate events before the memory of a slave seeking manumission.

22. Statement of Faraj bin Saif aged about 60 recorded at the PA, Bahrain, January 9, 1930; IOR R/15/1/205.

23. Statement of slave Farhan bin Mubarak aged about 45 years recorded in the PA Bahrain, July 23, 1931; IOR R/15/1/205.

24. Statement of slave Omar bin Ali Somali, aged about 22 years, recorded in the PA Bahrain, August 23, 1931; IOR R/15/1/205.

25. Statement of slave Bilal bin Rashid, aged 40 years, recorded at Bahrain, February 7, 1938; IOR R/15/1/207.

26. Statement made by Faraj bin Sulaiman, aged about 34 years, recorded at Sharjah, October 10, 1939; IOR R/15/1/207.

27. Political Agent to Kuwait to Personal Secretary to H. E. the High Commissioner, Baghdad, May 13, 1921; IOR R/15/1/207.

28. Statement of Khamis bin Mubarak, age about 30 years, recorded in the Political Agency Bahrain, August 24, 1929; IOR R/15/1/204.

29. Statement of slave Sarur bin Unknown, age about 55 years, recorded at the Political Agency, Bahrain, September 4, 1929; IOR R/15/1/204. In the margin, the official recording the testimony wrote, "Negro, mother tongue is Habashi, of which he knows very little."

30. Statement of Faraj bin Nasib, age 50 years, recorded at the Agency, Bahrain, October 4, 1929; IOR R/15/1/204.

31. Political Resident in the Persian Gulf, "Notes on Manumission in the Gulf, 1895–1900" (ca. 1900), 90–92; IOR R/15/1/200.

32. Statement made by Sharifah bint Wekayu, Abyssinian, aged about 25 years, recorded on the 29th Rabi II 1344, November 16, 1925; IOR R/15/1/208. "KB Isa the RA Shargah" refers to Khan Bahadur Isa bin Abdul Latif, the British residency agent at Sharjah.

33. Statement of Faraj bin Razi, aged about 50, Abyssinian, May 31, 1927; IOR R/15/1/204.

34. Statement of Mubarak bin Salim, aged about 35 years, March 3, 1928; IOR R/15/1/204.

35. Statement of Faraj bin unknown, age 14 years ["negro"], August 8, 1929; IOR R/15/1/204.

36. Statement of Raihan bin Hussain, slave, about 34 years old, November 1, 1930; IOR R/15/1/205.

37. Statement of Marzooq bin Ali, aged about 30 years ["he looks to be a negro and talks Arabic"], August 8, 1934; IOR R/15/1/209.

38. Statement made by slave Walaid, a man of about 24, December 28, 1930; IOR R/15/1/208.

39. Statement of Mubarak bin Abdullah Swahili of Hamriyya, aged about 40 years, November 20, 1931; IOR R/15/1/217.

40. Statement made by Sa'id bin Ismail of Zanzibar, aged about 45 years, February 10, 1934; IOR R/15/1/218.

41. Statement made by Juma' bin Marzūk of Zanzibar, aged about 60 years, January 11, 1934; IOR R/15/1/218.

42. See, for example, Statement of slave Mubarak bin Othman, aged about 40 years, recorded at the Political Agency, Bahrain, April 25, 1931; IOR R/15/1/205.

43. Statement made by Mubarak bin Nār, originally from Zanzibar, aged about 40 years, November 24, 1930; Residency Agent, Sharjah, to Secretary to Political Resident, Persian Gulf, January 22, 1931; IOR R/15/1/217.

44. Statement of Hubaish bin Rashid, aged about 30 years, October 15, 1937; IOR R/15/1/219.

45. See, for example, Statement of slave Sangor bin Ahmed, aged about 30 years, September 5, 1938, and Statement of slave Bilal bin Mohammad, aged about 40 years, September 2, 1938; IOR R/15/1/220.

46. Statement of slave Musa'ad bin Zayed, aged about 34 years, recorded at the Political Agency, Bahrain, April 16, 1934; IOR R/15/1/209.

47. Statement of Khamīs bin Halais bin Barut Muwalid, aged about 22 years, October 26, 1921; IOR R/15/1/216.

48. Commander HMS *Crocus* to HBM Consul, Muscat, October 29, 1921; IOR R/15/1/216.

49. Statement of Khadia bint Mabrook, aged about 35 years, recorded at the Political Agency, Bahrain, January 11, 1929; IOR R/15/1/204.
50. Statement of Zubad bint (father unknown), aged about 20 years, February 19, 1937; IOR R/15/1/219.
51. RA Sharjah to Sect to PRPG, No. 182, June 22, 1932; IOR R/15/1/217.
52. Statement of slave Muhammad bin Sa'ad, aged about 30 years, January 23, 1938; IOR R/15/1/207.
53. Statement made by slave Walaid, a man aged about 24 years, December 28, 1930; IOR R/15/1/208.
54. Statement made by Bilāl bin Marzuq, born at Shamal of Ras el Khaimah, aged about 40 years, July 25, 1938; IOR R/15/1/211.
55. Residency Agent, Sharjah, to Captain R. C. Alban, Undersecretary to Political Resident, Persian Gulf, June 7, 1931; IOR R/15/1/205.
56. Harrison, *The Arab at Home*, 88.
57. Ibid., 89.
58. Ibid., 89–90.
59. Statement made by Farhan bin Bilal, born at Suwahil, aged about 40 years, May 19, 1939; IOR R/15/1/211.
60. Statement of Juma'h bin Ibrahīm, aged about 25 years, September 9, 1938; IOR R/15/1/220.
61. An expanded version of this section can be found in Hopper, "Slavery."
62. Statement of Sa'id bin Sanqur, born at Sharjah, aged about 25 years, August 13, 1938; IOR R/15/1/211.
63. See, for example, Statement made by Sa'ad bin Mubarak, aged about 40 years, January 31, 1938, and Statement made by Farhan bin Sa'ud, aged about 60 years, born at Suwahil, January 31, 1938; IOR R/15/1/210.
64. Statement of Mubarak bin Salmīn, born in Shaqra of Nejd, aged about 50 years, April 13, 1940; IOR R/15/1/212.
65. Statement made by Zainab bint Mubarak, aged about 30 years, place of birth Saibiyeh of Yemen, June 27, 1927; IOR R/15/1/208.
66. Statement of slave Sadullah bin Sālem, aged about 45 years, January 25, 1927; IOR R/15/1/204.
67. See, for example, Statement of Marzook bin Hassan, aged about 27 years, October 22, 1927; IOR R/15/1/204.
68. Statement of Sulaiman bin 'Abdullah, aged about 30 years, October 13, 1928; IOR R/15/1/204.
69. Statement of slave Mabrūk bin 'Ali aged about 30 years, October 29, 1928; IOR R/15/1/204.
70. Statement of Zahra bint Mubarak Swahili, aged about 30 years, December 2, 1929; IOR R/15/1/208.
71. Statement made by Salhuh bint Ahmad, aged about 35 years, July 23, 1938; IOR R/15/1/211.

72. Statement of Walaid (father's name unknown) aged about 50 years, May 15, 1929; IOR R/15/1/204.

73. Statement of Hilaweh bint Rashid, born in Za'ab Island, aged about 35 years, February 18, 1942; IOR R/15/1/207.

74. Statement made by Faraj bin Sulaiman, aged 34 years, October 10, 1939; IOR R/15/1/207.

75. Wikan: *Behind the Veil in Arabia* and "Man Becomes Woman."

76. "News of the Trucial Coast, August 1–15, 1936," No. 15, "Local News," 306–307, Residency Agent, Sharjah, News Reports, vol. 2, 1935–36; IOR R/15/2/1865.

77. Statement made by Khamīs bin Johar, born in Dubai, aged about 21 years, June 6, 1925; IOR R/15/1/208.

78. Statement made by Maryami bint Jumah Swahili, aged about 30 years, May 17, 1931; IOR R/15/1/209.

79. Statement made by Zainab bint Mubarak of Sabiyeh of Yemen, aged about 30 years, June 27, 1927; IOR R/15/1/208.

80. Statement made by Rafia'h bint Marzūq Baluchi, aged about 25 years, October 21, 1925; IOR R/15/1/208.

81. Statement made by Khamīs bin Abdur Rahman, born at Dubai, aged about 34 years, July 27, 1933; IOR R/15/1/218.

82. Residency Agent Sharjah to Secretary to Political Resident, Persian Gulf, September 30, 1933; IOR R/15/1/218.

83. Statement made by Zamzam bint Wadh, originally from Dhohar, aged about 55 years, April 4, 1934; IOR R/15/1/209.

84. 'Abd al-'Azīz and 'Abd ar-Rahmān bin 'Abd al-Latīf Al-Mana' to Nāsir bin Muhammad Al-Mani', 21 Muharram 1354 (April 25, 1935); copy in attachment to Political Agent, Bahrain to Lt. Col. T. C. Fowle, Political Resident, Persian Gulf, May 2, 1935; IOR R/15/1/226.

85. Hanretta, *Islam and Social Change in French West Africa*, 212.

86. Statement made by Belal bin Khamīs, aged about 30 years, November 6, 1925; IOR R/15/1/208.

87. Statement made by Gharib bin Said, negro, April 19, 1925; IOR R/15/1/216.

88. Statement made by Zainab bint Mubarak Swahili, aged about 40 years ["negress"], October 10, 1926; IOR R/15/1/208.

89. Statement made by Rab'a bin Firuz Swahili, aged 20 years, October 10, 1926; IOR R/15/1/208.

90. Storm, "Glimpses from My Window," 12–13.

91. See, for example, Statement of Medinah daughter of Wekayu of Selali in Abyssinia, aged about 20, November 16, 1925; she stated, "I do not want to go back to my country, Abyssinia, lest slave traders will re-kidnap me." IOR R/15/1/208.

92. See, for example, case of Juma' referenced in Telegram from HMS *Hastings*, Henjam Radio, to Political Resident, Bushehr, No. 1350, April 2, 1931; IOR R/15/1/209. See also Alpers, "Recollecting Africa."

93. Statement made by Juma' bin Raihan, negro, aged about 55 years, Suwahili, slave of Rashid bin Khalifah Suwaidi of Khan near Dubai, November 29, 1926; IOR R/15/1/216.

94. J. Cantine, "Field Notes—Arabian Mission," *The Mission Field* 11 (October 1898): 184–187.

95. "Rev. James Cantine Writes from Muscat Regarding the Freed Slaves' School," *The Mission Field* 12, no. 6 (October 1899): 200–201.

96. Samuel M. Zwemer to British Consul General, Bushehr, November 27, 1936; IOR R/15/1/203.

97. "Muscat," *The Arabian Mission: Quarterly Letters from the Field* 32 (October–December 1899): 6–8.

98. J. C. Wilson, *Apostle to Islam*, 232.

99. Cited in Cantine, "The Boys of the Freed Slave School," 19–20.

100. Ibid., 17–18. Zwemer and Cantine, *The Golden Milestone*, 103.

101. Cantine, "The Boys of the Freed Slave School."

102. *Fourteenth Census of the United States: 1920—Population*, New York, NY; Borough of Manhattan, 1st NY, Dist. 964, sheet 4B, line 89.

103. "Personalia," *Neglected Arabia* 134 (1925), 16. (A story related to me by a number of people in several ways goes variously as follows: the missionary Wells Thoms was aboard a touring boat in New York harbor when he encountered Solomon at random working aboard; Wells Thoms randomly ran into Solomon in New York city, where he worked as a cook; and finally Samuel Zwemer, in retirement living in New York City, was called by the doorman of his apartment building and informed that a black man was in the lobby claiming to be his son; Zwemer, curious, descended to the lobby to discover Solomon waiting for him. In spite of my best efforts I have been unable to confirm any of these colorful stories.)

104. S. M. Zwemer to Political Resident, Muscat, January 17, 1934; IOR R/15/1/202.

105. W. King Solomon to British Consul-General, Bushehr, January 17, 1934; IOR R/15/1/202.

106. Vice Consul Frank H. Todd to Samuel M. Zwemer, March 13 1937; IOR R/15/1/203.

107. Secretary to PRPG to Samuel M. Zwemer, June 18, 1934; IOR R/15/1/202.

108. Washington, DC: National Archives and Records Administration, n.d. World War II Draft Cards (4th Registration) for the State of New York, Borough of Manhattan; GS Film Number: 2368783; Digital Folder Number: 004126353; Image Number: 01333.

109. For additional discussion on this topic, see Hopper, "Globalization and the Economics of African Slavery."

Chapter 5. Antislavery and Empire

1. It is possible that the name recorded as "Joah" by Captain Guthrie aboard the *May Frere* was a rendering of "Juma'," a common name for enslaved men in the Gulf and in East Africa.

2. J. S. Saldanha, "Précis on the Slave Trade in the Gulf of Oman and the Persian Gulf, 1873–1905 (With a Retrospect into Previous History from 1852) [Secret]," (1906), 63–64; IOR L/PS/20/C246.

3. Captain Guthrie, Officer Commanding the *May Frere* to Acting Political Resident in the Persian Gulf, September 6, 1873; Enclosure 4 in Sir Louis Mallet to Lord Tenterden (March 9, 1874); in Great Britain, Royal Commission on Fugitive Slaves, *Report of the Commissioners*, 165. Guthrie was concerned on the night of the incident that the pearling captains might be fearful of "a second *Thetis* affair," a reference to an incident in the Red Sea in May 1873 when the boats of the HMS *Thetis* under Captain Ward had reportedly robbed a number of pearling boats on the pretext of seizing slave dhows. The prolonged court case in Aden in 1873–1874 produced volumes of evidence condemning the apparently unscrupulous crew and damaging the reputation of the Royal Navy in the region. The incident would have been very fresh in the minds of both naval officers and pearling captains. See File Sa. 68 Court of Inquiry into circumstances attending the destruction of dhows by HS *Thetis* in May 1873 Captain Ward (1874); PRO ADM 1/6301.

4. Acting Political Resident in the Persian Gulf to Mr. Aitchison, September 19, 1873; Enclosure 2 in Sir Louis Mallet to Lord Tenterden (March 9, 1874); in Great Britain, Royal Commission on Fugitive Slaves, *Report of the Commissioners*, 165.

5. First Assistant Political Resident to Acting Political Resident in the Persian Gulf, September 3, 1873; Enclosure 3 in Sir Louis Mallet to Lord Tenterden (March 9, 1874); in Great Britain, Royal Commission on Fugitive Slaves, *Report of the Commissioners*, 165.

6. Robert Bourke to Secretary of Admiralty, April 30, 1875; in Great Britain, Royal Commission on Fugitive Slaves, *Report of the Commissioners*, 167–168.

7. Circular No. 33, Robert Hall, Admiralty, to all Commanders-in-Chief, Captains, Commanders, and Commanding Officers of Her Majesty's Ships and Vessels, July 31, 1875; NMM MLN/160.

8. "English Affairs: Topics of the Day. A Tempest in a Tea-Pot, The British Navy and Fugitive Slaves, Effect of an Admiralty Circular, Consequences of Popular Indignation," *New York Times*, October 24, 1875.

9. Shaw, "Recall to Life," 153–177.

10. Miers, "Slavery to Freedom in Sub-Saharan Africa."

11. Miers, *Britain and the Ending of the Slave Trade*, 317.

12. Miers, "Slavery and the Slave Trade as International Issues," 16.

13. Bondarevsky, "Turning the Persian Gulf into a British Lake"; W. R. Lewis, "The British Withdrawal from the Gulf, 1967–71," 86; Schofield, "Old Boundaries for a New State," 27, 35; Adelson, *London and the Invention of the Middle East*, 7; Cornish, "Notes," 372. Alternatively, the Indian Ocean as a whole has been described as a "British lake" in Panikkar: *India and the Indian Ocean*, and "Regional Organization," 246; Gallagher, "Nationalisms and the Crisis of Empire, 358; and Zinkin, "The Commonwealth and Britain East of Suez," 214.

14. Viscount Palmerston, Foreign Secretary, to Col. Atkins Hamerton, Political Agent, Zanzibar, December 18, 1846; ZNA AA 1/2.

15. "Memorandum on the Use of the French Flag by Suri and Muscat Dhows"; Enclosure 2 in Marquess of Landsdowne to Sir E. Monson, April 16, 1902; IOR R/15/1/552; Greville, Acting British Consul (Beira), "Report on the Capture, Trial, and Sentence of Certain Muscat Slavers by the Portuguese Authorities at Mozambique under the Provision of the General Act of the Brussels Conference, and of Section 162 of the Portuguese Penal Code," October 17, 1903; PRO FO 54/34.

16. The text of the law was thorough: "All manner of dealing and trading in the Purchase, Sale, Barter or Transfer of Slaves, or Persons intended to be sold, transferred, used or dealt with as Slaves, practiced or carried on, in, at, to or from any Part of the Coast of Countries of Africa, shall be, and the same is hereby utterly abolished, prohibited and declared to be unlawful" (47 Geo. III, c. 36.); cited in Lloyd, *The Navy and the Slave Trade*, 11. The question of why the British, who had been the major proponents of the Atlantic slave trade in the eighteenth century, became the chief opponents of the slave trade in the nineteenth century has elicited a substantial historical literature since Eric Williams's thesis in 1944 and is beyond the scope of this book. See Williams, *Capitalism and Slavery*; D. B. Davis, *Problem of Slavery*; Drescher: *Econocide* and *Capitalism and Antislavery*; Eltis, *Economic Growth*; Genovese, *The Political Economy of Slavery*; Bender, ed., *The Antislavery Debate*.

17. Lloyd, *The Navy and the Slave Trade*, 275–276.

18. Ibid., 203–204.

19. Ibid., 203–216, 229–232.

20. Viscount Palmerston to Atkins Hamerton, December 18, 1846; ZNA AA 1/2.

21. Secretary of the Government of India to Government of Bombay, February 18, 1842; IOR R/20/A/118.

22. Atkins Hamerton to Secret Committee, Bombay Government, March 19, 1844, and Atkins Hamerton to Secret Committee, Bombay Government, April 3, 1847; ZNA AA 12/29.

23. Atkins Hamerton to Secret Committee, Bombay Government, March 19, 1844; ZNA AA 12/29.

24. Seyyid Sa'id bin Sultān to PRPG; ZNA AA 12/29.

25. Sultan Seyyid Sa'id bin Sultān to Atkins Hamerton; cited in Hamerton to Secretary to Bombay Government, February 1, 1842; ZNA 12/29.

26. Foreign Office to Seyyid Sa'id bin Sultān, December 31, 1844; ZNA AA 1/2.

27. "While I was at Muscat I did not know of a single instance in which a salute was fired that from three to five men were not destroyed"; Hamerton to Secret Committee (BEIC), n.d. [ca. June 1841]; ZNA AA 3/1.

28. Atkins Hamerton to Secret Committee, Bombay Government, March 20, 1848; ZNA AA 12/29.

29. Atkins Hamerton to Chief Secretary, Bombay Government, May 20, 1850; ZNA AA 12/29

30. Lloyd, *The Navy and the Slave Trade*, 241–242.

31. Felix Jones (PRPG) to Commodore Griffith Jenkins, July 2, 1859; IOR R/15/1/168.
32. Commodore Griffith Jenkins to Felix Jones (PRPG), July 2, 1859; IOR R/15/1/168.
33. Felix Jones (PRPG) to Commodore Griffith Jenkins, July 5, 1859; IOR R/15/1/168.
34. Viscount Palmerston to Lord John Russell, December 9, 1860; cited in Lloyd, *The Navy and the Slave Trade*, 243.
35. Lloyd, *The Navy and the Slave Trade*, 242–243.
36. Devereux, *A Cruise in the "Gorgon,"* 122.
37. Lloyd, *The Navy and the Slave Trade*, 282–286.
38. Testimony of Rear Admiral Arthur Cumming, examined March 11, 1876; in Great Britain, Royal Commission on Fugitive Slaves, *Report of the Commissioners, Minutes of the Evidence, and Appendix* [C-1516-L], 1–7; Lloyd, *The Navy and the Slave Trade*, 283–284.
39. Admiral Cockburn to Secretary of Admiralty, Whitehall, July 17, 1871; PRO ADM 1/6190.
40. Sheriff, *Slaves, Spices and Ivory*, 35–41, 223–235.
41. Campbell: "Madagascar and Mozambique in the Slave Trade," and "The East African Slave Trade."
42. Leopold G. Heath to Secretary of Admiralty, March 1, 1869; PRO ADM 1/6093.
43. C. P. Rigby to Anderson, "Report on the Zanzibar Dominions," No. 39 of 1860, n.d. (ca. June 1860); ZNA AA 3/19.
44. C. P. Rigby to Secretary to Government of Bombay, May 14, 1861; ZNA AA 12/2.
45. W. M. Coghlan to R. L. Playfair, August 24, 1863; STA MsDep14, MS 38502–5.
46. E. D. Ropes, Jr., letter to his parents, May 1, 1883; cited in Gilbert, *Dhows and the Colonial Economy of Zanzibar*, 65.
47. Sheriff, *Slaves, Spices and Ivory*, 235–238.
48. G. Keith Gordon, "HMS *Briton*, 1873"; unpublished memoir, MS 79/176; NMM FIE/43.
49. Kirk Diaries, vol. 5 (Malindi, September 23, 1873); NLS Acc. 9942/25.
50. Rear Admiral Arthur Cumming to Secretary of Admiralty, December 5, 1874; PRO ADM 1/6301.
51. Rear Admiral Arthur Cumming to Secretary of Admiralty, January. 10, 1873; PRO ADM 1/6261.
52. Captain Sullivan (HMS *London*) to Rear Admiral Arthur Cumming, April 6, 1875; PRO ADM 1/6301.
53. Rear Admiral MacDonald to Admiralty, "Report on East Africa Slave Trade to 31st May 1876," June 1, 1876; PRO ADM 1/6379.
54. Corbett to Secretary of Admiralty, October 1, 1877; PRO ADM 1/6412.
55. Rear Admiral Arthur Cumming to Secretary of Admiralty, July 1, 1874; PRO ADM 1/6301.

56. Kirk Diaries (1875); NLS Acc. 9942/25.
57. Rear Admiral Arthur Cumming to Secretary of Admiralty, January 10, 1873; PRO ADM 1/6261.
58. Captain Malcolm to Secretary of Admiralty, July 1, 1873; PRO ADM 1/6261. On the final point, see Hopper, "Imperialism and the Dilemma of Slavery."
59. "Slave Trade Report from 1st Jan. 1874 to 19th May 1875. East Indies Station." PRO ADM 1/6341.
60. Annual Report, 1875 (January 1, 1876); PRO ADM 1/6379.
61. Young, "On a Recent Sojourn."
62. F. Elton to Earl of Derby, August 17, 1876; ZNA BK 4/1.
63. Kirk, "A Visit to the Mungao District," 588–589.
64. Rear Admiral Corbett to Secretary of Admiralty, August 8, 1879; PRO ADM 1/6484.
65. Lloyd, *The Navy and the Slave Trade*, 271.
66. Gilbert, *Dhows and the Colonial Economy of Zanzibar*, 63. Gilbert gives 1880 as the termination date but acknowledges occasional flare-ups of the slave trade around Zanzibar in the late 1880s.
67. Captain Luxmore (HMS *London*), June 3, 1882; cited in Admiral W. Hewett to Secretary of Admiralty, June 25, 1882; PRO ADM 1/6622.
68. Commander in Chief, East Indies Station, to Secretary of Admiralty, February 18, 1884; PRO ADM 1/6714.
69. Leopold G. Heath to Secretary of Admiralty, March 1, 1869; PRO ADM 1/6093.
70. John G. Haggard to Ella Haggard, December 13, 1883; RHO Emp. S. 465.
71. Rear Admiral Richards to Secretary of Admiralty, August 30, 1886; PRO ADM 1/6807.
72. John G. Haggard to his Father, March 18, 1884; RHO Emp. S. 465.
73. John G. Haggard to Ella Maddison Green, March 15, 1884; RHO Emp. S. 465.
74. John G. Haggard to William Haggard, December 20, 1884; RHO Emp. S. 465.
75. A good starting place is Higgins, *Rider Haggard*, 53–107, and M. N. Cohen, *Rider Haggard*, 85–137.
76. Cooper, *Plantation Slavery on the East Coast of Africa*, 132–133.
77. See, for example, David Livingstone to Thomas Livingstone, December 26, 1863; NLS MS 10701, f. 142–143, and Young, "On a Recent Sojourn." When James Grant accompanied Joseph Thomson to Lake Nyasa, he recorded seeing dhows active on the lake. See James Augustus Grant, "Grant's Journal on Voyage with Thompson" (1890); NLS MS 17918. See also Thomson, "To Lake Bangweolo." But when Joseph S. Kellet Smith visited in 1895, he saw and photographed the remains of what was said to be the last slave dhow in use on the lake, which had only recently been destroyed. Officers of the Royal Navy on Lake Nyasa (consisting of two "small craft built somewhat on the lines of an upriver picnic steamer"), Smith wrote, "exhibited with pride" the partly submerged remains of the dhow at Monkey Bay, which "had been run down and captured only a little time before." See Smith, "Memoirs." See also Money and Smith, "Explorations."

78. Campbell, "The East African Slave Trade."

79. Numerous factors have limited the number of testimonies that were recorded. As mentioned in the preface, enslaved Africans who sought manumission certificates were overwhelmingly male. The format of manumission testimonies also varied over time. British agents did not always ask those who appealed to them for manumission for details about their arrival in Arabia, and the information may not have been recorded. Some cases of Africans who were kidnapped are missing too much information to be included in this survey. Furthermore, not all manumission testimonies have been preserved or were accessible at the time of this research. I am unable to accurately judge the proportion of slaves these records represent. Thus the figures provided here are intended to be suggestive rather than authoritative.

80. For a detailed and more complete survey of the manumission testimonies in the India Office Records, see Zdanowski, "The Manumission Movement."

81. G. Keith Gordon, "HMS *Briton*, 1873"; unpublished memoir, MS79/176, NMM FIE/43.

82. Atkins Hamerton to Commodore C. Wyvill, March 13, 1852; ZNA AA 12/29.

83. Gilbert, *Dhows and the Colonial Economy of Zanzibar*, 63.

84. Sultan Mājid warned Playfair in 1863 that if British cruisers continued to capture slaves, Arab captains would begin using the French flag and had in fact already begun to do so. See Seyyid Mājid bin Saʿīd to Robert L. Playfair, September 8, 1863; ZNA AA 3/18. A Swahili author in the 1880s described this phenomenon as follows: "And persons who trade in slaves often use the flag of the French to ship them, because the British are not permitted to enter any ship that sails under the French flag. This is the reason why some Muslims seek the protection of the French nation. And if they want to hoist the French flag they pay for it. They pay an annual flag fee. . . . Among those who hoist the French flag are many Arabs who are called Wasuri. They frequently ship slaves with their vessels." From Bromber, ed. and trans., *The Jurisdiction of the Sultan of Zanzibar*, 25.

85. C. P. Rigby to Anderson, Government of India, April 18, 1861; ZNA AA 12/2.

86. Robert L. Playfair to Secretary of State for Foreign Affairs, May 30, 1865; ZNA AA 3/25.

87. Lt. Col. Merewether, Political Resident Aden, to Secretary of Government Bombay, May 17, 1865; ZNA AA 3/25. British naval captains also used false intelligence, frequently circulating false reports of their intended destinations, after which they left harbors in their alleged direction, only to change directions once clear of sight in hopes of capturing dhows attempting to take advantage of the ship's absence. See, for example, Captain Tucker to Rear Admiral James H. Cockburn, Commander in Chief, October 23, 1871; PRO ADM 1/6190. The captain wrote that he "determined to quit Zanzibar as soon as possible, leaving behind me the impression that I should sail from the Seychelles for Marsheck. This ruse succeeded beyond my expectation." The HMS *Columbine* caught a slave trader shortly after.

88. Mohammad ʿAli to P. E. de Roubaix, Consul General to the Sublime Porte, Cape of Good Hope, August 24, 1864; ZNA AA 3/25.

89. W. S. Field to Colonial Secretary, November 1, 1864; ZNA AA 3/25.

90. Mohammad 'Ali to P. E. de Roubaix, Consul General to the Sublime Porte, Cape of Good Hope, August 24, 1864; ZNA AA 3/25.

91. P. E. Roubaix to Governor of the Colony of the Cape of Good Hope, November 1, 1865; ZNA AA 3/25.

92. P. E. Roubaix to Governor of the Colony of the Cape of Good Hope, November 22, 1865; ZNA AA 3/25.

93. P. E Wodehouse to Political Agent, Zanzibar, November 23, 1865; ZNA AA 3/25.

94. Sultan Mājid's letter to the governor was sanitized slightly by British authorities, who objected to the idea that the already indebted sultan sponsor the Zanzibaris' return.

95. C. C. Saunders: "Between Slavery and Freedom"; "Liberated Africans in the Cape Colony"; and "'Free Yet Slaves'"; Watson, "'Prize Negroes.'"

96. Logbook of John G. Lynch, entry for January 13, 1869; RHO MSS Brit. Emp. S. 536.

97. John Kirk to Secretary of Government, Bombay, May 16, 1869; copy in Admiral L. G. Heath to Secretary of Admiralty, July 31, 1869; PRO ADM 1/6093. For extended discussion of this subject, see Gilbert, *Dhows and the Colonial Economy of Zanzibar.*

98. Lloyd, *The Navy and the Slave Trade;* Gilbert, *Dhows and the Colonial Economy of Zanzibar.*

99. John Kirk, Vice Admiralty Court, Zanzibar, May 1, 1869; ZNA AA 7/3.

100. Churchill, Vice Admiralty Court, Zanzibar, November 12, 1870; ZNA AA 7/3.

101. John Kirk, Vice Admiralty Court, Zanzibar, January 11, 1872; ZNA AA 7/4.

102. Gilbert, *Dhows and the Colonial Economy in Zanzibar.*

103. Colomb, *Slave Catching in the Indian Ocean,* 267–269.

104. Cited in Sullivan, *Dhow Chasing in Zanzibar Waters,* 83–96.

105. Ibid., 90.

106. Ibid., 88.

107. C. P. Rigby, "Report on the Zanzibar Dominions," No. 39 of 1860; ZNA AA 3/19.

108. Playfair to Foreign Office, May 30, 1865; ZNA AA 3/25.

109. Bishop Tozer to Rear Admiral Cockburn, June 7, 1871; PRO ADM 1/6190.

110. Ibid.

111. These statistics include all captures of ships found to contain ten or more captives.

112. E. C. Ross, "HMS *Vulture* v. an Arab Dhow Named *Yasmeen,* in the Instance Court of Vice Admiralty of Muscat," September 10, 1872; IOR R/15/6/5; Political Agency, Muscat—Slave Trade Correspondence, 1847–1872.

113. Hill, *Fifty Days on Board a Slave-Vessel,* 21–24, 48–51.

114. L. G. Heath, Commander in Chief, to Secretary of Admiralty, January 16, 1869; PRO ADM 1/6093 Sa. 33.

115. Logbook of John G. Lynch; RHO MSS Brit. Emp. S. 536. During adjudication it was discovered that thirty-six of the supposed slaves the *Star* brought to Aden were in fact captains and crew of legitimate trading vessels—casualties of the overeager interpreters. See John Kirk to Gonne, May 16, 1869; enclosure in L. G. Heath to Secretary of Admiralty, July 31, 1869; ADM 1/6093 Sa. 140.

116. L. G. Heath, Commander in Chief, to Secretary of Admiralty, January 16, 1869; PRO ADM 1/6093 Sa. 33. Great Britain, *Correspondence Respecting the Condition of Liberated Africans at the Seychelles, Parliamentary Papers*, L (1873), 1–3; cited in Nwulia, *Britain and Slavery in East Africa*, 113.

117. Sullivan, *Dhow Chasing in Zanzibar Waters*, 94.

118. Instructions for the Guidance of Naval Officers Employed in the Suppression of the Slave Trade, November 6, 1869; in Great Britain, Royal Commission on Fugitive Slaves, *Report of the Commissioners*, 220–221.

119. Admiral L. G. Heath to Admiralty, March 25, 1870; PRO ADM 1/6149 Sa. 70.

120. Noted in Nwulia, *Britain and Slavery in East Africa*, 115–116.

121. Statement of Disposal of Slaves Captured by HMS *Garnet* and Forfeited to Her Majesty, July 16, 1888; enclosure in Commander in Chief, East Indies to Secretary of Admiralty, August 22, 1888; PRO ADM 1/6917 Sa. 146.

122. Ben Campion's "The Lost Pinnace," in Hutcheson, *The Penang Pirate and The Lost Pinnace*, 73–192 (quote at pp. 83–84).

123. Great Britain, Royal Commission on Fugitive Slaves, *Report of the Commissioners*, 9.

124. Rev. Price, "Sunday, November 14th" (1875); cited in Stock, *The History of the Church Missionary Society*, 87.

125. Statistics of the E. Africa Mission (1876); CMS/B/OMS/C A5 O23/47a.

126. Commander Mather Byles to Charles J. Brownrigg, SNO East Africa, July 12, 1881; in William Gore Jones, Commander in Chief, East Indies, to Secretary of Admiralty, September 8, 1881; ADM 1/6577 Sa. 188.

127. Stock, *The History of the Church Missionary Society*, 90–91.

128. Bromber, *The Jurisdiction of the Sultan of Zanzibar*, 21.

129. Chancellor to Gray, April 3, 1877; CMS/B/OMS/C MA O10.

130. Hunter, *The Imperial Gazetteer of India*, vol. 18: *Nasik District Gazetteer*.

131. Parliamentary Papers, XII (1871), 5–6; cited in Nwulia, *Britain and Slavery in East Africa*, 114.

132. E. Russell to Bombay Government, December 24, 1864; enclosure in Heath to Admiralty, April 5, 1869; *Parliamentary Papers*, LXI (1870), 77; cited in Nwulia, *Britain and Slavery in East Africa*, 114–115.

133. C. C. Saunders: "Between Slavery and Freedom," and "Liberated Africans in the Cape Colony."

134. Harries, "Culture and Classification."

135. Great Britain, Royal Commission on Fugitive Slaves, *Report of the Commissioners*, 5.

136. Nwulia, *Britain and Slavery in East Africa*, 113–114.

137. Cited in Great Britain, Royal Commission on Fugitive Slaves, *Report of the Commissioners*, 17–18.

138. Ibid., 7–9.

139. Chancellor to Gray, April 3, 1877; CMS/B/OMS/C MA O/28.

140. Sister Mary St. Ignatius Superior to Sir Bartle Frere, January 11, 1873; IOR R/20/A/405.

141. Reverend William Sadler Price, Journal for 1875; CMS/B/OMS/C/A5 O23.

142. Huzzey, *Freedom Burning*, 209.

143. Holt, "The Essence of the Contract," 56. On the Morant Bay Rebellion, see Heuman: "*The Killing Time*"; "Riots and Resistance"; and "The British West Indies." See also Huzzey, *Freedom Burning*, 184–186.

144. D. A. Lorimer, *Colour, Class and the Victorians*, 181.

Chapter 6. Globalization and the End of the East African Slave Trade

1. Nixon, "First Dates," 50–51; Kearney, "Date Varieties and Date Culture in Tunis."

2. Fairchild, "Persian Gulf Dates."

3. Fairchild, *The World Was My Garden*, 226–244.

4. Diary, February 5–27, 1902; FTBG David G. Fairchild Papers.

5. Scheibinger, *Plants and Empire*, 35–43.

6. Nixon, "First Dates," 50–51.

7. Popenoe, *Date Growing*, xiv, 64, 92, 256.

8. Popenoe to F. O. Popenoe, October 21, 1912, and Wilson Popenoe to F. O. Popenoe, October 29, 1912; AHC PPP, Box 2, ff. 2; Paul B. Popenoe, "With the Natives of Maskat," *Los Angeles Times*, December 14, 1912.

9. Homer Brett to Paul Popenoe, October 8, 1912; AHC PPP, Box 2, ff. 2.

10. Paul Popenoe to F. O. Popenoe, October 29, 1912; AHC PPP, Box 2, ff. 2.

11. Homer Brett to Paul Popenoe, January 12, 1913; AHC PPP, Box 2, ff. 3.

12. Paul Popenoe to F. O. Popenoe, October 29, 1912; AHC PPP, Box 2, ff. 2.

13. Paul Popenoe to F. O. Popenoe, November 3, 1912; AHC PPP, Box 2, ff. 2.

14. Wilson Popenoe to F. O. Popenoe, November 8, 1912; Paul Popenoe to F. O. Popenoe, November 9, 1912; AHC PPP, Box 2, ff. 2.

15. David Fairchild, "Travels in Arabia and along the Persian Gulf," *National Geographic Magazine* 15, no. 4 (April 1904): 139–151.

16. Paul Popenoe to F. O. Popenoe, November 18, 1912; AHC PPP, Box 2, ff. 2.

17. Paul Popenoe, "Competition in Dates: Oriental Countries Have Heard of the New Industry in California," *Coachella Valley News*, February 23, 1913.

18. Wilson Popenoe to F. O. Popenoe, November 22, 1912; AHC PPP, Box 2, ff. 2.

19. Paul Popenoe to F. O. Popenoe, December 14, 1912; AHC PPP, Box 2, ff. 2.

20. Contract between A. G. Tomlinson and Paul Popenoe, December 16, 1912; AHC PPP, Box 2, ff. 2.

21. Paul Popenoe to F. O. Popenoe, January 1, 1913; AHC PPP, Box 2, ff. 3.
22. Paul Popenoe to F. O. Popenoe, January 15, 1913; AHC PPP, Box 2, ff. 3.
23. Paul Popenoe, "To Baghdad for Date Palms," unpublished manuscript, 1913; AHC PPP, Box 174, ff. 3.
24. Agreement between Peshaga ibn Sagakia and Paul Popenoe, January 25, 1913; AHC PPP, Box 2, ff. 3.
25. Paul Popenoe to F. O. Popenoe, February 19, 1913; AHC PPP, Box 2, ff. 3.
26. Wilson Popenoe to F. O. Popenoe, February 13, 1913; AHC PPP, Box 2, ff. 3.
27. Carne, "Notes on Date Culture in America," 805.
28. Eunson, *The Pearl King*.
29. Cited in ibid., 23–24.
30. Rosenthal, *The Pearl and I*, 115–117; Cariño: "The Cultured Pearl Polemic," 42–44, and "The Great Debate," 49–51.
31. Banque Nationale de Crédit, *Répertoire de la BNC en liquidation*, Affaires Diamantaires (AQ 120 666, 668, 674 and 675); available at Centre des Archives du Monde du Travail, Roubaix, France.
32. Rosenthal, *The Pearl Hunter*, 179–193.
33. "Paris Jews Face New Terror," *New York Times*, September 2, 1941.
34. "Leonard Rosenthal Dies at 83; Authority and Dealer in Pearls," *New York Times*, July 18, 1955.
35. Stein, *Plumes*, 23–26.
36. Acting Political Agent, Bahrain to Political Dept., Government of India, July 25, 1935; IOR R/15/2/346; Police v. Khalil Ibrahim al-Bakr (Cheating, importing, selling, and being in possession of cultured pearls), Case no. 398, October 8, 1933; IOR R/15/3/7012.
37. India Office to Political Resident, Persian Gulf, October 28, 1935; PRO FO 371/18918.
38. This topic is addressed in more detail in Hopper, "Imperialism and the Dilemma of Slavery."
39. Political Agent to Political Resident, Persian Gulf, May 30, 1932; IOR R/15/2/848 [and PRO FO 371/16838]. This incident is also described in a different context in Bose, *A Hundred Horizons*, 90–92.
40. Marques of Lansdowne to Sir E. Monson, April 16, 1902; IOR R/15/1/552.
41. Greville, Acting British Consul (Beira), "Report on the Capture, Trial, and Sentence of Certain Muscat Slavers by the Portuguese Authorities at Mozambique under the Provision of the General Act of the Brussels Conference, and of Section 162 of the Portuguese Penal Code," October 17, 1903; PRO FO 54/34. O'Neill, "On the Coast Lands," 596. Alpers mentions the chief of Samuco in 1831 as Nampustamuno (*Ivory and Slaves*, 256).
42. Greville, Acting British Consul (Beira), "Report on the Capture, Trial, and Sentence of Certain Muscat Slavers by the Portuguese Authorities at Mozambique under the Provision of the General Act of the Brussels Conference, and of Section 162 of the Portuguese Penal Code," October 17, 1903; PRO FO 54/34.

43. Ibid. See also Capela, *O tráfico de escravos*, 121–122.

44. Greville, Acting British Consul (Beira), "Report on the Capture, Trial, and Sentence of Certain Muscat Slavers by the Portuguese Authorities at Mozambique under the Provision of the General Act of the Brussels Conference, and of Section 162 of the Portuguese Penal Code," October 17, 1903; PRO FO 54/34.

45. Martin Gosselin to Marquess of Lansdowne, November 1, 1903; Wenceslau de Lima to Martin Gosselin, October 28, 1903; PRO FO 54/34. Of the 103 Omanis imprisoned from the raid on Samuco, 40 were listed as from Sur, 53 from Muscat (although Muscat may serve as a placeholder for portions of the Batinah Coast under the rule of the sultan of Muscat), and 3 from Khaḍra'. Of the same group 38 were listed as members of the Janebah tribe, 24 Gerahdee, 7 Sardee, 4 Seehabee, 4 Saʻidi, 2 Benu Bu Ali, 2 Khamisi, and 1 from each of the following: Baluchi, A'mari, Maadi, and Fahamsi. Their professions are listed in the court records as well. Fifty-four of the prisoners claimed to be sailors, 9 merchants, and 6 fishermen; 6 stated that they had no particular profession, 4 were captains of dhows, 2 were listed as carriers, 2 as property owners, 1 as a cook, 1 as a rope maker, and 1 as the sheikh of a mosque. Of the 17 Omani prisoners taken at Moma Bay, all claimed Suri origin except 1, who came from Muscat. Among these prisoners, 9 men were in their twenties, 3 in their thirties, 1 man was forty, and 2 were in their fifties. There was also 1 nine-year-old boy in the group, who accompanied his father. See Wenceslau de Lima to Martin Gosselin, October 28, 1903; Enclosures 1 and 2, PRO FO 54/34.

46. In addition, in the midst of the Anglo-Boer War, in August 1899 Britain had signed a secret agreement with Portugal—the Treaty of Windsor—in which the Portuguese pledged to attempt to prevent the transport of contraband firearms through Mozambique to the Transvaal in exchange for British reaffirmation of its five-century alliance with Portugal and a commitment to protect Portuguese territory where it lay, including its African colonies, which were increasingly under question. The Omani merchants at Moma Bay and Samuco were, in addition to purchasing slaves, delivering some small pieces of artillery from India and large amounts of Martini and Schneider ammunition, which was in high demand on the coast and in the interior. The presence of the *São Rafael*, the newest ship in the Portuguese Navy (and one of only four cruisers produced between 1895 and 1921), may be seen as partly connected to the enforcement of the treaty. On these points see Langhorne, "Anglo-German Negotiations"; Gooch and Temperley, eds., *British Documents*, vol. 10, part 2, "The Last Years of Peace"; Lains and Costa, "Portugal and the Boer War."

47. Hafkin, "Trade, Society, and Politics," 253–281.

48. Ibid., 266.

49. Ibid., 359–363.

50. Bonate, "The Ascendance of Angoche."

51. Ibid., 133–140. Paes d'Almeida, the engineer who had reported the presence of the Omani ships to the district governor, was killed at Buela near Angoche within a year of the Omani dhow incident. Almeida had been drafting a map of the Angoche region as part of the "new" Portuguese efforts to bring the area under administrative

control, and he had arranged to visit the Maca-*mwene*, a lesser chief of the Mogovollas. After repeatedly ignoring warnings from the paramount chief of the Mogovollas, the Cabula-*mwene*, that he needed formal permission to enter his lands, Almeida and Pitta Simoes, an ex-sergeant who accompanied him, were surrounded and killed on orders from the Cabula. The map that Almeida was commissioned to draw bears the publication date of February 21, 1903, and is understandably vague on the land of the "Mogobulla." See de Almeida, *Esboço geographico de Angoche;* Bonate, "The Ascendance of Angoche," 132.

Plans for an expedition to bring the Makua territory and the coast between Mozambique Island and Quelimane into submission were laid in 1905–1906, when Joao de Azevedo Coutinho was governor-general. The memory of Almeida and Simoes was repeatedly invoked in Portuguese demands to "avenge the death of our brothers and co-citizens." The actual expedition, delayed until 1910, was led by Massano de Amorim, who succeeded in gaining the submission of the Makua chiefs one by one. The same year, Farallahi and Ibrahimu were captured and sent into exile on the Cape Verde Islands. The capture of the Omani dhows at Samuco and Moma must also be seen as part of a wider effort by the Portuguese colonial government to extend its rule over the Makua people and dominate the trade of the entire coast of Mozambique. See Newitt, "Angoche, the Slave Trade and the Portuguese"; Bonate, "The Ascendance of Angoche," 133–140; Hafkin, "Trade, Society, and Politics," 390.

52. Abrahamian, *Iran between Two Revolutions;* Gelvin, *The Modern Middle East*, 172; Majd, *The Great Famine and Genocide in Persia.* See also John Foran, ed., *A Century of Revolution*, and Najmabadi, *The Story of Daughters of Quchan*.

53. Sykes, *History of Persia*, 515; cited in Majd, *The Great Famine and Genocide in Persia*, 40.

54. Mohammad Ali Jamalzadeh, cited in Hafez Farmanfarmaian, "Farmanfarma and the Famine of 1917 in Shiraz," 3–4; cited in Majd, *The Great Famine and Genocide in Persia*, 40.

55. A. P. Trevor to E. B. Howell, December 16, 1923; IOR R/15/1/222.

56. Political Agent, Muscat to Political Resident, Persian Gulf, n.d.; no. 69-C of 1929, IOR R/15/1/225.

57. For a thorough discussion of the Muscat arms trade, see C. H. Allen, "Sayyids, Shets and Sultans," 140–177.

58. "Notes on Slave Trade by Wazir Thomas," August 1929; P. 7418/29, IOR L/PS/12/4091.

59. Political Agent, Kalat, to Governor General, Baluchistan, January 28, 1928; IOR L/PS/12/4091.

60. H. Boyes, Senior Naval Officer, Persian Gulf, to Commander in Chief, East Indies Station, September 12, 1929; IOR L/PS/12/4091.

61. "Notes on Slave Trade by Wazir Thomas," August 1929; P. 7418/29, IOR L/PS/12/4091.

62. "Statement made by Dashok bin Gezi of Suruk of Karavan" and "Statement made by Nakbat son of Gondoo of Balak," October 31, 1929; IOR, R/15/1/217.

63. "Statement made by Muti son of Frao, Born in Lucknow," November 20, 1926; IOR R/15/1/222.
64. "Statement made by Qasim bin Abdullah," October 30, 1922; IOR R/15/1/222.
65. Political Resident in Persian Gulf to Government of India, no. 1095, June 10, 1928; IOR L/PS/12/4091.
66. Statement of Gharib bin Sayeed, place of birth Shinas (Batinah District) aged about 38 years, name of master Sultan bin Zayed, chief of Abu Dhabi, November 30, 1924; IOR R/15/1/216.
67. Statement of Taaib bin Bilal, manumitted slave of Muhammad bin Said of Bani Nimk, resident of Muslamat, Wadi Muawal, Oman, age 40 years, January 26, 1927; IOR R/15/1/216.
68. Immigration Officer's Report, Port of Liverpool, Subject: Sulaiman bin Yusuf, Certificate of Identity S. 392, Bahrain, March 23, 1927; IOR R/15/1/204.
69. Statement of Bahkit bin Muhammad, age 23 years, Iraqi subject, recorded at Bahrain, August 5, 1929; IOR R/15/1/204.
70. Seven people reported being kidnapped between 1900 and 1904, fourteen between 1910 and 1914, twelve between 1915 and 1919, eleven between 1920 and 1924, and three between 1925 and 1929.
71. Barth, *Sohar*, 184–186.
72. Political Agent Bahrain to Political Resident, Persian Gulf, January 16, 1936; IOR, R/15/1/226.
73. Barth, *Sohar*, 42–49; Valeri, *Le sultanat d'Oman*, 33–36; Montigny, "L'Afrique oubliée des noirs du Qatar," 219–220.

Conclusion

1. Sebiane, "Le statut socio-economique de la pratique musicale."
2. R. Cohen, *Global Diasporas*, 162–167.
3. El-Mallah, *Die Musik einer alten Hochkultur*, 46–47.
4. Ibid., 20.
5. Al-Khan, *Laiwa Music of the Gulf*, 2.
6. Sultanat 'Omān, *Ashkāl Mu'āsira li-Alfunūn Al-Sha'biyat*, vol. 3, 14–15, 31–32.
7. Smithsonian Institution, "Connecting the Gems of the Indian Ocean: From Oman to East Africa"; http://africa.si.edu/50years/oman/; accessed May 28, 2014.
8. Trouillot, *Silencing the Past*, 48–49.
9. Ibid., 96–98.
10. Sheriff, *Dhow Cultures*, 53–64.
11. Barth, *Sohar*, 48.
12. Valeri, *Oman*, 15.
13. Barth, *Sohar*, 48.
14. Valeri, *Oman*, 15.
15. Bristol-Rhys, *Emirati Women*, 99–102.
16. Rosenwaks, *The Film Class*.
17. Limbert, *In the Time of Oil*, 143–148.

18. Ibid., 147.
19. Ibid., 143.
20. Ibid., 144–145. See also Limbert, "Marriage, Status and the Politics of Nationality in Oman," 167–179.
21. Glassman, "Creole Nationalists." See also Glassman, *War of Words*, 23–64, 141, and Ho, *The Graves of Tarim*.
22. Barth, *Sohar*, 46.
23. Gramsci, *Prison Notebooks*, 333; Genovese, *Roll, Jordan, Roll*, 147.
24. Larson, "Reconsidering Trauma, Identity, and the African Diaspora."
25. Golash-Boza, *Yo Soy Negro*, 1–58.

BIBLIOGRAPHY

Archival Resources

American Heritage Center, University of Wyoming (AHC)
Paul Popenoe Collection (Acc. 4681) (PPP)

Bahrain National Museum, Manama, Kingdom of Bahrain (BNM)
Arabic Documents Collection

Beit Al-Zubair Museum Library, Muscat, Sultanate of Oman (BAZ)
Neglected Arabia
Persian Gulf Administration Reports: 1873–1947
Persian Gulf Trade Reports: 1905–1940

Bodleian Library of Commonwealth and African Studies at Rhodes House, Oxford University, UK (RHO)
Haggard, John George, Papers (Mss. Brit. Emp. S. 465)
Logbook of HMS *Star* kept by John G. Lynch, 1866–1869 (MSS. Brit. Emp.S. 536)
Lugard, Fredrick, Papers (Mss. Brit. Emp. S. 71)

Church Missionary Society Archive, University of Birmingham, UK (CMS)
Buswell, Rev. Henry Dixon, Papers (CMS/B/OMS/C MA O8)
Chancellor, Rev. William Bartlett, Papers (CMS/B/OMS/C MA O10)
Price, Rev. William Salter, Papers (CMS/B/OMS/C A5 O23)

Centre for Documentation and Research, Abu Dhabi, United Arab Emirates (CDR)

Political and Secret Department Records (L/PS)
Records of the British Residency and Agencies in the Persian Gulf (R/15)
Records of the Foreign Office (FO)

Fairchild Tropical Botanic Garden, Coral Gables, FL (FTBG)

David G. Fairchild Papers

Historical Documents Center, Kingdom of Bahrain (HDC)

Ottoman Documents Collection
Portuguese Documents Collection

India Office Records, British Library, London, UK (IOR)

Pelly, Lewis, Papers (Mss. Eur./F126/54)
Political and Secret Department Records (L/P&S)
Records of the British Residency and Agencies in the Persian Gulf (R/15)
Records of the British Administration in Aden (R/20)

Mystic Seaport Museum, Mystic, CT (MSM)

VFM 264 Horace Coombs Papers (1893–1898)
Log 579 Imaum (Bark) Journal, 1858–1859
Log 315 Taria Topan (Bark) Logbook, 1892–1893
Log 325 Warren White (Bark) Journal, 1852–1853

National Archives, London (Kew), UK (PRO)

Records of the Admiralty (ADM)
Records of the Foreign Office (FO)

National Archives, College Park, MD (NARA)

General Records of the Department of State (RG 59)
Records of the Foreign Service Posts of the Department of State (RG 84)

National Library of Scotland, Edinburgh, Scotland, UK (NLS)

Kirk, Sir John and Lady Helen Cooke, Papers (Acc. 9942)
Cameron, Verney Lovett, Papers (Acc. 10120)
Grant, James Augustus, Papers (MS 17918)
Livingstone, David, Papers (MS 10701–10704)

National Maritime Museum, Greenwich, UK (NMM)

Field, Admiral Sir Arthur Mostyn, Papers (FIE/43)

Gilbert-Cooper, Lt. C. M., Papers (BGY/G/5)
Milne, Sir Alexander, Papers (MLN/160)

Newberry Library Chicago, IL (NL)

Neglected Arabia
Quarterly Letters from the Arabian Mission

Peabody Essex Museum, Essex, MA (PEM)

Charles Benson Papers (MSS 15)
John Bertram Papers (MSS 104)
LOG 1851E2 Elizabeth Hall, Bark
LOG 1857A Arthur Pickering, Bark
LOG 1855E2 Emily Wilder, Bark
LOG 1855I2 Iosco, Bark
LOG 1853I3 Iosco, Bark
LOG 1884T Taria Topan, Bark
LOG 1845E Exchange, Iosco, Madagascar, Sophronia Barks
LOG 1855I Iosco, Bark

Ratansi Purshotum Papers, private collection, Muscat, Sultanate of Oman (RPP)

Ratansi Purshotum Papers

Reformed Church in America Archives, New Brunswick, NJ (RCA)

Arabian Mission Papers
Samuel Zwemer Papers
Scudder Files

Royal Geographical Society, London, UK (RGS)

Cox, Percy Z., Papers
Elton, J. F., Papers
Smith, Joseph S. Kellett, Papers

St. Andrews University Library, Special Collections, St. Andrews, Scotland, UK (STA)

Playfair, Robert Lambert and family, Papers (MS 38502)

University of Miami, Special Collections, Library, Coral Gables, FL (UM)

Walter T. Swingle Papers (ASM 0188)

Yale Divinity School, New Haven, CT (YDS)

Lyman Hoover Papers (RG 9)
John R. Mott Papers (RG 45)
Student Volunteer Movement for Foreign Missions Papers (RG 42)
Horace Waller Papers (RG 72)
Robert Parmelee Wilder Papers (RG 38)
The Mission Field
The Arabian Mission Field Report

Zanzibar National Archives, Zanzibar, Tanzania (ZNA)

Foreign Office Correspondence, 1838–1890 (AA 1)
General Correspondence, 1837–1890 (AA 2)
Bombay Correspondence, 1840–1884 (AA 3)
Arabic Correspondence, 1841–1944 (AA 5)
Court Records, ca. 1855–1891 (AA 7)
Vice-Consulate Archives: Mombasa, Lamu, 1883–1890 (AA11)
Miscellanea, 1837–1914 (AA 12)
General Correspondence, 1890–1911 (AC 2)
Foreign Publication: Miscellaneous, 1825–1910 (BK 1)
Command Papers: Slavery and Slave Trade, 1877–1919 (BL 10)

Published Sources

'Abd al-Jalīl, Muḥammad Midḥat Jābir. *Al-ʿUmrān al-taqlīdī fī Dawlat al-Imārāt al-ʿArabīyah al-Muttaḥidah*. Al-ʿAyn: Markaz Zāyid lil-Turāth wa-al-Tārīkh, 2000.

Abdulaziz, Mohamed H. *Muyaka: 19th Century Swahili Poetry*. Nairobi: Kenya Literature Bureau, 1979.

Abrahamian, Ervand. *Iran between Two Revolutions*. Princeton, NJ: Princeton University Press, 1983.

Abu-Lughod, Janet. *Before European Hegemony: The World System, A.D. 1250–1350*. New York: Oxford University Press, 1989.

Adelson, Roger. *London and the Invention of the Middle East: Money, Power, and War, 1902–1922*. New Haven: Yale University Press, 1995.

Agius, Dionisius A. *In the Wake of the Dhow: The Arabian Gulf and Oman*. Reading, UK: Ithaca Press, 2002.

Albion, Robert Greenhalgh. *The Rise of New York Port, 1815–1860*. New York: Charles Scribner's Sons, 1939.

Al-Fahim, Mohamed. *From Rags to Riches: A Story from Abu Dhabi*. London: London Centre of Arab Studies, 2004.

Al-Harbān, Jāsim bin Mohammad. *Al-Fijrī*. Bahrain: Mu'sesa al-Tabaʿa wa al-Nashar, 1994.

Al-Hijji, Yacoub Yusuf. *Kuwait and the Sea: A Brief Social and Economic History.* Trans. Fahad Ahmad 'Isa Bishara. London: Arabian Publishing, 2010.

Al-Khan, Waheed. *Laiwa Music of the Gulf.* Qatar: GCC Folklore Centre, 2002.

———. *Aghānī al-Ghaūs fī al-Bahrayn.* Doha: Markaz al-Turāth Ash-Sha'bī, 1990, 2002.

Allen, Calvin H. "Sayyids, Shets and Sultāns: Politics and Trade in Masqat under the Al Bū Sa'īd, 1785–1914." PhD diss., University of Washington, 1978.

Allen, Richard B. "The Constant Demand of the French." *Journal of African History* 49, no. 1 (March 2008): 43–71.

———. "The Mascarene Slave Trade." In Campbell, *The Structure of Slavery in the Indian Ocean and Asia.*

———. *Slaves, Freedmen, and Indentured Laborers in Colonial Mauritius.* Cambridge: Cambridge University Press, 1999.

Allina, Eric. *Slavery by Any Other Name: African Life under Company Rule in Colonial Mozambique.* Charlottesville: University of Virginia Press, 2012.

Almeida, Paes de. *Esboço geographico de Angoche, Lourenço Marques, 1903.* Cota local: C.C. 144 P2. Biblioteca Nacional, Portugal. Available at Biblioteca Nacional Digital, Portugal: PURL 1426/2, http://purl.pt/1426.

Alpers, Edward A. "The African Diaspora in the Northwestern Indian Ocean: Reconsiderations of an Old Problem, New Directions for Research." *Comparative Studies in South Asia, Africa and the Middle East* 17, no. 2 (1997): 61–80.

———. *The East African Slave Trade.* Nairobi: Published for the Historical Association of Tanzania by the East African Publishing House, 1967. Historical Association of Tanzania Papers Series, no. 3.

———. "Introduction: Slave Routes and Oral Tradition in Southeastern Africa." In Zimba, Alpers, and Isaacman, *Slave Routes and Oral Tradition in Southeastern Africa.*

———. *Ivory and Slaves: Changing Pattern of International Trade in East Central Africa to the Later Nineteenth Century.* Berkeley: University of California Press, 1975.

———. "Mozambique and 'Mozambiques': Slave Trade and Diaspora on a Global Scale." In Zimba, Alpers, and Isaacman, *Slave Routes and Oral Tradition in Southeastern Africa,* 39–61.

———. "The Other Middle Passage: The African Slave Trade in the Indian Ocean." In *Other Middle Passages,* ed. Marcus Rediker, Cassandra Pybus, and Emma Christopher. Berkeley: University of California Press, 2007.

———. "Recollecting Africa: Diasporic Memory in the Indian Ocean World." *African Studies Review* 43, no. 1 (2000): 83–99.

———. "Slave Trade: Eastern Africa." In *Encyclopedia of Africa South of the Sahara,* vol. 4, ed. John Middleton. New York: Charles Scribner's Sons, 1997.

———. "The Story of Swema: Female Vulnerability in Nineteenth-Century Zanzibar." In Robertson and Klein, *Women and Slavery in Africa,* 185–201.

———. "The Western Indian Ocean as a Regional Food Network in the Nineteenth Century." In Edward A. Alpers, *East Africa and the Indian Ocean,* 23–38. Princeton, NJ: Markus Wiener, 2009.

Alpers, Edward A., and Matthew S. Hopper. "Parler en son nom? Comprendre les témoignages d'esclaves africains originaires de l'Océan Indien (1850–1930)" [Speaking for themselves? Understanding African freed slave testimonies from the Western Indian Ocean, 1850–1930]. *Annales: Histoire, Sciences Sociales* 63, no. 34 (July–August 2008): 799–828.

Al-Shamlan, Saif Marzooq. *Pearling in the Arabian Gulf: A Kuwaiti Memoir*. Trans. Peter Clark. London: London Centre of Arab Studies, 2001 [originally published 1975].

Al-Zayyani, Rashid. *Al-Ghaūs wa at-Tawāsha: Min Mū'lif Zhakriyāt wa Tārīkh*. Manama, Bahrain: Al Ayam Publishing, 1998.

Andrade, Tonio. "A Chinese Farmer, Two African Boys, and a Warlord: Toward a Global Microhistory." *Journal of World History* 21, no. 4 (December 2010): 573–591.

Anscombe, Frederick F. *The Ottoman Gulf: The Creation of Kuwait, Saudi Arabia, and Qatar*. New York: Columbia University Press, 1997.

Anstey, Roger. "The British Slave Trade, 1751–1807: A Comment." *Journal of African History* 17, no. 4 (1976): 606–607.

———. "Review: Numbers and the Slave Trade." *Journal of African History* 11, no. 3 (1970): 457–459.

Ashe, Irma. "Smart Dress Accessories." *Pictorial Review*, November 1906, 17.

Ashmore, A. T. "Early Summer Fashions." *Harper's Bazaar*, May 12, 1900, 103.

Atwood, Edward S. "Memorial of John Bertram." *Historical Collections of the Essex Institute* 21, nos. 4–6 (April–June 1884): 81–96.

Austen, Ralph A. "From the Atlantic to the Indian Ocean: European Abolition, the African Slave Trade, and Asia Economic Structures." In *The Abolition of the Atlantic Slave Trade: Origins and Effects in Europe, Africa, and the Americas*, ed. David Eltis and James Walvin, 117–140. Madison: University of Wisconsin Press, 1981.

———. "The Islamic Slave Trade out of Africa (Red Sea and Indian Ocean): An Effort at Quantification." Paper presented to the Conference on Islamic Africa: Slavery and Related Institutions, Princeton University, 1977.

———. "New Theories for Old Zanzibar." *Journal of African History* 29, no. 2 (1988): 333–334.

———. "The 19th-Century Islamic Slave Trade from East Africa (Swahili and Red Sea Coasts): A Tentative Census." In Clarence-Smith, *The Economics of the Indian Ocean Slave Trade in the Nineteenth Century*.

Ayalon, David. *The Mamluk Military Society*. London: Variorum Reprints, 1979.

Balsan, Consuelo Vanderbilt. *The Glitter and the Gold*. New York: Harper, 1952.

Banton, Mandy. "The 'Taint of Slavery': The Colonial Office and the Regulation of Free Labour." In K. Hamilton and Salmon, *Slavery, Diplomacy and Empire*.

Barth, Fredrik. *Sohar: Culture and Society in an Omani Town*. Baltimore and London: Johns Hopkins University Press, 1983.

Barton, Clara. *The Red Cross: A History of This Remarkable International Movement in the Interest of Humanity*. Washington, DC: International Red Cross, 1898.

Bauer, Raymond A., and Alice H. Bauer. "Day to Day Resistance to Slavery." *Journal of Negro History* 27 (October, 1942): 388–419.

Baur, R. P. *Voyage dans l'Oudoe et l'Ouzigua*. Tours: A. Mame, 1887.

Beachey, R. W. *The African Diaspora and East Africa: An Inaugural Lecture Delivered at Makerere University College (University of East Africa), Kampala, Uganda, on 31st July, 1967*. Nairobi: 1967.

———. *A Collection of Documents on the Slave Trade of Eastern Africa*. New York: Harper and Row, 1976.

———. *The Slave Trade of Eastern Africa*. New York: Harper and Row, 1976.

Beckles, Hilary. "Down but Not Out: Eric Williams' 'Capitalism and Slavery' after Nearly 40 Years of Criticism." *Bulletin of Eastern Caribbean Affairs*, May–June 1982.

Belgrave, Charles. *Personal Column*. London: Hutchinson, 1960.

Bender, Thomas, ed. *The Antislavery Debate: Capitalism and Abolitionism as a Problem in Historical Interpretation*. Berkeley: University of California Press, 1992.

Benjamin, Walter. *The Arcades Project*. Cambridge, MA: Belknap Press of Harvard University Press, 2002.

Bennett, Norman Robert. *Arab versus European: Diplomacy and War in Nineteenth-Century East Central Africa*. New York: Africana Publishing, 1986.

———. *New England Merchants in Africa: A History through Documents, 1802 to 1865*. Boston: Boston University Press, 1965.

———. "Review: Abdul Sheriff, Slaves, Spices and Ivory in Zanzibar." *American Historical Review* 94, no. 1 (February 1989): 191–192.

Berg, F. J. "Mombasa under the Busaidi Sultanate: The City and Its Hinterland in the Nineteenth Century." PhD diss., University of Wisconsin, 1971.

Berg, L. W. C. van den. *Le Hadhramaut et les colonies arabes dans l'Archipel Indien*. Westmead, UK: Gregg International Publishers, 1969.

Berlioux, Étienne Félix. *The Slave Trade in Africa in 1872 Principally Carried on for the Supply of Turkey, Egypt, Persia and Zanzibar*. London: Frank Cass, 1872 [1971 reprint].

Bernal, Victoria. "Cotton and Colonial Order in Sudan: A Social History, with Emphasis on the Gezira Scheme." In *Cotton, Colonialism, and Social History in Sub-Saharan Africa*, ed. Allen Isaacman and Richard Roberts, 96–118. Portsmouth, NH: Heinemann, 1995.

Bhacker, Reda. *Trade and Empire in Muscat and Zanzibar: Roots of British Domination*. New York: Routledge, 1992.

Bird, Christiane. *The Sultan's Shadow: One Family's Rule at the Crossroads of East and West*. New York: Random House, 2010.

Bishara, Fahad Ahmad. "A Sea of Debt: Histories of Commerce and Obligation in the Indian Ocean, c. 1850–1940." PhD diss., Duke University, 2012.

Blackburn, Robin. *The Making of New World Slavery: From the Baroque to the Modern 1492–1800*. London: Verso, 1997.

Blassingame, John W. *The Slave Community: Plantation Life in the Ante-Bellum South.* New York: Oxford University Press, 1972.

Bligh, Arthur C. V. *Golden Quest: The Roaring Days of West Australian Gold Rushes and Life in the Pearling Industry.* Sydney: Publicity Press, 1955.

Blumenfeld, Ralph D. "London Topics from Our Special Correspondent." *Town and Country*, August 8, 1903, 15.

Boersma, Jeanette. *Grace in the Gulf.* Grand Rapids, MI: Wm. B. Eerdmans Publishing, 1991. Historical Series of the Reformed Church in America, no. 20.

Bonate, Liazzat J. K. "The Ascendance of Angoche: The Politics of Kinship and Territory in Nineteenth Century Northern Mozambique." *Lusotopie* (2003): 115–140.

Bondarevsky, Grigori L. "Turning the Persian Gulf into a British Lake: British Domination in the Indian Ocean in the Nineteenth and Twentieth Centuries." In *The Indian Ocean: Explorations in History, Commerce and Politics*, ed. Satish Chandra. Newbury Park, CA: Sage Publications, 1987.

Bose, Sugata. *A Hundred Horizons: The Indian Ocean in the Age of Global Empire.* Cambridge, MA: Harvard University Press, 2006.

Bradley, Keith, and Paul Cartledge, eds. *The Cambridge World History of Slavery*, 2 vols. New York: Cambridge University Press, 2011.

Bristol-Rhys, Jane. *Emirati Women: Generations of Change.* New York: Columbia University Press, 2010.

British Parliamentary Papers. Irish University Press Series. Slave Trade, 95 vols. Shannon, Ireland: Irish University Press, 1969.

Brode, Heinrich. *Tippoo Tib: The Story of His Career in Central Africa.* London: Edward Arnold, 1907 [reprint, Chicago: Afro-Am Press, 1969].

Bromber, Katrin, ed. and trans. *The Jurisdiction of the Sultan of Zanzibar and the Subjects of Foreign Nations.* Würzburg: Ergon Verlag 2001. Bibliotheca Academia: Sammlung Interdisziplinarer Studien, vol. 8.

Brunschvig, R. "'Abd." In *Encyclopedia of Islam*, 2nd ed., vol. 1. Leiden: Brill, 1960.

Buckingham, James Silk. *Travels in Assyria, Media, and Persia, Including a Journey from Bagdad by Mount Zagros, to Hamadan, the Ancient Ecbatana, Researches in Ispahan and the Ruins of Persepolis, and Journey from Thence by Shiraz and Shapoor to the Sea-Shore. Description of Bussorah, Bushire, Bahrein, Ormuz, and Muscat, Narrative of an Expedition against the Pirates of the Persian Gulf, with Illustrations of the Voyage of Nearchus, and Passage by the Arabian Sea to Bombay.* Farnborough: Gregg International Publishers, 1971. First published 1829 by H. Colburn.

Burdett, Anita L. P., ed. *Records of the Persian Gulf Pearl Fisheries, 1857–1962*, 4 vols. London: Archive Editions, 1995.

Burke, Edmund, ed. *Struggle and Survival in the Modern Middle East.* Berkeley: University of California Press, 1993.

Busch, Briton Cooper. *Britain and the Persian Gulf, 1894–1914.* Berkeley: University of California Press, 1967.

Bush, M. L., ed. *Serfdom and Slavery: Studies in Legal Bondage.* New York: Longman, 1996.

Busia, Abena P. A. "Silencing Sycorax: On African Colonial Discourse and the Unvoiced Female." *Cultural Critique* 14 (Winter 1989–1990): 81–104.
Cable, James. *Gunboat Diplomacy, 1919–1979: Political Applications of Limited Naval Force*. New York: St. Martin's Press, 1981.
Campbell, Gwyn, ed. *Abolition and Its Aftermath in Indian Ocean Africa and Asia*. New York: Routledge, 2005.
———. "The East African Slave Trade, 1861–1895: The 'Southern' Complex." *International Journal of African Historical Studies* 22, no. 1 (1989): 1–26.
———. *An Economic History of Imperial Madagascar, 1750–1895: The Rise and Fall of an Island Empire*. New York: Cambridge University Press, 2005.
———. "Introduction: Slavery and Other Forms of Unfree Labour in the Indian Ocean World." In Campbell, *The Structure of Slavery in Indian Ocean Africa and Asia*.
———. "Madagascar and Mozambique in the Slave Trade of the Western Indian Ocean, 1800–1861." *Slavery and Abolition* 9, no. 3 (1988): 165–192.
———. "Slavery in the Indian Ocean World." In *The Routledge History of Slavery*, ed. Gad Heuman and Trevor Burnard, 56–61. London: Routledge, 2011.
———, ed. *The Structure of Slavery in Indian Ocean Africa and Asia*. New York: Frank Cass, 2004.
Cantemir, Dimitrie. *Histoire de l'empire Othoman, ou se voyent les causes de son aggrandissement et de sa décadence*. Paris: Despilly, 1743.
Cantine, James. "The Boys of the Freed Slave School." *Neglected Arabia* 57 (1906): 15–21.
Capela, José. *O tráfico de escravos nos portos de Moçambique, 1733–1904*. Porto: Edições Afrontamento, 2002.
Cariño, Micheline. "The Cultured Pearl Polemic." *World Aquaculture* 27, no. 1 (1996): 42–44.
———. "The Great Debate: The Cultured Pearl Polemic." *Pearl Oyster Information Bulletin* 10 (August 1997): 49–51.
Carmichael, Tim. "The Diaspora in Yemen." In R. S. Hamilton, *Routes of Passage*, vol. 1, part 1.
Carne, W. M. "Notes on Date Culture in America with Some Consideration of Its Possibilities in New South Wales." *Agricultural Gazette of New South Wales*, September 2, 1914.
Carter, Robert A. *Sea of Pearls: Seven Thousand Years of the Industry That Shaped the Gulf*. London: Arabian Publishing, 2012.
Catlin-Jairazbhoy, Amy, and Edward A. Alpers. *Sidis and Scholars: Essays on African Indians*. New Delhi: Rainbow Publications, and Trenton, NJ: Africa World Press, 2003.
Chakrabarty, Dipesh. *Provincializing Europe: Postcolonial Thought and Historical Difference*. Princeton, NJ: Princeton University Press, 2000.
Chamberlain, James F. "The Fruit Industry in California." *Overland Monthly and Out West Magazine* 82, no. 7 (July 1924): 304–305.

Chase-Dunn, Christopher, and Thomas D. Hall. *Rise and Demise: Comparing World-Systems.* Boulder, CO: Westview Press, 1997.

Chatterjee, Indrani. "Abolition by Denial? Slavery in South Asia after 1843." In Campbell, *Abolition and Its Aftermath in Indian Ocean Africa and Asia,* 150–168.

Chiang, Bien. "Market Price, Labor Input, and Relation of Production in Sarawak's Edible Birds' Nest Trade." In Tagliacozzo and Chang, *Chinese Circulations.*

Clarence-Smith, William Gervase. "The British 'Official Mind' and Nineteenth-Century Islamic Debates over the Abolition of Slavery." In K. Hamilton and Salmon, *Slavery, Diplomacy and Empire.*

———, ed. *The Economics of the Indian Ocean Slave Trade in the Nineteenth Century.* London: Frank Cass, 1989.

———. *Islam and the Abolition of Slavery.* London: C. Hurst, 2006.

Clements, F. A. *Oman, the Reborn Land.* New York: Longman, 1980.

Codrai, Ronald. *The Emirates of Yesteryear.* London: Stacey International, 1990, 2001.

———. *Seafarers of the Emirates: An Arabian Album—A Collection of Mid-20th Century Photographs.* Dubai: Motivate Publishing, 2003.

Cohan, Steven. "Victorian Power." *NOVEL: A Forum on Fiction* 22, no. 3 (Spring 1989): 350–353.

Cohen, Ariel. Introduction to lecture by Robert Bostom, Heritage Foundation, Lehrman Auditorium, Washington, DC, May 9, 2006. Available at http://multimedia.heritage.org/content/wm/Lehrman-050906.wvx (accessed Aug. 26, 2006).

Cohen, Morton N. *Rider Haggard: His Life and Works.* New York: Walker, 1961.

Cohen, Robin. *Global Diasporas: An Introduction.* New York: Routledge, 2008.

Colley, Charles C. *The Century of Robert H. Forbes: The Career of a Pioneer Agriculturalist, Agronomist, Environmentalist, Conservationist and Water Specialist in Arizona and Abroad.* Tucson, AZ: Arizona Historical Society, 1977.

Colomb, Philip Howard. *Slave Catching in the Indian Ocean: A Record of Naval Experiences.* London: Dawsons of Pall Mall, 1968. First published 1873 by Longman, Green.

Cooper, Frederick. "Conditions Analogous to Slavery: Imperialism and Free Labor Ideology in Africa." In Cooper, Holt, and Scott, *Beyond Slavery.*

———. *From Slaves to Squatters: Plantation Labor and Agriculture in Zanzibar and Coastal Kenya, 1890–1925.* Portsmouth, NH: Heinemann, 1997. First published 1980 by Yale University Press.

———. *Plantation Slavery on the East Coast of Africa.* Portsmouth, NH: Heinemann, 1997. First published 1977 by Yale University Press.

Cooper, Frederick, Thomas C. Holt, and Rebecca J. Scott, eds. *Beyond Slavery: Explorations of Race, Labor, and Citizenship in Postemancipation Societies.* Chapel Hill: University of North Carolina Press, 2000.

Cornish, Vaughan. "Notes on the Historical and Physical Geography of the Theatres of War." *Geographical Journal* 45, no. 5 (May 1915).

Cottrell, Alvin J., ed. *The Persian Gulf States: A General Survey.* Baltimore: Johns Hopkins University Press, 1980.
Coupland, Reginald. *The British Anti-slavery Movement.* London: T. Butterworth, 1933.
———. *East Africa and Its Invaders, from the Earliest Times to the Death of Seyyid Said in 1856.* Oxford: Clarendon Press, 1938.
———. *The Exploitation of East Africa, 1856–1890: The Slave Trade and the Scramble.* Chicago: Northwestern University Press, 1967.
———. *Wilberforce: A Narrative.* Oxford: Clarendon Press, 1923.
Creasy, Edward Shepherd. *History of the Ottoman Turks from the Beginning of Their Empire to the Present Time.* London: Richard Bentley, 1856.
Critz, José Morilla, Alan L. Olmstead, and Paul W. Rhode, "'Horn of Plenty': The Globalization of Mediterranean Horticulture and the Economic Development of Southern Europe, 1880–1930." *Journal of Economic History* 59, no. 2 (June 1999): 316–352.
Crone, Patricia. *Slaves on Horses: The Evolution of the Islamic Polity.* New York: Cambridge University Press, 1980.
Curtin, Philip D. *The Atlantic Slave Trade: A Census.* Madison: University of Wisconsin Press, 1969.
———. "Measuring the Atlantic Slave Trade Once Again: A Comment." *Journal of African History* 17, no. 4 (1976): 595–605.
Dale, Robert. "The Water Resources of Oman." Unpublished report for TetraTech International, ca. 1980. James H. Critchfield Papers, private collection, Williamsburg, VA.
Damluji, Salma Samar. *The Architecture of Oman.* Reading, UK: Garnet, 1998.
———. *The Architecture of the United Arab Emirates.* Reading, UK: Garnet, 2006.
Daniel, Norman. *Islam and the West: The Making of an Image.* Edinburgh: University Press, 1960.
D'Antonio, Michael. *Hershey: Milton S. Hershey's Extraordinary Life of Wealth, Empire, and Utopian Dreams.* New York: Simon and Schuster, 2006.
Davis, David Brion. *Problem of Slavery in the Age of Revolution, 1770–1823.* Ithaca, NY: Cornell University Press, 1975.
Davis, Mike. *Late Victorian Holocausts: El Niño Famines and the Making of the Third World.* New York: Verso, 2001.
Devereux, W. Cope. *A Cruise in the "Gorgon."* London: Dawsons of Pall Mall, 1968. First printed 1869 by Bell and Daldy.
De Waal, Alex. *Famine That Kills.* New York: Oxford University Press, 2005.
De Waleffe, Maurice. *Quand Paris était un paradis: Mémoires 1900–1939.* Paris: Société des Éditions Denoël, 1947.
Dodge, Toby. *Inventing Iraq: The Failure of Nation Building and a History Denied.* New York: Columbia University Press, 2003.
Donkin, R. A. *Beyond Price: Pearls and Pearl-Fishing, Origins to the Age of Discoveries.* Philadelphia: American Philosophical Society, 1998.

Dooling, Wayne. *Slavery, Emancipation and Colonial Rule in South Africa*. Athens, Ohio University Press, 2008.

Dowson, V. H. W. *Dates and Date Cultivation of the 'Iraq. Part I: The Cultivation of the Date Palm on the Shat Al 'Arab*. Cambridge: Agricultural Directorate of Mesopotamia, 1921.

Dowson, V. H. W., and A. Aten. *Dates: Handling, Processing and Packing*. Rome: Food and Agricultural Organization of the United Nations, 1962.

Drescher, Seymour. *Abolition: A History of Slavery and Antislavery*. New York: Cambridge University Press, 2009.

———. "Abolitionist Expectations: Britain." In Temperley, *After Slavery*.

———. *Capitalism and Antislavery: British Mobilization in Comparative Perspective*. New York: Oxford University Press, 1987.

———. *Econocide: British Slavery in the Era of Abolition*. Pittsburgh: University of Pittsburgh Press, 1977.

———. "Eric Williams: British Capitalism and British Slavery." *History and Theory* 26, no. 2 (1987): 180–196.

Dunn, Ross E. *The Adventures of Ibn Battuta: A Muslim Traveler of the Fourteenth Century*. Berkeley: University of California Press, 1989.

Edwards, Holly, ed. *Noble Dreams, Wicked Pleasures: Orientalism in America, 1870–1930*. Princeton, NJ: Princeton University Press, 2000.

Elkins, Stanley M. *Slavery: A Problem in American Institutional and Intellectual Life*. Chicago: University of Chicago Press, 1959.

———. "The Slavery Debate." *Commentary* 60, no. 6 (December 1975): 40–54.

El-Mallah, Issam. *Die Musik einer alten Hochkultur: Das Sultanat Oman* [The music of an ancient civilization: The Sultanate of Oman]. Muscat, Oman: Ministry of Information, 1994.

Eltis, David. *Economic Growth and the Ending of the Transatlantic Slave Trade*. New York: Oxford University Press, 1987.

———. *The Rise of African Slavery in the Americas*. New York: Cambridge University Press, reprint edition, 1999.

———. "The Transatlantic Slave Trade: Revised Estimates of the Volume and Direction Derived from the Second Edition of the Cambridge Database of Voyages." Paper presented to American Historical Association annual meeting, January 6, 2006.

Engerman, Stanley. "Comparative Approaches to the Ending of Slavery." In Temperley, *After Slavery*.

Engerman, Stanley, Seymour Drescher, and Robert Paquette, eds. *Slavery*. New York: Oxford University Press, 2001.

Enstad, Nan. *Ladies of Labor, Girls of Adventure: Working Women, Popular Culture, and Labor Politics at the Turn of the Twentieth Century*. New York: Columbia University Press, 1999.

Erdem, Y. Hakan. *Slavery in the Ottoman Empire and Its Demise, 1800–1909*. New York: St. Martin's Press, 1996.

Eunson, Robert. *The Pearl King: The Story of the Fabulous Mikimoto.* Tokyo: Charles E. Tuttle, 1963.

Evans, Brad. *Before Cultures: The Ethnographic Imagination in American Literature, 1865–1920.* Chicago: University of Chicago Press, 2005.

Ewald, Janet J. "Africa: East Africa." In *A Historical Guide to World Slavery*, ed. Seymour Drescher and Stanley L. Engerman, 41–46. New York: Oxford University Press, 1998.

———. "Crossers of the Sea: Slaves, Freedmen, and Other Migrants in the Northwestern Indian Ocean, c. 1750–1914." *American Historical Review* 105, no. 1 (February 2000): 69–91.

Facey, William. *Riyadh: The Old City from Its Origins until the 1950s.* London: Immel Publishing, 1992.

Fage, J. D., and Roland Oliver, eds. *The Cambridge History of Africa*, vol. 4: *From c. 1600 to c. 1790.* London: Cambridge University Press, 1975.

Fairchild, David G. "Persian Gulf Dates and Their Introduction into America." *USDA Bureau of Plant Industry*, Bulletin 54. Washington, DC: GPO, 1903.

———. *The World Was My Garden: Travels of a Plant Explorer.* New York: Charles Scribner's Sons, 1938.

Farmánfarmáian, Hafez. "The Fall of the Kajar Dynasty, a Crisis in Persian History, 1918–1925." Master's thesis, Stanford University, 1950.

Fattah, Hala. *The Politics of Regional Trade in Iraq, Arabia, and the Gulf, 1745–1900.* Albany: State University of New York Press, 1997.

Fischel, Oskar, and Max von Boehn. *Modes and Manners of the Nineteenth Century as Represented in the Pictures and Engravings of the Time*, 4 vols. London: J. M. Dent and Sons, 1927.

Fisher, Martin, and David A. Membery. "Climate." In *Vegetation of the Arabian Peninsula*, ed. Shahina A. Ghazanfar and Martin Fisher, 5–38. Norwell, MA: Kluwer Academic Publishers, 1998.

Fogel, Robert William. "Cliometrics and Culture: Some Recent Developments in the Historiography of Slavery." *Journal of Social History* 11, no. 1 (Autumn 1977): 34–51.

Foran, John, ed. *A Century of Revolution: Social Movements in Iran.* Minneapolis: University of Minnesota Press, 1994.

Foucault, Michel. *Discipline and Punish: The Birth of the Prison*, 2nd ed. New York: Vintage Books, 1995.

Frank, Andre Gunder. *ReOrient: Global Economy in the Asian Age.* Berkeley: University of California Press, 1998.

Frazier, E. Franklin. *The Negro Church in America.* New York: Schocken Books, 1963.

Gallagher, John. "Nationalisms and the Crisis of Empire, 1919–1922." *Modern Asian Studies* 15, no. 3 (1981): 355–368.

Gavin, R. J. "The Bartle Frere Mission to Zanzibar, 1873." *Historical Journal* 5, no. 2 (1962): 122–148.

Gelvin, James L. *The Modern Middle East: A History.* New York: Oxford University Press, 2005.

———. "Modernity, Tradition, and the Battleground of Gender in Early Twentieth-Century Damascus." *Die Welt des Islams* 52, no. 1 (Winter 2012): 1–22.

Gelvin, James L., and Nile Green, eds., *Global Muslims in the Age of Steam and Print*. Berkeley: University of California Press, 2014.

Genovese, Eugene. *The Political Economy of Slavery*. New York: Vintage Books, 1965.

———. *Roll, Jordan, Roll: The World the Slaves Made*. New York: Pantheon Books, 1974.

———. *The World the Slaveholders Made: Two Essays in Interpretation*. New York: Pantheon Books, 1969.

Gibb, H. A. R., and Harold Bowen. *Islamic Society and the West: A Study of the Impact of Western Civilization on Moslem Culture in the Near East*. London: Oxford University Press, 1950.

Gilbert, Erik. *Dhows and the Colonial Economy of Zanzibar, 1860–1970*. Athens, OH: Ohio University Press, 2004.

Gilroy, Paul. *The Black Atlantic: Modernity and Double Consciousness*. Cambridge, MA: Harvard University Press, 1993.

Glahn, Richard von. *Fountain of Fortune: Money and Monetary Policy in China, 1000–1700*. Berkeley: University of California Press, 1996.

Glassman, Jonathon. "Creole Nationalists and the Search for Nativist Authenticity in Twentieth-Century Zanzibar: The Limits of Cosmopolitanism." *Journal of African History* 55, no. 2 (July 2014): 229–247.

———. *Feasts and Riot: Revelry, Rebellion, and Popular Consciousness on the Swahili Coast, 1856–1888*. Portsmouth, NH: Heinemann, 1995. Social History of Africa Series.

———. *War of Words, War of Stones: Racial Thought and Violence in Colonial Zanzibar*. Bloomington and Indianapolis: Indiana University Press, 2011.

Golash-Boza, Tanya Maria. *Yo Soy Negro: Blackness in Peru*. Gainesville: University Press of Florida, 2011.

Goldschmidt, Louis. "Pearl Fisheries in Venezuela." *Forest and Stream: A Journal of Outdoor Life*, July 13, 1901.

Goldstone, Jack. "The Rise of the West—or Not? A Revision of Socio-Economic History." *Sociological Theory* 18 (2000): 175–194.

Gooch, G. P., and Harold Temperley, eds. *British Documents on the Origins of the War, 1898–1914*, 10 vols. New York: British Library of Information, 1938.

Gordon, David M. "The Abolition of the Slave Trade and the Transformation of the South-Central African Interior during the Nineteenth Century." *William and Mary Quarterly* 66, no. 4 (October 2009): 915–938.

Gordon, Frances Linzee, Jenny Walker, Anthony Ham, and Virginia Maxwell. *Lonely Planet: Arabian Peninsula*. Oakland, CA: Lonely Planet Publications, 2004.

Gordon, G. Keith. "HMS Briton, 1873." Unpublished manuscript, MS79/17. Admiral Sir Arthur Mostyn Field Papers, National Maritime Museum, Greenwich, UK.

Gordon, Murray [Murray Gordon Silberman]. *Slavery in the Arab World*. New York: New Amsterdam Books, 1989. Originally published in France as *L'esclavage dans le monde arabe* (Paris: Éditions Robert Laffont, 1987).

Graf, Charles C. "The Batinah Hydrologic Area." In *The Hydrology of the Sultanate of Oman: A Preliminary Assessment.* Sultanate of Oman, Public Authority for Water Resources, PAWR 83:1, 28–43. Muscat, Oman: Public Authority for Water Resources, 1983.

Graham, Helga. *Arabian Time Machine: Self-Portrait of an Oil State.* London: Heinemann, 1978.

Gramsci, Antonio. *Selections from the Prison Notebooks of Antonio Gramsci,* ed. Quintin Hoare and Geoffrey Nowell-Smith. New York: International Publishers, 1971.

Grant, Kevin. *A Civilised Savagery: Britain and the New Slaveries in Africa, 1884–1926.* New York: Routledge, 2005.

Great Britain, Royal Commission on Fugitive Slaves. *Report of the Commissioners, Minutes of the Evidence, and Appendix, with General Index of Minutes of Evidence and Appendix* [C–1516-L]. London: H. M. Stationary Office, 1876.

"Great Britain v. France." *American Journal of International Law* 2, no. 4 (October 1908): 921–928.

Guha, Ranajit. *Dominance without Hegemony: History and Power in Colonial India.* Cambridge, MA: Harvard University Press, 1997.

Gutman, Herbert G. *The Black Family in Slavery and Freedom, 1750–1925.* New York: Vintage Books, 1976.

———. *The Invisible Fact: The Black Family in American History, 1850–1930.* New York: Pantheon, 1974.

Hackney, Ki, and Diana Edkins. *People and Pearls: The Magic Endures.* New York: Harper, 2000.

Hadary, Gideon. "The Candy-Consumer: How Much Will He Buy in the Postwar Period?" *Journal of Business of the University of Chicago* 18, no. 2 (April 1945): 96–100.

Hafkin, Nancy. "Trade, Society, and Politics in Northern Mozambique, c. 1753–1913." PhD diss., Boston University, 1973.

Hall, Gwendolyn Midlo. *Africans in Colonial Louisiana: The Development of Afro-Creole Culture in the Eighteenth Century.* Baton Rouge: Louisiana State University Press, 1992.

Hamilton, Alexander. *A New Account of the East Indies.* Edinburgh: John Mosman, 1727.

Hamilton, Keith. "Zealots and Helots: The Slave Trade Department of the Nineteenth-Century Foreign Office." In K. Hamilton and Salmon, *Slavery, Diplomacy and Empire.*

Hamilton, Keith, and Patrick Salmon, eds. *Slavery, Diplomacy and Empire: Britain and the Suppression of the Slave Trade, 1807–1975.* Brighton and Portland, OR: Sussex Academic Press, 2009.

Hamilton, Ruth Simms. *Routes of Passage: Rethinking the African Diaspora.* East Lansing: Michigan State University, 2007.

Hancock, Michael. "The Stones in the Sword: Tennyson's Crown Jewels." *Victorian Poetry* 39 no. 1 (2001): 1–24.

A Handbook of Arabia, vol. 1: *General, Compiled by the Geographical Section of the Naval Intelligence Division, Naval Staff, Admiralty*. London: H. M. Stationary Office, 1919.

Hane, Mikiso. *Peasants, Rebels, Women, and Outcastes: The Underside of Modern Japan*, 2nd ed. Lanham, MD: Rowman and Littlefield, 2003.

Hanretta, Sean. *Islam and Social Change in French West Africa: History of an Emancipatory Community*. Cambridge: Cambridge University Press, 2009.

Hansman, John. *Julfar, an Arabian Port: Its Settlement and Far Eastern Ceramic Trade from the 14th to the 18th Centuries*. London: Royal Asiatic Society, 1985.

Harbān, Jasim Mohammad. *Al-Fijri*. Bahrain: Mu'sesa al-Taba'a wa al-Nashar, 1994.

Hardy-Guilbert, Claire, and Christian Lalande. *La maison de Shaykh ʿIsáà Baḥrayn*. Paris: Éditions ADPF, 1981.

Harms, Robert W. *Rivers of Wealth, River of Sorrow: The Central Zaire Basin in the Era of the Slave and Ivory Trade, 1500–1891*. New Haven: Yale University Press, 1981.

Harries, Lyndon. *Swahili Poetry*. Oxford: Clarendon Press, 1962.

Harries, Patrick. "Culture and Classification: A History of the Mozbieker Community at the Cape." *Social Dynamics* 26, no. 2 (2000): 29–54.

Harris, Joseph E. *The African Presence in Asia: Consequences of the East African Slave Trade*. Evanston, IL: Northwestern University Press, 1971.

———. *Recollections of James Juma Mbotela*. Nairobi: East Africa Publishing House, 1977.

Harrison, Paul W. *The Arab at Home*. New York: Thomas Y. Crowell, 1924.

Hasanovitz, Elizabeth. *One of Them: Chapters from a Passionate Autobiography*. Boston: Houghton Mifflin, 1918.

Hawley, Donald. *Oman and Its Renaissance*. London: Stacey International, 1977.

Heard-Bey, Frauke. *From Trucial States to United Arab Emirates*. Dubai: Motivate Publishing, 2004. First published 1982 by Longman.

Herdman, W. A. *Report to the Government of Ceylon on the Pearl Oyster Fisheries of the Gulf of Manaar*. London: Royal Society, 1903.

Herskovits, Melville J. *The Myth of the Negro Past*. Boston: Beacon Press, 1941.

Heude, William. *A Voyage up the Persian Gulf and a Journey Overland from India to England in 1817*. London: Longman, Hurst, Rees, Orme, and Brown, 1819.

Heuman, Gad. "The British West Indies." In *The Oxford History of the British Empire*, vol. 3: *The Nineteenth Century*, ed. Andrew Porter, 470–493. New York: Oxford University Press, 1999.

———. *'The Killing Time': The Morant Bay Rebellion in Jamaica*. London: Macmillan, 1994.

———. "Riots and Resistance in the Caribbean at the Moment of Freedom." In Temperley, *After Slavery*, 135–149.

Higgins, D. S. *Rider Haggard: A Biography*. New York: Stein and Day Publishers, 1983.

Hill, Pascoe Grenfell. *Fifty Days on Board a Slave-Vessel in the Mozambique Channel, April and May, 1843.* Baltimore: Black Classic Press, 1993. [Originally published 1848.]
Hills Brothers Company. *Dromedary Cook Book.* New York: Hills Brothers, 1912.
———. *One Hundred Delights.* New York: Moore Press, 1923.
———, Department of Food Research. *Dates in the Healthful Diet.* New York: Hills Brothers, 1928.
Ho, Engseng. *The Graves of Tarim: Genealogy and Mobility across the Indian Ocean.* Berkeley: University of California Press, 2006.
Holloway, Joseph E., ed. *Africanisms in American Culture.* Bloomington and Indianapolis: Indiana University Press, 1990.
Holt, Thomas C. "The Essence of the Contract: The Articulation of Race, Gender, and Political Economy in British Emancipation Policy, 1838–1866." In Cooper, Holt, and Scott, *Beyond Slavery,* 33–60.
Hooper, Jane, and David Eltis. "The Indian Ocean in Transatlantic Slavery." *Slavery and Abolition,* 34. no. 3 (2013): 353–375.
Hopper, Matthew S. "The African Presence in Arabia: Slavery, the World Economy, and the African Diaspora in Eastern Arabia, 1840–1940." PhD diss., University of California at Los Angeles, 2006.
———. "East Africa and the End of the Indian Ocean Slave Trade." *Journal of African Development* 13, no. 1 (2011): 27–54.
———. "Globalization and the Economics of African Slavery in Arabia in the Age of Empire." *Journal of African Development* 12, no. 1 (2010): 125–146.
———. "The Globalization of Dried Fruit: Transformations in the Eastern Arabian Economy, 1860s–1920s." In Gelvin and Green, *Global Muslims in the Age of Steam and Print,* 158–182.
———. "Imperialism and the Dilemma of Slavery in Eastern Arabia and the Gulf, 1873–1939." *Itinerario: International Journal on the History of European Expansion and Global Interaction* 30, no. 3 (2006): 76–94.
———. "Slavery, Family Life, and the African Diaspora in the Arabian Gulf, 1880–1940." In *Sex, Power and Slavery: The Dynamics of Carnal Relations under Enslavement,* ed. Gwyn Campbell, 167–181. Athens, OH: Ohio University Press, 2014.
Hourwich, Isaac. "The Crisis in Russian Agriculture." *Yale Review: A Quarterly Journal of History and Political Science* 1 (May 1892–February 1893): 411–433.
Howard, Arthur. "Selling Jewels to Multimillionaires: The Duchess of Montrose's Necklace." *McClure's Magazine,* July 1913, 56–65.
Howard, Douglas A. "Ottoman Historiography and the Literature of 'Decline' of the Sixteenth and Seventeenth Centuries." *Journal of Asian History* 22, no. 1 (1988): 52–77.
Hull, Clifton E. "River Pearls." *Rural Arkansas,* April 1981.
Hunter, W. W. *The Imperial Gazetteer of India.* London: Trubner, 1883.
Hunwick, John O., and Eve Troutt Powell. *The African Diaspora in the Mediterranean Lands of Islam.* Princeton, NJ: Markus Wiener Publishers, 2002.

Hutcheson, John Conroy. *The Penang Pirate and the Lost Pinnace*. London: Blackie and Son, 1885.

Huzzey, Richard. *Freedom Burning: Anti-Slavery and Empire in Victorian Britain*. Ithaca, NY: Cornell University Press, 2012.

———. "Minding Civilisation and Humanity in 1867: A Case Study in British Imperial Culture and Victorian Anti-Slavery." *Journal of Imperial and Commonwealth History* 40, no. 5 (December 2012): 807–825.

Inalcik, Halil. "Military and Fiscal Transformation in the Ottoman Empire, 1600–1700." *Archivum Ottomanicum* 6 (1980): 283–337.

India. Commercial Intelligence Department. *Annual Statement of the Sea-Borne Trade of British India with the British Empire and Foreign Countries*. Calcutta: Department of Statistics, 1885–1930.

Inikori, Joseph E. *Africans and the Industrial Revolution in England: A Study in International Trade and Economic Development*. New York: Cambridge University Press, 2002.

———. "Measuring the Atlantic Slave Trade: An Assessment of Curtin and Anstey." *Journal of African History* 17, no. 2 (1976): 197–223.

———. "Measuring the Atlantic Slave Trade: A Rejoinder." *Journal of African History* 17, no. 4 (1976): 607–627.

Issawi, Charles. *An Economic History of the Middle East and North Africa*. New York: Columbia University Press, 1982.

———. "Middle East Economic Development, 1815–1914: The General and the Specific." In *The Modern Middle East*, ed. Albert Hourani, Philip S. Khoury, and Mary C. Wilson. Berkeley: University of California Press, 1993.

Izzard, Molly. *The Gulf: Arabia's Western Approaches*. London: John Murray, 1979.

Jayasuriya, Shihan de Silva. *African Identity in Asia: Cultural Effects of Forced Migration*. Princeton, NJ: Markus Wiener Publishers, 2008.

Jayasuriya, Shihan de Silva, and Richard Pankhurst, eds. *The African Diaspora in the Indian Ocean*. Trenton, NJ: Africa World Press, 2003.

Johnson, John. *A Journey from India to England through Persia, Georgia, Russia, Poland, and Prussia in the Year 1817*. London: Longman, Hurst, Rees, Orme, and Brown, 1818.

Johnson, Walter. *River of Dark Dreams: Slavery and Empire in the Cotton Kingdom*. Cambridge, MA: Belknap Press of Harvard University Press, 2013.

———. *Soul by Soul: Life inside the Antebellum Slave Market*. Cambridge, MA: Harvard University Press, 1999.

Joselit, Jenna Weissman. *A Perfect Fit: Clothes, Character, and the Promise of America*. New York: Owl Books, 2002.

Joyce, Kristin, and Shellei Addison. *Pearls: Ornament and Obsession*. New York: Simon and Schuster, 1993.

Kafadar, Cemal, "The Question of Ottoman Decline." *Harvard Middle Eastern and Islamic Review* 4, nos. 1–2 (1997–1998): 30–75.

Kearney, Thomas H. "Date Varieties and Date Culture in Tunis." *USDA Bureau of Plant Industry*, Bulletin 92. Washington, DC: GPO, 1906.

Kelly, J. B. *Britain and the Persian Gulf, 1795–1880.* Oxford: Clarendon Press, 1968.

Kennedy, Hugh. *The Prophet and the Age of the Caliphates: The Islamic Near East from the Sixth to the Eleventh Century.* New York: Longman, 1986.

Keppel, George. *Personal Narrative of a Journey from India to England.* London: H. Colburn, 1827.

Kilekwa, Petro. *Slave Boy to Priest: The Autobiography of Padre Petro Kilekwa.* London: Universities' Mission to Central Africa, 1937.

Killick, Victor M. "Laughing Riches: Great Profits of Producers." *Los Angeles Times*, January 1, 1914, V130.

Kinross, Patrick Balfour. *The Ottoman Centuries: The Rise and Fall of the Turkish Empire.* London: Jonathan Cape, 1977.

Kirk, John. "A Visit to the Mungao District, near Cape Delgado." *Proceedings of the Royal Geographical Society of London* 21, no. 6. (1876–1877).

Kroeber, A. L., and Clyde Kluckhohn. *Culture: A Critical Review of Concepts and Definitions.* New York: Vintage Books, 1952.

Kunz, George Frederick, and Charles Hugh Stevenson. *The Book of the Pearl: The History, Art, Science and Industry of the Queen of Gems.* New York: Century, 1908.

Kurlansky, Mark. *Salt: A World History.* New York: Penguin Books, 2003.

Lains, Pedro, and Fernando Costa. "Portugal and the Boer War." In *The International Impact of the Boer War*, ed. Keith Wilson. New York: Palgrave, 2001.

Lal, Kishori Saran. *The Legacy of Muslim Rule in India.* New Delhi: Aditya Prakashan, 1992.

———. *The Mughal Harem.* New Delhi: Aditya Prakashan, 1988.

———. *Muslim Slave System in Medieval India.* New Delhi: Aditya Prakashan, 1994.

Landen, Robert G. *Oman since 1856: Disruptive Modernization in a Traditional Arab Society.* Princeton, NJ: Princeton University Press, 1967.

Langhorne, Richard. "Anglo-German Negotiations Concerning the Future of the Portuguese Colonies, 1911–1914." *Historical Journal* 16, no. 2 (1973): 361–387.

Larson, Pier M. "Horrid Journeying: Narratives of Enslavement and the Global African Diaspora." *Journal of World History* 19, no. 4 (December 2008): 431–464.

———. *Ocean of Letters: Language and Creolization in an Indian Ocean Diaspora.* New York: Cambridge University Press, 2009.

———. "Reconsidering Trauma, Identity, and the African Diaspora: Enslavement and Historical Memory in Nineteenth-Century Highland Madagascar." *William and Mary Quarterly* 56, no. 2 (April 1999): 357–361.

Lears, T. J. Jackson. "The Concept of Cultural Hegemony: Problems and Possibilities." *American Historical Review* 90, no. 3 (June 1985): 567–593.

Lemelle, Sidney, and Robin D. G. Kelley. *Imagining Home: Class, Culture and Nationalism in the African Diaspora.* New York: Verso, 1994.

Lewis, Bernard. *Islam and the West.* New York: Oxford University Press, 1993.

———. "Other People's History." In *Islam and the West*, ed. Bernard Lewis, 119–131. New York: Oxford University Press, 1993.
———. "Ottoman Observers of Ottoman Decline." *Islamic Studies* 1 (1962).
———. *Race and Slavery in the Middle East: An Historical Enquiry*. New York: Oxford University Press, 1990.
Lewis, William Roger. "The British Withdrawal from the Gulf, 1967–71." *Journal of Imperial and Commonwealth History* 31, no. 1 (2003): 83–108.
Limbert, Mandana E. *In the Time of Oil: Piety, Memory and Social Life in an Omani Town*. Stanford, CA: Stanford University Press, 2010.
———. "Marriage, Status and the Politics of Nationality in Oman." In *The Gulf Family: Kinship Policies and Modernity*, ed. Alanoud Alsharekh. London: Saqi Books, 2007.
———. "The Senses of Water in an Omani Town." *Social Text* 19, no. 3 (Fall 2001): 35–55.
Livingstone, David. *Last Journals of David Livingstone in Central Africa*. New York: Harper and Brothers, 1875.
Lloyd, Christopher. *The Navy and the Slave Trade: The Suppression of the African Slave Trade in the Nineteenth Century*. London: Longmans, Green, 1949.
Lorimer, Douglas A. *Colour, Class and the Victorians: English Attitudes to the Negro in the Mid-Nineteenth Century*. New York: Holmes and Meier Publishers, 1978.
Lorimer, J. G. *Gazetteer of the Persian Gulf, Oman and Central Arabia*, 4 vols. Calcutta: Superintendent Government Printing, 1907, 1915.
Lovejoy, Paul E., ed. *The Ideology of Slavery in Africa*. Beverly Hills, CA: Sage Publications, 1981.
———, ed. *Slavery on the Frontiers of Islam*. Princeton, NJ: Marcus Wiener Publishers, 2004.
———. *Transformations in Slavery: A History of Slavery in Africa*. New York: Cambridge University Press, 1983.
———. "The Volume of the Atlantic Slave Trade: A Synthesis." *Journal of African History* 23, no. 4 (1982): 473–501.
Lovejoy, Paul E., and Jan S. Hogendorn. *Slow Death for Slavery: The Course of Abolition in Northern Nigeria, 1897–1936*. New York: Cambridge University Press, 1993.
Lybyer, Albert Howe. *The Government of the Ottoman Empire in the Time of Suleiman the Magnificent*. Cambridge, MA: Harvard University Press, 1913.
Magee, Gary B., and Andrew S. Thompson, eds. *Empire and Globalisation: Networks of People, Goods and Capital in the British World, c. 1850–1914*. London: Cambridge University Press, 2010.
Majd, Mohammad Gholi. *The Great Famine and Genocide in Persia, 1917–1919*. Lanham, MD: University Press of America, 2003.
Malcolm, John. *Sketches of Persia*. London: John Murray, 1845.
Mandel, Robert. "The Effectiveness of Gunboat Diplomacy." *International Studies Quarterly* 30, no. 1 (March 1986): 59–76.
Mann, Kristin. *Slavery and the Birth of an African City: Lagos, 1760–1900*. Bloomington: Indiana University Press, 2007.

Manning, Patrick. *Navigating World History: Past, Present, and Future of a Global Field*. New York: Palgrave Macmillan, 2003.

———. *Slavery and African Life: Occidental, Oriental, and African Slave Trades*. New York: Cambridge University Press, 1990.

Marmon, Shaun E. *Eunuchs and Sacred Boundaries in Islamic Society*. New York: Oxford University Press, 1995.

———, ed. *Slavery in the Islamic Middle East*. Princeton, NJ: Markus Wiener Publishers, 1999.

Martin, Esmond B., and T. C. I. Ryan. "A Quantitative Assessment of the Arab Slave Trade of East Africa, 1770–1896." *Kenya Historical Review* 5, no. 1 (1977): 71–91.

Mason, Silas C. "Date Culture in Egypt and the Sudan." *USDA Department Bulletin* 1457. Washington, DC: GPO, 1927.

———. "The Saidy Date of Egypt: A Variety of the First Rank Adapted to Commercial Culture in the United States." *USDA Bulletin* 1125. Washington, DC: GPO, 1923.

Maxon, Robert M. *East Africa: An Introductory History*. Morgantown: West Virginia University Press, 2009.

Mbotela, James Juma. *The Freeing of the Slaves in East Africa*. London: Evans Bros., 1956.

———. *Uhuru wa Watumwa (Waliokamatwa Mateka)*. London and Nairobi: Eagle Press/EALB, 1951. First printed 1934 by Sheldon Press.

McCusker, John J., and Russell R. Menard. *The Economy of British America, 1607–1789*. Chapel Hill: University of North Carolina Press, 1985.

McDow, Thomas Franklin. "Arabs and Africans: Commerce and Kinship from Oman to the East African Interior, c. 1820–1900." PhD diss., Yale University, 2008.

McGinnis, A. C. "Pearl Search Began in 1897." *Independence County Chronicle*, July 1968, 25–29.

McKnight, Kathryn Joy. "'En su tierra lo aprendió': An African Curandero's Defense before the Cartagena Inquisition." *Colonial Latin American Review* 12, no. 1 (2003): 63–85.

McLauchlan, Keith. "Oil in the Persian Gulf Area." In Cottrell, *The Persian Gulf States*.

Médard, Henri, and Shane Doyle, eds. *Slavery in the Great Lakes Region of East Africa*. Athens, OH: Ohio University Press, 2007.

Meillassoux, Claude. *The Anthropology of Slavery: The Womb of Iron and Gold*. London: Athlone, 1991.

Miers, Suzanne. "The Anti-Slavery Game: Britain and the Suppression of *Slavery in Africa and Arabia*, 1890–1975." In K. Hamilton and Salmon, *Slavery, Diplomacy and Empire*.

———. *Britain and the Ending of the Slave Trade*. New York: Africana Publishing, 1975.

———. *Slavery in the Twentieth Century: The Evolution of a Global Problem*. Lanham, MD: Alta Mira Press, 2003.

———. "Slavery and the Slave Trade as International Issues, 1890–1939." In *Slavery and Colonial Rule in Africa*, ed. Suzanne Miers and Martin Klein. Portland, OR: Frank Cass, 1999.

———. "Slavery to Freedom in Sub-Saharan Africa: Expectations and Reality." In Temperley, *After Slavery*, 237–264.
Miers, Suzanne, and Richard Roberts, eds. *The End of Slavery in Africa*. Madison: University of Wisconsin Press, 1988.
Mignan, Robert. *A Winter Journey through Russia, the Caucasian Alps and Georgia; Thence across Mount Zagros, by the Pass of Xenophon and the Ten Thousand Greeks, into Koordistaun*, vol. 2. London: Richard Bentley, 1839.
Miles, S. B. *The Countries and Tribes of the Persian Gulf*. London: Frank Cass, 1966.
Miller, John J. "The Unknown Slavery: In the Muslim World, That Is—And It's Not Over." *National Review* 54, no. 9 (May 20, 2002).
Miller, Joseph C. *The Problem of Slavery as History: A Global Approach*. New Haven: Yale University Press, 2012.
———. "A Theme in Variations: A Historical Schema of Slaving in the Atlantic and Indian Ocean Regions." In Campbell, *The Structure of Slavery in Indian Ocean Africa and Asia*, 169–171.
Mintz, Sidney W. *Sweetness and Power: The Place of Sugar in Modern History*. New York: Penguin Books, 1985.
Mirzai, Behnaz A. "Slavery, the Abolition of the Slave Trade, and the Emancipation of Slaves in Iran, 1828–1928." PhD diss., York University, 2004.
Mitchell, Dolores. "Images of Exotic Women in Turn-of-the-Century Tobacco Art." *Feminist Studies* 18, no. 2 (1992): 327–350.
Mitchell, Timothy. *Colonizing Egypt*. Berkeley: University of California Press, 1988.
Money, R. I., and S. Kellett Smith. "Explorations in the Country West of Lake Nyasa." *Geographical Journal* 10, no. 2 (August 1897): 146–172.
Montigny, Anie. "L'Afrique oubliée des noirs du Qatar." *Journal des africanistes* 72, no. 2 (2002): 213–225.
Moore, Thomas. *Lalla Rookh: An Oriental Romance*. New York: Hurd and Houghton, 1867.
More, Sheshrao. *Islam: Maker of the Muslim Mind*. Pune: Rajhans Prakashan, 2004.
Morton, Fred. *Children of Ham: Freed Slaves and Fugitive Slaves on the Kenya Coast, 1873 to 1907*. Boulder, CO: Westview Press, 1990.
Munro, J. Forbes. *Maritime Enterprise and Empire: Sir William Mackinnon and His Business Network, 1823–1893*. Rochester, NY: Boydell Press, 2003.
Muscat Dhows Arbitration in the Permanent Court of Arbitration at the Hague, Grant of the French Flag to Muscat Dhows: The Counter-Case on Behalf of the Government of His Britannic Majesty. London: Foreign Office, 1905.
Najmabadi, Afsaneh. *The Story of Daughters of Quchan: Gender and National Memory in Iranian History*. Syracuse, NY: Syracuse University Press, 1998.
Newitt, M. D. D. "Angoche, the Slave Trade and the Portuguese, c. 1844–1910." *Journal of African History* 13, no. 4 (1972): 659–672.
Nicholls, C. S. *The Swahili Coast: Politics, Diplomacy and Trade on the East African Littoral, 1798–1856*. New York: Africana Publishing, 1971.

Niebuhr, Carsten. *Travels through Arabia and Other Countries in the East.* Trans. Robert Heron. Edinburgh: R. Morison and Son, 1792.

Nisbet, Robert A. *Social Change and History: Aspects of the Western Theory of Development.* New York: Oxford University Press, 1969.

Nixon, Roy. "First Dates Imported 78 Years Ago." In *Coachella Valley's Golden Years: The Early History of the Coachella Valley County Water District and Stories about the Discovery and Development of This Section of the Colorado Desert,* ed. Ole Nordland. Coachella, CA: Coachella Valley County Water District, 1968.

Nwulia, Moses D. E. *Britain and Slavery in East Africa.* Washington, DC: Three Continents Press, 1975.

O'Neill, H. E. "On the Coast Lands and Some Rivers and Ports of Mozambique." *Proceedings of the Royal Geographical Society and Monthly Record of Geography* 4, no. 10 (October 1882).

Onley, James. "Britain's Native Agents in Arabia and Persia in the Nineteenth Century." *Comparative Studies of South Asia, Africa and the Middle East* 24, no. 1 (2004): 129–135.

O'Rourke, Kevin, and Jeffrey Williamson. *Globalization and History: The Evolution of a Nineteenth-Century Atlantic Economy.* Cambridge, MA: Harvard University Press, 2000.

Otte, T. G. "'A Course of Unceasing Remonstrance': British Diplomacy and the Suppression of the Slave Trade in the East." In K. Hamilton and Salmon, *Slavery, Diplomacy and Empire.*

Ouf, Ahmed M. Salah. "Reconstructing a Historic Image: Techniques and Process in Sharjah City." In *The Conservation of Historic Images,* ed. Ahmed M. Salah Ouf. Berkeley: Center for Environmental Design Research, International Association for the Study of Traditional Environments, University of California at Berkeley, 1998.

Ovington, John. *A Voyage to Suratt in the Year 1689.* London: Jacob Tonson, 1696.

Owen, Roger. *Cotton and the Egyptian Economy, 1820–1914: A Study in Trade and Development.* Oxford: Clarendon Press, 1969.

———. *The Middle East in the World Economy, 1800–1914.* New York: I. B. Tauris, 1993.

Palgrave, William Gifford. *Personal Narrative of a Year's Journey through Central and Eastern Arabia, 1862–63.* London: Macmillan, 1883.

Palmer, Dewey H., and Frederick J. Schlink. "Education and the Consumer." *Annals of the American Academy of Political and Social Science* 173 (1934): 188–197.

Panikkar, K. M. *India and the Indian Ocean: An Essay on the Influence of Sea Power on Indian History.* Bombay: George Allen and Unwin, 1951.

———. "Regional Organization for the Indian Ocean Area." *Pacific Affairs* 18, no. 3 (September 1945).

Pankhurst, Richard, and Douglas Johnson. "The Great Drought and Famine of 1888–92 in Northeast Africa." In *The Ecology of Survival: Case Studies from Northeast African History,* ed. Douglas Johnson and David Anderson, 47–73. Boulder, CO: Westview Press, 1988.

Parker, Rose W. "Beautiful English Women of Title: Their Personal Traits, Interests and Amusements, and Their Superb Jewels." *Town and Country*, October 24, 1903, 16.

Parsons, Abraham. *Travels in Asia and Africa*. London: Longman, Hurst, Rees and Orme, 1808.

Patterson, Orlando. *Freedom in the Making of Western Culture*. New York: Basic Books, 1991.

———. *Slavery and Social Death: A Comparative Study*. Cambridge, MA: Harvard University Press, 1982.

Perri, Michael. "'Ruined and Lost': Spanish Destruction of the Pearl Coast in the Early Sixteenth Century." *Environment and History* 15 (2009): 129–161.

Persian Gulf Administration Annual Reports, 1873–1905. Gerrards Cross: Archive Editions, 1986.

Peterson, Derek R., ed. *Abolitionism and Imperialism in Britain, Africa, and the Atlantic*. Athens, OH: Ohio University Press, 2010.

Philips, John Edward. "The African Heritage of White America." In Holloway, *Africanisms in American Culture*.

Pierce, Leslie. *The Imperial Harem: Women and Sovereignty in the Ottoman Empire*. New York: Oxford University Press, 1993.

Pipes, Daniel. *Slave Soldiers and Islam: The Genesis of a Military System*. New Haven, CT: Yale University Press, 1981.

Plekhanov, Sergey. *A Reformer on the Throne: Sultan Qaboos bin Said Al Said*. London: Trident Press, 2004.

Pomeranz, Kenneth. *The Great Divergence: China, Europe, and the Making of the Modern World Economy*. Princeton, NJ: Princeton University Press, 2000.

Popenoe, Paul B. *Date Growing in the Old World and the New*. Altadena, CA: West India Gardens, 1913.

———. "The Distribution of the Date Palm." *Geographical Review* 16, no. 1 (1926): 117–121.

———. "The Home of the Fardh Date." *Monthly Bulletin* [of the California State Commission of Horticulture] 3, no. 1 (January 1914).

———. "The Promising Outlook for the Date Industry in California." *Los Angeles Times*, May 23, 1920, IX8.

Porter, Andrew, ed. *The Oxford History of the British Empire*, vol. 3: *The Nineteenth Century*. New York: Oxford University Press, 1999.

Porter, John. *Remarks on the Bloachee, Brodia and Arabian Coasts, by Lieutenant John Porter in the Dolphin Brigg*. London: George Bigg, 1787.

Potter, Lawrence G., ed. *The Persian Gulf in History*. New York: Palgrave Macmillan, 2010.

Pouwels, Randall L. "Eastern Africa and the Indian Ocean to 1800: Reviewing Relations in Historical Perspective." *International Journal of African Historical Studies* 35, nos. 2–3 (2002): 385–425.

Prakash, Gyan. "Subaltern Studies as Postcolonial Criticism." *American Historical Review* 99, no. 5 (1994): 1475–1490.

———. "Writing Post-Orientalist Histories of the Third World: Perspectives from Indian Historiography." *Comparative Studies in Society and History* 32, no. 2 (1990): 383–408.
Prestholdt, Jeremy. *Domesticating the World: African Consumerism and the Genealogies of Globalization*. Berkeley: University of California Press, 2008.
———. "East African Consumerism and the Genealogies of Globalization." PhD diss., Northwestern University, 2003.
———. "On the Global Repercussions of East African Consumerism." *American Historical Review* 109, no. 3 (2004): 755–782.
Putnam, George Granville. *Salem Vessels and Their Voyages: A History of the George, Glide, Taria Topan and St. Paul in Trade with Calcutta, East Coast of Africa, Madagascar and the Philippine Islands*. Salem, MA: Essex Institute, 1924.
Quataert, Donald. "Ottoman Manufacturing in the Nineteenth Century." In *Manufacturing in the Ottoman Empire and Turkey, 1500–1950*, ed. Donald Quataert, 87–121. Albany: State University of New York Press, 1994.
R. J. Reynolds Tobacco Company. *Golden Leaves: R. J. Reynolds Tobacco Company and the Art of Advertising*. Winston-Salem, NC: R. J. Reynolds Tobacco Company, 1986.
Ranke, Leopold von. *The Ottoman and the Spanish Empires in the 16th and 17th Centuries*. London: Wittaker, 1843.
Razik, Salil ibn. *Al-fath al-mubin al-mubarhim sirat al-sadat Al bu Saʿidiyin*. Trans. G. P. Badger as *History of the Imams and Seyyids of Oman*. London: Hakluyt Society, 1871.
Reusch, Richard. *History of East Africa*. New York: F. Ungar, 1961.
Richardson, Neil, and Marcia Door. *The Craft Heritage of Oman*, 2 vols. Dubai: Motivate Publishing, 2003. Ministry of Information, Sultanate of Oman, No. 255/2001.
Ricks, Thomas M. "Slaves and Slave Traders in the Persian Gulf, 18th and 19th Centuries: An Assessment." In Clarence-Smith, *The Economics of the Indian Ocean Slave Trade in the Nineteenth Century*.
Riggs, Oscar Willoughby. "The Fruit-Ships at New York." *Frank Leslie's Popular Monthly* 21, no. 5 (May 1886): 599–609.
Riverside County Fair and National Date Festival home page. Available at http://www.datefest.org/default.aspx (accessed June 20, 2006).
Robertson, Claire C., and Martin Klein, eds. *Women and Slavery in Africa*. Madison: University of Wisconsin Press, 1983.
Rosenthal, Leonard. *The Pearl Hunter: An Autobiography*. New York: Henry Schuman, 1952.
———. *The Pearl and I: The Diary of an ex-Millionaire*. New York: Vantage Press, 1955.
Rosenthal, Rachel, and Una Chaudhuri. *Rachel's Brain and Other Storms: The Performance Scripts of Rachel Rosenthal*. New York: Continuum, 2001.
Rosenwaks, Uri. *The Film Class*. Israel: New Foundation for Cinema and TV and Channel 10, 2006.

Rycaut, Paul. *The History of the Turkish Empire from the Year 1623 to the Year 1677*. London: Printed by J. M. for J. Starkey, 1680.

Said, Edward W. *Orientalism*. New York: Vintage Books, 1978.

Salman, Michael. *The Embarrassment of Slavery: Controversies over Bondage and Nationalism in the American Colonial Philippines*. Berkeley: University of California Press, 2001.

Saunders, Charles Francis. "The California Desert as a Pleasure Resort." *Outlook*, August 22, 1914, 997.

Saunders, Christopher C. "Between Slavery and Freedom: The Importation of Prize Negroes to the Cape in the Aftermath of Emancipation." *Kronos* 9 (1984): 36–43.

———. "'Free Yet Slaves': Prize Negroes at the Cape Revisited." In *Breaking the Chains: Slavery and Its Legacy in the Nineteenth-Century Cape Colony*, ed. Nigel Worden and Clifton C. Crais, 99–115. Johannesburg: Witwatersrand University Press, 1995.

———. "Liberated Africans in the Cape Colony in the First Half of the Nineteenth Century." *International Journal of African Historical Studies* 18 (1985): 223–239.

Saunders, Daniel. *A Journal of the Travels and Sufferings of Daniel Saunders, a Mariner on Board the Ship Commerce of Boston, Samuel Johnson, Commander, Which Was Cast Away near Cape Morebet, on the Coast of Arabia, July 10, 1792*. Leominster, MA: Charles Prentiss, 1791.

Scheibinger, Londa. *Plants and Empire: Colonial Bioprospecting in the Atlantic World*. Cambridge, MA: Harvard University Press, 2004.

Schofield, Richard. "Old Boundaries for a New State: The Creation of Iraq's Eastern Question." *SAIS Review* 26, no. 1 (2006).

Schultz, J. R. "Button-Cutter Speech." *American Speech* 16, no. 2 (April 1941): 154–156.

Scott, James C. *Domination and the Arts of Resistance: Hidden Transcripts*. New Haven: Yale University Press, 1990.

Scudder, Lewis R., III. *The Arabian Mission's Story: In Search of Abraham's Other Son*. Grand Rapids, MI: Wm. B. Eerdmans Publishing, 1998. Historical Series of the Reformed Church in America, no. 30.

Sebiane, M. M. "Le statut socio-économique de la pratique musicale aux Emirats arabs unis: La tradition du leiwah a Dubai." *Chroniques yemenites* 14 (2007): 117–135.

Segal, Ronald. *Islam's Black Slaves: The Other Black Diaspora*. New York: Farrar, Straus and Giroux, 2001.

Serels, Steven. "Famines of War: The Red Sea Grain Market and Famine in Eastern Sudan, 1889–1891." *Northeast African Studies* 12, no. 1 (2012): 73–94.

———. "Watering Slaves and Growing Grain: The Expansion of Slave Labour in Northern Sudan, 1896–1913." Presentation to international conference on Enslavement, Bondage and the Environment in the Indian Ocean World, Indian Ocean World Centre, McGill University, Montreal, April 28–30, 2011.

Shaw, Caroline E. "Recall to Life: Imperial Britain, Foreign Refugees and the Development of Modern Refuge, 1789–1905." PhD diss., University of California, Berkeley, 2010.

Shepperson, George. "The African Abroad or the African Diaspora." In *Emerging Themes of African History*, ed. Terrance O. Ranger, 152–176. Nairobi: East African Publishing House, 1968.

Sheriff, Abdul. *Dhow Cultures of the Indian Ocean: Cosmopolitanism, Commerce and Islam*. New York: Columbia University Press, 2010.

———. "Localisation and Social Composition of the East African Slave Trade, 1858–1873." In Clarence-Smith, *The Economics of the Indian Ocean Slave Trade in the Nineteenth Century*, 131–145.

———. "The Rise of a Commercial Empire: An Aspect of the Economic History of Zanzibar, 1770–1873." PhD diss., University of London, 1971.

———. *Slaves, Spices and Ivory in Zanzibar: Integration of an East African Commercial Empire into the World Economy, 1770–1873*. London: James Currey, 1987.

———. "Slaves, Spices and Ivory in Zanzibar Reconsidered." Paper presented to conference on Reasserting Connections, Commonalities, and Cosmopolitanism: The Western Indian Ocean since 1800, Yale University, November 3–5, 2000.

———. "The Slave Trade and Its Fallout in the Persian Gulf." In Campbell, *Abolition and Its Aftermath in Indian Ocean Africa and Asia*.

———. "Slave Trade and Slave Routes of the East African Coast." In Zimba, Alpers, and Isaacman, *Slave Routes and Oral Tradition in Southeastern Africa*, 13–38.

Shumway, Nina Paul. *Your Desert and Mine*. Los Angeles: Westernlore Press, 1960.

Sikainga, Ahmad Alawad. *Slaves into Workers: Emancipation and Labor in Colonial Sudan*. Austin: University of Texas Press, 1996.

Silberman, Murray Gordon. "Switzerland and the Unfinished Business of World War II." *Jerusalem Letters: Newsletter of the Jerusalem Center for Public Affairs* 377 (March 1, 1998). Available at http://www.jcpa.org/cjc/jl-377-silberman.htm (accessed August 31, 2006).

Silverman, Debora L. *Art Nouveau in Fin-de-Siècle France: Politics, Psychology, and Style*. Berkeley: University of California Press, 1989.

Sluglett, Peter. *Britain in Iraq: Contriving King and Country, 1914–1932*. New York: Columbia University Press, 2007.

Smallwood, Stephanie E. *Saltwater Slavery: A Middle Passage from Africa to American Diaspora*. Cambridge, MA: Harvard University Press, 2007.

Smith, Joseph S. Kellett. "Memoirs." Unpublished manuscript, AR-GB-402-JSS. London: Royal Geographical Society Archives.

Sobel, Robert. *They Satisfy: The Cigarette in American Life*. Garden City, NY: Anchor Books, 1978.

Sokolow, Michael. *Charles Benson: Mariner of Color in the Age of Sail*. Amherst and Boston: University of Massachusetts Press, 2003.

Solow, Barbara L. "Caribbean Slavery and British Growth: The Eric Williams Hypothesis." *Journal of Development Economics* 17 (1985): 99–115.

———, ed. *Slavery and the Rise of the Atlantic System*. New York: Cambridge University Press; reprint edition, 1993.

Speece, Mark. "Aspects of Economic Dualism in Oman, 1830–1930." *International Journal of Middle East Studies* 21, no. 4 (November 1989): 495–515.
Spivak, Gayatri Chakravorty. "Can the Subaltern Speak?" In *Marxism and the Interpretation of Culture*, ed. Cary Nelson and Lawrence Grossberg, 271–313. Urbana and Chicago: University of Illinois Press, 1988.
Stampp, Kenneth M. *The Peculiar Institution: Slavery in the Ante-Bellum South*. New York, Alfred A. Knopf, 1956.
Stein, Sarah Abrevaya. *Plumes: Ostrich Feathers, Jews, and a Lost World of Global Commerce*. New Haven: Yale University Press, 2008.
Sterling, Ada. "At the Opera." *Harper's Bazaar*, January 13, 1900, 27.
Stock, Eugene. *The History of the Church Missionary Society: Its Environment, Its Men and Its Work*, 3 vols. London: Church Missionary Society, 1899.
Storm, Mrs. Harold. "Glimpses from My Window." *Neglected Arabia* 189 (1940): 12–13.
The Story of a Pantry Shelf: An Outline History of Grocery Specialties. New York: Butterick Publishing, 1925.
Stuart, Amanda Mackenzie. *Consuelo and Alva: Love and Power in the Gilded Age*. London: HarperCollins, 2005.
Sullivan, G. L. *Dhow Chasing in Zanzibar Waters*. Zanzibar: Gallery Publications, 2003. First published 1873 by Sampson Low.
Sultanat 'Omān Wizārat Al-Turāth Al-Qūmī wa Al-Thaqāfa. *Ashkāl Mu'āsira li-Alfunūn Al-Sha'bīyat Al-'Omānīya, Al-Juz' Al-thālith*. Muscat: Wizārat Al-Turāth Al-Qūmī wa Al-Thaqāfa, 1991.
Sutton, Keith. *Arkansas Wildlife: A History*. Fayetteville: University of Arkansas Press, 1998.
Suzuki, Hideaki. "Enslaved Population and Indian Owners along the East African Coast: Exploring the Rigby Manumission List, 1860–61." *History in Africa* 39 (2012): 1–31.
Sykes, Percy. *History of Persia*. London: Macmillan, 1930.
Tagliacozzo, Eric, and Wen-Chin Chang, eds. *Chinese Circulations: Capital, Commodities, and Networks in Southeast Asia*. Durham and London: Duke University Press, 2011.
Talhami, Ghada Hashem. "The Zanj Rebellion Reconsidered." *International Journal of African Historical Studies* 10, no. 3 (1977): 443–461.
Tannenbaum, Frank. *Slave and Citizen: The Negro in the Americas*. New York: A. A. Knopf, 1947.
Temperley, Howard, ed. *After Slavery: Emancipation and Its Discontents*. Portland, OR: Frank Cass, 2000.
———. *British Antislavery 1833–1870*. London: Longman, 1972.
———. "Capitalism, Slavery and Ideology." *Past and Present* 75 (May 1977): 94–118.
———. "The Delegalization of Slavery in British India." In Temperley, *After Slavery*.
"That Unpopular Question Again." *The Friend: A Religious and Literary Journal*, February 2, 1901, 228.

Thieme, Otto Charles. "The Art of Dress in the Victorian and Edwardian Eras." *Journal of Decorative and Propaganda Arts* 10 (1988).
Thomas, Bertram. *Alarms and Excursions in Arabia.* London: Allen and Unwin, 1931.
Thomson, Joseph. "To Lake Bangweolo and the Unexplored Region of British Central Africa." *Geographical Journal* 1, no. 2. (February 1893): 97–115.
Thornton, Michael C. "African Diaspora Passages from the Middle East to East Asia." In R. S. Hamilton, *Routes of Passage.*
Toledano, Ehud. *As If Silent and Absent: Bonds of Enslavement in the Islamic Middle East.* New Haven: Yale University Press, 2007.
———. "The Concept of Slavery in Ottoman and Other Muslim Societies: Dichotomy or Continuum." In Toru and Philips, *Slave Elites in the Middle East and Africa,* 159–175.
———. *The Ottoman Slave Trade and Its Suppression, 1840–1890.* Princeton, NJ: Princeton University Press, 1982.
———. *Slavery and Abolition in the Ottoman Middle East.* Seattle: University of Washington Press, 1998.
Toru, Miura, and John Edward Philips, eds. *Slave Elites in the Middle East and Africa: A Comparative Study.* New York: Kegan Paul International, 2000.
Townsend, John. *Oman: The Making of the Modern State.* London: Croom Helm, 1977.
———. *Proconsul to the Middle East: Sir Percy Cox and the End of Empire.* London: I. B. Tauris, 2010.
Trivellato, Francesca. "Is There a Future for Italian Microhistory in the Age of Global History?" *California Italian Studies* 2, no. 1 (2011): 1–24.
Trouillot, Michel-Rolf. *Silencing the Past: Power and the Production of History.* Boston: Beacon Press, 1995.
Troutt Powell, Eve M. "Slaves or Siblings? Abdallah al-Nadim's Dialogues about the Family." In Walz and Cuno, *Race and Slavery in the Middle East,* 217–228.
———. *Tell This in My Memory: Stories of Enslavement from Egypt, Sudan, and the Ottoman Empire.* Stanford, CA: Stanford University Press, 2012.
———. "Will That Subaltern Ever Speak? Finding African Slaves in the Historiography of the Middle East." In *Middle East Historiographies: Narrating the Twentieth Century,* ed. Israel Gershoni, Amy Singer, and Y. Hakan Erdem. Seattle: University of Washington Press, 2006.
Tucson, Penelope, ed., *Persian Gulf Trade Reports 1905–1940,* vol. 5. Gerrards Cross, UK: Archive Editions, 1987.
Ulaby, Laith. "Performing the Past: Sea Music in the Arab Gulf States." PhD diss., University of California at Los Angeles, 2008.
U.S. Department of Agriculture. *Yearbook of the United States Department of Agriculture,* 1894–1935. Washington, DC: GPO, various years.
U.S. Federal Trade Commission. "Hills Brothers Co. (et al.) v. FTC." In *Federal Trade Commission Decisions: Findings, Orders, and Stipulations* 31 (June 1, 1940–November 30, 1940). Washington, DC: GPO, 1941.

Valeri, Marc. *Le sultanat d'Oman: Une révolution en trompe-l'oeil.* Paris: Karthala, 2007.

———. *Oman: Politics and Society in the Qaboos State.* New York: Columbia University Press, 2009.

Veblen, Thorstein. *The Theory of the Leisure Class.* New York: Penguin Classics, 1994.

Vernet, Thomas. "East Africa: Slave Migrations." In *Encyclopedia of Global Human Migration*, ed. I. Ness. Oxford: Wiley-Blackwell, 2013.

———."Le commerce des esclaves sur la côte swahili, 1500–1750." *Azania* 38 (2003): 69–97.

———. "La première traite française à Zanzibar: Le journal de bord du vaisseau l'Espérance, 1774–1775." In *Civilisations des mondes insulaires (Madagascar, canal de Mozambique, Mascareignes, Polynésie, Guyanes)*, ed. C. Radimilahy and N. Rajaonarimanana, 477–521. Paris: Karthala, 2011. Mélanges en l'honneur du Professeur Claude Allibert.

———. "Slave Trade and Slavery on the Swahili Coast (1500–1750)." In *Slavery, Islam and Diaspora*, ed. Paul Lovejoy, Behnaz A. Mirzai, and Ismael M. Montana, 37–76. Trenton, NJ: Africa World Press, 2009.

Villiers, Allan. *Sons of Sinbad: An Account of Sailing with the Arabs in Their Dhows in the Red Sea, around the Coasts of Arabia, and to Zanzibar and Tanganyika: Pearling in the Persian Gulf; and the Life of the Shipmasters, the Mariners and Merchants of Kuwait.* New York: Charles Scribner's Sons, 1940.

———. *Sons of Sinbad: The Photographs*, ed. and intro. William Facey, Yacoub Al-Hijji, and Grace Pundyk. London: Arabian Publishing, 2006.

Wagener, Mary L. "Fashion and Feminism in 'Fin de Siecle' Vienna." *Woman's Art Journal* 10, no. 2 (1989–1990): 29–33.

Wāli, Ṭāriq. *Al-Muḥarraq, 1783–1971: 'Umrān Madinah Khalijiyah.* Al-Baḥrayn: Maṭbū'āt Bānūrāmā al-Khalij, 1990.

Walker, Julian. *Tyro on the Trucial Coast.* Durham, UK: Memoir Club, 1999.

Walker, Lydia Le Baron. "Fashions in Jewelry." *Harpers Bazaar*, May 1909.

The Walled Oasis of Biskra in the Coachella Valley: An Interpretation of the American Desert in the Algerian Manner, Chas. H. Jonas, Founder. Los Angeles: Hoag and Ford Advertising, ca. 1928.

Waller, Horace. *The Last Journals of David Livingstone in Central Africa from 1865 to His Death*, vol. 1. London: John Murray, 1874 [reprint Westport, CT: Greenwood, 1970].

———. *Paths into the Slave Preserves of East Africa: Being Some Notes on Two Recent Journeys to Nyassa-land Performed by Right Rev. Bishop Steere of the Universities Mission and Mr. E. D. Young, R.N., attached to the Scotch Missions.* London: William Clowes and Sons, 1876.

Wallerstein, Immanuel. *The Modern World-System I: Capitalist Agriculture and the Origins of the European World-Economy in the Sixteenth Century.* New York: Academic Press, 1974.

———. "The West, Capitalism, and the Modern World-System." *Review* 15, no. 4 (1992): 561–619.
Wallerstein, Immanuel, et al. "The Incorporation of the Ottoman Empire into the World Economy." In *The Ottoman Empire and the World-Economy*, ed. Huri Islamoğlu-Inan, 88–97. New York: Cambridge University Press, 1987.
Walz, Terence, and Kenneth M. Cuno, eds. *Race and Slavery in the Middle East: Histories of Trans-Saharan Africans in Nineteenth-Century Egypt, Sudan, and the Ottoman Mediterranean.* Cairo: American University in Cairo Press, 2010.
Warsh, Molly. "Adorning Empire: A History of the Early Modern Pearl Trade, 1492–1688." PhD diss., Johns Hopkins University, 2009.
Watson, James L. "Slavery as an Institution: Open and Closed Systems." In *Asian and African Systems of Slavery*, ed. James L. Watson, 9–13. Berkeley: University of California Press, 1980.
Watson, R. L. "'Prize Negroes' and the Development of Racial Attitudes in the Cape Colony, South Africa." Paper presented to Southeastern Regional Seminar in African Studies, Western Carolina University, Cullowhee, NC, April 14–15, 2000.
Westlake, John. "The Muscat Dhows." *Law Quarterly Review* 23 (1907): 83–87.
White, Hayden. *Metahistory: The Historical Imagination in Nineteenth-Century Europe.* Baltimore: Johns Hopkins University Press, 1973.
White, Landeg. *Magomero: Portrait of an African Village.* New York: Cambridge University Press, 1987.
Whitehead Consulting Group. *Sultanate of Oman Economic Survey, 1972.* Windsor: Harold Whitehead and Partners, 1972.
Whitmarsh, Huber Phelps. "Fishing for Pearls in Australia." *The Century: A Popular Quarterly* 43, no. 6 (April 1892): 905–913.
Wikan, Unni. *Behind the Veil in Arabia: Women in Oman.* Baltimore: Johns Hopkins University Press, 1982.
———. "Man Becomes Woman: Transsexualism in Oman as a Key to Gender Roles." *Man* (New Series) 12, no. 2 (August 1977): 304–319.
Wilkinson, J. C. *The Imamate Tradition in Oman.* Cambridge: Cambridge University Press, 1987.
———. *Water and Tribal Settlement in South-East Arabia: A Study of the Aflaj of Oman.* Oxford: Clarendon Press, 1977.
Williams, Eric E. *Capitalism and Slavery.* Chapel Hill: University of North Carolina Press; reprint edition, 1944.
Wilson, Elizabeth. *Adorned in Dreams: Fashion and Modernity.* London: I. B. Tauris, 2003.
Wilson, J. Christy. *Apostle to Islam: A Biography of Samuel M. Zwemer.* Grand Rapids, MI: Baker Book House, 1952.
Wilson, Joseph H. *United States Telegraphic Cipher Adapted to the Use of Dealers in Fruit and Produce and Merchandise Brokers.* New York: Charles H. Parsons, 1893.
Winseck, Dwayne Roy, and Robert M. Pike. *Communication and Empire: Media, Markets, and Globalization, 1860–1930.* Durham, NC: Duke University Press, 2007.

Winter, Frank H. *The First Golden Age of Rocketry: Congreve and Hale Rockets of the Nineteenth Century.* Washington, DC: Smithsonian Institution Press, 1990.

Wisnicki, Adrian S., et al. *Livingstone's 1871 Field Diary: A Multispectral Critical Edition;* http://livingstone.library.ucla.edu/1871diary/index.htm (accessed February 2012).

Wittek, Paul. *The Rise of the Ottoman Empire.* London: Royal Asiatic Society, 1938.

Wong, R. Bin. *China Transformed: Historical Change and the Limits of European Experience.* Ithaca, NY: Cornell University Press, 1997.

Worger, William H. *South Africa's City of Diamonds: Mine Workers and Monopoly Capitalism in Kimberley, 1867–1895.* New Haven: Yale University Press, 1987.

Worsley-Gough, Barbara. *Fashion in London.* London: Allan Wingate, 1952.

Young, E. D. "On a Recent Sojourn at Lake Nyassa, Central Africa." *Proceedings of the Royal Geographical Society of London* 21, no. 4. (1876–1877): 225–233.

Zahlan, Rosemarie Said. *The Making of the Modern Gulf States: Kuwait, Bahrain, Qatar, the United Arab Emirates and Oman.* Reading, UK: Ithaca Press, 1998.

Zdanowski, Jerzy. "The Manumission Movement in the Gulf in the First Half of the Twentieth Century." *Middle Eastern Studies* 47, no. 6 (2011): 863–883.

———. *Slavery in the Gulf in the First Half of the 20th Century: A Study Based on Records from the British Archives.* Warsaw: Wydawnictwo Naukowe Askon, 2008.

———. "Slaves, Pearls and the British in the Late Colonial Time." *Hemispheres: Studies on Cultures and Societies* 23 (2008): 5–29.

Zilfi, Madeline C. *Women and Slavery in the Late Ottoman Empire: The Design of Difference.* New York: Cambridge University Press, 2010.

Zimba, Benigna, Edward Alpers, and Allen Isaacman, eds. *Slave Routes and Oral Tradition in Southeastern Africa.* Maputo, Mozambique: Filsom Entertainment, 2005.

Zinkin, Maurice. "The Commonwealth and Britain East of Suez." *International Affairs* 42, no. 2 (April 1966): 207–218.

Zwemer, Samuel M., and J. Cantine. *The Golden Milestone: Reminiscences of Pioneer Days Fifty Years Ago in Arabia.* New York: Fleming H. Revell, 1938.

INDEX

Abbasid Caliphate, 31
'Abd ur-Rahman bin Khalfan al-Mutawwa', 131–132
Abdul 'Aziz Ar Ruwaihi, 207
Abdülaziz, Sultan, 163
abolitionism, 11, 21, 145
abolitionists, 107
Abu Bakr Effendi, 163–164
Abu Dhabi, 25; slavery in, 132, 134, 206
abuse, 42, 46, 65, 116, 119–123, 174
Act for the Abolition of the Slave Trade (1807), 20
aflāj. See *falaj*
African Americans, 28, 51, 108, 225n30
African diaspora, 5, 9, 10–17, 22, 110, 212–213, 220
African population in Gulf, 9, 19, 22–25, 27–28, 203
agricultural labor, 11, 31, 60–68, 148
Ahmad bin Rashid Al Mu'alla, 123
Ahmed bin Sa'id (Imam), 28
'Ajmān, 124, 125, 133
Al-Bidda, 26, 87
Al-Hasa, 26, 54, 89, 114, 120, 127, 181
Al-Hofūf, 26
al-Jahiz, 31

Al-Khaḍra'. *See* Khaḍra'
Al-Laiwa, 212–214
Allen, Calvin H., 60
Allen, Richard, 33–34
Al-Musna'ah, 18, 25
Alpers, Edward, 12, 15, 33, 35, 40, 44
Al-Satwa quarter (Dubai), 212
Al-Wakrah, 26
amendoim, 197
Andrade, Tonio, 15, 226n46
Anglo-Boer War, 257n46
Anglo-Egyptian Condominium, 117
Angoche, 46, 198fig, 199, 201, 257n50, 258n51
anti-piracy treaties, 25
antislavery in the Indian Ocean, 146–148
antislave-trade measures, 11, 37, 49–50, 67, 111, 148–180
Arabian (Persian) Gulf (the Gulf), 22fig, 22–50, 52–53, 80–86, 93, 153–154
Arabian Mission (RCA), 135–137, 188
Arcades des Champs-Élysées, 81, 95, 96
Asfar, Albert, 59, 235n25
asylum, 142, 145
Atlantic paradigm, 12–15, 108, 119, 220–221
Atlantic slavery, 6–7, 33–36, 53, 64, 108

293

Atlantic slave trade, 152, 169. *See also* transatlantic slave trade
Atlantic world, 12–15, 29, 110–112, 216, 220–221
Austen, Ralph, 13, 39

Badgaon, 176
baghla, 1
Baluchi slave trade, 203–206
Baluchis, 24, 28, 80, 86, 113, 131, 159, 203–206, 212, 217
Baluchistan, 22, 181, 183, 196, 203–207, 210
baracoons, 151
barhi (date variety), 188
barks, 51, 55–56, 69–70
Barth, Fredrik, 209–210, 216–217, 219
Basra, 3, 21, 27–28, 31, 52, 54, 59, 68–79, 89, 105, 129, 138, 181, 186fig, 187–191
Bassidu, 80
Batinah, 5, 18–20, 24–25, 49, 53, 60–66, 80, 86, 88, 102, 114, 117, 120, 125–129, 135, 204–206, 213–214, 216–219
Battle of Omdurman, 117
Bauer, Alice, 108
Bauer, Raymond, 108
Baur, R. P., 36
Bazza bint Sultan, 105–106
Beachey, R. W., 36
beatings. *See* abuse
Belgrave, Charles, 86
Beni Yas, 25
Benson, Charles, 51–52
Berlin Conference, 200
Bertram, John, 51, 57, 70
Beville, F. G., 3–4
bidār, 62
bihar, 59
biopiracy, 183
Birkat Khan, 205
Biyaban, 205

Black Atlantic paradigm, 108
Black Studies, 108
bodyguards, 31, 105, 119
Bonate, Liazzat, 202
Boston, 57
Boston Journal, 70
branding, 121–122
Brett, Homer, 185–187
Brooklyn fruit docks, 69–75, 191
Bu 'Abali, 18
Budeyya', 26
Bunjī, 22fig, 204
Buraimi, 114, 124, 204, 209
Bureau of Plant Industry (USDA), 181
Bureau of Plant Propagation (USDA), 184
Bushehr, 4, 22fig, 40, 87, 118, 136, 138, 150, 207, 208
Byles, Mather, 174–175

calumba, 197
Campbell, Gwyn, 14–15, 35, 159
Cantine, James, 3, 136–138, 188
Cape Colony, 4, 163–164
Cape Guardafui, 2fig, 37
Cape Town, 162–164, 171, 176
capitalism, 9–10, 15, 21, 35
cash bounties (head money), 143, 167
cash crops, 11, 16, 52, 67, 78, 175
Chahbar Bay, 22fig, 205
chains, 62, 125, 134. *See also* manacles
Chakrabarty, Dipesh, 13
Chalk, H. P., 73, 187–188
Challaq, 205
childbirth, 106, 128–132
cholera, 68, 136
Circular No. 33 (1875), 143–145, 248nn7–9
cloth, 40, 42, 43, 53–56, 103
clothing, 11, 18, 30, 46, 83, 120, 123–124, 147, 175, 208–209
Coachella Valley, 181–183, 190
Codrai, Ronald, 87

Colomb, Philip, 167–168
Comorians, 31
Comoro Islands, 162, 202
concubines, 31, 106, 113, 128–132
conspicuous consumption, 7–8, 31, 46
contradictory consciousness, 109, 219
Cooper, Frederick, 15, 67–68, 146
corvee labor, 14
Coupland, Reginald, 21, 36
creoles, 13–14, 177, 219
cultured pearls, 10, 182, 191–194, 196, 210
cyclones, 65–57

Daily News, 143
d'Almeida, Paes, 197, 202, 258n51
dār sha'bīa, 90
Darīn, 120, 127
date packing, 16, 52, 59–60, 73, 187
date race, 73–75
date trade, 51–69, 72–79; volume of, 55, 58, 71–72
dates: as ballast, 56–57; boiling of, 62; drying of, 62–63; harvesting of, 23, 28, 52, 57–62, 75; and hygiene, 59, 187–188; irrigation for, 60–64; and labor, 60–68; marketing of, 73–77; North African varieties, 184, 186, 190; and orientalism, 76; and profits, 55, 59, 66, 70–71; recipes for, 58; and wages, 59–60; women and, 59–60
Davis, Mike, 67
de Albuquerque, Mousinho, 202
De Kantzsow, Commander, 170–171
de Waleffe, Maurice, 96
debt, 81, 101–104, 107, 121, 127, 132, 195
debt pawnage, 40, 204
dependence, on global markets, 8–9, 11, 15, 82; on slave labor, 11, 145
Devereux, W. Cope, 152–153
Dhahirah, 204
dhows, 1, 3–4, 6, 38–44, 49–50, 58, 63–64, 67, 80, 87–88, 128–129, 136, 143, 151–173, 196–199, 202–205

disease, 68, 93, 130–131, 136, 169–171
"disposal" (of liberated slaves), 169–180
Doha, 9, 26, 122, 132, 142
domestic slavery, 6–8, 11, 31, 52, 105, 113, 119, 135
"domestic" slaves, 111–114, 143, 196
Dowson, V. H. W., 62
Dromedary dates, 73–78, 74fig
Durand, E. L., 86
Dutch Reformed denomination. *See* Reformed Church in America (RCA)

East African slave trade, 18–50, 181–211
East Indies Station, 37, 153–154, 158, 170, 175
eastern Arabia, 3, 5, 7, 9, 15, 20, 22, 24, 25, 31, 49, 52–54, 60, 64, 72, 78, 82, 105, 113, 121, 128, 146–147, 160, 196, 203–205
Edwards, Holly, 76
elite slavery, 6–8, 52, 119
Elkins, Stanley, 108–109
El-Mallah, Issam, 213
Eltis, David, 33–35
Elton, J. Fredric, 156–157
Emperor Meiji, 191
Evans, Brad, 76, 239n92
exoticism, 76, 100
ex-slaves. *See* former slaves

Fairchild, David, 181–184, 187, 191
Faisal bin Tūrkī, 185
falaj (pl. *aflāj*), 60, 62
family life, 106, 126–133, 177
Faraj bin Sa'id, 105–106
fardh (date variety), 53, 57, 66, 70–71, 75, 77, 181, 184, 186
Farelay. *See* Muha-Muheva Farallahi
Field, W. S., 163
Fifth Avenue, 99, 194
fijrī, 90

fishing, 23, 119
forked sticks. See *gorees*
former slaves, 17, 23, 133–135, 179, 209–210, 220–221
Francklin, Philip, 1–3
free labor, 9–10, 81, 107
free markets, 9–10
Freed Slave School, 3–6, 136–140
freedom, purchase of, 134
freedom papers. *See* manumission certificates
Frere, Bartle, 155, 158, 178
Frere Town, 171–175, 178–179
Fugitive Slave Commission, 111, 145, 173, 177

Garvey, Marcus, 5, 12, 139
Gelvin, James, 68–69
General Act of Brussels Conference, 19, 146
Genovese, Eugene D., 108–111, 219
Ghaūs al-Bard, 85
Ghaūs al-Kabīr, 85
ghawāwīs (sing. *ghawwās*), 83
Gissing, Charles E., 158
Glassman, Jonathon, 218–219
Glide, 51–52, 57, 70
global capitalism, 9–10, 15, 21, 35
global history, 15
global markets, 7–11, 15–16, 20, 34–35, 52–53, 78–79, 81–82, 184, 210
globalization, 9–10, 50, 68–69, 78–79, 81, 160, 183, 210
godowns, 23, 59–60, 72, 125
Gohurt, 205
Gordon, Murray, 21, 225n17, 227n8
gorees, 40, 42–44, 198
Great Depression, 17, 182, 194
Green, Nile, 68
Gujarat, 58, 72
Gulf of Oman, 1, 60, 63
gum copal, 51, 56, 70
Gwadur, 55, 205–206

Hadd (Bahrain), 26
Hadhramaut, 33
Hadhramis, 32
Haggard, John G. ("Jack"), 158–159
Haggard, Rider, 159
hajj, 68, 130, 133
Hajji Abdul-Rahmān, 189
halāwī (date variety), 181, 188
Hale's war rockets, 153, 156
Halfkin, Nancy, 199, 201
Hamad bin Sa'id Ahmed Ma'awli, 207
Hamerton, Atkins, 45, 55, 148–150
Hamilton, Alexander, 28
Hamriyya, 80, 118, 120
Harrison, Paul W., 86, 125
Hassani Yussuf, 201
Hathorne, William Hollingsworth, 57
Heath, Leopold G., 37, 154, 158, 170–171, 173–174
Hecht, J. A. H., 163
Hellespont, 57
Herskovits, Melville, 108
Hills Brothers Company, 72–77, 187–189
HMS *Cleopatra*, 170
HMS *Columbine*, 253n87
HMS *Crocus*, 122
HMS *Daphne*, 171
HMS *Dryad*, 167
HMS *Espiegle*, 204
HMS *Falkland*, 151
HMS *Forte*, 167
HMS *Fox*, 5, 137–138
HMS *Garnet*, 172
HMS *Gorgon*, 152
HMS *Hastings*, 80
HMS *Lapwing*, 1–3
HMS *London*, 67, 156, 157fig, 157–159, 161fig
HMS *Lupin*, 65
HMS *Lyra*, 38, 150–151, 161–162
HMS *May Frere*, 142
HMS *Menai*, 148

HMS *Nymphe*, 165
HMS *Osprey*, 64, 67
HMS *Penguin*, 161, 169
HMS *Philomel*, 64, 172fig
HMS *Ranger*, 67
HMS *Seagull*, 174
HMS *Seahorse*, 28
HMS *Sidon*, 38
HMS *Sphinx*, 3, 18–20, 23, 136
HMS *Star*, 165, 170
HMS *Teazer*, 166
HMS *Thetis*, 248n3
HMS *Vigilant*, 234n109
HMS *Vulture*, 63, 170
HMS *Wolverine*, 42, 166
homosexuality, 129
Hooper, Jane, 33–35
Hormozgān, 204–205
households, 106–108, 111–114, 119
hurricanes. *See* cyclones
Huzzey, Richard, 146, 179

Ibadhi Muslims, 25
Ibn Battuta, 21, 31
Ibn Sa'ud, 26, 207
identity, 111–119, 162–168, 216–217, 220
Imam Saif bin Sultan I, 28, 32
Imam Saif bin Sultan II, 28
Imamate Rebellion, 185
Imaum, 56–57
Imbamella, 201–202
Indian Mutiny, 69
Industrial School for Freed Slaves. *See* Freed Slave School
infant mortality, 128
Iraq, 21, 24, 53, 59–60, 70–73, 77–78, 187–191
Islam, and abolition, 113, 133; and concubinage, 129–132; and cosmopolitanism, 216–217; and manumission, 133; and race, 216–217; and slavery, 6–7, 21, 225n17, 227n8; spread of, 201

Jaafer, 189
Jabal Akhdar range, 25
Jahiz, 31
Jamalzadeh, Mohammad Ali, 204
Japan, 10, 17, 67, 153, 182–183, 191–196, 210
Jask, 22fig, 205
Jeddah, 88, 115, 118, 127, 130, 207–208
Jenkins, Griffith, 151
Jones, Felix, 151–152
Jumairah, 131

kafa'a, 218
Karbala, 181
kerosene, 24
khadhrāwī (date variety), 70, 188
khadim, 217
Khaḍra', 18, 25, 64–65, 204–205, 257n45
khal, 210
khalāsa (date variety), 181, 187, 190
khameyzi (date variety), 62
khamīs, 123
Khandesh, 176
Khargh Island, 22fig, 30
Khoja, 24, 25
kidnapping, in Arabia, 104, 114, 117–118, 122, 130–132, 206–208; in Baluchistan, 203–206; in Djibouti, 117; in East Africa, 31, 40–41, 44, 65, 88, 116, 118, 120, 122, 125, 128, 135, 159–160; in Ethiopia, 105, 118–119, 127, 159–160; in Mekran, 131; in Somalia, 115; in Sudan, 115, 118, 127, 159–160; in Suwakin, 115; in Zanzibar, 47–49, 65, 80, 118, 120–121, 134, 159–160
Kikutu, 42
Kilekwa, Petro, 42
Kilwa, vii, 31–35, 40, 42, 46, 150–151, 155–158
Kingdom of Nejd, 26, 114, 207
Kirk, John, 68, 155–158, 165–166, 231n76

Kobayashi, Rikiya, 192
Konārak, 22fig, 205
Kotakota, 43–44

Laiwa, 212–214
Lake Nyasa (Lake Malawi), 42–44, 46, 157, 159, 201
Lamu, 32, 46, 150, 155, 158–159
Larson, Pier, 13–14, 32–35, 39, 220
Lavigerie, Cardinal, 107
League of Nations, 11, 195, 208
Lears, T. J. Jackson, 109
legal status (of slaves), 21, 104, 129–131, 209
Leima, Antonio d'Almeida, 197
Leiwa. *See* Laiwa
liberated Africans, 169–180
Lindi, 158
Lingah, 87, 93, 118
Litchfield, F. Shirley, 18
Lloyd, Christopher, 158
Lorimer, J. G., 9, 86
Lourenço Marques, 200
Lovedale, 4
Lovejoy, Paul, 32, 34–35, 39, 45
Lynch, John G., 165

Madagascar, 9, 32–34, 70, 154, 156, 161, 200–201
Makua, 147, 176, 197–199, 201–202, 258n51
Malagasy slave trade, 32–34
Malcolm, John, 28–29, 112
Malindi, 114, 155–156
manacles, 18. *See also* chains
Manama, 24, 26
manjūr, 60–62
manumission certificates, xi–xii, 16, 65, 88–89, 107, 113, 117–121, 133–135, 159, 209, 252n79
Marave. *See* Suali bin Ali Ibrahimu
marriage, 105–106, 126–131, 177–179, 217–218

Martin, Esmond, 39
Mascarene Islands, 9, 33–34, 149–150, 154
maseybili (date variety), 62
Masira Island, 151
Maviti, 42
Mbweni, 49
McKnight, Kathryn Joy, xi
Mekran, 22, 56, 80, 86, 131, 203–205
Mesopotamia Persia Corporation, 138
Mikimoto, Kokichi, 182–183, 191–193, 192fig
Miles, S. B., 64
Miller, Joseph, 14
Mintz, Sidney, 15
mobility, 133–141
Mohammerah, 187
Mokha, 55–57
Moma Bay, 197, 198fig, 199, 201
Morant Bay Rebellion, 179
Moresby, Fairfax, 148, 150
Moresby Treaty, 150
mortality rates, 169–171
Mozambique, 4–5, 33–35, 43–44, 57, 147, 170, 197–203
Mozambique Channel, 9, 31, 154, 159, 198fig
Mozambique Island, 35, 197, 198fig, 199–201, 258n51
Mrima, 4, 116, 128
Muha-Muheva Farallahi ("Farelay"), 201–202
Muharraq, 26, 196
Mujannah, 85
Mukallah, 117
Mullah Naji al-Hajj, 189, 190fig
Musa Mohammad Sahib Quanto, 201
Musendam Peninsula, 25
Mutrah, 9, 24, 30, 58–60, 64, 66, 73, 185, 206, 213
muwalid, 114, 120, 122–123, 126–127, 131–133, 159, 166
mzalia, 166

nākhudha (pl. *nawākhida*), 83
Namarral, 201
Nampuito Muno, 197–199
Napoleonic Wars, 6, 9, 34
Nasuri bin Anton al-Baghdadī, 189
National Review, 21
Nattan, Émile, 93
natural disasters. *See* cyclones
Nazis, 194
neoliberal economics, 9
New York City, 5, 8, 53–59, 69, 73, 75, 99, 138–141, 190, 192, 194
New York Times, 95, 143
Ngindo, vii, 46, 167
nihām, 90
Nizwa, 28,
Nosy Bé, 150, 161

oil industry, 208–211, 220–221
Oldfield, R. B., 150
Oman ophlolite, 60
Omar bin Cacogo Farallahi, 202
O'Neill, H. E., 197
orientalism, 7, 76. *See also* exoticism
Oromos, 32, 168
Ottoman Empire, x, 8, 26–27, 52, 54, 69, 107, 162–163, 188
overland route, 155–158

Palgrave, William, 9, 82
Palmerston, Viscount, 146, 149, 152
Pan-Africanism, 12, 141, 220
Panic of 1907, 92–93
Pārak, 205
Paris, 81, 92–96, 97, 191–194
Parsons, Abraham, 28
Pate, 32, 34
paternalism, 109–111
paternity, 106, 132
pearl diving, 82–91, 100–101
pearl exports, 91–96, 100–101, 194–196
pearl fashion, 81–83, 96–99, 193
pearl production, global, 100–101

pearling. *See* pearl diving
pearling music, 90
pearling seasons, 85
pederasty, 129
Pemba, 4–5, 31, 35, 40, 44–46, 63, 67, 115, 150, 155–156, 166, 170
Persian Gulf. *See* Arabian (Persian) Gulf
Peshaga ibn Sagakia, 189
petit marronage, 107
piracy, 25, 87, 111, 234n108
plague, 93, 130–131
plantation complex, 6, 34–35
plantations (Atlantic), 29, 112, 202; clove, 46, 173; date, 23–24, 28, 33, 52, 62, 66–67, 119, 205; grain, 45, 68; mission, 175; South African, 176; sugar, 33, 35
Playfair, Robert Lambert, 154, 162, 169
polygyny, 127–128
Popenoe, Paul, 58–59, 70, 182–191, 186fig, 190fig
Popenoe, Wilson, 184–185, 189–190
porters, 40, 43, 182
pregnancy, 106, 129–132
Prestholdt, Jeremy, 46, 243n15
prices of slaves, 9, 34, 67, 81, 103, 162
Prince Komatsu, 191
Princeton Theological Seminary, 140
Purshotum, Ratansi, 73
Puzim, 22fig, 205

qādhis, 129, 133
Qarmatians, 31
Qāsimī (pl. Qawāsim), 25, 38, 149, 151, 234n108
Qatar, 9, 26, 82, 88–89, 114–115, 117–120, 122, 127–129, 132, 134, 205, 209
Qatīf, 26, 123
Qishm Island, 22fig, 80
Quelimane, 35, 199, 201, 258n51
Quitangonha, 199–201
Quran, 21

Qurum, 213

radhafa (sing. *radhīf*), 83
Ras al-Hadd, 24, 49, 63, 159, 170, 233n108
Ras al-Khaimah, 25, 29–30, 120, 124, 130, 234n108
Ras Madraka, 64
re-enslavement (of freed slaves), 113, 119, 130, 133–135, 169, 195
re-export (of slaves), 30, 46, 205
Reformed Church in America (RCA), 3–5, 134–138, 188
resistance (to slavery), 106–111, 119, 124–125
Reusch, Richard, 36
Rhodes, Cecil, 201
Rigby, Christopher P., 38, 46, 48–49, 55, 154
Rosenthal, Leonard, 92–96, 193–194
Rosenthal et Frères, 93, 95, 194
Rosenwaks, Uri, 217
Ross, Edward C., 143, 170
Roubaix, Petrus, 163–164
Royal Commission on Fugitive Slaves, 145, 173–174, 177
Royal Navy, 1, 6, 11, 20, 36–37, 67, 111, 122, 138, 142, 147–148, 148–154, 158, 160, 162, 164, 167, 170
Russell, Edward, 165, 176
Russo-Turkish War, 71
Rustaq, 28
Ruvuma River, 42
Ryan, C. I., 39

Sagara, 46
saib (pl. *siyūb*), 83–84, 86–87, 91, 120, 135
Said, Edward, 7
Saʿid bin Sultan. *See* Seyyid Saʿid
Salalah, 214, 216
Salem, 8, 28, 51, 55–57, 69–70
Salil ibn Razik, 28

Salton Basin, 183
Samuco Bay, 197–199, 202, 257nn45–46
Sancul, 199, 201
Sangage, 199
Sangone Bay. *See* Samuco Bay
Scott, James C., 109–111
Sebiane, Maho, 212
self-identification, 111
Semail Valley, 58, 66, 181, 185, 187
Seyd Rawf, 189
Seyyid Bargash, 155, 173
Seyyid Mājid, 164, 252n84
Seyyid Saʿid, 45, 92, 149–150
Shafik, Ahmed, 107
Sharjah, xi, 25, 30, 47, 80, 87–88, 115–116, 120, 124–125, 126–131, 134, 159, 209, 234n108
Shat al-Arab, 187
Shaw, Caroline, 145
Sheibinger, Londa, 183
Sheikh Muhammad bin Thānī, 8–9, 82
Sheriff, Abdul, 7, 13, 21, 31, 33–34, 36, 39, 45, 216
Shiʿi Islam, 26, 90, 181
Shinas, 25, 206
Shire River, 201
Shirs, 205
siyūb. *See saib*
slave labor, demand for, 6–7, 10, 15–16, 20, 31, 33, 35, 50, 52–53, 64–65, 82, 104, 182, 196, 203
slave market (Muscat), 29, 228n34; (Zanzibar), 46–49, 149–150, 155
slave raiding, 41–44, 116, 157, 201–202, 232n83
"slave sticks." *See gorees*
"slave track." *See* overland route
slave trade, size of, 30–39; to Americas, 33–35; to Arabia, 36–39; to Brazil, 33–35, 170; to Madagascar, 9, 32–34, 154, 200; to Mascarene Islands, 9, 33–35, 149–150, 154; to Oman, 156; to Sur, 4–5, 58–49, 63–64, 67, 88, 116,

118–125, 128, 147, 159, 197, 202; to Wudam, 135, 204–205; to Zanzibar, 4–5, 33–38, 45–50
slavery, in Arabia, 60–67, 86–91, 105–141
slaves, lives of, 44–50, 105–141; provision for, 104, 123; sale of, 21, 29, 33, 65, 114, 119, 126, 132–133, 149, 205–206
smallpox, 170–171
Sohar, 22fig, 25, 60, 63–65, 114, 209, 216
Spanish Asiento, 33
Spivak, Gayatri, x
S.S. *Kasara*, 184
Stampp, Kenneth, 108
Standard, 143, 179
stevedores, 23, 75
Strait of Hormuz, 25, 96
Suali bin Ali Ibrahimu ("Marave"), 201–202, 258n51
Sudaich, 205
Sullivan, J. G., 167–168, 171, 173–174, 177
Sur, 1, 4–5, 24, 216, 217; in manumission testimonies, 88, 116, 118, 120, 121, 124, 125, 128, 132; Portuguese attack on slave traders from, 202–203, 257n45; role in East African slave trade, 48–49, 63–64, 67, 147, 159, 197, 233n108
Suris (people of Sur, Oman), 38, 48, 120, 203, 233n108, 252n84, 257n45
Suwaiq, 25, 63–64, 66, 204–205, 216
Suwakin, 115
Suzuki, Hideaki, 46
Swema, 44–45
Sykes, Percy, 204

Taimur bin Faisal, 62
Talhami, Ghada, 31, 228n40
Taria Topan, 70
Tatoku Island, 183, 191
tawwāsh (pl. *tawāwīsh*), 23, 86, 90

Thomas, Bertram, 62, 86, 112
Thoms, Sharon, 73, 137
Thoms, Wells, 185, 247n103
The Times (London), 143, 177, 179
Toledano, Ehud, x–xi, 107, 225n22
Townsend, William H., 56
transatlantic slave trade, 13, 49. *See also* Atlantic slave trade
Trans-Saharan slave trade, 13
Treaty of Windsor, 257n46
Trincomalee, Ceylon, 153
Trivellato, Francesca, 15
Trouillot, Michel-Rolf, 215–216
Troutt Powell, Eve, xi, 107
Trucial Coast (Trucial Oman), xi, 9, 25–26; pearling on, 91, 101; and slave trade, 47–49, 114, 149–150, 204–205; slavery on, 86, 118, 122, 225, 134, 252n79
Trucial Oman Levies, 209

Umm al-Quwain, 25, 65, 120, 123, 128
United States: and date trade, 16, 51–60, 66, 69–79; and importation of date palms, 10, 181–191; and Indian Ocean slave trade, 9; and pearl production, 100; and pearl trade, 97–100, 193–194
United States Department of Agriculture (USDA), 181–187
ushenzi, 218
ustaarabu, 218

Vernet, Thomas, 31–34, 229n43
Vice Admiralty courts, 171; Aden, 165; Cape Town, 163; Muscat, 254n112; Zanzibar, 42, 165–166, 169, 176, 231n76
Villiers, Allan, 86
Viscount Palmerston, 146, 149, 152

Wadi Ham, 204
Wadi Muawal, 207, 259n67
Wahabism, 25

wali (governor), 25, 205
Ward, Lawrence Pierson, 56
Washington, DC, 181, 182, 215
West Africa, 148, 152
White, Frank H., 73
Wikan, Unni, 129
World War I, 95, 191, 207; effect on Baluchi slave trade, 22, 203, 210; Solomon in, 5, 137, 140
World War II, 141
Wudam, 22fig, 132, 135, 204–205

Yao, 4, 46, 167, 198, 202, 234n109
Ya'rubi dynasty, 28
Yasmeen, 170
Yusef bin Ahmed, 188

Zairku Island, 22fig, 142
Zanj Revolt, 21, 31
Zanzibar, as center of slave trade, 4–5, 33–38, 45–50; ethnicity of slaves, 43, 46; kidnapping from, 47–49, 65, 80, 118, 120–121, 134, 159–160; liberated slaves deposited, 171–176; Omani rule 33–34, 45; passage to, 44–45, 49; slave life, 46; slave market, 46
Zanzibaris (mistaken for slaves), 162–164
zaygra, 60, 61fig, 236n31
zijrah, 60–62, 236n31
Zilfi, Madeline, 107–109
Zwemer, Peter, 4–5, 67, 135–137, 141
Zwemer, Samuel, 3–4, 137–141, 247n103